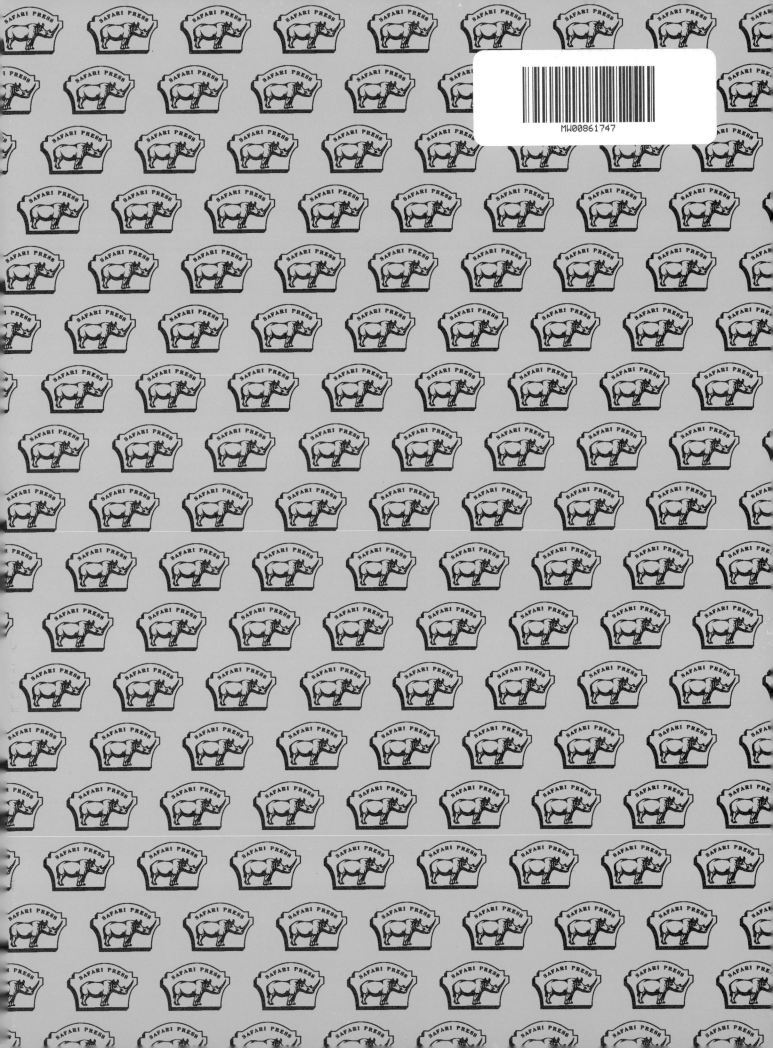

MW00861747

PARKER GUNS

THE "OLD RELIABLE"

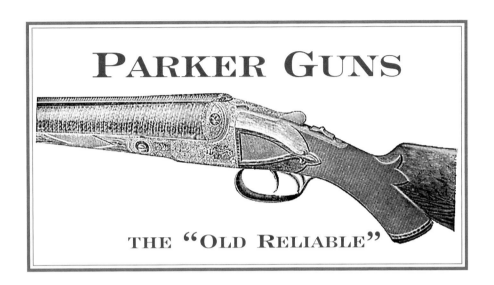

PARKER GUNS

THE "OLD RELIABLE"

ED MUDERLAK

Safari Press Inc.

P.O. Box 3095, Long Beach, CA 90803-0095, USA

The trademark Safari Press ® is registered in the U.S. Patent and Trademark Office and in other countries.

Muderlak, Ed

Safari Press Inc.

Second edition

ISBN 1-57157-054-3

Library of Congress Catalog Card Number: 96-70050

1997, Long Beach, California

10 9 8 7 6 5 4 3 2

Readers wishing to receive the Safari Press catalog, featuring many fine books on big-game hunting, wingshooting, and sporting firearms, should write to Safari Press, P.O. Box 3095, Long Beach, CA 90803, USA. Tel: (714) 894-9080, or visit our web site at http://www.safaripress.com.

CONTENTS

CHAPTERS

I didn't start out to write a book about the "Old Reliable" Parker gun, as I would rather read than write any day. However, all the reading led to jotting down random notes, which led to correlating and rewriting notes, which led to . . . well, you get the picture. This book deals with Parker guns put into historical context, with particular emphasis on people and the times. I've avoided a simple litany of manufacturing dates and serial numbers in favor of creating a looking-glass to the past with material gleaned from contemporary sources. I rely heavily on rare old books, period magazines and newspapers, factory correspondence, and catalogs and the like to define the Parker gun through pictures and words of those who were present and accounted for at the time of manufacture. I've gone to original sources rather than paraphrase last year's book or article on the same topic. As casual reading and jotted notes evolved to be serious research and formal writing, sometimes it seemed I had pulled the thread that would unravel the entire American experience.

Charles Parker's best-known product was essentially unchanged from the end of the Civil War through World War II. The Parker shotgun remained a double-barrel "tipping" breechloader for seventy-five years of production. Meanwhile, the times they were a-changin', as Tin Lizzy displaced the horse and buggy, and commercial air carriers attracted passengers and mail away from the railroads. Women were allowed to vote. Parker shotguns were the "age of progress" and the "golden age of shotgunning" personified for the later years of the nineteenth century, and they survived the early 1900s' preoccupation with repeaters to become the shooting connoisseur's weapon of choice and the Holy Grail for collectors. This is the story of the people, the times, and the "Old Reliable" Parker gun.

Ed Muderlak
Blackacre Farms
Durand, Illinois

FOREWORD

When I was a young boy growing up on an East Texas farm in the early 1950s, my favorite guns were a Model 10 Remington pump 12 gauge and a Model 12 Remington pump .22 L.R. My father owned these two guns, and I thought they were the best two guns in the world. I was allowed to use them when I became old enough, and I could not imagine anything better. Eventually, I was given a Mossburg bolt action .410, which I enjoyed using for several years. I shot my first rabbit, squirrel, turkey, and duck with it.

When I was married in 1956, I thought I would graduate to the ultimate, in my opinion at that time, and I bought a Remington Sportsman 58 automatic. This gun served me well for several years, and I thought indeed I did have the ultimate gun for everything that flew, as well as a lot of things that ran on the ground. Somewhere in the years beginning in 1970, I attended my first gun show in Dallas, Texas. It was there I was smitten. Over the years I had seen a lot of old doubles, but I had never been impressed; in fact, I viewed them as old relics without much appeal, something to hang over the fireplace. I never will forget when I, heart and mind, was jerked to attention.

On a table at one of the gun shows I saw a gun, standing up in a rack, that grabbed my attention as I walked down the aisle. This old double had Damascus barrels and some engraving on the receiver, which I thought was excellent, but what caught my eye was the recessed hinge pin area. I asked the man if I could look at it, and he asked me if I liked Parkers. If I remember correctly, my reply was "I don't know. Do you have one?" and he said, "You are holding one."

I looked at that gun with amazement. There was something about that recessed hinge pin! Something about the way the receiver was filed and fitted, something about the overall ambiance of the gun just reached out and hollered at me, the way my father would do at times to get my attention, only I heard no audible words, only my mind being grabbed to full attention. I remember asking another man at the gun show for his opinion of the gun, and he said "That's a fine ole gun all right, but it should have steel barrels."

I bought the gun anyway. What an education that gun gave me. I think I paid $150 for it, which was plenty to pay at the time, but it was nearly new. In about the fall of 1972, I read a book by Peter Johnson that was entitled, *Parker, America's Finest Shotgun*. Well, that did it. I was hooked, I was entranced, *I was in love*.

One of my first thoughts was how I would be able to buy a steel-barreled Parker. Since I had a wife and three children to support on a mediocre income, how could I do this while keeping food on the table for my family, and not ending up divorced? I thought if I could only find the right gun, then I could find a way to pay for it: I could get a night job to provide both for my family responsibilities and my Parker habit. After two or three months, I had saved enough money to buy my dream: I bought a two-barrel set V.H.E. 20-gauge Skeet Gun advertised by its owner, a man in Maryland. It had been redone by Mr. Del Grego of Ilion, New York. I was highly satisfied with my purchase, but I was only able to keep the gun for a year because when tax time rolled around, somehow we had forgotten to provide for the tax on our home, and our only hope to raise enough money was to sell the gun. I hoped I could recover my investment, and advertised the gun in the *Shotgun News*. A doctor from Honolulu wanted the gun worse than I did, and was willing to pay me a $700 profit. I was flabbergasted. I had stumbled on a bonanza. For years I had been looking for a way to make an extra $100 a month, and this gun allowed me seven months of fulfilled wishes in one fell swoop.

And, I guess as they say, more or less, the rest is history. I bought several guns from then on thinking I would keep each one because I really didn't want to part with my treasures, but finances being as they were, I had to sell them to acquire a new one and to pay off debts. So, I did that. A definite changing point in my life came when I discovered I couldn't borrow enough money at the bank to buy all the Parkers that I kept finding—all of which were good buys. I managed to talk my loving, understanding wife into allowing me to sell our house to recover our $10,000 equity. This was difficult for us both, but I truly believed at the time it was the right thing to do. I did it, she cried, we worried, we prayed, and it all worked out for the best. In 1976, I even quit my job working for Texas Power & Light Co. in order to pursue my lifelong ambition, which, of course, was to buy and sell guns for a living.

Since then it's been a never-ending love affair for me with Parkers. I have bought and sold some of the finest guns in the world of other makes, and I do like other makes very well, especially the fine German, English, Belgium, and some of the fine Italian guns, and of course, some of the other fine American guns. But, there is no replacing in my heart and mind my love affair with Charlie Parker's wonderful creation.

Up until now, there have been two books written about Parkers, one by Mr. Baer, and another by Mr. Johnson. Both books are good in their own right, but they leave out so much information that I am surprised it has taken so long for someone to finally do the job, and do it right. I hope this new book on Parkers will not only contribute to, but further excite the imagination of American sportsmen. Further, I hope these sportsmen will discover, as I have, that the double shotgun is truly the finest type of arm in the pursuit of feathered game.

Parker shotguns are not just well-made, they are the epitome of Yankee ingenuity, American craftsmanship, and downright genius on the part of an American entrepreneur, namely Charlie Parker. I have examined with great interest every major, and almost all minor gunmakers in the world in the past twenty-three years. All of them have their advantages, all of them have their drawbacks, all of them have their own individuality, but the Parker is the ultimate shotgun—in a class by itself. There is no better gun when stranded in the backwoods; there is no gun more reliable; there is no gun more dependable; and there is no gun upon which I would prefer to make my livelihood.

I dearly wish my father could have afforded to have owned a Parker and to have passed it down to me as one of my family's heirlooms—a treasure in terms of American arms making. The good Lord willing, I will be able to pass down two or three to my grandsons so that they can enjoy and appreciate the quality and heritage of America's finest.

For years Colts and Winchesters have dominated the market as far as antique or collectable firearms in the United States. They were well-made guns, they were made in vast quantities, and they were aesthetically pleasing to the eye. For some reason shotguns have not quite gained that level of appreciation to collectors, as much as it has to shooters. I am hoping with the new information by Ed Muderlak, this fine piece of American craftsmanship will be considered on the same level as Colts and Winchesters, not only for their collectability but also for their utilitarian purposes. You don't see many Winchesters and Colts being shot; they are cherished but not used. You pick up a nice Parker shotgun in good condition—there are thousands to be found—and you can use this gun for your lifetime, and the lifetime of your children, and grandchildren, and still have a serviceable arm that truly is as well made and collectable as any Colt or Winchester. I say to Ed and to others fortunate enough to have expertise and the desire to write: Keep up the good work. It is only through education that people can be informed of their options—and who knows, perhaps the information in this valuable book will jerk them into an awareness of America's finest, as I was back in 1970.

Herschel Chadick
Terrell, Texas
November 1996

ACKNOWLEDGMENTS

Parker Guns—The "Old Reliable" would not be in print but for the help of numerous Parker collectors, friends, acquaintances, and others whose contributions I cannot even begin to itemize. As the book progressed, I jotted down names of those who were particularly helpful. My list is strictly alphabetical. Some contributed more than others, and each knows the part he or she played by supplying information, access to guns, photographs, or maybe just answering my phone calls to clarify a point. My special thanks to Eddie Bauer Jr., Dan and Jane Behr, Bryan Bilinski, Geoffrey Boothroyd, Broadfoot Publishing, Herschel Chadick, Dan Coté, J.C. Devine, Inc., Larry Del Grego Jr., Lawrence Del Grego, Richard Fairchild, Jan Franco at the Meriden Public Library's local history room, Dr. Dave Fredrickson, Les Freer, Oscar Gaddy, Cdr. Roy Gunther, Richard Hoover, Ronald Kirby, Forrest Marshall, Pat McKune, Bill Mullins, Dave Mulvain, Bill Nitchmann, Louis C. Parker III, Charlie Price, John Puglisi, Lou Razek, Craig Reynolds, Dan Shuey, Doug Turnbull, Pete Wall, Robert White, and Al Weathers, curator of the Meriden Historical Society. The persons who declined to be helpful can be counted on the fingers of one thumb. Overall, the people part of writing this book has been a very pleasant experience. From the technical standpoint, Nancy put my words on disk and paper with a Compaq Presario 433, using Windows 3.1 Microsoft Works. Almost all of my photographs were taken with a Zeiss Contax 167MT using a Vario-Sonnar 3.4/35-70 lens and high-quality 100 ASA slide film. Thanks again to all who played a part in *Parker Guns—The "Old Reliable."*

DEDICATION

To Dad, for my first double gun, and

Dan, who sparked my interest in Parkers, and

Nancy, who makes all things possible.

PROLOGUE

SUMMER OF '54

My desire to own and shoot a fine hand-finished, double-barrel shotgun likely traces back to a hot summer day in 1954, when, at the impressionable young age of thirteen, I first visited the gunroom at VL&A. Summer-vacation high adventure, for boys soon to be in eighth grade, was an all-day trip from Chicago's far north side to the Loop for an air-conditioned matinee. Carl, Ed, and I would catch the early Countryside bus for the long ride downtown, take in a double feature or twenty-five color cartoons, feast on a rib-eye and baked potato at the "99 cent Steak House," and then wander around killing time until the afternoon bus left for Edgebrook, Niles, and points north.

Carl knew about the gunroom at VL&A. After some serious debate and advance planning, we decided to try for it. Again, this was the summer of '54. Kids knew their place. Kids were seen but not heard, and chewing a stick of Juicy Fruit or Blackjack was a classroom felony. Three boys venturing into the adult world of an upscale specialty store, without their parents, just to look at guns, wasn't to be taken lightly. We shifted to our best behavior mode—meaning no goosing or funny noises—and pushed through the heavy brass doors marked 9 North Wabash Street.

Our plan was to make it past the protective cadre of first-floor sales clerks without being challenged with the double meaning, "May I help you?" Picture three kids walking on eggs, just fast enough but not too fast. We didn't want to seem in a hurry, like, say, three pigs in a parlor. By prior agreement, our best response to almost any question would be, "No, thank you, we're just looking." If one of the straightlaced salesladies, wanting to have a little fun at our expense, had leaned across the counter and whispered, "Would you like to touch my bosoms?" we would have said at once, "No, thank you, ma'am, *we're just looking.*"

We ran what seemed to us the gauntlet of stern faces and cold stares of clerks and floor walkers. In retrospect, they were probably just bored and somewhat relieved we weren't picky-fussy customers' kids needing to be indulged or dealt with. Carl led our parade down the main aisle without incident and quickly turned and headed to the relative safety of the elevator. We were well aware that "elevation engineers" weren't persons with authority. In the '50s, all elevators were run by timid old men playing out their golden years by opening and closing the door, cranking the control, and practicing their limited vocabulary of "Watch your step" and "Floor please." As I recall, VL&A had a mezzanine and the second-floor gunroom was at the end of the line.

We watched our step, politely said "Two," and were whisked off to the inner sanctum. As the door opened, we watched our step again and were sort of greeted by a gunroom clerk who acknowledged our presence by looking up from whatever he was doing but never said a word. This set the tone for the occasion. We complied by saying nothing—not even to each other. No questions were asked, no answers given, and no information volunteered. We simply were tolerated by a clerk whose demeanor was as if he had discovered three flies in his bowl of soup.

The gunroom was a feast for our young eyes. Although none of us was quite sure of what we he was seeing, we knew we were in the presence of guns that were, in Ed's words, ". . . far superior to the above average." For my part, the seed was planted; someday I'd make my mark on the world, I'd own a fine gun; and I would be a welcome customer at VL&A.

Forty years later, I bought a Spring 1955, Abercrombie & Fitch used-gun catalog at a gun show. Thus I learned that VL&A stood for Von Lengerke and Antoine. Some of the guns I had seen in the summer of '54 were listed and described. As would be expected, names like Purdey, Boss, Greener, Holland & Holland, Westley Richards, and Parker were well represented. I guess this is what a "shrink" would call *closure*. Later, another sort of closure would occur when VL&A went out of business in the 1980s.

The summer of '54 was a good time to be thirteen. The following summer, I spent $100 of my paper-route earnings to buy a Chris-Craft boat kit. With some help from my dad, I built the boat, used it once, and sold it for $225 in the fall. The following year, I would earn $50 on a real good weekend caddying at Tam O'Shanter Country Club. My 1955 VL&A used-gun list shows some Parkers that I could have owned with the hard-earned money at my disposal. For example:

> **PARKER C.H.E. GRADE. 12 ga., 32" barrels.** Double Barrel Hammerless Shotgun. Automatic ejectors. Acme steel barrels. 3" chambers. Right barrel, modified choke. Left, full. Drop at heel 2 7/8", comb 1 9/16". Stock 14 7/8". Full pistol grip. Pachmayr recoil pad. Metal bead front sight. Beavertail fore-end, solid rib, engraved action, gun does not have a safety. Weight 8 lbs. 5 oz. *Excellent* [new condition, implying little use, with no appreciable bore wear and only minor surface scratches or wear] $285.00

Too soon old—too late smart! Such a gun today would cost at least eight thousand after-tax dollars. I wonder if my life would have been different had I bought that CHE trap gun. My first gun, however, was a double, a Model 24 Savage .22/.410 over-under, a Christmas present in 1954. My first side-by-side 12-gauge was a loose Baker I bought in 1960 together with six boxes of shells for twenty-five dollars. It wasn't until 1974 that I acquired my first Parker, and I never spent a penny at VL&A.

My preference has always been for double guns. When I finally tuned in on the better type of double, it could as well have been a Belgian Browning O/U, Winchester Model 21, or Parker. But, fate such that it is, I met Dan Behr, and he was a Parker man. That was in 1973. My hunting gun at the time was an SKB 12-gauge. It kicked like a horse and looked like it had been built by a low bidder. Meanwhile, I had access to Dan's gun safe and could fondle his DHE 12-gauge and CHE 28 and other Parkers that I don't now exactly recall. I decided I had to own a Parker. Dan was gun-dealing, and I mentioned that if he ever ran across a nice 20-gauge with a straight grip, I'd be interested. A short time later he showed up with a Trojan 20, which I bought for $900; it had a straight grip, but that's another story. Thus began my Parker collecting career in 1974—and it seems like only yesterday. Time flies when you're having fun.

The thing about the "Old Reliable" is that Parker guns are inherently well owned and hence collectible in groups of one or more. You don't ordinarily think of a person with one stamp as having a collection or being a collector. However, with Parker guns it's different. Even the most beat-out shooter is considered a thing of beauty and a joy forever by its owner.

By 1980 I owned five Parkers and could claim threshold collector status. The dimension lacking, however, was the ability to expand my knowledge and sharpen my interest by networking with other Parker collectors. Dan had since sold out and moved away. I lost my mentor and found gun shows to be the only venue to further my Parker education. But gun shows and used-car lots are expensive places to get educated.

Meanwhile, prices for "investment" guns skyrocketed as runaway inflation on Jimmy Carter's watch made it possible for even the most unsophisticated investors to lock in sixteen percent interest on federally insured CDs. Prices in the late 1970s and well into the 1980s sidelined me as a collector; but with note pad in hand, I kept stalking a Parker to add to my collection—to no avail. Worse yet, by the last half of the 1980s, all those overpriced Parkers didn't even make it to the gun shows as the bottom fell out of the collector-gun market, and the "investors" suffered an acute case of the "I've got more than that in it" blues. The feast-and-famine cycle took about ten years, and by 1990 some pretty decent Parker guns started to be offered for sale at sensible prices. In April of '91, I added a sixth gun to my collection. It had been a long, dry eleven years, but prospects for the '90s seemed promising.

In the summer of '93, almost twenty years after I bought my first Parker gun and forty years since my first trip through the VL&A gunroom, I discovered the *Double Gun Journal* (*DGJ*) and everything started to fall into place. I wasn't alone. Other people had my level of interest in Parkers and other fine guns. About the same time, an ad appeared in the *DGJ* for the newly formed Parker Gun Collectors Association. I joined. Collecting thrives on the exchange of information. I got all fired up, bought all the back issues of the *DGJ*, and started studying. My immediate goal was to add a nice D-grade 12-gauge to my collection. This led to an avenue of inquiry documented in "Parker Guns—Supply Side Economics," an article first published in the *DGJ* and included as a chapter in this book.

My "Supply Side Economics" search for a high-condition, straight-grip DH or DHE led to Terrell, Texas, and a three-day total immersion in Parker guns at Chadick's, Ltd. I bought a DHE 12-gauge Trap with high original condition, good dimensions, and straight grip at a reasonable price. To make the trip pay, I also bought a high-original-condition, good-dimension, straight-grip, VHE 12-gauge Skeet and traded out of some past mistakes. As a bonus, I had the opportunity to examine and compare more good guns at one time in one place than I had seen over the previous several years of scrounging around gun shows.

Meanwhile, the Parker Gun Collectors Association started to pay dividends. I had the entree to more knowledgeable Parker people in my first year as a member than I had run across in twenty years of trying to make connections at gun shows. As noted, collecting thrives on information: more available information leads inevitably to more collector interest, more guns changing hands, greater overall activity, and better collecting.

Make no mistake, I didn't just fall off a hay wagon in 1993, bump my head on the *DGJ*, and go off in pursuit of Parker-related information so as to make my mark on the Library of Congress card catalog. I'm a consummate note-taker and bean-counter, and have been collecting and keeping track of Parker information for more than twenty years. My copies of Peter Johnson's book, *Parker—America's Finest Shotgun*, and Larry Baer's book, *The Parker*

Gun—An Immortal American Classic, are drenched with notes, annotations, elaboration, and corrections. Every encounter with a Parker gun, Parker catalog, or related memorabilia has been documented with copious notes. The events of the summer of '93 were a catalyst to bring twenty years of bits and pieces into focus.

When I began my search for a nice D grade, I put together some statistical information that I thought would be of interest to fellow collectors. The adverse logistics of having my "Supply Side Economics" article typed by a secretarial service in a city thirty miles from my farm home led to the purchase of a computer word-processor. My wife Nancy sharpened her computer and secretarial skills by typing up reams of accumulated Parker information. I dictated my notes to give them some semblance of order and ease the translation to the typewritten page. Slowly a mass of seemingly disparate raw material was transformed into what started to look like stand-alone articles. Some were published, and it seemed the results of my efforts were appreciated. Articles became chapters, and we reached the point of no return—a book was in the C drive!

A book about the Parker gun is in reality a history book. Facts are where you find them and often are gleaned from the works of other authors, then compared and tested by reference to an ever-expanding body of available original information such as Parker catalogs, technical booklets, advertising, hanging tags, letters to customers, and the like. Other sources of historical information are contemporary writings in trade publications, sporting papers, magazines, and books. None of the information is new or original, although most has not been published within the lifetime or recollection of today's collectors. Finding "new" Parker-related information isn't all that difficult. Blending and correlating the "new finds" with the old information and conventional wisdom is what *Parker Guns—The "Old Reliable"* is all about.

As more and more information becomes available, some of the facts and conclusions of other authors may be questioned or shown to be wrong—but not without value! The early Parker writings of Johnson and Baer give us a baseline of information from which to amplify or make corrections. Parker collectors owe a debt of gratitude to these pioneering authors. Their books stimulated collector interest and encouraged the exchange of information that made the next generation of articles and books possible.

A *caveat*—read this book in the spirit intended. My goal is to inform and entertain by passing along some of the various qualities of Parker information I have come to possess over my collecting career. Be careful to separate the wheat from the chaff, the hard facts from soft facts, and educated opinions from pure speculation and conjecture. When I write that my VHE 12-gauge Skeet weighs six pounds fifteen ounces, this is a *hard fact*. It will weigh six pounds fifteen ounces on any accurate scale. When I discuss small-bore Parkers in the context of other authors' opinions contrasted to my own, well, we all have the right to an opinion. When I speculate that "Best Gun Iron Barrels" on the early Parker guns were probably converted musket barrels, this is an "educated opinion" but an opinion nevertheless.

Parker Guns—The "Old Reliable" blends Bob Hinman's nostalgic approach to the *Golden Age of Shotgunning* with case-in-point scenarios specific to the Parker Gun. For example, on the issue of retrofit ejectors, I pull a 1903 customer letter from the archives to prove a point. On the worth of thirty-four-inch or longer barrels, Parker's office manager has his say from a 1927 factory letter. As to the Remington-Parker years, a DuPont executive assigned to manage Remington explains the rationale for the Parker acquisition in 1934, and gives reasons for not resuming production of the Parker gun after the war. While this manuscript was in final draft form, I spent three days in Meriden, Connecticut; a day with Larry "Babe" Del Grego Jr. in Ilion, New York; and a day with the nation's most knowledgeable shotshell collectors at Oak Brook, Illinois, just to ensure that certain nagging questions were not left unanswered. When I agree with conventional wisdom, my resources are applied to expand and amplify the various themes. When I disagree with what has been written, I state my version and reasoning so as to correct the record. Although I write here primarily about the "Old Reliable" Parker gun, I've woven in a wealth of "golden age" facts and nostalgia to put the gun in context and appeal to the broader interests of fine double-gun connoisseurs of all makers.

Read and enjoy. If you cracked a smile when the saleslady leaned across the counter and whispered, then maybe we're on the same wavelength, or at least of the same generation. For the more serious Parker students, there's plenty of new information and new twists, corrections, and amplifications of old information to add to the ever-expanding body of knowledge about the Parker gun. If you have facts in conflict with mine, or reach different conclusions on the same facts, make your notes and annotations in the margins and on the blank pages of this book, just as I have done with my copies of Johnson's and Baer's books. The only way we're ever going to get it right is by the cumulative effect of hard facts displacing soft facts and educated opinions correcting wild guesses. The essence of gun collecting is the study and appreciation of fine guns. Communication and exchange of information are the key. I submit *Parker Guns—The "Old Reliable"* as a part of the never-ending process by which we enhance the pleasure of owning and shooting our Parkers by savoring their history and provenance.

"Old Reliable"

Parker guru Larry Baer wrote that "Charles Parker created his shotgun with great deliberation and appropriately named it 'Old Reliable'"—but wait, wasn't the Sharps rifle trademarked "Old Reliable" in 1876? Sharps was based in Bridgeport, Connecticut; Parker Brothers in Meriden, Connecticut. How can this be? The use of "Old Reliable" is so closely identified with the Parker shotgun that it's hard to believe Parker Brothers simply appropriated a neighbor gunmaker's trademark.

Christian Sharps was an innovative gunmaker but not much of a businessman. He patented his famous single-shot breechloader chambered for a linen cartridge in 1848. The Sharps Rifle Manufacturing Company was organized with $100,000 capital and began building Sharps rifles in 1851 at Hartford, Connecticut, just eighteen miles north and thirty minutes by rail from Meriden. Christian Sharps wasn't an officer or shareholder but a technical advisor who collected a royalty of one dollar for each rifle built. Sharps left the company in 1853 and was involved in various other gunmaking ventures until he died in 1874 at age sixty-four.

The original Sharps Rifle *Manufacturing* Company was liquidated as a consequence of settlement of a lawsuit in 1874, and the next year, a new group of investors formed a *Sharps Rifle Company* to continue manufacturing the popular Sharps rifle. The new company moved from Hartford to Bridgeport (about forty miles south of Parker's gun works at Meriden), and adopted "Old Reliable" as its trademark in 1876. The following year, Sharps announced that it would produce ". . . a shotgun that should equal the Sharps rifle in excellence and we expect to be ready to fill orders about May 1, 1878."

Charles Parker, by comparison, was a hands-on industrialist with diversified hardware-manufacturing facilities in and near Meriden, Connecticut. His home, purchased the year Christian Sharps died, cost $162,000, while probate records show $341.25 to be Sharps's gross estate. Charles Parker was not a gunmaker. He licensed the patent for his first side-by-side

Soldiers, hunters, and marksmen have, as their estimate of its excellent qualities, long given the name of "Old Reliable" to the Sharps rifle, and the company have adopted that as their trademark, which will hereafter appear upon all of their productions.

Sharps Rifle Company, April 25, 1876

shotgun and began production at West Meriden in 1866. By the early 1870s, his Parker Brothers gun works had a good reputation as a maker of fine-quality double-barrel shotguns. Parker Brothers adopted a number of patented design improvements in 1875-1876 that ensured the reliability and consequent long-term success of the Parker gun. Parker's May 1, 1877, catalog announced:

> . . . Gents: The Parker shotgun has been known in the market for the last 12 years [since 1865?], and has gained an enviable reputation for workmanship and shooting qualities. After long experience and great expense in completing our improved machinery, we are able to offer the trade an interchangeable gun, thus producing the best breech-loading shotgun in the world, at the lowest price, the parts of which are all made to gauge, fit accurately, and are readily duplicated.

History shows Parker's announcement to be of substance while Sharps's was merely a matter of form. Parker performed and Sharps didn't. Despite the special announcement in Sharps's 1877 catalog and in shooting publications of the day, the Sharps Rifle Company never built a double-barrel shotgun, although a small number of 10- and 12-gauge imports marked with the Sharps name were sold during 1878-1879. Parker Brothers and Sharps were gunmakers and neighbors but were never in direct competition. Sharps failed in 1881, while Parker went on to become the premium maker of fine double-barrel shotguns in the United States for more than fifty years.

The key to Parker Brothers' success was that Parker shotguns were machine-built to rough but close specifications using the best materials, then hand-finished to extra-close "zero" tolerances with conservative dimen-

Parker Brothers began using The "Old Reliable" *in the mid-1890s. This ad is from the April 8, 1897 issue of* Shooting and Fishing, *and is the first in author's collection showing Parker's use of the trademark.*

sions and weights so as to stand the tests of time and hard use. For the first decade of production, prior to the advent of sized frames, Parker shotguns were rough-machined but mostly hand-built. The first "interchangeable" Parker guns (with frame size stamped on the barrel lugs) were built and sold in 1877, according to the above-quoted announcement. Frame size wasn't a special feature but simply a gauge from which close-machined barrels and fore-end metal took their dimensions as a first step in the manufacture of a gun of proper scale and balance. After 1877, Parker guns were machine-made and hand-finished—not hand-built like a London "best" gun.

Parker guns earned their good reputation for having a tight breech by the early 1880s, about the time the Sharps Rifle Company failed and production of the Sharps rifle ceased. But Parker Brothers didn't appropriate Sharps's "Old Reliable" trademark right away. It honored propriety and didn't start using Sharps's logo until the mid-1890s, but by the turn of the century, The "Old Reliable" was synonymous with The Parker Gun. Remington Arms Co., Inc. acquired rights to the Parker shotgun in 1934 and used The "Old Reliable" mark on catalogs, price lists, and advertising until the mid-1950s, when Remington gun mechanic Larry Del Grego Sr. left the company, bought the Parker parts inventory, and went into business for himself.

The Parker shotgun, like the Sharps rifle, earned a reputation for being reliable over more than twenty-five years. If the Sharps Rifle Company had successfully introduced a double-barrel shotgun using Sharps's trademark "Old Reliable," the name we consider synonymous with Parker guns would not have been. Today, generations after Remington discontinued production, The "Old Reliable" still means The Parker Gun. What's in a name? Everything! And did Charles Parker *personally* create the Parker shotgun ". . . with great deliberation and appropriately name it 'Old Reliable'"? Opinions differ, but I doubt it. More on this in "Charles Parker's Company."

Charles Parker's Company

Charles Parker was born January 2, 1809, at Cheshire, Connecticut, and died January 31, 1902, at Meriden in his ninety-fourth year. His obituary in the *Meriden Daily Journal* said, "Notwithstanding his age Mr. Parker had been in fairly good health until recently and therefore his death was a surprise and shock. Mr. Parker retained his full mental faculties until a few hours before his death. He was the ideal business man in his younger days and for many years after others of less energetic character would have given up all business affairs, he kept in thorough touch with the many lines in which the immense Parker Company was engaged. In his death Meriden loses its most distinguished citizen."

Charles Parker was the eleventh of twelve children of Steven Parker's two marriages, and was "apprenticed" with a farmer before he was ten years old. Charles continued with farm work until age eighteen, then moved to Meriden in 1828, and by 1832 established himself in the hardware-manufacturing business. According to local lore, he parlayed a blind horse and seventy dollars into his industrial empire. Charles married Abi Lewis Eddy in 1831, and they had ten children—two daughters and three sons survived childhood to play various roles in Charles Parker's company. His sons Wilbur Fisk Parker (born 1839, died December 25, 1876), Charles Eddy Parker (born 1842, died May 11, 1897), and Dexter Wright Parker (born 1850, died February 8, 1925) were the namesakes of Parker Brothers. While Charles Parker's various business interests were first and foremost manufacturers of household goods and hardware, he is best remembered for the Parker Brothers gun works and The Parker Gun.

The productive years of Charles Parker's life were the years of the American Industrial Revolution, and he rode the crest. According to the *Meriden Record Journal* for April 17, 1936, ". . . The present Parker Brothers factory was built in 1853 . . . [by] . . . the firm of Oliver Snow & Co., consisting of Oliver Snow and Charles Parker. . . ." Contem-

"The Charles Parker Company as incorporated has always been the sole owner of Parker Brothers, which was never an incorporated company, but was nothing more than a basic factory."

Walter A. King (1924)

SNOW, BROOKS & CO.

SUCCESSORS TO MERIDEN MACHINE COMPANY, WEST MERIDEN, CONNECTICUT,

MANUFACTURERS OF

STEAM ENGINES AND BOILERS,

MILL GEARING, SHAFTING, PULLEYS, WATER WHEELS,

MACHINISTS' TOOLS,

Farnham's Double Acting Lift and Force Pumps, and Lift Pumps, of all sizes, arranged in every form where large or small quantities of water or other liquids are required.

ORNAMENTAL CAST IRON FOUNTAINS IN GREAT VARIETY.

HEAVY OR LIGHT MACHINERY of any kind made to order at short notice.   STAMPING PRESSES of all sizes, for Tinners and other Plate Metal Manufacturers.

THE CELEBRATED FOWLER PUNCHING PRESSES,

(So called,) of all sizes, as well as various other kinds of PRESSES of the most approved construction, with Dies for the same when required.

N. B.—Cuts of most of our Tools will be furnished on application when desired.   We have in store, at 23 PLATT STREET, NEW YORK, a large assortment of MACHINERY, both of our own and other makers, which will be sold at the Manufacturers' Prices.

SNOW, BROOKS & CO.

POST OFFICE ADDRESS, WEST MERIDEN, CONN.

NEW YORK OFFICE AND DEPOT, 23 PLATT STREET.

Snow, Brooks & Co. factory built during the mid-1850s to manufacture railroad wheels. The name changed in the mid-1860s to Meriden Manufacturing Company and, in turn, Parker Brothers by 1869. The small building on the left was the office for Parker Brothers gun works.

porary advertising leaflets at the Meriden Historical Society show a succession of name changes from Meriden Machine Co., to Snow, Brooks and Co., to Parker, Snow & Co. to Meriden Manufacturing Company, and finally in 1869, to Parker Brothers.

Charles Parker's facilities in and around Meriden were strategically located and destined to prosper from the Civil War. Parker, Snow & Co. was a Civil War-era private contractor of Model 1861 U.S. percussion rifle-muskets. Charles Parker, however, was an industrialist and financier, not a gunmaker. According to a letter written to William Muir & Co. of Windsor Locks, Connecticut, in April 1862, Parker, Snow, Brooks & Co.'s bid to secure a subcontract for gunlocks and guard plates represented that "... Mr. Snow

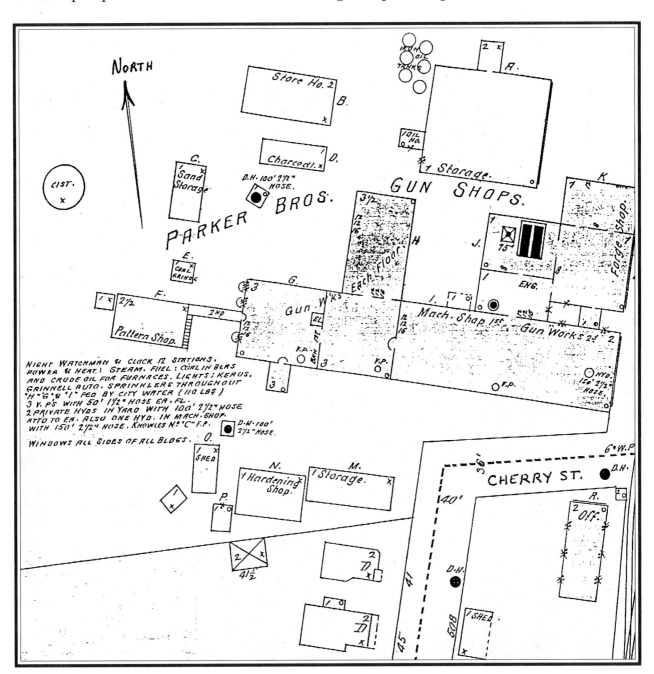

Fire map showing Parker Brothers gun works complex. The Cherry Street office is the only building remaining in 1996.

had been educated in the manufacture of arms and understood the business fully. . . ." After three days of reviewing almost every shred of evidence at the Meriden Historical Society and the local history archives at the Meriden Public Library, it's my opinion that Charles Parker had little or no hands-on knowledge of gunmaking and had little or nothing to do with the design, manufacture, refinement, and marketing of the Parker gun.

A summary of the history of Meriden Manufacturing Company at the library states that

> On Sept. 28, 1863, Parker, Snow & Company was awarded a contract for 15,000 rifle-muskets at $19 each and they delivered this number before November 1864. Price paid by the government for some of these arms was $18.50 each as they did not quite meet their rigid specifications, but still were serviceable. The government paid a total of $284,339.10 for the 15,000 muskets.

The roughly $285,000 received for one year's production of firearms may have been the highest *annual* gross revenues attributed to the manufacture of any and all Parker firearms through the last shotgun, built in 1947 by Remington. The Parker shotgun never was "big business."

The war between the states and westward expansion put development of firearms on the fast track, and as the war wound down, a large number of manufacturing companies had the capability to produce contract arms for the military. The question was, which gun manufacturers could survive the switch-over to nonmilitary peacetime production. Charles Parker's company survived while most others fell by the wayside. The *Meriden Chronicle* reported that during 1863, Parker, Snow & Co. employed upwards of 450 men and about 300 were building Springfield rifle-muskets. The Parker shotgun was simply a postwar product conceived to take advantage of the

gunmaking skills acquired by Charles Parker's employees while building government contract arms.

William H. Miller was forty years old in 1862, when he was hired as superintendent of the gun works. His younger brother George, then age twenty-four, was employed as a toolmaker. The gun works (called Meriden Manufacturing Company) contracted with the government in 1865 to build 5,000 Triplett & Scott (December 6, 1864, patent) breechloading repeating carbines for the Kentucky militia. Later Meriden Manufacturing converted some of its 1861 Springfields to breechloaders using William and George Miller's May 23, 1865, patent. These dates can be an aid to aging otherwise undated Parker literature by referring to the number of years of *manufacturing firearms* (since 1863), *breechloading arms* (since 1864-65), and *shotguns* (since 1865-66). The Triplett & Scott carbines were stamped "Meriden Man'fg. Co. Meriden, Conn." The first Parker shotguns, circa 1866, were marked "Meriden Man'fg. Co. Meriden, Conn. for Cha's Parker," and utilized William Miller's November 13, 1866 patent for a breechlock improvement. When Charles Parker gave the Miller brothers the go-ahead to start fooling around with musket barrels and breech-opening mechanisms toward the end of the Civil War, it's doubtful they had any idea the end result would become *the* American classic side-by-side, double-barrel shotgun.

William and George Miller left Meriden Man'fg. Co. in 1867 or 1868 to found the Miller Brothers Pocket Knife Company (sometimes called Miller Bros. Cutlery Company) as their next business. Although the knife company failed in 1878, William and George had continuing royalty income from their various patents, including William's lifter-opener used on Parker Brothers' guns for almost forty years. The Meriden Manufacturing Company gun works became part of Parker Brothers in 1868, and thus began a sixty-seven-year success story. A contemporary (1872) news story in a New York City newspaper had nothing but praise for Charles Parker's company:

The business of this veteran manufacturer and merchant was commenced in 1832, and his success is shown by the fact that he now owns no less than five large factories; one at Meriden Center, one at East Meriden, two at West Meriden, and one at Yalesville, Connecticut.

These factories cover several acres of ground, and employ a total force of 500 to 600 men. They comprise the Union Works, Machine and Gun Works, Britannia and German Silver Works, Iron Spoon Works, and the Hinge and Scale Works, and turn out about 120 different lines of goods. The value of tools and machinery is about $500,000. Two steam engines are used, each of 100 horse power; besides which there are three water powers, amounting to 200 horse power, to which steam engines are added whenever required, in times of drought. The amount of coal used in these factories in a year is about 2,500 tons. The average value of stock carried is from $400,000 to $500,000, while the annual sales already reach from $1,250,000 to $1,500,000. The great variety of articles there manufactured is of course the reason why the cost of tools and machinery is exceptionally large.

During the late 1860s and until the mid-1870s, Charles Parker's company seemed to lack corporate identity. However, American business and industry of the nineteenth century was, by today's standards, almost informal. Consolidations of productive assets were often owned outright by a patriarch for the benefit of his extended family. Written partnership agreements were usually reserved for non-family business relationships, articles of incorporation were not considered important

First model Parker shotgun built by Meriden Manufacturing Company for Charles Parker after patent date of November 13, 1866. This gun is serial number 90, originally owned by Wilbur F. Parker Jr., and now in the Meriden Historical Society collection.

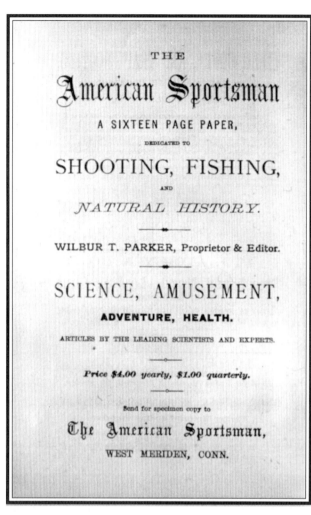

Charles Parker's oldest son, Wilbur F. Parker, founded The American Sportsman *in 1871, and placed this ad in Joe* Long's 1874 book, American Wild-fowl Shooting. *Notice the typo for Wilbur Fisk's middle initial.*

as a shield from personal liability, and income and estate taxation were not yet crucial survival issues for a family business. News reports through the mid-1870s called Charles Parker a *proprietor*—apparently he owned the company "lock, stock, and barrel." However, Charles Parker at age sixty-seven, perhaps coming to grips with his own mortality, incorporated his various holdings as The Charles Parker Company. The *History of New Haven County* for 1900 reported that ". . . in 1876 Mr. Parker partially retired from business and his extensive works have been in charge of his sons, Dexter W. and Charles E., and his son-in-law, William H. Lyon, under the corporate name of The Charles Parker Company.

The company now owns the Union Works on High and Elm Streets, the Parker Gun Factory on Cherry Street, the Iron Spoon Shop in East Meriden, the Box Shop in Yalesville, and the Clock Shop in the western part of the town."

According to the *Encyclopedia of Biography—Representative Citizens, the American Historical Society* (1917), "The business was incorporated in 1876, with a capital of $500,000 as The Charles Parker Company, and . . . the first officers were: Charles Parker, president; Charles E. Parker, vice-president; Dexter W. Parker, secretary and treasurer." At 67, Charles Parker was no doubt ready to pass the day-to-day management of the business to his sons. He had recently purchased an elegant residence on North Broad Street in Meriden for the astronomical price of $162,000; but to put this in context, plush private railway cars could cost as much as $50,000 at the time. Charles lived in his mansion with his wife Abi until she died in 1880—they had been married for forty-nine years. In 1882, he was stricken with some unspecified disease that kept him confined to his home most of the time; however, his obituary stated that his intellectual abilities weren't impaired until his last hours. Charles Parker died at home in January 1902, and the Meriden newspapers reported that his 1,500 employees had a few days off when the company shut down to mourn.

The *Meriden City Directory* listed Charles Parker as president of his company until the day he died. He outlived most of his children, including two of three Parker Brothers namesakes—second son Charles E. and oldest son Wilbur F. predeceased him. Charles was succeeded as CEO by his youngest and only surviving son, Dexter, an 1870 graduate of the U. S. Military Academy at West Point. Dexter was president until 1925, when he died at age seventy-five.

Wilbur Fisk Parker, general manager of Parker Brothers in the early 1870s, was creative and innovative and had a number of

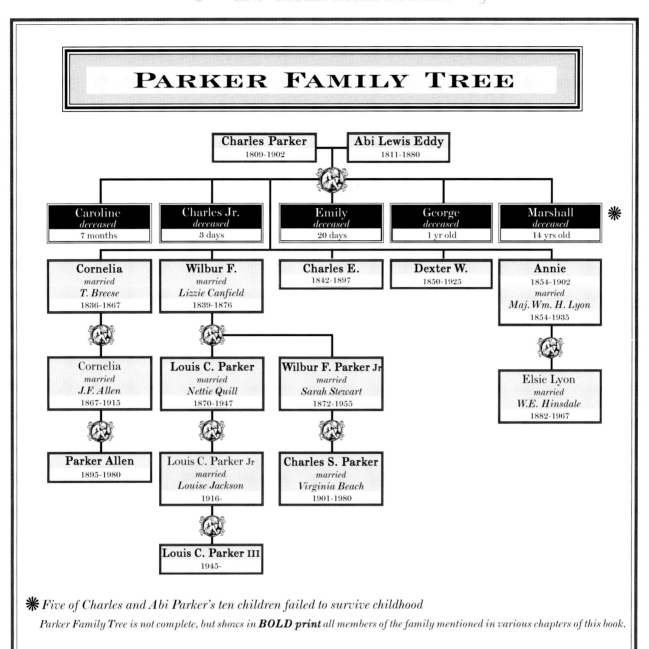

PARKER FAMILY TREE

Charles Parker
1809-1902

Abi Lewis Eddy
1811-1880

Caroline
deceased
7 months

Charles Jr.
deceased
3 days

Emily
deceased
20 days

George
deceased
1 yr old

Marshall
deceased
14 yrs old ✱

Cornelia
married
T. Breese
1836-1867

Wilbur F.
married
Lizzie Canfield
1839-1876

Charles E.
1842-1897

Dexter W.
1850-1925

Annie
1854-1902
married
Maj. Wm. H. Lyon
1854-1935

Cornelia
married
J.F. Allen
1867-1915

Louis C. Parker
married
Nettie Quill
1870-1947

Wilbur F. Parker Jr
married
Sarah Stewart
1872-1955

Elsie Lyon
married
W.E. Hinsdale
1882-1967

Parker Allen
1895-1980

Louis C. Parker Jr
married
Louise Jackson
1916-

Charles S. Parker
married
Virginia Beach
1901-1980

Louis C. Parker III
1945-

✱ *Five of Charles and Abi Parker's ten children failed to survive childhood*
Parker Family Tree is not complete, but shows in **BOLD print** *all members of the family mentioned in various chapters of this book.*

gun patents to his credit. He earned his management position by working in the shop, and served a three- or possibly five-year apprenticeship learning Charles Parker's various businesses from the bottom up. Rumor has it that he was jailed by the Confederacy at Richmond for the "crime" of being a northern industrialist, and he may have contracted tuberculosis ("consumption") in a southern prison. Wilbur founded his own weekly publication—*The American Sportsman*—in October 1871, and was referred to as "editor-proprietor" in the 1874 *Meriden City Directory*. The sixteen-page pulp tabloid was published at West Meriden, cost ten cents per copy (four dollars per year) payable in advance, and had a nationwide circulation among hunters, anglers, and other outdoorsmen. *The American Sportsman* was a natural advertising vehicle for Parker Brothers and Parker shotguns, and was eventually sold to the predecessor of *Forest and Stream*. Wilbur died on Christmas Day, 1876, at thirty-seven years of age in Florida, and his widow then returned to Meriden with their two children, Louis C. Parker and Wilbur F. Parker Jr., ages six and four respectively. The only mention I found of Louis C. (born 1870, died March 29, 1947) in all my research was that he managed Parker's New York City salesroom and was in charge of a Parker Brothers exhibit at a turn-of-the-century Madison Square Garden Sportsmen's Exposition. Wilbur F. Jr. (born 1872, died October 26, 1955) seemed to have a higher public profile than his older brother, was active in various trapshooting organizations, and was involved in management of the family business as vice president and chairman of the board. His son Charles S. Parker (born 1901, died September 3, 1980) was president of The Charles Parker Company when the assets of Parker Brothers were sold to Remington in mid-1934.

The centennial year of 1876 was a big year at Charles Parker's company and, in turn, Parker Brothers. The business was incorporated, Charles Sr. semiretired, and Charles E., then thirty-four years of age, succeeded to the day-to-day management of the business. As noted, his older brother, Wilbur F., died in Florida on Christmas Day of that year. Younger brother Dexter had graduated from the U. S. Military Academy at West Point in 1870, but due to the surplus of Civil War officers in a peacetime army, he served only one year of active duty and then returned to Meriden to serve his three- to five-year apprenticeship in the family business. Dexter was just starting to get involved in management when Charles E. assumed overall responsibility for the newly incorporated The Charles Parker Company. Charles E.'s twenty-one-year tenure, from 1876 to 1897, is best described in a story—"Death of Charles E. Parker"—on the front page of *Shooting and Fishing* for May 27, 1897, which so fairly characterizes the posture of Parker Brothers for the last quarter of the nineteenth century that I will quote it in its entirety:

On the evening of the first day's meeting at Peekskill [New York, May 11, 1897], while the shooting men were discussing the events of the day, a telegram which was handed to one of the sportsmen who had been competing in jolly fashion in the day's work caused a wave of regret to pass over the minds of all. The recipient was Wilbur F. Parker, and the telegram announced the death of Charles E. Parker, the head and business manager of the vast manufacturing interests of the company at Meriden, Conn. While few knew Charles E. Parker, thousands of men knew of the Parker Bros., whose shotguns made the firm name known the world over. Years ago I knew Wilbur F. Parker, the elder of the brothers, well. The manufactory had been just started, and if ever there was an enthusiast in all that regards American guns or the capabilities of American mechanics, that man was Wilbur F. Parker. He most certainly led the way in the work of making shotguns in this country and the development of the manufacture has been something to be talked about. Wilbur F. passed away many years ago, leaving all things to the management of [his brother] Charles. The latter was an entirely different type of man from Wilbur F. He was pushing, eager to adopt improved methods, leaving nothing unexamined which might lead to the bettering of anything produced at the Meriden manufactory. Charles was infinitely more conservative in thought and deed. Things had to be proved good before he would adopt them. I can recall an instance in point. It was when the nitro powders first came to be used. Sportsmen favored them, began to use them extensively, and they asked that guns be guaranteed; that is, that the barrels of guns made here should be of strength enough to resist all strain caused by the combustion of nitro powders. To the credit of L. C. Smith Co., it was one of the first to issue such guarantee. Charles E. Parker refused to do so for a long time, but ultimately realized it had to be done, and then of course did it, and did it thoroughly. I remember in those early days reading a paragraph of a letter written by Charles E. Parker in answer to an inquiry as to his guarantee of guns, which stated that "when the tail wagged the dog, then they would give such guarantee as was desired." I do not wish to give the impression that Charles E. Parker was not up to the character of modern business life. He was eminently so, but his conservatism in all things connected with the Parker Bros. gun made him more than cautious. The gun had made itself a name throughout the world as a model of strength and of shooting quality, and he did not intend to jeopardize its reputation by taking up any new idea; at least not until it had demanded by its proved excellence that it was desirable to make use of the improvement.

In person Charles E. Parker was of the New England type of manhood. Tall and spare, with a clean cut face, which resembled when seen in profile the heads upon a Grecian cameo. He was brown-haired and blue-eyed, the latter keen and expressive. He was in thought a sportsman, for while not fond of shooting himself, he was at all times ready to take part pecuniarily in a contest where some man he liked was to be one of the contestants. While his home was at Meriden, Conn., he resided so much in this city [New York] that he was a well-known figure in club life. His passing away cannot be said to be unexpected, yet it was a surprise for all that. He had been far from well for a year past, when an attack recently of something like pneumonia confined him to the house. He rallied from the attack, and he was thought to be in no immediate danger, and that while his illness was a serious one he would pull through. There came, however, a relapse, which was as sudden as it was unexpected, and which ended, as was told, in the telegram received at Peekskill.

Charles E. Parker was a bachelor, leaving as inheritors of the large interests at Meriden a number of near relatives, chief of whom are, I think, the sons of the late Wilbur F. The corporation was almost altogether a family one. The business will no doubt go right along without a hitch or break. As I saw somewhere recently, where the death of an individual was noticed, a man who occupied large space in the business interests of this country, "No man is necessary, but some are missed."
—signed Jacob Pentz

Charles and Abi Parker had two daughters. The older, Cornelia, died in 1867 at age thirty-one and was survived by two children. Cornelia and her children were outside of the managerial loop, but her grandson, Parker B. Allen, was president of the corporation in 1957, when the shareholders agreed to sell the last remnants of Charles Parker's company to Union Manufacturing Co., thus ending 125 years of family ownership.

Charles and Abi's younger daughter Annie (born 1854, died December 30, 1902) married Major William H. Lyon in 1880, and he became president of The Charles Parker Company in 1925, when Dexter died at the age of seventy-five (Dexter never married or had children). Much of the success of The Charles Parker Company and Parker Brothers was due to the efforts of Major Lyon. Charles Parker's obituary in the March 1902 issue of *Sports Afield* said

> . . . during the past few years the conduct and management of the immense industries he built up has rested with his son-in-law, William H. Lyon, to whose ability and business vim their present prosperity is largely due.

The Great Depression marked the end of Parker Brothers' gun works as the flagship example of an artisan-oriented manufacturing process. Meanwhile, the other divisions of The Charles Parker Company were becoming less competitive in the hardware business, and in 1932 a reorganization took place whereby the firm was split. The Meriden newspaper reported that

> . . . on September 1, 1932, The Charles Parker Company was separated into two corporations, Charles Parker Estate, Inc., and The Charles Parker Company.

Charles Parker Estate, Inc. is essentially a holding company, owning the real estate, buildings, and investments of the company. The Charles Parker Company is an operating company, engaged solely in the manufacture and sale of the company's products.

William H. Lyon became president of the real-estate company, and Charles S. Parker (Charles's great-grandson) took over as president of the operating company. Thus Charles S. was in a position to sell the assets of the Parker Brothers operation to Remington Arms Co., Inc., in mid-1934. Remington moved the manufacture of the Parker Gun to Ilion, New York, in late 1937, and the *Hartford Times* reported on September 10, 1938, that

The old Parker gun factory on Cherry Street . . . has been purchased by The International Silver Company . . . the plant was established in 1853-54 . . . no definite plans for its use have been made . . . good will, name, machinery and inventory of the Parker Brothers, long famous for their hunting rifles [sic], were bought by the Remington Arms Company in May, 1934, and the business was moved to Ilion, N.Y., last December, although the land and buildings remain in the Parker estate.

The Union Manufacturing Co. of New Britain, Connecticut, maker of Uno-Vac stainless-steel vacuum bottles, acquired The Charles Parker Company in 1957 as a wholly owned subsidiary. After the acquisition, the newspaper clipping file at the library documents a low-profile, "hanging-in-there" manufacturing operation producing insulated containers and commercial bathroom fixtures through the 1960s and 1970s. Then, in the early 1980s, the company was plagued by shutdowns, labor problems, layoffs, strikes, and both federal and civil environmental contamination lawsuits. The handwriting was on the wall. There were rumors of moving the manufacturing facilities to Taiwan.

Then, in July 1984, the company abruptly began manufacturing its products in Mexico. As happened with other manufacturing concerns that date back to the Civil War, the ground under the Parker factory was saturated with oil. By the 1980s, environmental concerns were a new challenge, and a federal lawsuit was filed. The Charles Parker Company eventually settled its environmental lawsuit with the federal government for a $1,000 nuisance value, but it continued to be involved in litigation in the federal courts with two environmental groups. The union contract lapsed in September, and on November 1, 1984, the last factory employees were laid off permanently. The *Meriden Record Journal* for November 8, 1984, reported that ". . . the layoffs last week represented the shutdown of the last local operating division of the 152-year-old company." Thus ended Charles Parker's company and the industrial prosperity of Meriden, Connecticut. The company had made Meriden an industrial city and Parker was its leading citizen. When the city incorporated in 1867, Charles Parker was the first mayor, and his legacy to Meriden was more than a century and a half of industrial wealth and employment. The Charles Parker Company wasn't a victim of the unions or the environmentalists in the 1980s, but had simply become obsolete and was a victim of the times.

During April 1996, Nancy and I spent three days in Meriden researching for this book, and the place is pretty bleak. The people we met were universally friendly, gracious, and eager to help; but the town itself is quintessential rust belt, with plywood covering the windows of vacant downtown stores and office buildings. The primary industry seems to be fast foods. The Parker Brothers gun works site, which once employed hundreds of skilled gun mechanics, is now occupied by government-subsidized housing. We overheard too many conversations among young people reflecting their desire to

Parker Brothers gun works office building as it looks in 1996. The office, along with the rest of the gun works, was sold to International Silver Company in 1938, after Remington moved the Parker gun operation to Ilion, New York. Five intrepid Parker collectors visited the old office building in summer 1996, and were allowed to scrounge around the attic. Beneath a hundred year's accumulation of coal dust they found a treasure trove of Parker memorabilia. Fortune favors those who are willing to travel long distances, knock on doors, roll up their sleeves, and risk black lung disease.

Larry ("Babe") Del Grego Jr. and son Lawrence carry on the family tradition of Parker gunsmithing and restoration in their shop at Ilion, New York.

leave for elsewhere as soon as possible. The older people seem to dwell in the past, and we heard repeated references to some unnamed but omnipotent "they" who had somehow changed their lives for the worse. Meriden is an American tragedy in 1996, but it is not alone. Our next stop was Ilion, New York, to touch base at the Remington Museum and visit master Parker gunsmiths Larry Del Grego Jr. and his son Lawrence. We asked our motel keeper in Ilion to recommend a good restaurant, and he suggested the Denny's in the next town, five miles away. Again, the people were wonderful, but the town itself was rust-belt depressing. The story of the Charles Parker company, Parker Brothers gun works, and The Parker Gun is really the story of the industrialization and subsequent de-indus-trialization of America. Perhaps if Charles Parker had been born a century later, he might have created a better burger rather than the Parker shotgun.

Charles Parker was born during the presidency of Thomas Jefferson and lived to see Theodore Roosevelt become the twenty-sixth president of the United States. He witnessed almost every significant development in sporting arms after the invention of gunpowder and ignition by match and flint. The history of the Parker gun is the history of the breechloading, side-by-side, double-barrel shotgun in the United States. However, Charles Parker and the Miller brothers didn't create the Parker shotgun in a vacuum. Let me digress to some of the preconditions that set the stage for development of the first Parker shotgun.

Setting the Stage

3

Geoffrey Boothroyd is the oracle when it comes to anachronistic fowling pieces of British and European origin. Not surprisingly, he wrote a book—*The Shotgun—History and Development* (1985)—that is definitive of the sixty-year period (1805 to 1865) preceding the design of the first Parker shotgun. According to Boothroyd:

> A simple view of the nineteenth century would be that flint ignition was replaced by percussion, following the Forsyth patent of 1807, and percussion muzzleloaders were rendered obsolete by the Lefaucheux pinfire breechloader which was first seen [in England] at the Great Exhibition of 1851. The pinfire, in its turn, was then replaced by the central-fire shotgun and the remainder of the development was concerned with mechanical detail such as extractors, ejectors and self-cocking actions.

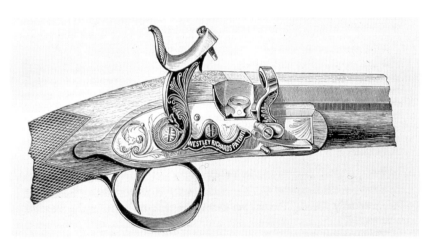

Wesley-Richards circa 1821 detonating gun could be used with loose fulminate powder, detonating patches, or paper caps. Note the connection between cock and pan cover. The gun is shown cocked and ready for priming. After a cap or patch was laid in the flash-pan, the cover was pressed down to protect the fulminate until firing when the falling hammer caused the cover to move away from the pan by means of the pivoted lever marked "Westley Richards Patentee." Dr. Maynard of Washington, D.C., refined this particular detonating method with his invention of a tape primer similar to a roll of paper caps used by a child's toy cap gun.

The first successful percussion priming system was invented in 1805 by the Reverend Alexander Forsyth, a Scotch clergyman. The merit of his invention was immediately recognized by the British military, and Forsyth was brought to the Tower of London Armory to develop and refine his process. The basic invention was a mixture of fulminate of mercury and gunpowder that would explode violently upon impact. Forsyth harnessed the flash of the fulminate to ignite the blackpowder charge. Letters of patent were issued on April 11, 1807, describing the invention of percussion ignition. Reverend Forsyth's original patent locks utilized *loose* oxymuriate of potash cut with charcoal and sulfur. A large number of derivative patent improvements—making the detonating compound more useful by capsulation in paper caps, pellets, tubes, balls, copper percussion caps, and finally primers as we know them today—provided a life's work for any number of English patent solicitors in the early 1800s. While the British were busy litigating percussion firearms to a high level of achievement, Charles Parker was building a hardware-manufacturing empire of financial strength to allow him the luxury of building expensive fine guns in his latter years. Fortune favors the well prepared.

Another innovation crucial to the development of the Parker gun was the evolving technique of mass production pioneered in America by Eli Whitney in 1798, when his machines rapidly produced large numbers of interchangeable parts for muskets. Samuel Colt and Elihu Root refined the idea in 1849 by dividing and simplifying steps in the manufacturing process to achieve faster and more uniform production of Colt revolvers.

There was wild rice along the Illinois River in 1870, when Joe Long and Fred Kimbell hunted ducks near Peoria. Artwork from Joe Long's 1874 first edition of American Wild-fowl Shooting.

Samuel Colt went to England for the Great Exhibition of 1851, at the invitation of the British government, to do a lecture tour expounding on his manufacturing techniques. The British, nevertheless, continued to favor hand-built "best" guns, while the American experience compelled almost universal adoption of Colt's semimass-production methods.

Edward Maynard, a doctor of dental surgery in and around Washington, D.C., patented a fulminate-tape priming device for muzzleloading muskets in 1845, and Christian Sharps patented his breechloading rifle for use with a linen cartridge in 1848. By 1851 Dr. Maynard had patented his first breechloading rifle for use with a metallic cartridge, and Sharps's rifle was in production and gaining popularity. The Sharps and Maynard rifles were breakthrough American weapons. The ability to disconnect the breech from the barrels and insert a pre-loaded, self-contained powder charge and projectile was the beginning of modern firearms. However, neither Sharps's linen cartridge nor Maynard's metallic cartridge would stand the test of time—both were externally primed. While the Maynard and Sharps rifles (with optional single shotgun barrels) may seem to be precursors of Charles Parker's breechloading doubles, I believe all close ancestors of 1860s Parker shotguns were strictly British and French.

The breechloading shotgun, as we know it today, traces to France in the 1830s, when Casimir Lefaucheux patented several break-action, breechloading, externally primed firearms. By 1836 Lefaucheux was building single-shot fowling pieces for use with a self-contained pinfire cartridge. Lefaucheux's gun, with its characteristic lever opener on the fore-end, was introduced to England in 1851 at the Great Exhibition. Some British gunmakers licensed the French patents, and a good number of pinfires were built; but after 1858 Schneider's (French patent) center-fire gun with snap-action, under-lever opener, and

shell extractors led British gunmakers into the last developmental phase of the double-barrel shotgun. Well-known London gunmaker G. H. Daw purchased Schneider's patents; however, all he got for his money was litigation. According to W. W. Greener in the 1910 edition of his tome, *The Gun and Its Development*:

> The central-fire cartridge, practically as now in use, was introduced into . . . [England] . . . in 1861 by Mr. Daw. It is said to have been the invention of M. Pottet, of Paris, and was improved upon by a M. Schneider, and gave rise to considerable litigation with reference to patent rights. Mr. Daw, who controlled the English patents, was defeated by Messrs. Eley Bros., owing, it is understood, to the fact that the patent had not been kept in force in France, where the invention was originally protected. Mr. Daw was the only exhibitor of central-fire guns and cartridges at the International Exhibition in 1862. . . .

French and British pinfires of the 1850s were too delicate and expensive for the American trade, and few examples found their way across the Atlantic. British improvements of Lefaucheux's breech-opening mechanism, and the move away from pinfire to "central" or center-fire shotshells, were still at the experimental stage when the South Carolina boys in gray declared open season on Fort Sumter. While Americans were busy deciding "one nation or two," the British developed the center-fire self-contained shotshell. Daw's center-fire cartridge, as it is shown in Greener's book, appears to be a low-brass paper shell with the primer having its own anvil. Thanks to Eley Bros., Daw's self-primed shotshell was in the public domain by 1862.

Self-primed paper shotshells were available from England soon after hostilities concluded in April 1865. J. H. Johnston's *Great Western Gun Works Catalog* for 1871 shows breechloading, side-by-side shotguns by W. W. Greener, Westley Richards, and

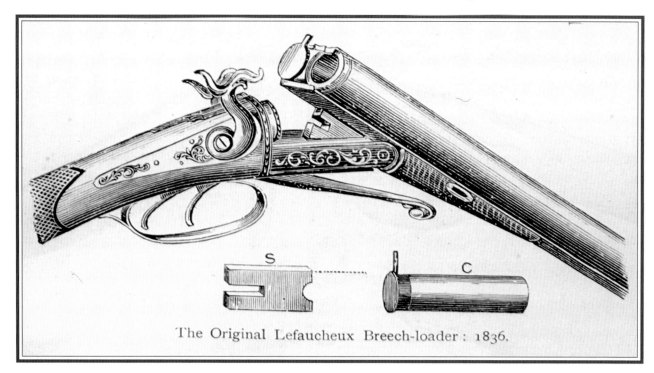

The Original Lefaucheux Breech-loader: 1836.

Lefaucheux's circa 1836 breechloader for pin-fire cartridge. The Lefaucheux "crutch gun" had a weak, clumsy, and inefficient breech-bolt. The Civil War spared most Americans the pin-fire inconveniences.

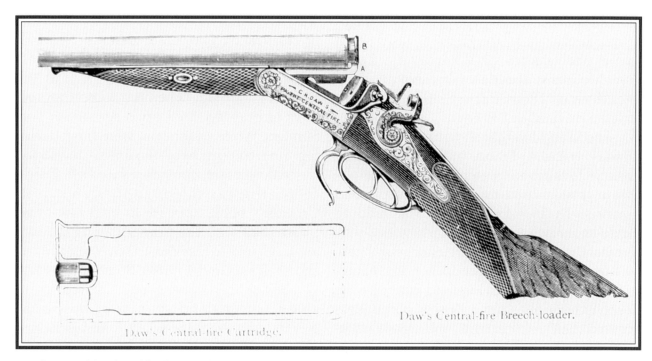

Daw's Central-fire Breech-loader.

Daw's Central-fire Cartridge.

Daw's central-fire breechloader introduced in England in 1861. The shotshell appears to be paper with a brass base and Boxer-type primer.

E. M. Reilly—and imported paper "cartridge shells," costing as little as a penny apiece, in 10-, 12-, 14-, and 16-bore—but no American-made breechloading doubles and no brass shotshells. The British referred to shotshells as "cartridges," and the reference to "cartridge shells" simply meant they were empty, ready to load. It wasn't until the 1890s that factory loads became universally available. The method prevailing in the U. S. during the 1860s and 1870s was that paper and brass shotshells and primers were bought mail-order, while the heavy and expensive-to-ship powder and shot were purchased locally. Imported British paper shells were difficult to load when new, and all but impossible to reload more than once. It's not surprising that Americans preferred brass shotshells early-on. John Bumstead wrote *On The Wing* in 1869 as a primer for the newly emerging class of post-Civil War sportsmen. He objected to paper shotshells and thought

> . . . the contrivances for fixing the ammunition for these tipping guns [British breechloaders] seems to have been constructed with the idea of making the manufacture of cartridges a highly professional operation.

Shotshell loading in England *was* a highly professional operation. The aristocratic British sportsmen bought factory loads and discarded the difficult-to-reload empties. While most British guns of the late 1860s were chambered for paper, American guns were special-ordered to shoot either paper or brass, but not both. (The 1869 Parker catalog offered guns chambered *A* for paper or *B* for brass.) American sportsmen and market hunters came to prefer brass shotshells for ease of reloading, wet-proofing, durability, and long life. By the early 1870s, brass shotshells were interchangeable with paper shells and were head-stamped *A* to distinguish them from the older-style, smaller- and out-side-diameter brass shells stamped *B*, which

fit the older B-chambered guns—such was the rapid development of shotgun ammunition from the late 1860s to the early 1870s.

The transition from muzzleloader to breechloader was a multistep process, and not without controversy. W. W. Greener and his father, William, had a serious falling out over the newfangled "tipping guns," William believing that

> . . . no fear need be entertained that the use of breechloaders will become general.

Peter Hawker had even gone so far as to

> . . . caution the whole world against using firearms that are opened and loaded at the breech—a horrid ancient invention, revived by foreign makers, that is dangerous in the extreme.

Lefaucheux's foreign-made breechloader was called "the French crutch gun" by its detractors. Conventional wisdom was that a muzzleloader shot harder than a breechloader, but this was quickly disproved in gun trials. There was, however, a certain attraction to loading the charge from the muzzle-end in the field. I'll let Joe Long, author of *American Wild-fowl Shooting* (1874), explain:

> To be brief, a man risks fewer long, wild shots with a muzzleloader, and consequently wastes less ammunition, has less extra bulk and weight to carry, as shells, loading-tools, etc. In boat-shooting, if he uses two muzzleloaders, he can, I think, kill more game the season through than with one breechloader, as he will frequently have opportunities to shoot both guns into the same flock of ducks before they get out of reach.

Long's most compelling argument, however, was

> . . . brought to . . . mind very forcibly, though rather unwillingly, and most frequently whilst sitting up at night loading shells and listening to the snoring of my fellow-hunters, votaries of the

"Tubs and Decoys" from an original 1884 etching, courtesy of Dan and Jane Behr.

muzzleloader, who, having eaten their supper, washed their guns, and refilled their pouches and flasks, had rolled up in their blankets to "woo tired nature's sweet restorer."

So there it is—the best argument in support of the muzzleloader was that the hunter could turn in early after a hard day's hunt, while his breechloader buddies burned the midnight oil loading shells.

Invention of the fulminate priming system by Rev. Forsyth led to development of a tape-fulminate priming device by Dr. Maynard. The Sharps breechloading rifle for use with a linen cartridge preceded Dr. Maynard's development of a breechloading rifle for use with a self-contained but externally primed brass cartridge. While the breechloading rifle was developed and refined by American gunmakers, the French-man Lefaucheux gets credit for the first breechloading shotgun using a self-contained (albeit pinfire) shotshell. Pinfire sporting ammunition was never popular in the United States, as this transitional cartridge became obsolete during the Civil War. The British improved the French-patent breechbolting and quickly adopted the center-fire cartridge after Eley Bros.' lawyers broke Daw's patent. Mass-production techniques and the interchangeable system of manufacturing gun components pioneered by Whitney and Colt were adopted by the British for the manufacture of self-primed paper shotshells circa 1862, and by American gunmakers to build shotguns after the Civil War. The stage was set for William Miller to assemble Charles Parker's first Parker shotgun.

First Parker Shotgun

The first Parker shotgun was built by Meriden Manufacturing Company for Charles Parker shortly after the Civil War. William H. Miller was then superintendent of Parker's Meriden Man'fg. Co. gun works and had overseen the production of upwards of 20,000 carbines and rifle-muskets during the war. Miller devised and patented what he considered to be an improved breech-locking mechanism on November 13, 1866, and immediately assigned the patent rights to his employer. The first series of Parker shotguns was built strictly to Miller's patent drawings. They were caplock breechloaders with a lifter-actuated clasp from top of breech to barrel rib ("T-Latch") breech-locking mechanism. The first "Lifter T-Latch" guns were chambered for a Maynard-type brass cartridge with a tiny hole in the center of the base. This specially manufactured metallic cartridge (more an auxiliary chamber than a shotshell) was the last refinement of Rev. Forsyth's method of external priming. Ignition was achieved with a common percussion cap, struck by a hammer, and the flash routed through the standing breech via a tube to a hole in the base of the cartridge to fire the black-powder charge. Various transitional shotshells and cartridges of the 1860s and 1870s are pictured in the first color section; however, examples of the two "auxiliary chambers" that accompanied each new T-Latch are the "missing link" of shotshell evolution.

Much care is bestowed to make it what the Sportsman needs—a good gun.

Charles Parker

Collectors agree that the first series of Parker shotguns was built by and marked *MERIDEN MAN'FG. CO., MERIDEN, CONN. FOR CHA'S PARKER* shortly after the Civil War. Peter Johnson wrote about the *first* Parker shotgun in his 1961 book, *Parker—America's Finest Shotgun*, and claimed that

> . . . this first Parker gun . . . [shown on frontispiece] . . . is, of course, a hammer gun, which is operated by a lifter bolting mechanism, and a fore-end fastened to the barrel by a key through a hole in the loop. *It is .14 gauge with a 29 inch barrel.* [*Emphasis mine*]

First model Miller-patent T-Latch Parker shotgun built by Meriden Man'fg Co., for Cha's Parker, *s/n 90 from the Meriden Historical Society collection. Notice the hole between the barrels is engaged by a* breech pin *when the gun closes. This breech pin was the germ of an idea for Wilbur Parker's improved bolting mechanism (bolt to slot at back of barrel lump) used throughout seventy plus years of "Old Reliable" production. Also notice the percussion cap nipple and "fence" which protected the shooter's eyes and face should a cap disintegrate.*

The gun pictured and referred to by Johnson was found among the personal effects of Wilbur F. Parker Jr. after his death in 1955, and now resides at the Meriden Historical Society. The problem is, the Meriden gun is *not* 14-gauge and the barrels are *not* twenty-nine inches long. Nevertheless, Johnson wrote the first book about Parker guns, and authors of Parker-related books and articles who followed, with few exceptions, simply repeated his misinformation.

David F. Butler in his 1973 book, *The American Shotgun,* had this to say about the first Parker shotgun:

> . . . [Parker's] . . . first models of a commercial double-barreled shotgun were completed and marketed in 1868. *It was a breechloading 14-gauge shotgun with 29-inch barrels [emphasis mine]* using "outside primed" ammunition.

This was a transitional ammunition with the powder charge, wads and shot contained in a brass case with a small hole in the base. Ignition was provided by conventional percussion caps, which were fitted on nipples similar to those on muzzle loading shotguns. The flame from the caps was directed through a small passage and passed through a hole in the head of the shell, igniting the main charge. This type of ammunition was quite similar to the Maynard rifle cartridge widely used during the Civil War.

According to Larry Baer in *The Parker Gun—An Immortal American Classic,* early Parker guns

> . . . were not of a center-fire primer type, but were fired by means of a percussion cap which traveled a spark through a nipple and detonated the powder in a brass

shotshell case . . . [and] . . . the early . . . Charles Parker guns were taken from the design of William H. Miller's improvement of breechloading firearms in 1866, which was originally invented for associated use with the center fire type cartridges invented by Maynard. Later, Isaac M. Milbank in 1867 developed the center fire primer type metallic shell as we know it today. The first Parkers were of a center fire type. But the use of a removable primer placed inside the case and detonated by percussion, as was the Milbank invention, was not added until later.

Let's take a short sidebar to clarify some cartridge issues that are not necessarily misstated but could be misinterpreted. First, Maynard didn't invent the center-fire-type cartridge, and he is not credited with the externally primed cartridge ignited through a tiny hole in its base. Ambrose E. Burnside, inventor of the Burnside rifle, gets credit for the "flash-hole" centered in the base of a metallic cartridge, and, in fact, Maynard credited Burnside in his own 1856 patent application. In this context, the reference to a "Maynard" cartridge in the letters patent for Miller's T-Latch explains his use of quotation marks. The second sidebar issue is the part Isaac M. Milbank played in the development of the self-contained cartridge fired by a removable primer. Milbank's innovation was *not* self-priming with a removable cap or primer, but was simply to reinforce the base of an existing center-fire cartridge with an internal disk, soldered in place, so as to mitigate the repeated impact of the hammer against the base of the reloadable cartridge.

Parker Brothers adopted Milbank's strengthener to use in conjunction with Hiram Berdan's priming system (anvil in the base of the cartridge rather than part of the primer), and the Milbank and Berdan patent dates were printed on boxes of circa 1870s "Parker's Patent Metallic-Shells." The next step was to eliminate the hammering of the shotshell base altogether by substituting British Boxer-type

primers with their own anvils. Milbank's base-strengthening patent became passé in the late 1870s with the advent of one-piece shotshells punched, annealed, and extruded from brass disks with thin walls and a thick base cupped for Boxer-type primers. For some strange reason, the American market gravitated to the British Boxer primer, while the British favored the American Berdan type. Sorry for the digression; now back to Parker's first shotgun.

Michael McIntosh joined the "14-gauge with 29-inch barrel" club in 1981 when he wrote *The Best Shotguns Ever Made in America*

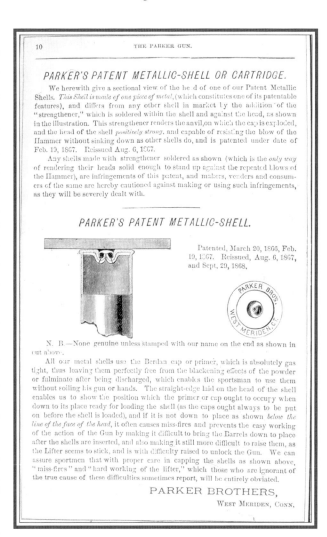

Parker Brothers 1872 catalog introduced the standard Berdan-primed, Milbank-strengthened, "Parker's Patent Metallic-Shell or Cartridge" manufactured by Union Metallic Cartridge of Bridgeport, Connecticut. Original catalog courtesy of Pat McKune.

and "Charlie Parker's Shotgun" (a chapter of the anthology *Second To None*). Colonel Charles Askins wrote about Parker's early years in an article, "The Classic Parker Shotgun" (1973 *Guns Annual*), but the closest he came to certifying the first Parker was to picture a hammer gun with lifter-opener and 1878-patent Deeley & Edge fore-end latch—a gun built more than ten years after Parker's first catalog. Parker Brothers, May 1, 1877, catalog claims that ". . . the Parker shotgun has been known in the market for the last twelve years . . . ." This may have been slight puffery as there's no evidence of a circa 1865 Parker shotgun. All five T-Latches I've seen display Miller's November 13, 1866, patent date on the upper tang. Suffice it to say that Parker literature has suffered from scant original research. Too many gunwriters took the path of least resistance by adopting Johnson's sometimes unreliable and mostly unverified information.

Norm Flayderman was correct when he wrote in the "American Shotguns and Fowling Pieces" section of *Flayderman's Guide to Antique American Firearms . . . and Their Values* (third to sixth editions) that ". . . [Parker's] . . . first side-by-side shotgun has yet to be positively identified; it has been variously reported by most researchers as being 14 gauge, however this seems unlikely as their earliest catalogs do not mention that gauge at all; the 14 gauge was not introduced until the 1880s." Flayderman refers to a copy of Parker Brothers' 1869 catalog, which offered guns in 10- , 11- , and 12-gauge. My research of collateral material (such as old gun catalogs and advertising) failed to disclose any contemporary American 14-gauge breechloading shotguns. However, .69-caliber smoothbore muskets were converted to fowling pieces, some were converted to breechloaders, and breechloading double-barrel shotguns were built using surplus musket barrels after the Civil War. When Johnson wrote of the ".14 gauge [*sic*]," he may have meant 14-bore, which is .69 caliber. My curiosity led me to his source—the Meriden Historical Society (MHS). I spoke to Al Weathers, curator, who undertook to do a little research for me. Here's what he reported:

> The *first* Parker at the Meriden Historical Society (MHS) is a breechloading, double-barreled shotgun with straight grip and a steel buttplate. Lock plates on both sides are stamped MERIDEN MAN'FG. CO., MERIDEN,

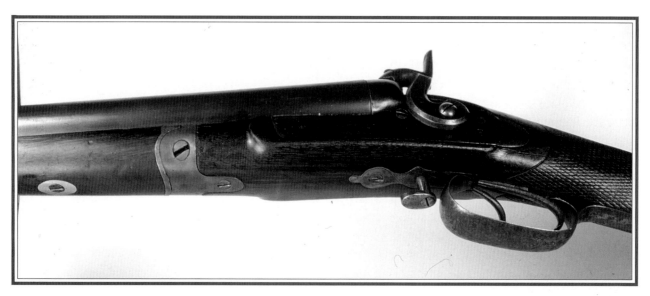

Bottom view of Meriden Man'fg for Cha's Parker T-Latch s/n 290, courtesy of Bob White and Greysolon Arms. Notice the old style lifter-opener and fore-end attached by a screw.

CONN., FOR CHA'S PARKER, and the gun is identical to the Lifter T-Latch shown on W. H. Miller's patent drawing. The Miller patent is memorialized on the tang behind the hammers as *Patented Nov. 13, 1866*, the barrel rib has no marking, and the barrels have no pattern. My guess is they are "Best Gun Iron" converted musket tubes.

Weathers measured the barrels to be exactly twenty-eight inches long. The MHS gun has a 13⅞-inch pull and is forty-four inches overall. He also measured the inside of the barrels and reported a rough measurement of ¾-inch. A dime (.705-inch) fits as loose as it would in a modern 12-gauge gun bored Skeet. The Meriden gun is chambered for a special 12-gauge brass shotshell consistent with the under .750-inch-diameter muzzle. The gun has percussion-cap geometry with flash tubes rather than firing pins. The right percussion tube is broken off, with nothing visible but a hole in the divot at the back of the breech. The left percussion tube is intact and stands above the divot, attached by a round metal nut having two flat sides. Early Parker catalogs offered a nipple wrench to fit this special nut. Flash tubes lead to ¹⁄₃₂-inch flash holes at center chamber to mate with corresponding flash holes of special Maynard-type shotshells that accompanied each gun. The chambers are two inches deep and terminate at a very definite ridge, rather than a tapered forcing cone. The sign with the first Parker shotgun at the Meriden Historical Society says:

> Double-barrel shotgun, developed by Meriden, Mfr. for Chas Parker about 1865. The gun opens at the breech by the old elevator type of lock. Two special shells loaded only with shot and powder were inserted. The firing was done in the conventional manner of cocking the hammer and releasing by the trigger pull. This type of percussion primer system of firing which is in general practice today. From estate of Wilbur F. Parker.

Weathers confirmed the gun to be serial number (s/n) 90. Later, when I personally examined the gun, I noticed that the serial number could also be read as 06, depending on which way it was held, but another single-digit T-Latch has no zero preceding. Of the lifter T-Latch guns I have actually handled, the lowest number is s/n 49 at the Puglisi Gun Room in Duluth, and this gun has been retrofitted with firing pins. One Parker researcher in the June 1990 issue of *The Gun Report* wrote that fourteen T-Latch serial numbers are known in the 2 to 729 range. Using an unspecified statistical projection, he was ninety-five percent confident that no more than 903 such guns were built by Meriden Man'fg. Co. for Cha's Parker.

Peter Johnson's claim that the *first* Parker gun had "14-gauge, 29-inch barrels" has no confirmed attribution. The Meriden Historical Society's Lifter T-Latch has twenty-eight-inch barrels, is chambered for special 12-gauge metallic cartridges of the auxiliary chamber type, and is externally primed according to Maynard's system. The fact that the Meriden Historical Society [MHS] gun was a Parker family heirloom may explain why it wasn't retrofitted with firing pins for conventional self-primed shotshells, as were most (if not all) of the other known Meriden Man'fg. Co. for Cha's Parker guns. It's possible that a patent model or prototype was, as a matter of expediency, built at 14-gauge (or bore), but I have my doubts. My facts aren't conclusive one way or the other, but my inside calipers favor an extremely thick-walled, two-inch-long, 12-bore cartridge of the auxiliary chamber type.

William Miller's T-Latch is a somewhat convoluted interpretation of what he no doubt had heard about British shotgun developments during the Civil War years. According to Geoffrey Boothroyd, ". . . in the ten years between 1857 . . . [and 1867] . . . no less than 56 different types of breechbolting were invented. Many were merely modifications of a previous system and some pursued a line of development which was a blind alley in view of later inventions." The evolutionary London and Birmingham guns were one-off, hand-built, and expensive. Few, if any, found their way to American shores, especially during the Civil War. Certain British guns such as Daw's Schneider-patent, Dougall's "Lock-Fast," and the Westley Richards with doll's-head snap-action bolt were truly innovative, but most of the fifty-six breechlock patents from 1857 to 1867 were redundant or dead ends. Time, distance, and the Civil War spared American gunmakers and the American market Lefaucheux's pinfire, but also left American fowling pieces seven to ten years behind state-of-the-art British shotguns.

was a design concept rather than a particular patentable breech-locking method. Miller's T-Latch was snap-action at a time when the Lefaucheux and most contemporary British guns had to be manually locked shut in a clumsy two-step process. (The Lefaucheux, for example, was first closed and then the fore-end lever had to be turned as much as ninety degrees to literally screw the breech shut.) Parker Brothers described its "snap-action movement" in the 1872 catalog:

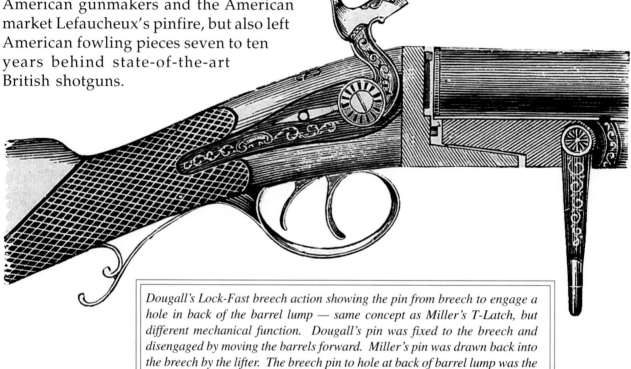

Dougall's Lock-Fast breech action showing the pin from breech to engage a hole in back of the barrel lump — same concept as Miller's T-Latch, but different mechanical function. Dougall's pin was fixed to the breech and disengaged by moving the barrels forward. Miller's pin was drawn back into the breech by the lifter. The breech pin to hole at back of barrel lump was the basis for Parker Brothers toggle-bolt to slot at back of barrel lump, which has to be the simplest, most effective breech-locking method of all time.

Miller's T-Latch seems to blend American ingenuity with misinterpretation of certain British innovations. You might say that Dougall's "Lock-Fast" and Westley Richards's Doll's Head lost something in the translation from "English." It's certain from reading his letters patent that Miller was aware of Daw's gun and the self-primed center-fire shotshell. The snap-action, however,

. . . by snap-action is meant that the locking drive works automatically, by simply bringing the barrels to place, thus dispensing with the extra operation of locking them, which many other breechloaders require. . . .

Miller was on the cutting edge with his snap-action feature, but his bolting mechanism was pure "Rube Goldberg." How could this be?

Well, time and distance had spared American gunmakers the pinfire dead end. The flipside, however, was that knowledge of British advancements came late and piecemeal as second- and third-hand hearsay. It's easy to see how the snap-action concept was incorporated in Miller's T-Latch, as a gun either snaps closed or it doesn't. But Dougall's "Lock-Fast" stud on the standing breech to engage a hole between the barrels (by moving the barrels back and forth with a lever) was interpreted by Miller to be a pin that his lifter moved in and out of the standing breech. Westley Richards's snap-action latch from the breech to engage a slot in a rib extension was interpreted by Miller to be a clasp (T-Latch) from the top of the breech to the rib itself. It's inconceivable Miller would have spent the time and incurred the expense to patent his dead-end T-Latch feature in 1866 if he had ever seen a circa 1864 Westley Richards gun.

The T-Latch patent "improvements" weren't particularly innovative. William Miller's letters patent acknowledge he was

> . . . aware that a latch upon the upper side of the frame has often been used to lock the barrel in its home position [Westley Richards?]. I do not, therefore, broadly claim a latch so constructed; but, having thus fully described my invention, what I do claim as new and useful, and desire to secure by letters patent, is . . . [see Miller's patent drawings and the following explanation].

William Miller's patent was by today's standards no big deal. His first "innovation" was simply putting orientation tabs (*a*) on the T-Latch; the second was a spring-loaded pin (*P*) to keep the lifter and T-Latch in the up position while the gun was broken open; and the third innovation was a "fail-safe" keeper (*N*) to hold the pin, which, in turn, held the lifter in the up position. The fact that the breech pin (*P*) moves forward to engage a matching hole between the barrels when the

gun closes (as does Dougall's "Lock-Fast") is not clearly shown on the patent drawings and doesn't seem to be considered important or patentable. This feature, however, was the germ of an idea that led to Parker's bolt-to-slot in the barrel-lump breech-locking mechanism adopted in 1868. Unfortunately, tabs (*a*) were superfluous while pin (*P*) and keeper (*N*) were not particularly sturdy or reliable; T-Latch guns suffered damage to the locking mechanism while opening and closing in the heat of the hunt and shot them-

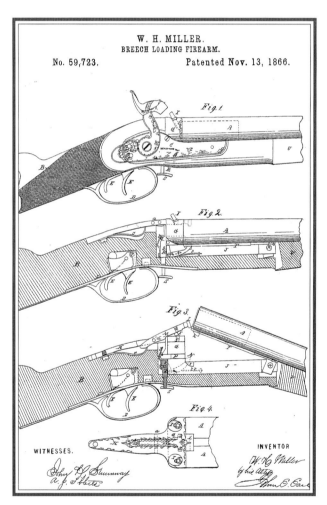

William H. Miller's November 13, 1866, T-Latch patent assigned to his employer Charles Parker. The patent drawings aren't just conceptual, but constitute mechanical drawings for Parker's T-Latch model right down to the engraving on metal parts. Compared to Dougall's Lock-Fast and Westley Richards's rib extension breech-bolting mechanisms, Miller's T-Latch was a fragile toy.

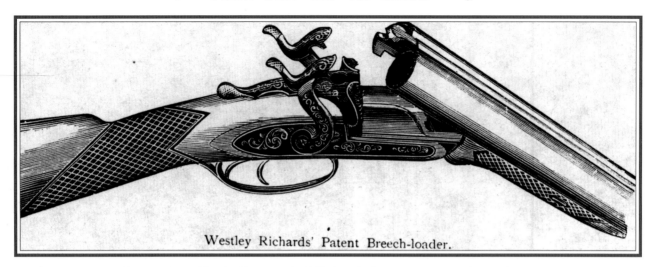

Westley Richards 1862-patent breechloader showing the doll's head rib extension gripped by a sliding bolt actuated by top-lever opener. The rib extension fastener would later be patented in America by F. S. Dangerfield in 1872, and assigned to Daniel Lefever, who refined the doll's head rib extension in 1878. Parker Brothers licensed Lefever's rib extension patent in 1881, for use with their new top-lever opener guns. Parker, however, never bolted through the rib extension.

selves loose all too soon. There must have come a day when Charles Parker regretted the decision to allow his good name to be conspicuously stamped on the side plates of his only bad gun.

Some insight into state-of-the-art circa 1866 can be gleaned from Miller's letters patent, as the inventor covered all bases.

> I have also described my arm as specially adapted to the use of the Maynard or other similar central-fire cartridge; yet the common fulminate-cartridge may be used, it only being required that the hammers so communicate with the cartridge that the blow of the hammer will explode the fulminate. If occasion requires that the arms should be used as a muzzleloader it is only necessary that a cartridge shell should remain in the barrel, so as to prevent the escape of gas at the joint between the rear of the barrel and the breechpiece.

Charles Parker's ad in the 1869 *Middleton Directory* explains the operation of the externally primed Miller T-Latch shotgun:

> The superiority of this breechloader over others consists of its simplicity, combined with great strength and superior workmanship. Two brass cartridges go with each

gun, which can be loaded and reloaded with ordinary ammunition any number of times. The ordinary cap is used, as we think it much safer than to transport ammunition with the cap on the cartridge. No accident can occur as the breech is fastened at the top and bottom of the charge. A simple pressure with the finger presents the barrels for receiving the cartridges. It can be loaded very rapidly, and will carry as accurately as any shot gun ever made. Try it.

A crude etching of what is clearly the T-Latch model is shown in the ad. Reference to the breech being ". . . fastened at the top and bottom of the charge . . ." means the $3/16$-inch pin from the standing breech to the back of the barrels below the charge and the T-Latch (clasp) from the standing breech to the barrel rib above the charge. The gun came with only two brass cartridges, which may seem like a short supply, but the two-inch chambers are cut extremely deep and must have been intended for brass shells of considerable thickness and durability. Miller's T-Latch wasn't chambered for a conventional paper or brass shotshell, but used special auxiliary chamber-type cartridges externally primed on Maynard's system. The diameter difference between the chamber and bore of guns for use

(right) Joe Long would burn the midnight oil ". . . while sitting up at night loading shells and listening to the snoring of my fellow hunters, votaries of the muzzleloaders. . . ." Parker Brothers 12-gauge back-action s/n 0895 with decarbonized steel barrels. Notice the old style lifter-opener and key-fastener fore-end. This gun was built circa 1870, weighs 7¾ pounds, and cost $75 new.

(left) Old cartridges left to right upper— Maynard .69 cal. "mule ear," Maynard "1865" 28-gauge, Maynard "1873" 20-gauge with Wilbur Parker's 1869-patent primer removal slots, Eley pinfire, Wills's patent 10-gauge "Draper;" and bottom left—one-piece Parker Bros' 10A size compared to Parker Bros' 12B, and two-piece 10-gauge Kynoch's Patent brass shotshell.

(left) Parker Brothers circa 1870 s/n 0895 back-action gun with John Bumstead's 1869 book, On The Wing. Bumstead surveyed late-1860s breechloaders and cast his vote in favor of Allen's New Patent lid-opening shotgun, but failed to mention the more popular and successful Parker gun.

(below) Meriden Man'fg Co. for Cha's Parker T-Latch s/n 290 showing early conversion firing pins for use with self-primed cartridges. Notice the absence of a percussion-cap "fence" as seen on the s/n 90 Meriden Historical Society externally primed gun.

(top) *Parker Brothers circa 1870 back-action 12-gauge s/n 0895 showing non-rebounding hammers, square-cut slot in barrel lump, and old-style lifter. Notice the hinge-pin is not recessed and compare this to s/n 9385 in the picture below.*

(bottom) *Parker Brothers circa 1877 front-action 10-gauge s/n 9385 with rebounding hammers. Notice Wilbur Parker's 1875 patent taper-bolt to angle slot in barrel lump, C. A. King's 1875 patent recessed hinge-pin, and Parker's improved one-piece lifter. This gun is Parker's field grade with plain twist barrels and is one of a surprising number that have survived 120 years in excellent condition.*

Parker VHE 12-gauge skeet s/n 239,826 date stamped XE (December 1936) by Remington. Choked skeet in and skeet out, this "lightweight" at 6 pounds, 15 ounces is useful for tracking tight-sitting pheasants in deep snow.

with early brass shotshells is slight; however, there is a visible ridge, which appears to be about $\frac{1}{32}$-inch deep, where the Meriden gun's chambers meet the bores. The Meriden T-Latch was intended for relatively light loads, so the short two-inch 12-gauge cartridges were no handicap. Parker's 1869 catalog recommended ". . . a fair charge for bird shooting with the 12-gauge guns is 2½ drams of powder and 1 ounce of shot."

The Miller-patent gun fit the mid-1860s shotgun market to a tee—no pun intended. One advantage of the Maynard-type shell was that it could be reloaded in the field by simply pouring a proper measure of powder into the cartridge, then push in a wad with one's finger, pour shot, and push in an overshot wad. Detonation was external, and the flash tubes could be kept clean and dry by simply firing a cap with an unloaded shotshell in the chamber. Parker's T-Latch ads touted that ". . . the ordinary cap is used, as we think it much safer than to transport ammunition with the cap on the cartridge." Perhaps they meant safer than contemporary pinfire cartridges, which had the risk of detonating in the hunter's pocket if he bumped into something or fell down.

Parker Brothers' 1869 catalog claimed the "Parker breechloading double-barreled shotgun . . . is the result of over four years of the most thorough experiments. . . ." This seemingly dates the first Parker shotgun to 1865. Various testimonial letters in the catalog have dates ranging from November 18, 1867, through April 10, 1868, and some refer back to guns purchased as early as summer 1867. Contrary to what has been written by other Parker researchers, I believe some (if not all) of the testimonials refer to the T-Latch. Ralph Worthington of Cleveland, Ohio, wrote on November 18, 1867,

> . . . I think, for convenience in loading and firing in the field or in a boat, it is the best I have ever seen. The metallic cartridges you use are far preferable to the paper ones commonly used, and they are not injured by moisture, can be shot any number of times, and are easily reloaded and recapped.

Reloading metallic cartridges ". . . in the field or in a boat . . ." was such a popular option that Wills's 1864 patent-threaded Draper self-primed shotshell continued to be offered by mail-order houses well into the 1870s. The base of the Draper could be unscrewed to insert the percussion cap, thus facilitating reloading in the field. However, Drapers weren't available in 1868, Wilbur Parker's slot-head wasn't patented until 1869, and it's inconceivable that Worthington would have found it convenient to recap Daw-type self-primed shotshells in the field, much less in his boat. He must have been referring to recapping the nipples of the externally primed T-Latch. Close reading of some of the other testimonials leads to this same conclusion.

Miller T-Latch guns were easily converted to use self-primed shotshells by fitting firing pins in drilled-out flash tubes. Most T-Latch guns in the hands of collectors have firing pins. Whether most or all T-Latches were built to be externally primed for use with the Maynard-type cartridge is problematical. William Miller's letters patent, however, clearly show that self-primed ammunition was contemplated:

> . . . the common fulminate-cartridge may be used, it only being required that the hammer so communicate with the cartridge that the blow of the hammer will explode the fulminate.

The "common fulminate cartridge" referred to by Miller may well have been the pinfire. The conversion of caplocks to pinfires was common in Great Britain. However, Parker and other American gunmakers skipped the transitional pinfire and quickly adopted the Daw-type self-contained shotshell.

By the time Meriden Manufacturing Company built the first T-Latch guns on the Maynard system, external priming was obsolete. The first Parker shotguns were sold to a market that had not yet settled on a particular type of self-primed ammunition. The two brass cartridges sold with each T-Latch were special to the Meriden Man'fg. for Cha's Parker gun, likely were made by Parker Brothers, and no doubt led to Wilbur Parker's 1869 patent slot-head innovation. Shotshell development was rapid in the late 1860s. Most caplock Parkers were fitted with firing pins to use self-primed brass shells. Of the few examples of Charles Parker's first gun known to exist today, only one is externally primed, and none, to my knowledge, show evidence of ever having been used with pinfire ammunition.

Early Parkers with the Lifter T-Latch breechlock had "Best Gun Iron Barrels"—likely converted .69-caliber smoothbore musket tubes oversized from nominal 14-bore to 12-, 11-, and 10-gauges. Parker's better-grade, second-model guns had "Laminated Steel" barrels and a different breechlock mechanism. The lifter-actuated T-Latch was re-engineered in 1867 to be a lifter actuated toggle bolt to engage a square slot at the back of the barrel lump. The lifter pin, which had pushed the T-Latch up to open the early guns, continued on as a useless protrusion through the standing breech until 1875, when Charles's son Wilbur F. Parker further improved the bolting mechanism. Early Parker guns were prone to a loose breech, and this was a real bone of contention between muzzleloader and breechloader advocates and critics. As late as 1870, Boston gunmaker Joseph Tonks sold his breechloaders with the promise to build a similar muzzleloader for free if the customer was dissatisfied.

William Miller or Wilbur Parker redesigned the bolting mechanism to eliminate the troublesome T-Latch in 1867, but the

toggle bolt to slot at the back of the barrel lump design wasn't new or patentable. Close review of Miller's patent does not necessarily lead to the conclusion that he claimed rights to the lifter mechanism itself, but often, collateral information in letters patent can be used as a basis to bluff the competition away from imitation or "infringement." While the lifter was a nifty way to open the relatively heavy-barrel early Parkers, the top lever adopted in 1882 was clearly superior.

Noted British gun-book author (and James Bond's weapons consultant) Geoffrey Boothroyd considers the breechloader to have been a chancy investment during the 1850s and 1860s on his side of the big pond, even though Lefaucheux had been building "tipping guns" since the 1830s in France. According to "Major" Boothroyd:

> The Lefaucheux radically altered the design of the British sporting gun by introducing hinged drop-down barrels. The barrels, of course, were open at both ends! Today you think little of this, but put yourself in the shoes of a man who for all his life had kept the explosive force of gunpowder in front of a two-inch long steel plug, screwed into the breech end of the barrel. All that was to be substituted for this was some paper wadding and a thin sheet of brass. No wonder the breechloader was not an instant success. Today it is difficult to appreciate what a lifelong user of a muzzleloader must have felt when asked to use a gun that "broke" in the middle. When opened, many of the breechloaders were loose and certainly some of the early bolting systems could not have given rise to a great deal of confidence.

The litmus test for any American breechloading gun in the 1860s was whether the breech would remain tight or shoot itself loose. John Bumstead discussed the pros and cons of muzzleloaders versus breechloaders in his 1869 book, *On The Wing*:

> I think a sportsman would very naturally inquire if such a gun [breechloader] was

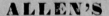

ALLEN'S
NEW PATENT BREECH-LOADING
DOUBLE-BARREL SHOT GUN,

MANUFACTURED BY

ETHAN ALLEN & CO.,
Worcester, Mass.

The cut below represents the gun with the lid open, the guard down, and a cartridge partly withdrawn. Also a longitudinal section of a loaded cartridge shell, showing the conical, or patent chamber form, which is acknowledged to be one of the most desirable features in all good guns.

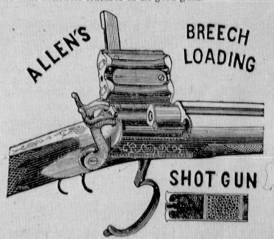

These guns are remarkably strong shooters, and use steel cartridge cases, which will last as long as the gun, and the cartridges can be inserted in the barrels quicker than in any other breech-loader made.

PRICE LIST.

12 GAUGE.	For **Fine Stub Twist**, Oiled or Varnished Stock, well Engraved	$100
	For **Fine Laminated and Damascus**, Oiled or Varnished Stock, finely engraved.	$150
10 GAUGE.	For **Fine Stub Twist**, Oiled or Varnished Stock, well Engraved	$115
	For **Fine Laminated and Damascus**, Oiled or Varnished Stock, finely Engraved	$165

A Cartridge Case, 24 Steel Shells, Loader and Brush, are furnished with each Gun.

Extra Shells, $6.00 per dozen. **Primers, $2.50** per M.

We also manufacture **Muzzle-Loading Double-Barrel Shot Guns** of all grades, from $35 upwards, and warranted superior to foreign-made guns of the same price.

JOHN P. LOVELL & SONS, Agents,
27 Dock Square and 15 Washington Street, Boston.

Allen's New Patent breechloading double-barrel shotgun ad from John Bumstead's 1869 book, On The Wing. *Note the cross section of Allen's 1865 patent shotshell that used a Flobert-type breech cap primer.*

considered perfectly safe. To which inquiry a dapper salesman standing by his side would very likely reply, "Perfectly safe, sir; no gun more so. Why, you could fire a solid, tight fitting ball out of these barrels without starting them a hair." Notwithstanding this very strong endorsement of the gun, the sportsman would still have his doubts about its safety; and I don't think he would give them up even on a still further examination. Indeed, I don't think any amount of assurance would convince him that the disconnecting of the barrels from their abutment; that the complete separation of the chambers from their bases, were not signs of weakness; while his knowledge of what constitutes fitness in any gun, whether muzzle or breechloader, would lead him to conclude that movable barrels would be very liable to get out of order in springing even but slightly at their joints.

Bumstead critiqued British "tipping" shotguns and then asked the rhetorical question: ". . . is there, then, no satisfactory breechloading shotgun, and have we only an impracticable theory for such a weapon?" Having found fault with tipping breechloaders, Bumstead discovers the fixed-barrel, lid-opening, Allen's New Patent breechloading double-barrel shotgun, manufactured by Ethan Allen & Co. (coincidentally advertised in the back of his book). The chapter ends with Bumstead giving his blessing to the new breechloaders: ". . . as between the muzzle and breechloading guns, . . . the latter is the more serviceable weapon, and that is to be the gun of the future." Thus spake American gunwriter John Bumstead. However, *On The Wing* makes no mention of the Parker gun. This probably had to do with loyalty to his advertising patron, Ethan Allen & Co., as it's hard to believe a company so well known as Charles Parker's could have built, advertised, cataloged, and sold almost a thousand guns without Bumstead taking notice. According to *Flayderman's Guide*, only "several hundred or more" Allen's New Patent guns were built and sold. The Parker gun, of course, was the success story of the 1870s and thereafter.

The one thing that sets Parker guns apart from every other side-by-side built in America or abroad is the bolting system. Other, lesser guns fell by the wayside because they closed like an old screen door; Parker guns close like a vault. The hot topic during the transition years from muzzleloaders to breechloaders was whether the newfangled guns would stay tight (i.e., *reliable*), or would quickly shoot themselves loose. When Wilbur F. Parker improved the bolting mechanism in 1875, he devised an angle cut on the barrel lump to match a tapered toggle bolt so as to allow Parker guns to wear themselves tight. This feature alone ensured the success of the "Old Reliable" and the Parker Brothers Gun Works.

Parker Brothers Gun Works

Parker Brothers' breechloading, side-by-side, double-barrel shotgun was built by a hardware manufacturer as a tool useful in reducing certain wild game to possession. Early Parker guns were a quantum leap in firepower compared to contemporary muzzleloading doubles and breechloading singles. The Parker shotgun was innovative in its early years, as was any 1860s breechloader. By the 1890s, however, the Parker gun lost its edge with the advent of repeating shotguns, particularly the popular Winchester Model 1897. After the turn of the century, Parker Brothers thrived by making fine hand-finished doubles for a niche market of connoisseurs and purists, until the Depression changed the nation's priorities.

Parker guns have always appealed to more than the base instincts of hunters and sportsmen. The guns built by the Parker Brothers shop of Charles Parker's hardware company weren't known for being on the cutting edge of technology and usually lagged the market in an era when "new and improved" could mean a manufacturer had cheapened existing production standards or devised a new but useless gimmick. Parker Brothers built a reputation for reliability with the conservative approach—not by being first but by getting it right the first time (Miller's T-Latch excepted). A remarkable aspect of the long-term success of the Parker gun was design continuity. Each change was for the better, and improvements were cumulative with no false starts or dead ends. The last gun, built in the 1940s, had evolved directly from the second gun, built in the 1860s.

The history of the Parker Brothers gun works and the Parker shotgun can be broken down into four periods: the beginning years from 1865 to 1876, before Charles Alonzo King had a significant impact on the company; the coming of age/industrialization years of 1876 to 1910, when King presided over Parker's gun works and had practically unbridled authority; the years from 1910 to 1930, when Parker Brothers coasted along on a good reputation while Walter A. King, Charles's son, presided; and finally the Depression years, when the company was on the skids.

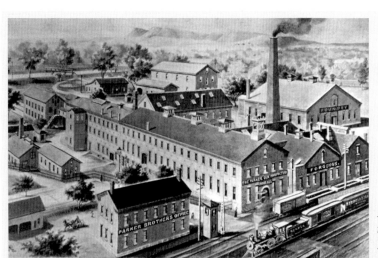

IN THE BEGINNING

Parker Brothers gun works circa 1870. Notice the crossing gate at Cherry Street and Parker Brothers Office, the only building remaining in 1996.

What follows is an overview of the evolution of the Parker gun. Serial numbers and exact manufacturing dates of the 1860s and early 1870s guns were lost to history, but are not particularly relevant. What does matter is that the beginning years of Parker Brothers, through 1876, served as harbinger of ultimate success for the Parker gun.

The years from 1865 through 1876 were marked by unprecedented political and financial turmoil. On April 14, 1865, just five days after General Lee's surrender at Appomattox, President Lincoln was assassinated. Vice President Andrew Johnson succeeded to the presidency and inherited all of the post-Civil War problems implicit in trying to restore "one nation, indivisible." President Johnson presided over one political crisis after another and was impeached in 1868, surviving conviction by one vote. The political crisis came to an end in 1869 with the election of Ulysses S. Grant, but seeds had been planted for the financial panic of 1873. The panic, in turn, was an excuse for the government to ignore violations of various Indian treaties by displaced Americans going west. One treaty in particular had to do with the Black Hills being Sioux Indian country, and the stage was set for Custer's untimely demise at Little Big Horn in 1876. Meanwhile, back in Connecticut. . . .

The history of the Parker gun is the history of the American Industrial Revolution insofar as it relates to the breechloading, side-by-side, double-barrel shotgun. The Parker

shotgun was one of the first useful breechloaders, but the real strength of Parker Brothers' gun works was that it comprised only a small part of Charles Parker's hardware empire. The gun works built roughly 10,000 guns from 1866 through 1877, less than 850 per year on the average. An advertisement dated May 1, 1874, shows Parker gun prices from $45 to $250. Using $100 as the average retail price, Parker guns with an annual retail value of $85,000 (but more likely $70,000 at wholesale) were but a fraction of the $1.5 million annual business revenues claimed by Charles Parker in contemporary news accounts of his company. Early on, guns sold as hardware and Charles Parker's lines of distribution were in place. Parker Brothers didn't need a gimmick to market guns. They could "lie behind the log" and let the innovators (Dan Lefever, for example) stick their necks out on new developments. The gun works had financial backing to simply acquire patent rights for proven advancements in gun manufacture (as with Lefever's patented doll's-head rib extension). The Parker gun could fairly be called the well-heeled tortoise in the race with the innovative hare.

1865 TO 1867

The first Parker shotgun (Miller's Lifter T-Latch) was developed in 1865 and patented in 1866, and several hundred were put in the hands of hardware jobbers and sportsmen at least as early as the summer of 1867. Parker shotguns were sold on approval— "One day for examination and trial"—much the same as the three-day examination typically allowed for mail-order collector guns today. In other words, Charles Parker's first shotguns were built on speculation that a post-Civil War demand for breechloading fowling pieces could be encouraged. Before the Civil War, America was pretty much a rifle and pistol country with scattershot weapons relegated to "squaw gun" status. The end of the Civil War left Charles Parker with 300 to 350 soon-to-be-unemployed gunmakers, along with inventory, machinery, and a factory adapted to building long guns. The switch from wartime production of Springfield rifle-muskets to peacetime production of Miller's T-Latch built by Meriden Man'fg. Co. for Cha's Parker was bridged by the Kentucky militia contract for Triplett & Scott carbines and another contract to modify Model 1861 rifle-muskets to be breechloaders. The first few T-Latches likely were sold in late 1866, and all through the 1860s Charles Parker was the only American commercial maker of a "tipping" breechloading shotgun.

1867-1868

William Miller and his brother George left Charles Parker's employ in 1867 to found the Miller Brothers Pocket Knife Company. By 1868 the Meriden Manufacturing Company gun works along the railroad tracks at Cherry Street was known as Parker Brothers. The first trade mention of Parker guns is considered to be a listing in the March 1868 Folsom Brothers & Co. of Chicago catalog, which showed three guns:

Laminated Steel Barrels $100.00

Best Gun Iron Barrels,
 superior finish .... $ 75.00

Best Gun Iron Barrels,
 plain finish .... $ 50.00

The fifty- and seventy-five-dollar guns with *Best Gun Iron Barrels* are believed to be T-Latch models. The one hundred-dollar gun with laminated steel barrels likely had the improved breechlock with lifter-actuated toggle bolt engaging a square slot at the back of the barrel lump. Some of the first "improved breechlock" guns were marked *CHARLES PARKER MAKER*, rather than Parker Brothers. The shortcomings of Miller's T-Latch system were recognized almost immediately. I don't believe anyone knows exactly who redesigned the T-Latch, but my guess is William Miller in collaboration with Wilbur F. Parker. One thing for sure, the breech-bolt improvement first seen on Charles Parker guns with laminated barrels circa 1867-68 was essential to the success of Parker Brothers and the Parker gun.

"Laminated steel" barrels on Parker Brothers' circa 1868 hundred-dollar gun may have been "fancied-up" musket barrels, which were only cosmetically different from gun iron barrels on lower-priced guns. I've handled a back-action s/n 129, and the owner—expert antique arms dealer David Condon—is of the opinion that the "laminated" pattern appears to have been applied to his seemingly original Parker by using a Damascene process. This is a tough call on a gun 125 years old, and could be proved or disproved only by semi-destructive removal of finish from an otherwise pristine antique. However, the barrel flats are attached to (rather than an integral part of) the barrel tubes—the same process used on my s/n 0895 with decarbonized steel barrels (which *are* converted musket tubes). Parker's gun works imported "provisional" or "first proof" Damascus, laminated, and twist barrels from England and Belgium, but I don't recall seeing any proofmarks on Condon's gun. It's interesting to note that Parker Brothers' circa 1869 catalog deemed "Laminated or Damascus Steel Barrels" equivalent (prices equal) on top-end guns, but "Laminated" barrels weren't offered on low-end back-action models (exposed hammer guns with the mainspring behind the bar). Omission of a Damascus-barrel gun from Folsom Brothers' catalog may reflect that Folsom was advertising the Parker line as it appeared in Charles Parker's 1867 or 1868 catalog, before the gun works was given the name Parker Brothers. In any case, s/n 129 *may* contradict conventional wisdom that Parker *never* made a gun with applied Damascene pattern.

1869-1870

Parker Brothers issued what is considered to be its first gun catalog in 1869 (the prior year's catalog was Charles Parker's). Parker Brothers' 1869 catalog offered five "grades" (by barrel quality and finish) in 10-, 11-, and 12-gauges with standard barrel lengths of twenty-four to thirty-two inches. Reprints of Parker's undated circa 1869 and 1870 catalogs are at the Meriden Historical Society. Larry "Babe" Del Grego believes that Cecil Martin, a Parker collector from Florida, reprinted these earliest Parker Brothers catalogs back in the late 1960s or early 1970s. Each of the Meriden reprints has a date handwritten on the cover, and the one marked "1869 catalog" has Cecil Martin's signature. Both catalogs have identical content but different cover pictures.

Although both catalogs are undated, there are certain clues: A medallion dated 1869, engraved with *Awarded To Parker Bros for Shot Guns,*" together with a number of testimonial letters with dates ranging from November 18, 1867, through August 10, 1868, dovetails with the dates

handwritten on the reprints. Also, the gun pictured has Miller's lifter but not the T-Latch, and is front-action (exposed hammer action with the mainspring inletted into the bar); and the reprints refer to the Parker shotgun as being

> . . . the result of over 4 years of the most thorough experiments, and is offered to the public in the fullest confidence, the manufacturers believing it to be the best gun in use in this or any other country.

Parker Brothers considered 1865 to be the first year for the Parker shotgun in various dated catalogs, so it seems pretty clear that those reprint catalogs at the Meriden Historical Society are in fact from 1869 and 1870.

All the guns in the Meriden reprints are 10-, 11-, or 12-gauge, and the "improved" breechlock description says, ". . . the barrels are securely locked by a bolt entering from the breech pin"—this in contrast to Charles Parker's ad in the *Middletown Directory* for 1869, describing the T-Latch mechanism whereby ". . . the breech is fastened at the top and bottom of the charge." My opinion is that all the guns with laminated, Damascus, and decarbonized steel barrels in Parker's 1869 and 1870 catalogs were built with the improved (bolt to slot) breechlock system. The 1869 and 1870 catalog price lists refer to "Improved Solid Breech." Parker's least expensive (fifty-dollars) circa 1869-70 gun had "Best Gun Iron Barrels, plain finish," and likely was the run-out of T-Latch inventory, but chambered for self-primed shotshells.

A testimonial letter written by Judge George S. Green of Trenton, New Jersey, to Charles Parker dated July 24, 1868, published in Parker Brothers' 1869 and 1870 catalogs, says, "I understand . . . you are manufacturing some fine laminated steel breechloader, with your improvements. . . ." The reference to "improvements" meant the toggle bolt to slot breechlock mechanism. While the one-hundred-dollar gun with laminated-steel barrels shown in Folsom's 1868 catalog *may* have incorporated the improved breechlock, all the guns offered in Parker's 1869 and later catalogs (with the exception of the Best Gun Iron, plain finish, 12-gauge T-Latch) used the new bolting system. The toggle bolt to square-cut slot in the barrel lump eliminated the troublesome T-Latch but wasn't unique or patentable. In fact, the "improvement" was simply the T-Latch's lower breech-pin concept redesigned for greater strength and reliability. Close reading of Miller's letters patent doesn't necessarily lead to the conclusion he sought patent protection for the lifter itself. Nevertheless, Parker Brothers continued to stamp *Pat'd Nov. 13, 1866* on lifter-opener guns well into the 1880s, even though the last vestige of what Miller claimed to be "new and useful" had disappeared by 1876 with the adoption of Wilbur Parker's taper-bolt breechlock improvement.

While the lifter was a nifty way to open the relatively heavy-barrel early guns, the top-lever opener was clearly superior. Parker's use of Miller's patent stamp after 1875 may have been to bluff the competition away from the lifter-opener until the somewhat belated adoption of top-lever openers in 1882. Patent protection was exclusive for only seventeen years, so Miller's November 13, 1866, patent would have expired during 1883.

1871

Wilbur F. Parker created *The American Sportsman* weekly newspaper in 1871, and it was a natural advertising vehicle for the Parker gun. Wilbur's sixteen-page pulp tabloid had a national circulation and was sold to the predecessor of *Forest and Stream*.

1872

Perhaps flushed by the success of having built and sold approximately 3,000 guns in seven years of production, Parker Brothers announced in its 1872 catalog that

. . . this gun, so heartily endorsed by the sportsmen of this country, has arrived, after a series of the most thorough experiments of over four years ['improved breechlock' since 1868], and an experience in its manufacture of nearly seven years [shotguns built since 1865], at a point so near perfection that we see no chance for further improvement. It now stands preeminently The Breech Loader of this, an age of progress. . . .

About the same time, there were serious discussions in Congress about closing the U. S. Patent Office for the reason that everything had been invented.

S. A. Tucker of Delavan, Illinois, signed on with Parker Brothers as their on-the-road salesman in the early 1870s. He was then considered one of the best live-bird shots in the United States. His contemporaries were Bogardus, Kimbell, and Doc Carver, so his shooting skills were tested in fast company. "Tuck" had a long career with the gun works and was still mentioned by the trade press as a Parker salesman after the turn of the century.

S. A. Tucker of Delavan, Illinois, was hired by Parker Brothers as its on-the-road salesman in the early 1870s. Tucker, born in Rhode Island in 1846, established himself as an expert shot at an early age, according to a biographical sketch in the October 11, 1888, issue of *Shooting and Fishing*, which went on to say:

> . . . his reputation is far from being local as he made a name largely by contesting in tournaments. In fact, he is classed as a tournament shot [professional], and he does not object to the classification but enjoys it. It is said that Mr. Tucker will travel farther and work as hard to attend a live bird tournament as any man in the country. Inanimate targets have no attraction for him when live bird shooting can be secured. Mr. Tucker has won many friends by his honorable conduct in tournaments . . . [and] . . . has for a number of years represented Parker Brothers, the manufacturers of the well-known Parker guns, visiting nearly every section of the country from Maine to California.

Peddling fine shotguns from Maine to California during the 1870s and 1880s must have been high adventure. A May 11, 1885, letter to *Forest and Stream*, from a Californian said,

> . . . we lately had the handsome, entertaining Tucker, of Parker gun fame, with us, and now he's down among the Texas cowboys. (I wonder if there are any cowgirls down that way.) 'Tuck' is a jolly good fellow, a fine shot, and all that: but he's a better businessman than either. He has a good gun to work for, it is true; but he's the chief in his line.

Tuck's sales approach was detailed in a May 13, 1913, letter to the *American Field*:

> Forty or more years ago there lived in a southern Illinois town a physician who was very fond of hunting and . . . one day in the middle of summer, S. A. Tucker then, as now, with the Parker Brothers gunmakers, visited the town for the purpose of introducing the breechloader and, as a matter of course, when he inquired of the landlord of the hotel where in the village he could find an influential sportsman, the landlord at once directed him to the office of the physician . . . he went as directed and found

the doctor in and, introducing himself and stating the object of his visit, he and the doctor conversed for an hour or so about guns, the doctor in the meantime taking quite a fancy to the first American-made breechloader he had ever seen, and before Mr. Tucker had left town the doctor had ordered one of the guns turning in his muzzleloading gun in part payment for the new arm.

Parker Brothers' 1872 catalog stated that

> . . . in reply to correspondents wishing muzzleloaders altered to breechloaders, we would say that it is not practicable. We sometimes take them in exchange for Parker Guns, and if sportsmen will inform us the kind and quality of their muzzleloaders, as well as the style of Parker Gun desired, we will be pleased to open negotiations with them.

Such was the way Parker guns were sold in the 1870s, by "negotiations" and on one day's approval with trade-ins accepted. The point of Parker Brothers' trade-in offer was to get Parker guns in the hands of sportsmen—not to become dealers in obsolete muzzleloaders. In this context, it's not unlikely that Parker Brothers received back most (perhaps all) of the externally primed T-Latches taken in trade on latter models, which, in turn, may explain why there is only one known caplock T-Latch—Wilbur F. Parker Jr.'s heirloom at the Meriden Historical Society.

1874

Parker Brothers' May 1, 1874, price list offered guns from $45 to $250, with rebounding locks included. A notation in Parker's order book for April 30, 1873, says, "rebounding throwed [sic] in for gratis." Parker Brothers considered rebounding locks so essential for safety that starting in 1873 they were no longer a $10 option but were installed free of charge on even the least expensive guns. Parker Brothers used J. C. Dane's March 26, 1872, patent for front-action rebounding locks, and J. Stokes's November 24, 1868, patent for rebounding hammers on back-action guns (see Patent Appendix). Parker's 1872-73 catalogs specifically refer to Stokes's rebounding lock "patented Nov. 24, 1868;" however, the four locks pictured are front-action, and the price list says, ". . . rebounding locks put on none but front action guns . . . $10.00." The debits never seem to equal the credits when researching the Parker gun.

Charles Alonzo King made the Parker Gun all that it was and is. He hired on as superintendent of Parker Brothers in 1874, semi-retired when his son Walter took over in 1910, but continued to drop by the gun works regularly until he passed away in 1914.

The Parker Brothers gun works really came on line in 1874, when Charles Alonzo King was hired away from Smith & Wesson. Notwithstanding the "age of progress" idea

in Parker Brothers' 1872 catalog that the Parker gun was ". . . at a point so near perfection that we see no chance for further improvement," King went to work to make a "near perfect" gun even better. The first result of his efforts was the March 16, 1875, patent of a spherical recess around the hinge pin, which can be spotted by Parker collectors from a mile away. Fifty years later, his son, Walter A. King, wrote that

> . . . in 1874 my father came to the Parker Co. from Smith & Wesson, and until his death in 1914 was employed by the Parker Co. as manager of the gun shop. He designed the Parker guns, built the tools and had practically a free hand in management.

Walter King went to work in the factory in 1889, and at one time or other worked in every department. He began to assume complete charge of the shop from his father in about 1910. Charles King died in 1914, after forty years with the company.

1875-1876

The key to Parker Brothers' success was the sound basic design achieved by Wilbur F. Parker with his March 23, 1875, patent of a taper bolt to matching barrel-lump slot, thus establishing one bolt-locking mechanism for all Parker guns manufactured through the end of production (see Patent Appendix).

The reader is referred to the color picture of my circa 1870 back-action Parker s/n 0895 with decarbonized-steel barrels, which according to one writer are actually *wrought steel* made by mixing molten metal with an oxidizing agent to reduce carbon (hence "decarbonized"). Wrought-steel barrels were considered to be less brittle than gun-iron barrels and were supposed to bulge rather than split along the grain of the metal if subjected to an overload. Guns with decarbonized-steel barrels were dropped from the line in 1874, and by 1878 Parker catalogs stated that

. . . we use no decarbonized or plain iron barrels in which the grain of the metal runs lengthwise.

My belief is the early guns with plain-steel, best-gun-iron, and decarbonized steel barrels were built with converted musket tubes of random metallurgical origins. The breech end of the barrels are round, with flats soldered on as an afterthought. Backlock s/n 0895 doesn't have the Stokes-patent

rebounding locks. The hammers rest against the firing pins, thus showing it to be a "half-cock" gun—certainly built before 1873, when Parker Brothers "throwed in" rebounding hammers for "gratis." Notice the absence of the characteristic 1875 King-patent spherical recess at the hinge pin. Also, the lifter extension pin protrudes above the standing breech when the gun is open (and sometimes when the gun is closed). Parker rationalized that an "up pin" served to warn that the

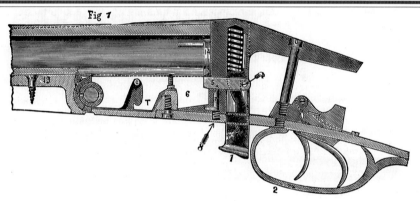

FIG. 7. REPRESENTS THE GUN CLOSED.

When the barrels are brought to place for firing, the bottom of the lug 6 strikes the trip 7, withdrawing it from the bolt 5, which then enters the mortise in the lug 6 and securely locks the gun, as shown in Fig. 7.

The taper bolt 5 locks the barrels positively firm, and the use of a taper bolt for fastening our gun gives it a decided advantage over others, as it does not allow a little dirt (which is very liable to get under barrels when open) to prevent the gun from locking. Many times, when shooting, sportsmen are balked this way, but our gun closes with the same ease, and locks as securely should there be a little dirt in the way.

WHEN GUN IS OPEN, AS SHOWN IN FIG. 8, THE CHECK HOOK T COMES IN CONTACT WITH THE PIN E, WHICH AVOIDS ANY STRAIN ON THE JOINT 13, AND THUS PREVENTS THE GUN BECOMING SHAKY BY CONSTANT USE.

In ordering any PARTS for these guns, should repairs be necessary, always state from which page of catalogue you order.

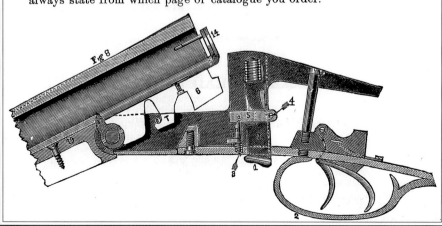

Cross section of lifter gun from Parker Brothers 1899 catalog. The location of the lifter spring chamber precludes use of Lefever's doll's head rib extension. Check-hook "T" is Dangerfield's 1872 patent, and the circular recess around the hinge-pin is Walter King's 1875 patent.

breech had not fully snapped shut. The thought passed in 1875, because Wilbur figured out how to get rid of the obstructive pin when he improved the breechlock mechanism.

Next, take a close look at the picture of my s/n 9385 bar-action lifter-opener gun. This is Parker's lowest grade with plain twist barrels and exhibits certain manufacturing details dating the gun to 1877. Serial number 9385 has Wilbur Parker's 1875- patent angle slot at the rear of the barrel lump (in contrast to the square slot on s/n 0895). The latter gun has the number 2 stamped on the barrel lump denoting frame size, as was typical throughout Parker production after the announcement in the 1877 catalog about retooling to produce an interchangeable gun. The fore-end is attached with a pre-1878 sliding key to barrel loop, and the locks have J. C. Dane's patent rebounding feature. Refer to the Patent Appendix if you need to clarify once and for all the difference between front-action and back-action guns. If the mainspring is forward of the hammer and fits into the action bar, then it's bar-action or barlock or front-action; if the mainspring is behind the hammer, it's a back-action or backlock. After 1870, the front-action barlock had almost universal application to shotguns, both here and abroad.

The illustration on the previous page shows a cross-section of the post-1875 lifter mechanism from Parker's 1899 catalog. Notice the angle slot on the barrel lump and the check hook marked *T* on the bottom drawing. This check hook, patented by F. S. Dangerfield on September 3, 1872, was assigned to D. M. Lefever, and reassigned to Parker Brothers in 1881, but not used until 1882, and then only on lifter and top-lever hammer guns (see Patent Appendix). I examined a cheap imported "Parker" knockoff at a gun show recently. The gun

didn't have a check hook, and I could have snapped it in two by putting pressure on the barrels. Dangerfield's patent check hook kept the hinge pin on Parker hammer guns from being damaged by rough handling. As an aside, Dangerfield's 1872 patent claimed the doll's-head rib extension usually credited to Lefever. Parker licensed "Lefever's" doll's head for use with top-lever opener guns built after 1882, so let's give credit where credit is due—Parker's highly touted doll's head is Dangerfield's 1872 rip-off of Westley Richards's circa 1864 British patent, but Lefever collected the royalties.

The first ten years of Parker Brothers' gun works were of no immediate historic importance, but were given meaning retroactively by post-1880 successes of the Parker gun. If Charles Parker had decided to close down the gun works in 1875, Parker guns would be nothing more than a footnote in *Flayderman's Guide*. However, the American Industrial Revolution was well under way, and Charles Parker's company had the capital, machinery, plant facility, and cash flow to give C. A. King a free hand in the manufacture and continued development of Parker shotguns. Wilbur Parker was sufficiently interested in his father's project to devise and patent a shotshell in 1869 (see Patent Appendix), and to devise the 1875 patent of a taper-bolt improvement to the breechlock mechanism. Parker Brothers had King as its in-house innovator and Wilbur splitting the difference between engineering and ownership. The company had the wherewithal and Charles Parker had the desire to preside over (and perhaps subsidize) the manufacture of a shotgun that could be fairly called beyond reproach—or, better yet, The "Old Reliable."

COMING OF AGE IN MERIDEN

Parker Brothers circa 1900 "Blue Ink" sixteen-page pocket catalog pictures the entire hammerless line. Original catalog courtesy of Craig Reynolds.

From 1866 until mid-1875, the Parker gun had little to commend it other than the innovation of being a workable breechloading double-barrel shotgun. After Charles King signed on in 1874, Parker Brothers went on to become the clear leader in the manufacture of fine doubles in the United States. By the early 1890s, Parker Brothers advertised itself as ". . . the oldest manufacturer of double-barreled shotguns in America." The competition had fallen by the wayside. The Charles King years of 1875 through 1910 made the Parker gun all that it was—and is.

1876

Charles Parker incorporated his various businesses as The Charles Parker Company with stated capital of $500,000. The Parker Brothers gun works was a division of the corporation and not a separate manufacturing entity–"nothing more than a basic factory," according to W. A. King.

1877

Parker Brothers' May 1, 1877, catalog showed all three 1875 patent improvements: first, Wilbur's taper bolt to angle slot at the back of the barrel lump, which allowed the gun to wear itself tight; second, the lifter pin no longer protruded gratuitously from the top of the standing breech (the up-pin was considered to be a safety feature on early guns as it served to indicate whether the breech-bolt had not fully engaged); and third, King's recessed hinge pin is clearly visible on the high-grade hammer gun shown on the

Parker Brothers circa 1877 "interchangeable" hammer gun of a higher grade. This ad is from Joe Long's 1879 revised edition of American Wild-fowl Shooting.

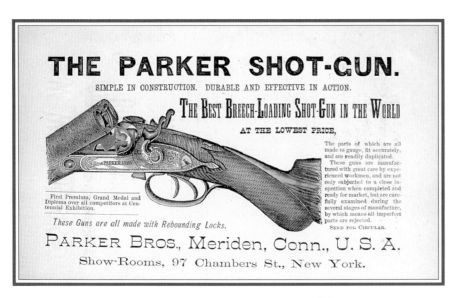

catalog cover. The Parker line was described by barrel quality, with prices ranging from $50 for plain twist to $300 for the top of the line with finest Damascus-steel barrels, finest English-walnut stock, gold medallion, finest checking and engraving, combined with the finest workmanship and finish throughout in 10- or 12-gauge. The finest Damascus gun would ultimately be designated Quality A, and the $300 price (without ejectors) would persist until about 1910, when the AHE (with ejectors) was reduced to $250 and prices for BH and lower grades were cut 25 percent. Thirty-three years of stable prices contributed to the success of the Parker gun insofar as gunmakers rather than cost accountants were in charge. As will be seen, this changed in the late 1920s.

1878

Parker Brothers adopted the British Deeley & Edge-style fore-end latch, patented in the United States by Charles King on March 26, 1878 (see Patent Appendix). King's fore-end latch together with his patent recess around the hinge pin are the "trademark" visual clues that identify Parker guns in a crowd. The fore-end latch superseded the sliding-key fore-end fastener and was used on all post-1878 Parker guns except Trojan grade. (If my reference to "Trojan grade" didn't strike a responsive chord, I suggest the reader skip forward to Chapter 7, "Grades of Quality," so as to be brought up to speed on the Parker grading system.)

1880s

Parker Brothers catalogs for the 1880s offered a full line of gunning equipment, supplies, and even clothing. The forty-two-page circa 1888 catalog devotes twenty pages to loading and cleaning equipment, gun and ammunition cases, clothing, pigeon traps, and the like; and Parker continued to ship guns on one day's approval:

Mrs. Eddie Bauer Jr. (known to her friends as "Stine"), an accomplished sportswoman who was as adept as her husband with shotgun and fishing rod. She and Ed were married for 56 years. Parker's "trademark" 1878 patent fore-end latch (used on all grades but Trojan) identifies "Stine's" fowling piece as the "Old Reliable." Photo courtesy of Eddie Bauer Jr.

Any person desiring to examine and test the Parker Gun can have one of them sent C.O.D., through any express company, with the following "special instructions" to their agent: "Allow one day for examination and trial; then if the gun suits, send the money to us; if it does not suit, return the gun to us and the money to the depositor.

The gun sent on approval was probably a sample to be kept or returned, buyer's choice. I doubt Parker Brothers would have built a special-order gun on speculation that an unknown purchaser in a distant state would elect to be satisfied. If the customer was satisfied with the sample gun but wanted special features or a higher grade, the sample could have been returned and his money applied to the special-order gun. Based on the full line of shooting accessories and approval terms offered in the 1888 catalog, I believe Parker Brothers was still selling guns pretty much one at a time direct to customers through the 1880s. However, by the 1890s the situation had changed, and the 1897-99 catalog encouraged retail customers to buy locally if possible: "The Parker Gun can be found in all the leading gun stores in the country, and is sold by dealers at factory prices. If your dealer does not keep them in stock, send your order direct to the factory." The times they were a-changin'.

Parker Brothers ad from the December 17, 1885, issue of Forest and Stream. *Notice "Doc" Carver, A. H. Bogardus, and "Buffalo Bill" Cody are mentioned. Carver originated the wild west show and was Buffalo Bill's partner the first year of "Cody and Carver's Wild West." Carver was a buffalo hunter in his frontier days and is said by some historians to have accounted for more buffalo with a rifle than any other American. Doc Carver defeated Bogardus in a six-day shootout, smashing 58,892 moving targets out of 60,000 shots. Bogardus, recognized at the time as the world's champion, used a shotgun—Carver fired a rifle! Carver died at age eighty-seven in 1927, and the preceding was taken from his obituary in the December 1927 combined issue of* Outdoor Life *and* Outdoor Recreation.

1881-1882

D. M. Lefever patented his refinement of Dangerfield's 1872-patent doll's-head rib extension in 1878. (Remember—Westley Richards's circa 1864 pinfire had a doll's-head-type rib extension gripped by a sliding bolt from the breech.) Parker Brothers acquired Lefever's patent rights in 1881, to be used in conjunction with the soon-to-be-adopted top-lever opener. The lifter-opener's spring chamber occupied the same area of the breech as the doll's-head cutout, so the two couldn't be used together. By 1884 the top lever was considered standard and the lifter-opener became a special-order item available through at least 1899, and possibly until 1905 and later. The adoption of Lefever's rib extension should have been the death knell for lifter-opener guns as Parker's 1880s catalogs touted the taper bolt as being ". . . supplanted by the top fastener upon the end of the extension rib which prevents the springing of the breech from the barrels and any lateral movement of the barrels at the time of discharge." If "springing of the breech" and "lateral movement of the barrels" were a real problem, and Lefever's rib extension was the real solution, then it's surprising that Parker would continue to build and sell lifter guns, which, by their own advertising, could be considered defective. As will be seen, the doll's head was more a matter of form than substance. Major Charles Askins, in his 1910 book *The American Shotgun*, discussed the second coming of the doll's-head rib extension:

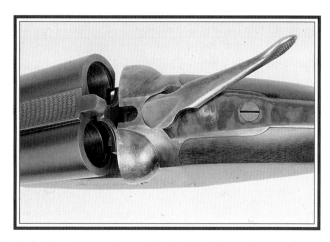

Parker Trojans are often credited with having a rib extension—some collectors even consider it to be "rare." A critical look will show the Trojan's rib extension to be purely cosmetic and not Lefever's doll's head type. Cost saving was the name of the game with Trojan grade so the "false" doll's head soon disappeared at behest of the accounting department.

By and by, when extension ribs came, the conservative gun makers took a hand, declaring that the gun was strong enough and handsomer without the ugly extension. Moreover, when these ribs were at last bolted through, or wedge-bolted from the rear, this entailed further contention, and one of our most popular manufacturers [Parker] still absolutely refuses to bolt through the rib of his gun, though, in the nature of things, he will have to yield finally to the demands of his patrons.

Notwithstanding Askins's compelling argument, Parker Brothers never bolted through the rib extension and eventually abandoned the rib extension altogether on Trojan grade. A few special-order live-bird guns were built without the "ugly extension." For example, crack-shot Frank S. Parmelee special-ordered a DH, specifying "no safety no ext rib," and took delivery of s/n 95,820 without rib extension, according to Parker Brothers' April 9, 1900, order book [Remington Museum, Ilion, New York].

1887 TO 1889

Charles King patented a series of improvements to the basic Anson & Deeley circa 1875 boxlock (see Patent Appendix). His first patent, filed August 30, 1886, alerted the trade

The Parker Hammerless Shotgun.

At the Annual Tournament of 1889, held at Cannes, France, **the grand prize**, consisting of 2,000 francs and a valuable cup, was won with the Parker Hammerless.

The first Parker Hammerless gun made won the Championship of America at Decatur, Ill.

It is the safest Hammerless Gun ever made, as hammers cannot be let down to rest on loaded shells. The safety is automatic, also positive and absolutely safe, and the spiral mainsprings employed are guaranteed for twenty-five years.

SEND FOR ILLUSTRATED CIRCULAR.

PARKER BROS., MAKERS,

NEW YORK SALESROOM: 97 Chambers Street.

MERIDEN, CONN.

Parker Brothers's first series of ads for the new hammerless shotgun featured a DH grade with fine Damascus barrels. This ad is from the February 1891 issue of Outing *magazine, but the same ad had been running since May 1889, in* Shooting and Fishing.

to the long-overdue Parker hammerless shotgun. The Parker boxlock, concealed-hammer ("hammerless") model came on the market in late 1888, with low serial numbers in the range of 55,XXX. (DH grade s/n 55,797 is the lowest-numbered hammerless gun I've seen.) Parker built almost 57,000 hammer guns (including 700 to 900 separate serial-numbered T-Latch models) before the hammerless shotgun was introduced. The circumstances surrounding the introduction of Parker's first hammerless were described in the December 13, 1888, issue of *Shooting and Fishing*:

> The Parker hammerless gun has been shown to the trade in the shape of a few samples, and it will soon be ready for the market, although in limited quantities for some time yet. Perhaps no gun ever placed on the market has had so much advertising amongst gunners as this one, and numbers of would-be purchasers of hammerless guns have delayed buying one this season because they have heard that the Parkers were at work perfecting the hammerless gun of the future, and knowing the reputation of the makers, they have felt that it would pay them to await the advent of the new gun; and at last it has been placed upon the market as a candidate for honors, but it is in many ways a disappointment, as sportsmen had perhaps been led to expect too much of the gun, because of the reputation of the makers. It has the distinctive finish that is so characteristic of Parker guns, and while in the main it is as it will be made, it has a somewhat clumsy look at present through the head of the stock where the action joins the wood, but in the latter guns this will be, in a measure, modified so that it will be somewhat lighter in appearance. The gun cocks as easily as any on the market, but is open to the objection that but few of the operations are positive, and it is the opinion of some that it has too many small pieces to be durable. But time alone will tell the story, and develop what

are the strong and what the weak points of the system, but, while feeling a sense of disappointment in the gun, we can but predict a large sale for them, because of the well-known reputation of the makers, who were, in a measure, the pioneers, as gun manufacturers, in America.

Apparently the first Parker hammerless model didn't live up to its exaggerated expectations. (Engineering details and analysis of the defects of the first Parker hammerless are beyond the scope of this book; however, it is interesting to note that two of four Charles King hammerless-action patents were filed months after J. R. Stice demonstrated the "first" hammerless Parker at Decatur, Illinois) Notwithstanding the negative announcement, Parker Brothers first advertised its hammerless shotgun in the March 7, 1889, issue of *Shooting and Fishing*, which, along with Parker's ad in the *Meriden City Directory* for 1889, said:

> . . . the first Parker hammerless gun made won the Championship of America at Decatur, Illinois. It is the safest hammerless gun ever made, as hammers cannot be let down to rest on loaded shells. The safety is automatic, also positive and absolutely safe, and the spiral main springs employed are guaranteed for twenty-five years.

The earliest magazine advertising for a Parker hammerless in my collection is from an issue of the *Outing Book* for 1889, which says,

> . . . at the annual tournament of 1889, held at Cannes, France, the grand prize consisting of 2,000 francs and a valuable cup, was won with the Parker hammerless . . . [and] . . . the first Parker hammerless gun made won the Championship of America at Decatur, Ill.

CHAMPIONSHIP
OF
AMERICA

"Big Jim" Stice demonstrated the first Parker hammerless gun in December 1888 by winning the American Field Cup, emblematic of the Championship of America. Unfortunately, the gun pictured is not his Parker.

A headline in "The Gun" section of Shooting and Fishing *for December 13, 1888, states, "Stice Wins The Championship Cup," and the article went on to say:*

Decatur, Ill., Dec. 5, '88. The second shoot for the Field Championship cup valued at $500, was shot this afternoon at the base ball park, the contestants being the first winner, Mr. L. S. Carter of Hammond, Illinois, and Mr. J. R. Stice, the renowned trapshooter of Jacksonville, Ill. Each man shot at fifty live pigeons from five ground traps, set five yards apart, thirty yards rise, the fence surrounding the grounds being agreed upon as the boundary . . . [and] . . . the birds used were a very select lot, being mostly carriers, and costing the contestants to shoot at $1.00 each. They were so good that not one of their number refused to take wing the instant the trap was sprung. Between 300 and 400 enthusiasts witnessed the match. [Side bets were large, the crowd vociferous, and tempers short—a fistfight broke out after the tenth bird when] . . . one of the spectators, who claimed to hail from Pittsburgh, Pa., and a democrat, made his presence very obnoxious . . . and being, as it is termed "called down" by a Chicagoan present, took exception thereto and struck the "caller" full in the face. This, for a time stopped the shooting and the Pittsburgher and the gentleman from Illinois had it out, the Pittsburgher's face at the finish showing up like choice, fresh-cut Chicago beef.

After the altercation, Stice went on to win the match by killing forty-three birds to Carter's forty-two. Stice used a new 7-pound, 14-ounce, 32-inch hammerless Parker gun loaded with: first barrel, four drams new American Wood Powder; second barrel, four drams FF Dead Shot Powder, his killing circle being composed of 1¼ ounces of Number 7 chilled shot. Carter used an L. C. Smith hammerless of the same weight and gauge. Stice was then thirty-four years old. For many years he had been one of the nation's top trapshooters and,

. . . with the exception of one season, when he used a Winchester repeating shotgun, all the shooting he did at the trap was done with a 10-gauge, 34-inch, 12-pound Parker, which has been nicknamed the "churn," by reason of his having "churned" the boys up so many times with it in a tie. . . .

The feathers had barely settled when C. W. Budd of Des Moines, Iowa, challenged Stice for the cup by posting forfeit money.

James R. Stice and C. W. Budd shot their first challenge match to a tie on March 5, 1889, at Jacksonville, Illinois. They shot a second match on March 16, 1889, at Keokuk, Iowa, and Budd beat Stice ninety-four to eighty-eight to wrest possession of the Championship of America. He, in turn, was immediately challenged by Dr. W. F. ("Doc") Carver and L. C. Smith's man on the road, Harvey McMurchy. A champion had little time to rest on his laurels, and the rigors of nineteenth-century travel often extracted a toll. *Shooting and Fishing* reported in its April 18, 1889, issue, that "Mr. James R. Stice, the famous trap-shot, has been confined to his bed for several weeks with inflammatory rheumatism. He has considerably improved recently, but even now can only hobble about the house with the aid of a cane."

W. B. Leffingwell in his 1895 book, *The Art of Wing Shooting*, wrote of the man who shot the first Parker hammerless gun made:

A few years ago an advertisement appeared in all the sportsmen's journals to the effect that the first Parker hammerless made won the American Field Cup, emblematic of the championship of America. James R. Stice won the cup. He appeared among the galaxy of stars, and as a shooter he was inferior to none. He traveled from ocean to ocean with an aggregation of shooting experts, and when the final result was figured out, James R. Stice stood at the head of the list, for in the days and weeks of successive shooting he held the highest average of all. [Stice was laid low by sickness and quit while he was ahead] . . . retired from trapshooting . . . settled at Jacksonville, Illinois, and . . . engaged in a profitable business, participating but seldom in trap-shoots, and then only in the vicinity of his home.

Stice made a name for himself with his Parker 10-gauge hammer gun and reached the zenith of his shooting career with Parker's first hammerless twelve, but I have never seen his

name mentioned in a Parker ad. Parker Brothers was slow to recognize the benefits of name dropping in its advertising. To paraphrase Dale Carnegie, a person can read no sweeter words than to see his own name in print. My collection of Parker ads shows it wasn't until about 1900 that Parker started to disclose the identity of individuals who won tournaments or shot remarkable scores with the Parker gun. Captain A. W. du Bray joined Parker's road sales force in December 1890, and his late 1890s "Gaucho" letters published by the sporting press raised customer ego-stroking to high art. (The next chapter will detail the life of this fascinating character.)

Dr. W. F. ("Doc") Carver had hustler's credentials as a trick-shot and exhibitionist with rifle and gun. "Doc" was also a top professional live-bird specialist and would regularly challenge other "top guns" to big money shoots, but he was notorious for failing to post required forfeit money and as a no-show.

GOLDEN AGE OF TRAPSHOOTING

The automobile made sport hunting and trapshooting more accessible to persons of average means. "Tin Lizzie" had much to do with the shift of emphasis by Parker Brothers from high grades to lower grades after the turn of the century.

The American Shooting Association was organized as a stock corporation by a number of leading cartridge, powder, and shot manufacturers in 1889, and S. A. Tucker of Delavan, Illinois, and A. W. du Bray, of Walla Walla, Washington Territory, (among others) were named to the advisory board. Tucker's exploits on behalf of Parker Brothers have already been described. Du Bray would move east during 1890 to join Parker's on-the-road sales staff and become a legend in his own time. Although the American Shooting Association was short-lived, the advent of nationally sanctioned live-bird and inanimate-target tournaments coincided with the introduction of the Parker hammerless shotgun and marked the beginning of the Golden Age of Trapshooting (which the Parker gun would dominate).

The best way to introduce Capt. A. W. du Bray is to republish his biography from the Christmas 1905 edition of *Shooting and Fishing*:

A. W. du Bray is an Englishman by birth and parentage. He was educated in France. At an early age he went to South America, where he spent several years on the Patagonian frontier. There he had good sport, shooting and chasing deer and ostriches, with an occasional puma and plenty of feathered game. He speaks both the French and Spanish languages, and at one time, when using them frequently, was as fluent in them as in his own tongue.

Upon reaching the United States Mr. du Bray devoted a good deal of his time to his favorite sport of game shooting, and subsequently went west, where he enjoyed fine sport afield in Minnesota, in the days when duck, snipe, woodcock, and prairie chicken were plentiful in that section.

In 1875 Mr. du Bray, having met with financial reverses, joined the Army, and in 1876 was stationed at Fort Seward, North Dakota, near the present site of Jamestown. It was here he first met General Custer, and at their meeting, the General, himself a thorough sportsman, offered to take him on the fatal campaign that ended so disastrously to himself and his famous crack regiment, the Seventh United States Cavalry. Owing to an unlooked for delay, occasioned by General Custer not being in command of that memorable campaign, orders for Mr. du Bray to join it were never issued, as in the meantime the General with over half of his valiant men were annihilated.

Upon the return of the survivors of the Seventh Cavalry to their winter quarters at Fort Abraham Lincoln, Mr. du Bray received the appointment in the Quartermaster's Department at that post. In the spring of 1877 he went afield with it on the Nez Perces expedition. It was here that he figured conspicuously in an engagement with these Indians and on the occasion Colonel F. W. Benteen, commanding a battalion of the Seventh Cavalry and one of the best and greatest Indian fighters ever known, took occasion after the fight to make special mention of Mr. du Bray in a general order read at the head of his battalion. This, coming from so eminent a source and from so grand a warrior, he regards as the greatest compliment ever paid him.

In the following year he again took the field with his cherished regiment and comrades, this time in pursuit of the fugitive Cheyennes.

During these two campaigns Mr. du Bray enjoyed exceptionally good shooting at antelope, deer, elk, buffalo, and all sorts of game birds, and his mess and many of the others was always well supplied with game, even when in an Indian country.

In December, 1890, Mr. du Bray left the Army and accepted the position of traveling salesman with Parker Bros., of Meriden, Conn., his fondness for guns and shooting causing him to take this step. His territory includes all of the southern states, part of Michigan, North Dakota, and all of Canada, and he spends approximately ten months of the year on the road among his business acquaintances and friends. . . .

. . . Beyond and above all else, after his own immediate family, he pins his faith to the old reliable Parker gun and on those whose name it bears, a quarter of a century having convinced him that like Shakespeare they are the best in their lines.

1892

The American Shooting Association had fizzled by 1892, and various manufacturers chose up sides among two new organizations—the American Manufacturers Associa-

tion, to which Parker Brothers was a subscriber, and the Interstate Manufacturers and Dealers Association. Organizational meetings were held simultaneously during November and December of 1892, and membership in one organization did not necessarily preclude membership in the other, although there was rivalry and some bad feelings. The American Manufacturers Association initially seemed the stronger group, and Thomas Hunter of the Hunter Arms Company, the chair at the first meeting of shareholders, placed the name of Arthur W. du Bray in nomination as a governor or director. The Interstate Manufacturers and Dealers Association was the survivor of the two, however, and Parker Brothers would soon become an active member, with Wilbur F. Parker Jr. sitting on the board.

1893

The Interstate Manufacturers and Dealers Association (soon to be renamed the Interstate Trapshooting Association—"Interstate Association" for short) held its inaugural Grand American Handicap at Dexter Park, Long Island, New York, in April 1893. Four of twenty-one guns were Parkers, and they placed second, fifth, twelfth, and seventeenth. The Parker gun would later come to dominate live-bird tournaments in the golden years before the ascendancy of repeaters.

1894

The Interstate Association held its second Grand American Handicap (GAH) at live birds at Dexter Park the first week of April 1894 with fifty-four entries. Although none of the winners used a Parker gun, the report of the event in the April 26, 1894, issue of *Shooting and Fishing* gave first notice that Parker Brothers was about to introduce a fluid-steel-barrel gun especially adapted to live-bird shooting:

Arthur W. du Bray, the more than popular representative of the Parker Bros. Gun . . . [announced that] . . . his firm proposed to put upon the market in the near future a gun for trap work with which nothing so far produced in this country could compete. It was to have steel barrels of the very highest quality, heavily metaled barrels at the breech where the greatest bursting pressure is exerted; altogether to be a model gun and one especially adapted for the use of any of the better nitro powders of the day.

This announcement would prove prophetic as the Parker gun took first prize in a field of fifty-eight at the next GAH in 1895; first and second in a field of 105 at the 1896 GAH; first, second, and third at the 1900 GAH; and first in 1901 at both live birds and targets. Not a bad record for a gun that would soon be "outmoded" by single-barrel repeaters.

1895

Parker Brothers exhibited its line at the Sportsmen's Exposition at Madison Square Garden during May 1895, and the exhibit was described in the May 16, 1895, issue of *Shooting and Fishing*:

On the right, as you enter from the Madison Square side of the garden, one of the first attractions that will be noticed by a lover of guns is the case containing the exhibit of that old firm—one of the first to manufacture a breechloading gun in this country—Parker Bros. The guns are shown in one of the handsomest cases in the exhibition . . . [and] . . . within this case are seventy guns varying from the $50 one with its twist barrels up to the one with barrels of [Whitworth] fluid steel, and costing $400. These higher priced guns are slowly but surely pushing their way to the front . . . [with seven recent sales mentioned]. In the case is contained samples of smallest and largest bored guns made by the Parker Brothers; 20-gauges, weighing from 5 to 5½ pounds, and heavyweight duck guns running from 11 to 13 pounds. The shooting quality of the Parker gun needs no mention from me here—it is known of all. The exhibit is in charge of Arthur W. du Bray, who is as popular as any "knight of the trigger" that ever grasped a gun in his hands.

Pigeon Gun: Parker Brothers fit its $300 Quality A with 12-gauge Whitworth fluid-steel barrels, marked the price up to $400, and dubbed it the Pigeon Gun. Whitworth

Parker Brothers ad from February 19, 1898 issue of Forest & Stream. *The gun is AAH Pigeon grade with Whitworth fluid steel barrels. Reference to "nearly 100,000 in use" was puffing as Parker didn't reach s/n 100,000 until the turn of the century.*

shotgun tubes had been available in England since 1885 or prior. A letter from "AH-PE" in the September 3, 1885, issue of *Forest and Stream* reported that ". . . on some of the finest English guns, barrels of Whitworth's fluid-compressed steel are used. They are by no means handsome, hardly presenting so neat an appearance as a good quality of stub-twist, but they are very strong and serviceable, and the most expensive barrels with which I have an acquaintance." Pigeon Guns were introduced in late 1894, with 79,XXX being a low serial number.

1896

The second Madison Square Garden Sportsmen's Exposition was held during March 1896, and as reported in the March 19, 1896, issue of *Shooting and Fishing:*

> . . . to the right, as you enter the building, will be seen at the head of the second aisle the handsome case containing the exhibit of [Parker Bros.], the first of the successful manufacturers of guns in America. Arthur du Bray has charge of the temporary home of the Meriden plant, and is as affable and polite as when in the old days he made hosts of friends by his entertaining letters about field sports, written for the *American Field* over the signature of Gaucho. The number of guns shown comprises between seventy-five and a hundred, and these of every grade and cost. The prices of these weapons run from $50 to $400. Among the first of the American manufacturers to realize that there was in this country a class of wealthy men fond of shooting, and to whom the mere price of a gun was a secondary condition, so long as the gun itself appealed to them.

1897

Charles E. Parker died at age fifty-five, survived by his father, younger brother Dexter (age forty-seven), and sister Annie Parker Lyon. Dexter succeeded as CEO, but Annie's husband, William H. Lyon, was the "hands-on" day-to-day manager. Wilbur F. Parker Jr. was twenty-five at the time, and although referred to as "a member of the firm" in connection with his "professional" status at live-bird shoots, his actual title and duties weren't specified. Wilbur Jr. was an active trap-shooter, and represented Parker Brothers on the board of the Interstate Association.

The third annual Sportsmen's Exposition at Madison Square Garden was held, as usual, in early March, and according to the March 18, 1897, issue of *Shooting and Fishing:*

> . . . Arthur W. du Bray is in charge [of Parker Brothers' exhibit], and what he does not know about shooting and guns is scarcely worth learning. The excellence of the Parker Bros. gun is known to every sportsman in the land for the good material that enters into lock, stock, and barrel. In its shooting capacity it has no superior and few equals. The firm for some years past has made a specialty of small-bore guns. At present its sales at the south show without contradiction that the small bores are fast becoming favorites for field work. The range of guns made by the firm is not equaled by any manufacturer of guns in the United States, for the factory turns out each year 8, 10, 12, 14, 16, 20, and 24 gauge breechloading guns. The sportsmen of Texas particularly seem to desire the smaller bores . . . [and various Houston sportsmen were listed as owners of 24-gauge Parkers]. Two guns of the Parker Bros. make to be seen at the space in charge of du Bray are more than worth the time taken in their examination. The first is a 16 gauge weighing 7 pounds 7 ounces. This gun has barrels of Damascus steel, but they are blued to resemble fluid steel . . . the other arm is what is known as the pigeon gun, being made especially for work at the traps where live birds are used. The barrels are of the Whitworth steel known the world over for its wonderful tenacity under the greatest strain . . . this gun must be seen to be appreciated, and I am sure Arthur du Bray will take pleasure in showing it to any lover of a high grade arm.

1898

Vulcan Grade: Jacob Pentz, well-known columnist for *Shooting and Fishing*, wrote in the July 21, 1898, issue that while

> . . . walking down Chambers Street last Friday I passed the New York store of the Parker Bros., and seeing Mr. Hunt inside it was a very natural thing to drop in and enquire if there was anything new in the Parker gun. The answer came quickly:
>
> "Most assuredly, I have just received samples of our new $50 hammerless gun, and we look upon it as a daisy for that money."
>
> The gun was shown to me. It is certainly an arm that will appeal most strongly to any lover of the shotgun. While absolutely plain, it looks all over a gun to wear well and to last. In the last point the guns of the Parker Bros. have ever borne most enviable reputation. It is only recently that two guns of this make have been mentioned in these columns that have been in constant use for a quarter of a century [since 1873] and are still in prime shooting condition. But to return to the new arm. In measurements the gun is: Barrels, 30 inches; weight, 7 pounds 14 ounces; drop at butt of stock, 2½ inches; drop at comb, 1⅝ inches. The barrels are of vulcan steel, and the barrels of this steel have answered every test required of them in most satisfactory manner. This gun is especially adapted to the use of the various nitro powders of the day. Most certainly the strength of the barrels at the chamber is assured by the amount of metal at that spot. The new departure looks a very serviceable gun and cannot help but meet the approval of sportsmen, especially those who are devoted to trap work. One feature of the gun, and a most desirable one, is that every piece of the gun is interchangeable. If through accident, anything gives way, the part can be duplicated without any delay by sending same to the Meriden factory and asking that a new one be forwarded.

Titanic fluid-steel barrels were offered as a no-cost option on BH, CH, and DH grades, priced at $200, $150, and $100 respec-

---

Parker Brothers special announcement of April 1, 1899, introduced VH grade for $50.00, and called attention to newly available Titanic steel barrels on B, C, and D grades. The game had quickly changed. A short four years prior, fluid steel barrels were exclusively a $100 option on Parker's finest gun; but by 1899, Quality VH complete with functionally equivalent black "Vulcan" barrels could be had for fifty bucks.

tively, at least by mid-1898 and possibly as early as 1897. The lowest-serial-number Parker with original Titanic steel barrels I've seen is BH No. 90,XXX. First mention of Titanic barrels in a Parker ad is in the May 4, 1899, issue of *Shooting and Fishing*, referring back to Guy Grimsby, age thirteen, killing forty-nine of fifty pigeons on November 24, 1898, at a Kentucky live-bird shoot.

1899

The Madison Square Garden Sportsmen's Exposition was gravitating away from being a manufacturers' show and was on its way to becoming the venue of hunting and fishing guides, taxidermists, and fishermen. Brief mention of Parker Brothers in the March 16, 1899, issue of *Shooting and Fishing* said

> . . . two of the prettiest guns I've seen in a long while were shown in the exhibit of Parker Bros. Each was a 20-gauge, 26-inch barrels. The weight was an ounce or so over 6 pounds. The barrels were of a high grade of Damascus steel, while the fittings, the wood of the stock, in fact, the whole appearance of both guns left nothing to be desired.

Of interest here is the lack of mention of Whitworth or Titanic or Vulcan fluid-steel-barrel guns. Apparently small bores were so much on the ascendancy that barrel quality was not considered an important topic, or at least not one that Parker Brothers chose to tout in the small editorial space allotted.

Parker's fifty-dollar VH grade, with standard Vulcan fluid-steel barrels, was formally introduced by an April 1, 1899, catalog insert. The company's order book for October 1899 shows low VH- grade serial numbers in the range of 92,XXX, which validates the dated serial numbers for 1898-99 in the Appendix. Arthur W. du Bray, writing as "Gaucho" in the August 16, 1900, issue of *Shooting and Fishing*, reported on some ballistic testing of his 20-gauge (s/n 82,403) and 12-gauge (s/n 86,637) Parkers with Titanic steel barrels. The 20-gauge serial number would push the advent of Titanic barrels back to 1894-95, so it's likely du Bray's small bore was rebarreled. However, it's clear the advent of Titanic steel barrels fell between the 1894 introduction of Pigeon Guns with Whitworth compressed-steel barrels and the mid-1898 availability of Vulcan grade at Parker's New York salesroom. Du Bray's 12-gauge was probably built during 1897, with original Titanic fluid-steel barrels. Parker Brothers gravitated toward modern "black" barrels beginning with

Whitworth steel in 1894, followed by Titanic steel barrels in 1897-98, and then Vulcan steel barrels on the fifty-dollar "knockabout" grade in mid-1898. Except for picturing an AAH Pigeon Gun with black barrels in its contemporary advertising, Parker Brothers hardly mentioned the move away from forged iron-and-steel composition, Damascus, and twist-patterned barrels.

I believe "Titanic steel" barrel tubes were imported at an initial cost that compelled their use on guns priced at $100 (DH grade) and up. Almost immediately, competition and economies of scale drove the price of raw tubes down to where a fifty-dollar gun could be profitably manufactured and sold—hence the introduction of VH grade. Apparently turn-of-the-century shotgunners were left to make their own decisions regarding the desirability of fluid steel versus Damascus. Parker Brothers didn't then tout one over the other, although experiments had been under way since at least 1894 to make Damascus barrels suitable for nitro powder. According to an article in the September 27, 1894, issue of *Shooting and Fishing*,

> . . . the well known firm of Parker Bros. [is] about to increase the strength of their gun barrels by doing away with the concave system [swamping?] of finishing their guns. This is most assuredly a step in the right direction. Manufacturers, to gain strength at the breech, have, of course, added weight. In order to do away with this increased weight, the barrels have in many instances been cut away just forward of the chamber to such an extent as to leave the metal at that point of a dangerous thinness—a thickness so light that at any undue strain they must give way. The step about to be taken is one to be commended.

Experiments with stronger forged iron-and-steel-composite "Damascus" led to the gun with ". . . barrels of Damascus steel . . . blued to resemble fluid steel. . . ." exhibited at the Sportsmen's Exposition in

1897—the same year Parker adopted Titanic fluid-steel barrels as an option on DH, CH, and BH grades. It would be another thirty years, however, before Damascus barrels were completely phased out at Parker Brothers.

Parker Brothers circa 1900 "Blue Ink" pocket catalog.

1900

The Charles Parker Company employed approximately 1,500 workers at the turn of the century, and as many as 300 were considered employees of the gun works. Assuming annual production of 4,000 guns, each of Parker Brothers's 300 employees would have represented production of thirteen guns of various grades wholesaled for $1,000 to jobbers and the trade. Manufacture of the Parker gun was extremely labor-intensive, and skilled labor came relatively cheap. Peter Johnson wrote of his 1960 interview with a Mrs. Hanson, who had been employed as a stock and fore-end checkerer at Parker in the early 1900s, that she earned fifty cents for a ten-hour day as an apprentice. Skilled gunmakers were called contractors by Parker Brothers and were considered such in their individual listings in the *Meriden City Directory*. However, the concept of contract labor was more a matter of piecework bookkeeping than an indication that the contractors had a degree of independence implied by the usage today. The *Meriden City Directory* for 1900 shows that C. A. King was superintendent of the Parker gun works, Walter King was a "contractor" in the barrelmaking department, and although Charles Parker continued to be listed as president, the business was run by his son Dexter and his son-in-law, William H. Lyon.

Early Parker Brothers automatic ejector ad from September 1903 issue of Recreation *magazine. The "latest attachment" to "Old Reliable" was* latest *in more than one sense of the word. Greener's guns had ejectors since 1885, and every American maker of fine double barreled shotguns offered ejectors years before Parker joined the club.*

1901

Automatic ejectors were patented by C. A. King and J. P. Hayes on March 7, 1901 (see Patent Appendix), and were offered, somewhat belatedly, in 1902, thus making the doll's-head rib extension more a matter of substance than form. The rib extension served to catch the ejectors on VH grade and above. The Trojan grade, introduced in 1913, omitted Lefever's doll's-head rib extension, but never seemed to have a problem with springing barrels shooting loose. Whether this had to do with advances in metallurgy by 1913, as contrasted to the state-of-the-art in the 1880s, when Parker Brothers adopted Lefever's rib extension is problematical.

1902

Charles Parker died on January 31, 1902, in his ninety-fourth year, and his daughter Annie Lyon died in December. The stage was set for Charles Parker's descendants to choose sides in the management of the company. My research didn't disclose any evidence of actual discord in the "public record," but Parker's family would have been the exception if the day-to-day concerns of salaried family members within management weren't at odds with the quarterly or annual concerns of Parker outsiders living off remittances of shared profits.

1903

Parker is credited with introducing and popularizing the 28-gauge in the United States. According to Parker's brochure titled "Congratulations On Your Choice of a Parker Gun," the first 28-gauge hit the market in 1903. Wrong! A report on the Boston Sportsman Show in the March 1, 1900, issue of *Shooting and Fishing* stated that

> . . . the Parker gun is too well-known to need a description. There are found here

all grades and bores of this famous gun, including 8, 10, 12, 16, 20, and last, but not least, except in bore, is a new 28 bore double hammerless shotgun, which has just been finished and placed on exhibition. If we mistake not, this is the first 28 bore factory gun made in America.

The Parker factory order book for June 27, 1900, shows an order for three 28-gauges with serial numbers 97,218, 97,219, and 97,220, so even the history of Parker written by Parker misses some dates by a few years. Note that a contemporary gunwriter could not state absolutely that Parker Brothers was the first to introduce an American 28-gauge, and the gun works missed the date by three years—please don't hold me to a higher standard.

1904

Parker Brothers, according to a story in the March 19, 1896, issue of *Shooting and Fishing*, was

> . . . among the first of the American manufacturers to realize that there was in this country a class of wealthy men fond of shooting, and to whom the mere price of a gun was a secondary condition, so long as the gun itself appealed to them.

Parker Brothers circa 1906 P grade hammer gun s/n 140,009 shows the "fishtail" top-lever opener and C. A. King's 1905-patent wear insert on barrel lump. This 16-gauge has plain twist barrels and is exceptional insofar as P grade hammer guns weren't offered in Parker catalogs after the early 1890s.

The writer didn't seem to grasp the fact that "appeal" and "price" were not mutually exclusive, as evidenced by the A No. 1 Special, introduced about 1904. While Quality A was top-of-the-line with finest everything, and Pigeon Guns added Whitworth barrels to the equation, the A-1-S seemed to have nothing incremental to commend it other than price—a vanity grade, pure and simple.

1905-1910

The last weak link in the Parker mechanical function was made right in 1905 with the addition of C. A. King's patented replaceable tool-steel insert on the barrel lug, which matched the hardness of the tapered bolt to mitigate wear (see Patent Appendix). Before 1905, loose-breech Parkers needed the factory or a skilled gunsmith to rework the barrel lump. Although some do-it-yourself practitioners achieved short-term results with a metal punch, the wear insert was a simple fix for even the most unhandy Parker owners. The insert was described in Parker's 1906 catalog:

> Our patent-locking-device for locking barrels to the frame is a new feature . . . the points of bearing are of hardened steel, bolt is square and fits into lug of barrels over a plate of hardened steel, locking barrels to frame absolutely tight, and providing for the minimum of wear of these parts.

Parker Brothers ad from September 1931 issue of Hunting & Fishing. *Notice J. P. Hayes's modification to the top-lever opener, making it operate directly as a cam rather than indirectly as a multi-piece lever. Also note the multi-facet wear plate and matching slot in the taper bolt.*

The remarkable thing about King's improvement to the barrel lug is that no one had thought of it before. The wear insert was introduced coincidentally with the first availability of English vanadium steel in the United States. Henry Ford's Model T would not have had a reliable engine but for this light steel with tensile strength triple that of steel then in use. Vanadium steel was first produced at Canton, Ohio, by United States Steel in 1905, and was used by Ford for crankshafts, rods, piston pins, etc.—and likely by Parker Brothers for the 1905 patent insert and for other internal parts subject to wear.

The taper-bolt mechanism was re-engineered so as to be actuated by the top lever, functioning as a cam rather than a lever. This reduced the number of parts and simplified the mechanism. These improvements and some faulty recollection may have been the remarkable event referred to by an aging J. P. Hayes when he was interviewed by Peter Johnson and quoted in his book: ". . . eighteen parts, yes eighteen, were reduced to four." Larry Del Grego Jr. is the nation's preeminent Parker gunsmith and has specialized in the Parker gun since the 1950s. When asked about this seemingly remarkable reduction of mechanical parts, he shrugged his shoulders and volunteered that perhaps it had something to do with the improved top-lever mechanism. I don't believe any Parker gunsmith can make head or tail out of Johnson's quote; however, I understand Hayes developed a working model with fewer parts, but his "simplifications" were never adopted by Parker.

The last basic mechanical improvement to the Parker gun was J. P. Hayes's 1910-patent modification of the tool-steel insert (see Patent Appendix). One could argue that by 1910 the Parker side-by-side double-barrel shotgun was perfection personified; another view would be that the Parker gun had reached the end of the line. In either case, 1910 was the watershed year for Parker guns now considered "modern and safe" for continued regular use with store-bought shotshells.

During the 1890s and early 1900s, it was a matter of genuine dispute whether any repeating shotgun could be made to balance and shoot as smoothly and reliably as a side-by-side double. Ansley Fox was working for Winchester, shooting its Leader shells through his Parker as late as 1900, but he put down the "Old Reliable" in favor of a Winchester 97 for the Grand American Handicap at Live Birds in 1902—a change not made in haste, given the big money at risk. Within ten years,

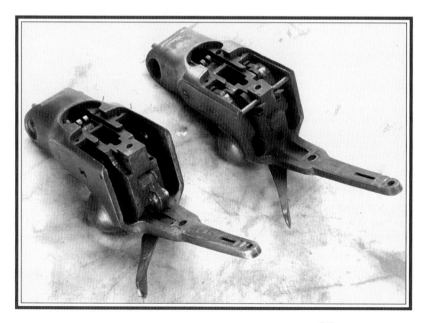

Two Parker boxlocks with different top-lever opener mechanisms. On the left is the old style linkage which was superseded in 1905, by the simplified cam-action opener shown on the right. See Patent Appendix A for cross-sectional drawings that clarify the improvements.

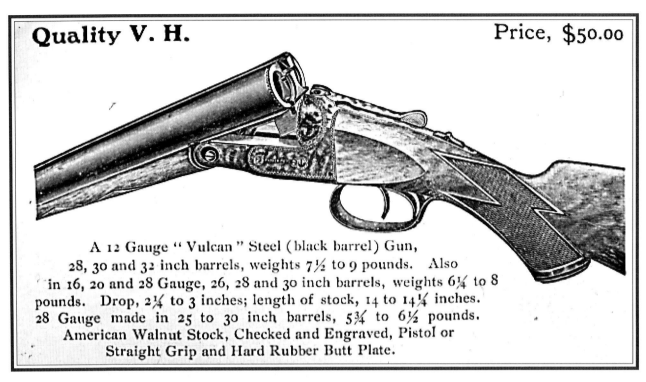

Quality V. H.   Price, $50.00

A 12 Gauge " Vulcan " Steel (black barrel) Gun,
28, 30 and 32 inch barrels, weights 7½ to 9 pounds. Also
in 16, 20 and 28 Gauge, 26, 28 and 30 inch barrels, weights 6¼ to 8
pounds. Drop, 2¼ to 3 inches; length of stock, 14 to 14¼ inches.
28 Gauge made in 25 to 30 inch barrels, 5¾ to 6½ pounds.
American Walnut Stock, Checked and Engraved, Pistol or
Straight Grip and Hard Rubber Butt Plate.

Parker Brothers offered VH grade priced at $50 in their rare circa 1900 "Blue Ink" pocket catalog. But the print was hardly dry on Parker Brothers circa 1908 (brown cover) Pine Cone catalog when it became apparent that Parker guns could no longer be sold at pre-existing prices and reductions began with VH grade.

all issues of effectiveness, reliability, and suitability for purpose were resolved in favor of the repeating shotgun. Major Charles Askins's book, *The American Shotgun*, is a window to the past circa 1910. Although Askins personally preferred side-by-side doubles, he was quite candid about repeaters:

The pump gun is the favorite trap gun in America today. If I am not mistaken it holds all amateur records at the trap, the longest run on clay birds, the best annual professional average, and odds the greatest number of first place wins either amateur or professional. As a trap gun for clay birds under present conditions it is unrivaled. It balances as well as a double arm, shoots more evenly, and will fire 5,000 shots for every dollar that it cost and still be ready for business.

This was a pretty stiff dose of wake-up medicine for "gun cranks" who would argue that side-by-side doubles had some mystical superiority that was shrouded by the fog of

highly suspect—but overwhelming—statistics favoring the repeater. Fortunately for Parker Brothers, the game was not zero sum. Loyal customers and those of conservative inclinations continued to buy Parkers at the rate of about 4,000 per year from 1900 until 1930—the same rate as between 1880 and 1900. Demand persisted for top-quality American-made doubles; what changed was the creation of a whole new market for good-quality American-made repeaters. Henry Ford's Model T was an important part of the new equation as increased mobility and a shorter work week allowed average working people the luxury of ranging out to do some hunting or spend leisure time at the gun club.

While it may seem that Americans had a long history of hunting for the table, if the truth be told, we've probably blown this colorful but narrow aspect of our heritage all out of proportion. Market hunters got all the press, while sharecroppers and clerks working six or seven days a week had little or no opportunity to hunt. The cost of live-bird shooting was prohibitive, and inanimate-target shooting didn't really catch on until after 1905. Meanwhile, game was getting scarce anywhere within easy travel of population centers.

Consider this: Deer were all but extinct in Illinois in 1902. The season was closed. Most people hadn't seen a whitetail in years, except maybe in a private game park or zoo. Fifty-five years later (in 1957), over the protest of the usual class of protectionists, the season was opened for a one-day shotgun hunt. Things got better and the hunt was extended to three days; then there was a split season of three days twice a year, plus three months for bowhunting. The times they were a-changin'—for the better!

This is not to say hunting had dried up by the 1900s. There was always plenty of game for those with time, money, and access. Game laws were almost nonexistent, particularly those protecting migratory birds, as no state wanted to protect a transient bird population by imposing seasons and bag limits on its own hunters, only to see the birds move on to be taken by unregulated gunners out of state.

1908-1909

Charles G. Spencer, using a twenty-seven-dollar grade Winchester repeating shotgun, broke 96.77 percent of 11,175 clay targets at registered tournaments during 1908 for top professional average. The low-end Parker was VH grade priced at $50.00, but an advertised price reduction to $37.50 in the February 29, 1908, issue of the *American Field* was a sign of the times. Nevertheless, the Parker gun survived the early 1900s just fine. The gun works kept busy at the average of 4,000 guns per year (as contrasted to Winchester 97s at approximately 45,000 per year). Small-bore guns were on the ascendancy, and the availability of ejectors after

1902 sold any number of new guns to Parker owners who wanted to "upgrade." The sentiment prevailing in 1910 was expressed by Major Askins: "Self ejectors are of such a positive advantage to the sportsmen afield that it is a matter of wonder any shotgun of good or medium grade should ever be made without them." Askins became America's best-known and most authoritative gun writer. He was gun-department editor for *Outdoor Life* in the 1920s and 1930s, and his opinions influenced the wants, needs, and expectations of several generations of double gunners. By the 1920s, Askins had elevated ejectors from simply a "positive advantage" to being "essential," and had this to say about ejectors in his 1928 book, *Wing Shooting*:

> We are terming ejectors a refinement, though in all reality they should be considered a necessity. All our better makes of firearms, like the Fox, Smith, Ithaca, Parker, have ejectors that have been tried and tested in long and strenuous service. They work and keep working. Ejectors should be considered standard and placed on all double guns. A double gun lacking ejectors is deficient in a feature essential to perfect service.

Suffice it to say that ejectors were always *the* most popular option. Parker devoted two pages to a cutaway picture and description of the new automatic ejector mechanism in their 1908 Pine Cone catalog. The extra cost

This ad appeared in the February 29, 1908, issue of American Field, *just after Parker Brothers cut VH price to $37.50 list. Price cuts on the rest of the line were soon to follow.*

of a gun with automatic ejectors was twenty-five dollars without regard to grade. The earliest ad for Parker ejectors in my collection is from the September 1903 *Recreation* magazine. By comparison, W. W. Greener offered ejectors as early as 1885, Lefever had been advertising automatic ejectors since 1891, and by 1898 all makers of premium doubles offered ejectors *except* Parker.

Parker Brothers refused to retrofit ejectors to extractor guns until about 1913, which surely helped sales of new guns catering to the American fascination with gimmicks. The 1908 Pine Cone catalog states that ". . . ejectors cannot be fitted to any guns now in finished condition." A letter published in *Recreation* magazine for December 1903 said this:

> I noticed in *Recreation* an inquiry as to Parker shotguns. I have owned and used many of them, from the $50.00 grade up to $175.00 ejector. They all shoot evenly and hard. In balance, finish, the Parker beats the world. The Parker people are not very accommodating about putting extra work on a gun; for instance, they will not accept an order to put an ejector on one of their own guns. I sent a $50.00 Parker to Chris Fisher, Grand Forks and he put on it the best automatic ejector I ever saw. It works perfectly with any shell and is simple in construction, there being but three pieces to it. I do not see why the Parker Company do not put ejectors on all grades. Other gun makers will put on all the extras you are willing to pay for
>
> —R. F. Billings, Corona, Cal.

Billings wrote about his $175 ejector gun, which would have been a $150 CH with $25 ejectors. Apparently he wanted his almost new $50 VH retrofitted with automatic ejectors, but the factory declined. Parker's refusal shouldn't have been a surprise as ejectors weren't offered on *new* GH, PH, and VH grades in 1903. Billings's letter verifies that itinerant gunsmiths were installing non-

factory ejectors on Parker guns almost coincidentally with the factory offering ejectors as an option. Retrofit automatic ejectors were doubly expensive when you consider that all the owner of a perfectly good extractor gun got for his money was a high-maintenance device capable of littering the ground with spent shotshells. ("High maintenance" means that ejector guns need to be broken open [cocked] before the fore-end is removed to avoid the uncocked ejector-hammer problem, so common that most Parker owners consider a malfunctioning ejector mechanism normal.) Nevertheless, automatic ejectors were *the* most popular option. The 1908 catalog offered ejectors as a "new" twenty-five-dollar option on GH, PH, and VH grades, and by the circa 1913 Flying Ducks catalog, Parker Brothers decided that ". . . ejectors can now be fitted to guns in finished condition." Over 90 percent of the better Parker guns offered for sale to collectors from 1989 to 1994 had ejectors. (More on special features in Chapter 9.)

1910

The Parker hammerless gun, with or without ejectors, evolved to its final mechanical form in 1910. Damascus-barrel guns were pretty much out of style, but so were side-by-side doubles. Hammer guns were no longer popular, but were available on special order to Parker customers suffering from incurable nostalgia. The Charles King era ended in 1910 as his son, Walter A. King, took over management of the gun works. Charles stayed on until he passed away in 1914, but Walter was in charge. The Parker gun would coast through the 1910s and 1920s under the ever-decreasing influence of Walter, until the stock-market crash of October 1929 and ensuing Depression put an end to the Parker Brothers gun works as a profit center within The Charles Parker Company.

COASTING WITH WALTER KING

Walter and Charles King in the superintendent's office at the gun works. Charles had been superintendent since 1874, and semi-retired in 1910. Although Walter started at Parker Brothers as a young man in 1889, his first listing in the Meriden City Directory *was in 1900, as "machinist at Parker Bros." Walter's listing changed to "contractor Parker Bros." in 1904, and "asst. sup't Parker Bros." in 1909. Walter seems to be dressed the part of assistant superintendent in the picture.*

While Samuel Colt was extolling the virtues of interchangeable gun parts at the Crystal Palace in 1851, the yacht America *sailed around the Isle of Wight on the Solent near Southampton, England, to win the first "America's Cup." Queen Victoria asked prince consort Albert about second place; he replied, "Ma'am—there is no second place." Likewise, until about 1910, the Parker gun was so clearly the first choice of double gunners (who could afford the price) that it was of little consequence whether the Fox or Lefever or L. C. Smith was considered the distant second. Parker Brothers had tremendous goodwill at the turn of the century. The Parker gun was thought to be the best America could produce. The A. H. Fox Gun Company was incorporated and started to build guns in 1905 and promptly declared the A. H. Fox gun "The finest gun in the world." By comparison, Parker tooled up to produce shotguns as early as 1865, and earned its reputation as the "Old Reliable" over more than twenty-five years and almost 100,000 guns.*

Charles Parker was a consummate participant in the Industrial Revolution during the latter half of the nineteenth century. While his Parker Brothers gun works was quick to adopt the innovation of interchangeable parts to produce shotguns in 1877, Henry Ford's pioneering of the assembly line with interchangeable *labor* to produce his Model T, in 1908, wasn't technology that could be transferred to the hand fit and finish of the Parker gun. The economies of the assembly line—with semiskilled and unskilled labor doing simple repetitive tasks efficiently at a speed regulated by the line itself—left Parker Brothers standing in the dust alongside the makers of buggy whips and various other nineteenth-century relics. Despite what some economists call the early twentieth-century "industrial drive to maturity," the Parker gun remained a labor-intensive, artisan-built "collector's item." Walter A. King gets credit for the hand-finished Parker gun persisting as the connoisseur's weapon of choice well into the 1930s.

The early 1900s were years of adjustment for the American economy. Gold continued to be valued at twenty dollars per ounce, but the movement from an agricultural to an industrial economy disconnected the value of goods and services from the value of gold-denominated capital investments; the consequent economic disparities offered widespread opportunities to succeed or fail on a grand scale. Meanwhile, political and economic conditions in Europe were leading irreversibly to the Russian Revolution and World War I. The disruptions in Europe were added incentive for great numbers of the disenfranchised working class to seek a better life by emigrating to the land of freedom and opportunity—the United States of America.

The flood of immigrant workers during the early 1900s compounded the growing pains of the newly industrialized American economy and contributed to lower wages and higher basic living costs. Discretionary income fell, and so did the price of Parker guns. The VH had been introduced on April 1, 1899, at fifty dollars, and the price persisted through Parker's 1908 Pine Cone catalog. However, by 1908 it was down to thirty-seven fifty, and by 1910 Parker's "hundred dollar" DH cost seventy-five bucks.

Major Askins may have preferred a fine double in the field and at the traps, but he couldn't ignore the ascendancy of the relatively inexpensive repeaters. In 1910 he wrote in his book, *The American Shotgun,*

[the fact that] . . . nearly all shotguns perform alike with their charges had a rather unfortunate effect on gun building in this country . . . [and] . . . has undoubtedly caused a large demand for the cheaper class, preventing any, even our best manufacturers, from making a specialty of high grade weapons. The pump gun is the favorite trap gun in America today.

1910

Charles Alonzo King had been largely responsible for success of the Parker gun since he hired on in 1874. The *Commemorative Biographical Record* for Meriden circa 1900 gave him his due:

Probably no house in the United States is better or more favorably known in its line

than that of Parker Brothers and it was as superintendent of their gun and their machine shops that Mr. King came to Meriden. For the past twenty-seven years he has been the efficient incumbent of that position. He is a designer and patentee of the hammerless breechloading shot gun now so widely known throughout the world. With from 200 to 300 men in his charge, Mr. King has not only satisfactorily performed the responsible duties of his office, but he has also earned the confidence and affection of both employers and employees. In these days of general business discontent he has so managed the affairs of Parker Brothers in his department that there has been little friction.

Charles King's tenure overlapped the years when Charles Parker controlled the hardware company and the years after control passed to his son Dexter. King had a relatively free hand in the management of the Parker gun works and, anticipating retirement in 1910, passed the superintendent position to his son, Walter A. King, who had been employed by Parker Brothers since 1889. Walter began as a "gofer" in the shop, and the *Meriden City Directory* called him a "Machinist at Parker Bros" in 1900, "Contractor" in 1904, and "Asst. Sup't Parker Bros" in 1909. With twenty-one years of experience and his father staying on in semi-retirement, Walter King was primed and ready for the tasks ahead. Walter's response to the challenges of the day gave the Parker gun the best twenty years of its existence.

Challenge number one—Parker Brothers and other makers of fine hand-finished double-barrel shotguns had a self-image that didn't include cheap guns for the masses. However, it was no secret that repeating shotguns were swamping the market. Winchester was selling eleven machine-made, machine-finished Model 97s for every hand-finished Parker. By 1912 Parker found it necessary to reduce prices of all guns by about 25 percent. The A-1 Special with ejectors, which had cost $525 in 1908, could be bought for $393.75 in 1912 and $400 in 1915. However, price reductions of higher-grade guns couldn't paint over the fact that Parker's customer base had changed.

Challenge number two—Ansley H. Fox was the first manufacturer of premium double-barrel shotguns to make a serious

Parker Bros. Quality VH and the competition in 1911. Discounting was a fact of life after the turn of the century. Quality VH was introduced at $50.00 list in 1898, and Parker reduced the price to $37.50 in February 1908. Evans Brothers, Cincinnati, discounted the reduced price to $34.50. Ansley Fox's Sterlingworth was a $25.00 gun when introduced in 1910, and was likewise discounted $3.00 by Evans Brothers.

play for the low end of the double-gun market. Fox was caught up in the "fine gun" panache and tentatively introduced the Sterlingworth in 1910, not as a Fox but rather as a product of the "Sterlingworth Company of Philadelphia." The introductory price was $25 without ejectors. By 1911 the Fox Sterlingworth could be had for $37.50 with ejectors. Meanwhile, Parker's VH grade cost $37.50 without ejectors and $56.25 with the popular option.

There may have been some technological advances in the manufacturing process that allowed Parker Brothers to reduce the price of VH grade from $50 to $37.50 in 1908, but likely there wasn't much profit left in the gun at the lower price. Walter King confronted a situation best exemplified by prices for knockabout double-barrel guns in the 1911 Evans Brothers catalog. Although the VH was discounted $3 from factory list to $34.50, the Sterlingworth was likewise discounted by $3 to $22. Meanwhile, Ansley Fox's A grade with Krupp fluid-steel barrels was $2.50 less than the Parker VH, and the Lefever and L. C. Smith low-end guns were $12 to $13 cheaper. Parker Brothers had a problem. The Trojan grade, introduced at $27.50 in early 1913, was part of the solution.

A second strategy was to create demand for small-bore Parkers among those true believers who were already banging birds with the company's 12-bore. To this end, Parker Brothers came out with a booklet, *The Small-Bore Shotgun,* in at least four versions from 1912 to 1922. The company got serious about selling small-bore shotguns after 1910, although one version of the booklet claims the 20-gauge was ". . . made popular by Parker in 1895," and 20s were available as early as 1878 on special order.

In the early years of the twentieth century, Parker popularized the 28-gauge, a bore size that today is sure to draw a blank almost everywhere except the skeet club. Parker Brothers started building 28-gauge guns in

Damascus and fluid steel with low serial numbers reputed to be 94,XXX, and factory records show at least three 28s on order as early as June 1900. The earliest 28-gauge I've actually seen is s/n 102,168, a VH on a standard 20-gauge size 0 frame. While 20-gauge was standard in the 1880s catalogs, the 28-gauge

Parker Brothers 1915 advertising gave unspoken credit to the dominance of repeaters and increasing popularity of single barrel trap guns. The twice emphasized reference to "Double" can be taken in the context of Parker Brothers protesting too much. Meanwhile, the push was on for Parker smallbores and in 1916, the gun works introduced its own Single Barrel Trap Gun (SBT).

The

Small Bore
Shot Gun

Parker Brothers

Master Gun Makers

MERIDEN, CONN., U.S.A.

Latest version of Parker's smallbore booklet has increased collector value because of Parker's "trademark" woodcock on the cover. However, some experts have called it a snipe. Author once shot a bird resembling this along a creek in northern Illinois, and it tasted more like dead fish than dead worms so it probably was a snipe.

was first mentioned in Parker's 1902 catalog, and the 1906 Pine Cone catalog pictures s/n 120,404, a 28-gauge A No.1 Special.

Small bores were a marketing ploy to sell second and third guns to Parker Brothers' existing customer base. Meanwhile, the Trojan grade targeted first-gun purchasers with relatively low price, consistent with maintaining production standards. In the Trojan grade, certain external metal-removal steps were simply omitted in making the boxlock, and the complicated and difficult-to-fit Deeley & Edge-style fore-end latch was eliminated altogether. Low serial numbers are in the range of 160,XXX, and early Trojans, perhaps as a result of Major Askins's advice, had a cosmetic ("false") rib extension. The highest serial number with a false rib extension I've seen is s/n 199,029, a 16-gauge built ten years after Trojan grade was introduced. The rib extension was soon eliminated to reduce cost. Aside from cost-saving elimination and omissions, the Trojan was built in large economical lots with standard barrel lengths, chokes, weights, measurements, and no special requests. By 1926 Parker Brothers advertised that 2,000 Trojan-grade guns were being built per year, or about 50 percent of the current annual production.

The "Old Reliable"
PARKER GUN

Last Call
for Trojans!

To be sure of Parker Trojans for next fall please get your orders in at once.

You do not need to disappoint your customers next fall if you'll heed this request to send your orders along right away.

With production on the Trojan limited to 2000 for the year and *more than half of them now gone*, the factory is on the jump taking care of increased orders on the higher grades, such as AH, BH, CH, DH, etc. We are following the policy of filling orders in rotation. We want to take care of you, but you must do your part first.

PARKER BROS., Master Gun Makers, 46 Cherry St., Meriden, Conn.
Pacific Coast Distributor, A. W. duBray, Box 102, San Francisco, Calif.

Parker Trojan ad from March 1926 issue of Sporting Goods Journal. *Trojans were popular from introduction in early 1913, and soon accounted for about half of Parker Brothers' production.*

The PARKER Single Barrel Trap Gun!

(A Chip of the "Old Reliable" Block)

THE GUN WITH A PEDIGREE!!

Price $150
The greatest scores ever recorded were made with
PARKER GUNS

For further particulars address PARKER BROS.
N. Y. Salesrooms, 32 Warren St. **Meriden, Conn.** Resident Agent, A. W. duBray Box 102, San Francisco, Cal.

Parker Brothers ad from May 1917 issue of American Field, *just after the Single Barrel Trap Gun was introduced. The last SBT ad in author's collection is from the October 1920 issue of* Field and Stream, *which brought to an end the three year advertising blitz for Parker's least popular gun.*

1914-1915

The First World War disrupted the supply of Damascus, laminated, and twist barrels from England and Belgium. Damascus barrels were in short supply, but by 1915 Damascus barrels were out of fashion and had slight demand. Nevertheless, the last Parker Brothers ad I've seen is in the 1934 *Meriden City Directory*, and the DH grade pictured has Damascus barrels. I wonder if this was conscious nostalgia or Depression-era indifference.

1916-1917

Target shooting experienced such rapid growth between 1905 and 1916 that an article in *Outers Book* boasted almost 4,000 registered trap clubs with 400,000 to 500,000 regular members. Trapshooting had become an Olympic sport, and J. R. Graham of Illinois won the 1912 Olympic Trap championship at Stockholm, Sweden. The exponential growth of trapshooting didn't escape the attention of Parker Brothers, and the Single Barrel Trap Gun (SBT) was introduced in 1916. Parker advertising from 1917 to 1920 touted the SBT almost exclusively.

The firm announced in its *Field and Stream* ad for October 1920 that ". . . some members of the Olympic team shooting for the United States used the OLD RELIABLE PARKER GUN." The next year, E. F. Haak won the Grand American Handicap at Chicago with his single-barrel Parker. The thought then passed, and Parker's SBT settled into relative anonymity, a condition that persists to this day. To my knowledge, no information has ever been published giving even the roughest estimate of how many SBT guns were built, but there weren't many. The Single Barrel Trap Gun had a ventilated rib standard as early as 1917, at least six years before the first vent-rib double.

1918

Parker Brothers' undated pocket catalog with references to shooting events of 1916 through June 22, 1917, shows the last of the hammer guns, ranging from Whitworth or Peerless-barrel AA Pigeon grade, which cost $381.25 to the lowly T grade, priced at $58.25 with Parker steel barrels. (What would a mint T grade with fluid-steel barrels be worth today?) The catalog's price-change insert dated June 3, 1918, doesn't mention hammer guns.

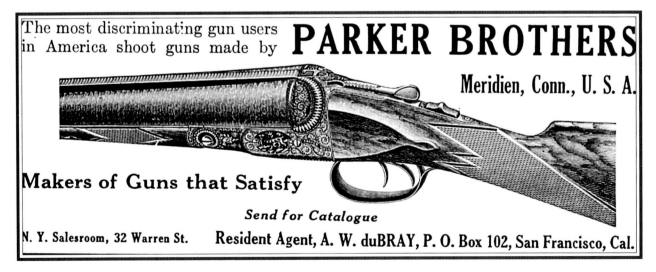

Parker Brothers ad from August 1916 issue of Outer's Book. *The gun is DH grade Damascus with straight grip. This is the last magazine ad showing a Damascus-barreled Parker in author's collection. Parker Brothers built Damascus guns on special order until about 1927.*

Thus ended the exposed hammer era at Parker Brothers. The highest-serial-number hammer gun I've seen is 156,XXX, a D grade circa 1912, with rare (but possibly retrofitted) Titanic barrels.

1921

Frank Lefler patented his single selective trigger (SST) on March 20, 1917 (see Patent Appendix), and Parker Brothers started offering the Lefler SST after 1921. According to Larry Del Grego Jr., Parker's Frank Fama reworked and refined the cranky Lefler SST; however, the Miller SST is preferred by most Parker people I know. Parker Brothers' December 1, 1920, pocket catalog (with an insert referring to Haak's GAH win at Chicago in August 1921) doesn't show or price the SST option. The SST first appears in the January 2, 1923, pocket catalog, as does the beavertail or trap-style fore-end. I have more than thirty magazine ads for the years 1921 through 1928, but none mentions the SST. The first ad I've seen for it is in the May 1929 issue of *Field and Stream*. Apparently the SST was a Parker secret. The incidence of Miller SSTs and articulated front triggers leads me to believe that a Parker SST is not necessarily a value-added item on anything other than a museum piece.

1922

Parker Brothers started a special gun to commemorate reaching s/n 200,000. Finished in early 1923 and originally designated "PP Superfine" in the fall 1922 stock book, the "Invincible" wasn't offered for sale until the January 1, 1926, large Flying Geese catalog, and even then, the price wasn't mentioned. According to J. P. Morgan, "If you need to ask what it costs, you can't afford it."

1923

The beavertail or trap-style fore-end became an extra-cost option in 1923, probably due to the demands of Parker's modern trapshooting clientele. Parker Brothers had produced a trap gun since before the turn of the century. AAH Pigeon grade was for "trap" shooting in the sense that live birds were released from plunge traps (some manufactured by Parker Brothers beginning in the 1870s). Parker's April 23, 1923, fold-up brochure was

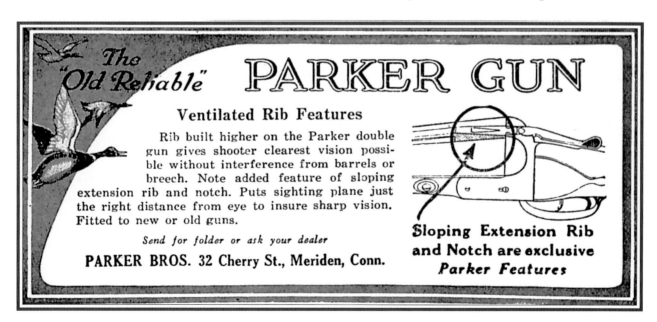

Parker Brothers ad from February 1926 issue of National Sportsman *magazine, showing Parker Brothers sloping ventilated rib and notch which somehow was supposed to help the eye focus on both rib and target. Remington-Parkers omit the notch on the vent-rib slope. Maybe the notch proved unnecessary or perhaps a dollar was saved; we'll never know.*

the first notice that a vent rib for double-barrel shotguns was in the works; however, it may have been 1926 before vent-rib doubles were built in any quantity.

1925

Dexter Parker died and was succeeded by his brother-in-law, William H. Lyon, as president of The Charles Parker Company. Parker Brothers began stamping OVERLOAD PROVED on the barrel flats, and a late 1920s booklet, A Trip Through Parker Bros., described the barrel-proofing procedure:

> Every Parker gun is tested for pattern and ability to withstand heavy loads. It is sent to the shooting and testing department where it is finish bored to the degree of choke called for. The gun is then tested with standard factory loads for accuracy and pattern and is finally proof tested with an abnormally heavy load which shows any latent defects of material or workmanship. Contrary to the general practice in proof testing barrels, Parker Brothers do not send their barrels for test while they are in the unfinished state, although that procedure would affect a considerable saving should the barrels fail to withstand the test. Parker Brothers defer the proofing until the barrels are completely finished inside and out and are down to the minimum thickness and weight. If barrels are tested while still unfinished, they are somewhat heavier and therefore to a certain degree, stronger than finished barrels. After proofing, the barrels are carefully inspected and if passed by the inspector, the proofmark is put on the flats of each tube. This is Parker Brothers' guarantee of good material and workmanship.

1926

Most collectors believe ventilated ribs were first offered in 1926, as a "new" extra-cost option on Parker doubles. Ventilated ribs, however, had been standard since 1917 on Single Barrel Trap Guns. Parker Brothers published a pocket-size folding brochure dated April 23, 1923, introducing "Parker Ventilated Rib Guns" and offering a special folder on these guns to be sent upon request. The picture of the new ventilated rib is strange insofar as the gun shown is an *unfinished* DH grade without engraving or checking. The gun must have been the prototype, photographed rush-rush to be included in the 1923 brochure. It took three years, however, for the Parker ventilated rib for double-barrel guns to become a popular option.

Meanwhile, Ithaca acquired a patent in 1926 for a ventilated rib on double-barrel guns and notified Parker of the "infringement." On May 31, 1927, Wilbur Parker wrote a letter to Lew Smith at Ithaca essentially saying that Parker's patent attorneys were smarter than Ithaca's. Another letter from Wilbur, dated July 15, 1927, put the matter to rest as it

> . . . was submitted to our patent attorneys for whose written opinion we were "soaked" good and proper, copy of which is enclosed.

Using a little 20/20 hindsight, I think Wilbur could have saved some attorney fees if he had forwarded a copy of Parker Brothers's 1923 brochure to Lew Smith at Ithaca.

The new sport of skeet started up in 1926, and renewed interest in the 28-gauge. Parker introduced the .410, which gained popularity as a skeet gun. By the early 1930s, skeet had become extremely popular, and Parker Brothers issued a pamphlet, For Your Best Scores At Skeet Shoot A Parker, touting both the VH with twenty-six-inch barrels and the Trojan with twenty-eight-inch barrels as skeet guns.

A woman from Montana won a hundred dollars in a magazine contest by coming up with the name *skeet*. I recall seeing the two-page contest announcement and entry form in National Sportsman and then turned the page to see an article titled "Skeeters————," referring to mosquitoes. In September 1937, EBW of British Columbia wrote a letter to the

W YORK SALESROOM
25 MURRAY ST.

THE PARKER GUN

PARKER BROTHERS

MASTER GUN MAKERS

MERIDEN, CONN.

August 22, 1927.

IN REPLY REFER TO

W. F. P.

Mr. Lou Smith
Ithaca Gun Company,
Ithaca, N. Y.

Dear Lou:

Yours of August 8th. You will have no trouble in getting
our affidavit as to when we made a ventilated rib gun for
W. E. Beers.

Walter intends to be in attendance at the G.A.H. We are
instructing him that he indicate to Steve, if he sees him,
that we have ample and conclusive evidence of ventilated ribs
being applied to double guns many years prior to the application for his patent, and further that with such information
in our hands it certainly would be extremely foolish on his
part to institute any legal proceedings.

Yours August 11th. Glad you have received an affidavit from
Bill Price covering ventilated rib on his Parker Gun. Sorry
he did not return the two affidavits properly signed so that
we might have one, but if you are in possession of one, it
hardly seems necessary for us to have you go to the trouble
of obtaining another.

Sincerely,

WFP-AN

Letter from Wilbur Parker to Lou (Lew?) Smith of the Ithaca Gun Company, resolving the dispute with Ithaca about whether Parker's use of a ventilated rib on double-barreled guns violated a certain patent licensed by Ithaca. Parker prevailed, but was "soaked" by their attorney, according to other correspondence in Herschel Chadick's file. Original Parker factory letter courtesy of Chadick's, Ltd.

editor of *Field and Stream* inquiring: "...As a sporting goods dealer, I have been asked several times recently by prospective Skeet shooters, just what the word 'Skeet' means—and where it originated." The gun editor's answer:

It was back in 1926, I believe, that the originators and sponsors of Skeet offered a $100 prize for an appropriate name for the new sport. Mrs. Gertrude Hurlbutt of Dayton, Montana, suggested "skeet," an old Scandinavian form of the word "shoot" and her suggestion received the award.

The following month, a number of letters from sportsmen of every Scandinavian descent disclaimed the word *skeet* as having anything to do with any shooting word known to any Scandinavian language. Yours truly put two and two together, seventy years after the fact, and perhaps I've come closer to the truth than the editor of *Field and Stream*, a short eleven years after skeet became a popular shooting game. In

a perfect blend of entomology and etymology, Gertrude named *skeet* after the non-Scandinavian word for *mosquitoes*!

Likewise the etymology (word derivation) of *trap* and *trapshooting*: many who shoot trap today don't know their game was named after the pigeon trap used to hold and release live birds, or that *Pull!* literally meant *Pull the line* attached to one of the five traps to eject a bird. One of Parker Brothers' earliest gun-related products was a plunge trap used for live-bird shooting. Captain Bogardus's 1878 book, *Field, Cover, and Trap Shooting*, advertised Parker's pigeon trap, which is also included with all sorts of other gunning equipment in 1880s Parker Brothers catalogs.

Also in 1926, Charles S. Parker (Wilbur F.'s son) was preparing himself to become president of The Charles Parker Company by working in the shop. Peter Johnson wrote about "...Mr. Charles S. Parker... [being]... in charge of the shop in the absence of Mr. Walter King who was recuperating from an illness...."

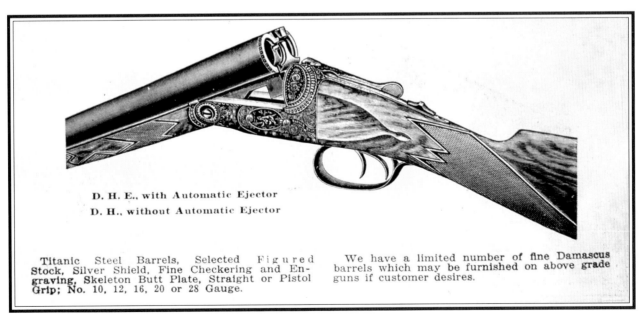

D. H. E., with Automatic Ejector
D. H., without Automatic Ejector

Titanic Steel Barrels, Selected Figured Stock, Silver Shield, Fine Checkering and Engraving, Skeleton Butt Plate, Straight or Pistol Grip; No. 10, 12, 16, 20 or 28 Gauge.

We have a limited number of fine Damascus barrels which may be furnished on above grade guns if customer desires.

Parker Brothers 1920 pocket catalog offered "...a limited number of fine Damascus barrels" on DH grade with or without automatic ejectors. Although Damascus-barrels weren't offered in Parker catalogs after 1920, a few Damascus-barreled guns were manufactured as late as 1927.

1927

Damascus barrels were offered after the Great War on special order for grades GH, DH, and CH in the December 1, 1920, pocket catalog, but not in the 1918 or 1919 pocket catalogs or in the 1923 or later catalog. I've seen two Damascus-barrel Parkers circa 1927—VHE s/n 227,XXX and DHE s/n 218,XXX—and both have original fine Damascus barrels stamped *OVERLOAD PROVED*, as was typical of post-1925 proof-tested guns. Some writers claim that PH grade was dropped from the line during 1927; however, the Parker Gun Price List No. 59, dated January 1, 1928, still listed the ejectorless PH with a suggested price of $77.25, and the PHE with single trigger for $124.75. The PH grade was hand-stamped "Discontinued" in the 1929 catalog. Collector tip—original January 1, 1929, large Flying Geese catalogs can be authenticated by the word "Discontinued" hand-stamped in magenta or green ink on the PH listing. Reprint catalogs, no matter the wear and tear or patina of age, have a halftone "Discontinued" the same color as the gun pictures.

1928

According to Peter Johnson, Charles S. Parker became president of The Charles Parker Company in 1928. I don't think so. The *Meriden City Directory* and contemporary news reports show that William H. Lyon was president until 1932. Charles S. Parker took over the operating company after the 1932 reorganization, and Lyon then became president of the real-estate holding company.

SEPTEMBER 1929

The "roaring twenties" hit their peak, and Parker Brothers delivered the first customer-ordered Invincible to A. C. Middleton of Moorestown, New Jersey, on September 13, 1929, according to an article by Dick Baldwin—"Parker's $100,000.00 Shotgun"—in the May 1971 issue of *Guns and Ammo*. Also, in a supreme example of poor timing, Parker started to place large ads in upscale magazines such as *The Sportsman* and *The Field*. A month later, captains of industry and finance were more likely to jump out a Wall Street window than to buy an expensive Parker gun.

OCTOBER 1929

"Stock Market Crashes": The excesses of the 1920s caught up with an economy that seemed more interested in paper profits than in producing goods and services. It wasn't imme-

By 1929, Parker Brothers had lost track of its own beginnings as shown by this ad from The Sportsman. *Notice the reference to ". . . eighty years of leadership in fine gunmaking. . ." which stretched the truth by about sixteen years.*

Parker Brothers "Bring Them Down" ad from November 1929 issue of Field and Stream, *which must have hit the newsstands and mailboxes coincidentally with the October 29, 1929 stock market crash. The depression "brought down" the Parker Gun.*

diately apparent that a worldwide depression would ensue, but things didn't bode well for the 1930s. Parker Brothers had coasted through the 1910s and 1920s with a good product and an even better reputation, but reversal of fortune would soon put The Charles Parker Company and the Parker Brothers gun works on the skids.

Parker Brothers ad from May 1929 issue of Field and Stream. *It could be the first owner of author's DHE trap gun saw this ad and placed his order. Perhaps he heard that Parker's single selective trigger was a bit troublesome and thus opted for more reliable double triggers; or one could speculate that some "market crash" belt tightening was in order and the $30 cost saving was purely economic.*

76

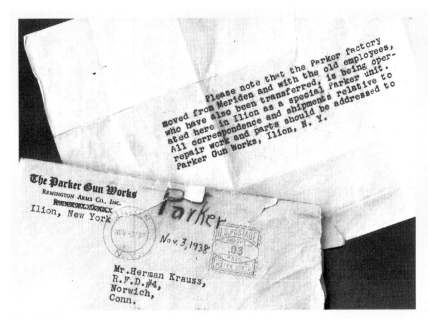

ON THE SKIDS

This letter came with a mint in-the-case BHE half-frame 12-gauge owned by Forrest Marshall, President of the Parker Gun Collectors Association. The special-order gun cost half as much as a low-priced automobile in 1938; but it's pretty clear that Parker's "hand-fit and finish" didn't extend to factory correspondence. The perception of the trade that Parker guns had been cheapened in the hands of Remington, and the reluctance of double-gun customers to pay high prices for Parker's of "doubtful origin," is best exemplified by the two pieces of paper pictured at left.

Something happened at the company in 1929 or 1930. The something was a Parker family/shareholder matter that likely preceded the stock market crash, or it could have been the slightly delayed impact of the economy grinding to a halt. Another possibility is that after Charles Parker's last surviving son, Dexter, died in 1925, Charles's descendants chose up sides and elected William H. Lyon as president of the family company. He had been involved in management since the 1880s, so there was nothing inherently upsetting with a "Parker by marriage," then age sixty-nine, running the business. Wilbur F. Parker Jr., then age fifty-two, could have coveted the position for himself—or maybe not. At any rate, the situation that had existed in 1925 wasn't all that uncommon for a family-owned business. Whether the changing of the guard involved a family power struggle is problematical. However, another action taken was to bring in an outside "efficiency expert" to manage the company while Wilbur Jr. stayed on as vice-president and his son Charles S. was in the shop learning the business.

1932

On September 1, The Charles Parker Company separated into two corporations, Charles Parker Estate, Inc., and The Charles Parker Company. Charles Parker Estate, was a holding company owning the real estate, buildings, and investments of the family company. The Charles Parker Company continued to be the operating entity engaged solely in the manufacture and sale of the company's products (including the Parker gun). William H. Lyon, widower of Charles's daughter Annie, became president of the estate as proxy for his line of descendants. Charles S. Parker took over the presidency of the operating company at the precocious age of thirty-one.

Meanwhile, Parker Brothers had been selling to a market that wanted, rather than needed, fine side-by-side shotguns. As the Depression wore on, the production of the gun works fell to less than 5 percent of average capacity. Walter King wasn't a happy man in 1933, when he wrote in a personal letter to an old customer and friend:

> . . . The great grandson . . . [Charles S.] . . .
> of the original owner . . . [Charles] . . . is
> now President. His father . . . [Wilbur F.

Jr.], who is just my age, and with whom I have been most closely associated for many years, is called chairman of the board, but has no power. The factory is run under the directions of a Jew from New York who came here about 4 years ago [1929] as an efficiency expert, installed his system in all the plants except the gun shop. He is now vice-president and general manager.

1933

One out of four Americans who had previously been working was unemployed in 1933, and 40 percent of the nation's commercial banks had failed. Banks in some states closed to stem a run on deposits, and one of

newly elected President Roosevelt's first moves after taking office was to declare a bank holiday. According to Walter King, the Parker family brought in outside help to try to straighten out the hardware business. Suffice it to say that all was not well at The Charles Parker Company, and the efficiency expert could not long ignore the shop within a shop. Walter continued to be in charge of the Parker Brothers gun works until the early 1930s, when he was replaced by his young assistant, who, in King's words, was ". . . a very fine young man, with a gift for charts, graphs, etc., but I must say that the practical parts of gun making are not of his education." When annual sales fell to about 300

Parker Brothers ad from May 1932 issue of Field and Stream. After two years of nominal advertising, Parker started placing bigger, better ads during 1932, and by then had acquired rights to manufacture and market the Hawes line of fishing rods. This particular ad is the first in author's collection to specifically advertise Parker's single trigger. The reference to "new" has to do with Frank Fama's refinement of the troublesome 1921 Lefler patent SST.

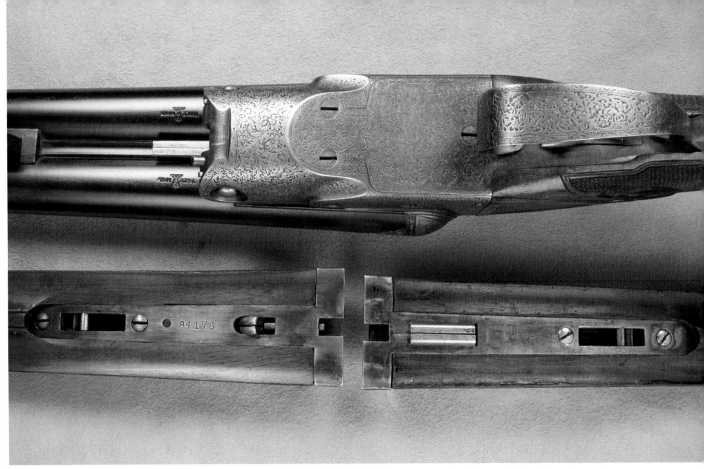

(top) *Bottom view of early AAH(E) Pigeon Gun s/n 84,176 showing Whitworth proof marks on the barrels and non-factory retrofit ejectors. Also notice the strange ejector mechanism on the VH(E) fore-end on right. Nonstandard ejectors are found with some frequency on turn-of-the-century guns, but are a double negative when it comes to collector value and function.*

(bottom) *Parker Brothers PH Damascus twist (top) and VHE s/n 223,581 (bottom). Notice how the ejectors fit into the thick rib extension on the VHE and compare this to the size and thickness of the PH rib extension. Early Parker hammerless guns could not be retrofitted with ejectors because of the "too small" PH-type rib extension. Parker soon standardized the tooling for all barrel rib extensions to be of the bigger, thicker type, so after about 1906, even guns ordered with extractors could be returned to the gun works for retrofit ejectors. Notice old-style (PH) and new-style (VHE) thumb safety slides.*

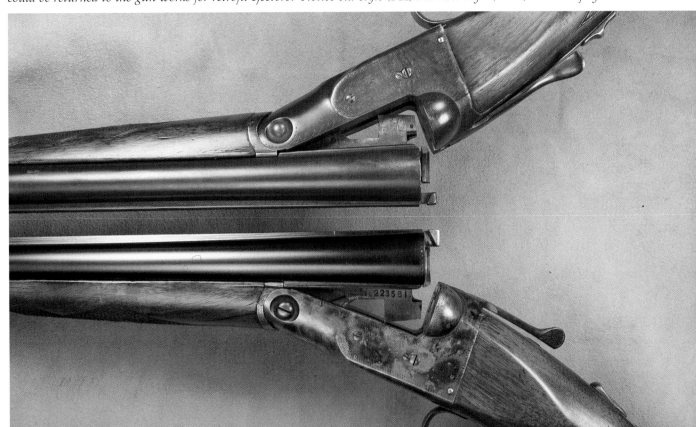

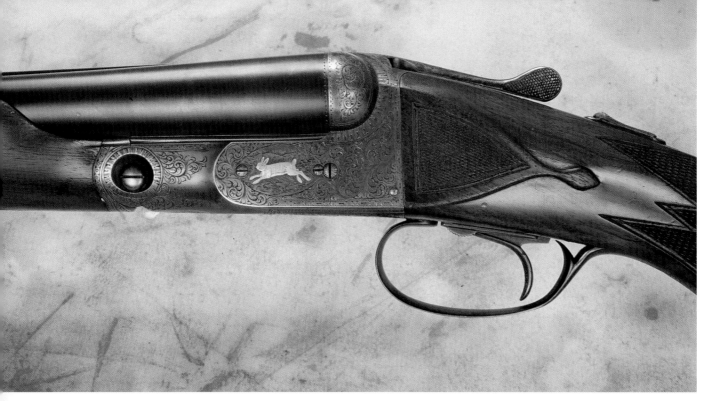

(top) Parker CHE with single trigger and a pedigree. This 12-gauge s/n 240,658 was a soft-fitted frame with rough barrels in Remington's parts department in 1960, when Larry Del Grego Sr. bought all of the Parker inventory. Del Grego Sr. finished the gun with help from Bob Runge in the 1970s. Notice the variation from usual C grade theme. The gold inlaid rabbit and checked side panel make this C-H-Exceptional! The engraved border at the back of the action identifies the gun as Quality C; however, the straight-line checking border on the grip is strictly D grade.

(bottom) Parker Brothers circa 1930 DHE trap gun s/n 232,754 has full and full choke 32-inch barrels, rare ventilated rib, No. 1½ frame, 14½-inch pull, Silver's pad, and weighs 8 pounds 4 ounces. Count me an infrequent trapshooter, but with a little attention to business I can break 23 and occasionally 24 clay flyers from 16 yards. What more could a Parker collector want? Well, maybe a nice Quality AH with straight grip and good dimensions, but that's another chapter.

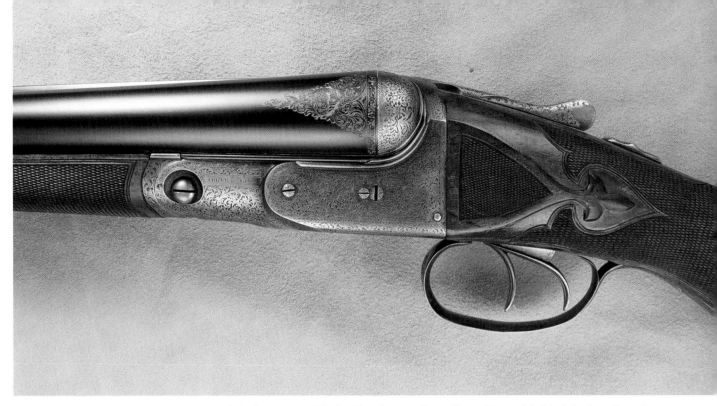

(top) *Parker Brothers circa 1896 AAH(E) s/n 84,176 with double triggers, three ribs or "fences" behind the breech, and suspicious barrel engraving. There is something about this restored Pigeon Gun that doesn't ring true—early AAHs had no barrel engraving. Also the fore-end checking does not conform to the turn-of-the-century style shown in Parker advertising.*

(bottom) *Parker Brothers circa 1928 GH 12-gauge s/n 224,176 with 30-inch barrels full and full, Miller single selective trigger, straight grip, and weighing a "perfect" all-round 7 pounds, 8 ounces.*

Parker Brothers circa 1893 trade card. If that isn't Captain A. W. du Bray at his usual 28-yard handicap, I'll eat his bowler hat. It makes sense that the gun works would promote their own people on the handout advertising. Parker Brothers produced a picture booklet with biographical sketches of various well-known Parker shooters in 1899, and I matched the pictures to the faces on the trade card as follows: The man poised and ready to pull one of the lines attached to a Parker patent plunge trap is S. A. Tucker, Parker's on-the-road salesman after the early 1870s; man standing with his arms crossed appears to be Parker shooting pro C. W. Budd, and the older gentleman sitting with his legs crossed is a dead ringer for Col. J. T. Anthony of Charlotte, N.C. The omission of AAH Pigeon grade from the price list on the back dates the trade card to 1893 or 1894, when the Grand American Handicap at Live-Birds was held at Dexter Park, New York.

hand-finished shotguns during 1932 and 1933, the handwriting was on the wall. King was banished to the office to reply to correspondence and enter orders for new guns and repairs. His 1933 letter shows him to be disgruntled and starting to sound like a grouchy old man. By then, King had been with the company almost forty-five years—perhaps he was ready for retirement.

The economy hit rock bottom in 1933, but unemployment and the Depression couldn't keep a young Larry Del Grego from eloping with Herman Shura's daughter. Fortunately for the newlyweds, Shura had some clout as a Parker barrelmaker, and Del Grego was soon working as his assistant. Another young man lucky to find a job in 1933 was Bob Runge (age sixteen), who apprenticed to his father in Parker Brothers' engraving shop. (As I write this, Runge at age seventy-nine is Parker Brothers' last known surviving employee.) Less than a year after Del Grego and Runge were hired, Remington Arms Co., Inc., bought the Parker name, inventory, and tooling from The Charles Parker Company, rented the Parker gun works from Charles Parker Estate, Inc., and set out to revive the Parker gun.

Remington: The DuPont Company bought a controlling interest in the Remington Arms Company during 1933. Remington had been hit hard by the Depression, and the profits of its ammunition business subsidized the losses of the firearms division. DuPont assigned Donald F. Carpenter and three other executives to manage Remington. Carpenter wrote "A Short History of the Remington Arms Company—1933-1940" as a retrospective in 1972, and the following was gleaned from that article: Remington was to be a stand-alone corporation with as little reliance on the credit of DuPont as possible. The ammunition line was prosperous, so attentions were first turned to resurrecting the firearms division at Ilion, New York. The factory buildings were Civil War-era construction, and the

machinery was old and outdated. DuPont moved Remington to a better set of buildings and tore down the old plant facility to make an employee parking lot. New equipment was purchased, and Remington began to develop its own special-purpose automatic machinery. Remington (like Parker Brothers) had a strong distribution network through hardware jobbers and wholesalers. It aggressively began to expand by acquiring all the assets of the Peters Cartridge Company of Ohio in May 1934, and Parker Brothers was next in line.

1934

Remington bought what was clearly distressed property in May or June 1934, and Remington-Parker production figures are not a success story. One needn't be clairvoyant to understand why Charles S. Parker was willing to sell the assets of Parker Brothers and rights to the Parker gun. Remington's motivation, however, has long been a puzzlement. Some light was shed on the issue by Carpenter's 1972 article. He was in the loop as director of Remington's manufacturing department in 1934, and wrote that ". . . it was felt the prestige of the gun line would be enhanced by the acquisition of the Parker gun. Parker was then in serious financial trouble, and a purchase was made. The immediate reaction of the trade was that whereas Parker had been the finest domestic gun, now that it was acquired by Remington, it would be 'cheapened.' Steps taken by Remington to offset the trade reaction were only partially effective." Carpenter explained how Remington had actually upgraded and refined the Parker gun, ". . . but still the trade had a hard time . . . to understand that Parker was actually improved and not deteriorating." My view is that the Parker gun was a well-kept secret after the acquisition by Remington.

An interesting aspect of the purchase and sale of the Parker gun was the low-key switchover of ownership. After twenty years

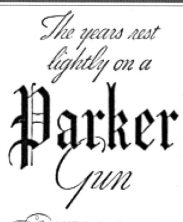

The years rest lightly on a

Parker Gun

SOME Parker Guns are their owners' proudest possessions after fifty years of service. Their mellow beauty, the smoothness of their action, the perfection of their fitting, the business-like ring with which they still snap shut, are fondly exhibited to an admiring younger generation.

Why don't you buy a Parker today? What pride you can take in its ownership! You may find a Parker at your dealer's that fits you exactly or we will custom build one to your own specifications.

Every part of every Parker is fitted and finished by hand. Possessing so fine a gun as a Parker brings out all the boyish joy that is left in a man of any age. Such a possession can not be measured by money.

Write now for information. Parker Gun Works, Remington Arms Co., Inc., Bridgeport, Conn.

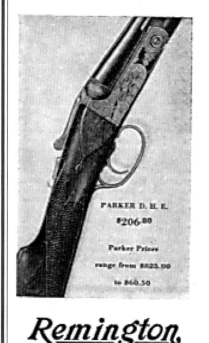

PARKER D. H. E.
$206.80

Parker Prices range from $825.00 to $60.50

Remington

DUPONT

of sifting through old magazines, searching for Parker-related information, I've yet to find any *contemporary* news account, announcement, or even an advertisement mentioning the transaction. When Remington moved the gun works to Ilion, the notice to customers was at best an insult to the owners of what had been one of America's most prestigious guns. Remington-Parker magazine ads from 1934 through the 1940s are all but nonexistent. Of more than 150 Parker magazine ads in my collection, the only post-sale advertisement is from the October 1935 issue of *Field and Stream*. Parker ads circa 1885 to 1934 are everywhere, but Remington-Parker ads are missing in action. The Meriden Historical Society and Meriden Public Library history room have rather complete files on The Charles Parker Company and Parker Brothers. I spent two days going through the information and couldn't find any contemporary mention of the sale of Parker to Remington.

World War II didn't put an end to the era of hand-finished guns or cause an irreversible shift from fine shotguns to wartime production. The Parker gun had been in serious trouble since 1930—the war simply put an end to Remington's failed attempt to trade on Parker's good name. Remington built approximately 4,000 guns at Meriden until the fall of 1937, and less than 1,800 guns after moving the Parker tooling to Ilion in 1938. Remington had leased the Parker Brothers gun works from Charles Parker Estate, Inc., and after the move, the Parker factory building, built back in 1853 along the railroad tracks at Cherry Street, was sold to the International Silver Company.

Walter King declined to move to Ilion with the gun works, and hired on as a quality-control inspector for The Charles Parker Company. He was given a gift of a special-order DHE, s/n 241,126, to honor the occasion and recognize his fifty years of service to the company. James Geary Jr., the barrelmaker who put his *JG* initials on so many Parker barrel flats, drifted off to become a

Of more than 150 different magazine ads in author's collection, this Remington-Parker ad from the October 1935 issue of Field and Stream *is the rarest of Parker advertising. Remington didn't advertise the Parker Gun. Information requests were directed to Parker care of Remington Arms Co., Inc., Bridgeport, Conn.; the Parker gun works was in Meriden, Conn.; Remington's home office was in Ilion, New York; and DuPont ran the overall operation from Delaware. No wonder the Parker Gun slipped in the crack.*

supernumerary policeman for the city of Meriden. Certain younger employees made the move to New York, including Larry Del Grego Sr., who, in turn, left Remington in 1955 to start his own business repairing and refurbishing the Parker gun. Larry Jr. ("Babe") joined his father's business in 1958, and his son Lawrence bought in for one dollar in 1993 after "Babe" had a stroke.

Parker Brothers, the shop within a shop, built approximately 237,000 fine shotguns from 1865 through May, 1934—about 3,500 per year on the average. The last year that could be called "full production" was 1930. The last Parker gun built by Remington is reputed to be a GH .410, s/n 242,387, assembled from parts in 1947. Using Parker Brothers' 1930 catalog to price the last full year's production at retail (assuming half the guns to be $55 Trojan grade and the average gun for the other half of production to be DHE grade at $160 retail, times 3,500 built and sold), the highest *retail* production in the history of Parker Brothers would have been roughly $375,000. However, Parker Brothers sold guns to jobbers at 75 percent of retail and to wholesalers at 85 percent of retail, and some guns sold directly from the gun works would have involved sales commissions to S. A. Tucker, A. W. du Bray, A. E. Perris, C. W. Budd, Fred Gilbert, and other factory representatives.

It's probable that Parker Brothers' gross revenues never exceeded $300,000 per year during its sixty-eight-year existence. Today,

three-hundred grand is hardly a speck of dust on the Dow Jones, minimum wage for a rookie ballplayer, corporate chicken feed. The flip side is that some of Parker's $500 guns are now inflation cost-adjusted to six figures, and should the elusive and reclusive s/n 200,000 Invincible ever change hands on the collector market, the price tag could be close to Parker's best-ever annual gross. After all, a two-gun, four-barrel BHE set was recently priced at $250,000. And remember, Charles Parker's company started gunmaking in 1864 with a $285,000 government contract for one year's production of rifle-muskets. In the final analysis, the famous Parker gun works was never more than a "nickel shop."

I can't think of any complex mechanical device in common use today that had its origins as early or remained as unchanged as the Parker gun. Fortunately, a good number of Parkers have survived, not just as collector's items but as fully functional windows to the past, so that we can know the pleasure of owning and shooting fine hand-finished examples of American design and manufacturing excellence. We can't claim they don't make guns like this anymore, because they do. During the 1980s, the Parker gun was machine-reproduced in Japan to jet-turbine tolerances using space-age technology. Considering that Parker Brothers' hammerless shotgun was visibly unchanged since 1889, and achieved final internal mechanical form by 1910, the Parker "imitation" stands as the sincerest form of flattery.

The Reincarnation of
A. W. du Bray

6

A friend of mine, when he gets in his cups, starts remembering things that may have happened only in one of his prior lives. Dave, it should be told, was always a ship's captain rather than an ordinary seaman. I became a little suspicious, however, when he helped me move my sailboat offshore from Key West to Charleston. He spent most of his time down below, developing a close personal relationship with a certain porcelain fixture. Apparently sea legs don't move from one life to another—at least not in Dave's case. But I gave him the benefit of the doubt. If Dave is a reincarnated ship's captain, then who would argue that I am not the reincarnation of A. W. du Bray? After all, I do own a number of Parker shotguns.

I think the way this reincarnation thing works is that random bits and facts strike a responsive but subconscious chord. The information is filed away, and with time, the source eludes conscious memory. As I began researching and writing this book, I would often see A. W. du Bray mentioned in the sporting and trade press of his day. He sometimes wrote long, stream-of-consciousness, literate but rambling letters about his exploits and signed them *Gaucho*. Captain du Bray was Parker Brothers' "good ol' boy on the road" from 1890 until about 1913, when he settled down as resident agent in San Francisco. His name appeared in Parker magazine ads from 1913 until 1926; then he retired after having sold Parker guns for thirty-six years.

As work on this book progressed, my notes became more scattered and less legible. I soon realized that du Bray had struck a responsive chord in me, and many of his experiences I wouldn't mind appropriating as my own. So I decided to play Dave's game and imagine myself as du Bray's alter ego. Although A. W du Bray was sometimes referred to as Captain in the same way auctioneers are sometimes called Colonel, he wasn't a captain of industry or the captain of a ship. He seemed to be an ordinary guy, just a peddler of Parker guns—as best I can reckon.

If you hold a certain fine English scrolled AA Pigeon Gun over the checkout scanner at the Wal-Mart in San Francisco, the ghost of Arthur du Bray may send you a message from the hereafter on your register receipt.

Psychic Advisor

A. W. du Bray,
Cincinnati, Ohio —

"Mr. du Bray has always been an ardent supporter of the Parker Gun, and has been acting as traveling salesman in its interest for the past nine years [since 1890]. He is a very fine live bird shot, and at inanimate targets has done excellent shooting with his trusted friend, The "Old Reliable." — From circa 1899 Parker Brothers booklet.

So there you have it. My interest in Parker guns may go back to prior-life employment by Parker Brothers as an on-the-road salesman. What follows are my best recollections of the sometimes interesting life of A. W. du Bray, who, like many of Charles Parker's employees, had a long career with the gun works. My memory spans the 1890s through 1920s, and has been refreshed from time to time by reference to the sporting press of the day.

I first made Captain du Bray's acquaintance in *Forest and Stream* for March 19, 1898, where he reported that

> . . . I usually make a trip through part of my territory, starting early in January and returning home in beginning of March. This jaunt carries me through most of the Southern States and Texas, where I go to see my friends and incidentally to say a few loving words anent the Parker gun. Of course there is very little on these lines to be said, so much having already been said, sung and whistled by 500,000 people more or less on that subject regarding that particular gun. Still none being so deaf as those who won't hear, it is just as well to keep ding-donging away, and sometimes with due diligence and perseverance one may

convert a doubting Thomas; hence my ramble, my peregrinations commencing this time very near home.

Louisville was "very near home," and in other correspondence du Bray mentioned close ties to Dayton, Kentucky. But back in 1898, he was operating out of Cincinnati, Ohio, and from there it was no small effort to call on Parker gun dealers and customers throughout the South and Texas. Travel was primitive, and du Bray earned no frequent-flyer miles. The first Model T did not come off Henry Ford's assembly line until ten years later. Railroads were the mode for long-distance travel, and du Bray relied heavily on Hertz rent-a-horse at various destinations where he went "ding-donging." Upon arriving at Louisville, he

> . . . came face to face with the unpleasant fact that the old Kentucky Gun Club had vacated its pleasant, historic and most accessible grounds, and that therefore the hospitality so freely extended to one and all by that splendid body of men would have to be dispensed in the future from other grounds. It is with feelings of regret that this announcement is made because

we all know how welcome any and all of us have been at the familiar old place, and while a club with so much wealth and unbounded enthusiasm can always find another location, yet the fact remains that in our memory will always dwell recollections of the championship events fought to a finish there, and the many enjoyable evenings spent seated about the grounds chatting on dogs and guns with a set of men who loved sport for its own sake and who moreover are cosmopolitan enough to understand that we all can't be rich nor yet college bred men, yet we should at least be gentlemen, failing in which we ought to have the common decency to be as gentlemanly as we can, and let it go at that.

In Charleston, South Carolina, du Bray waxed enthusiastic about some of Parker's best customers:

. . . Of course I saw the only Barney Worthen who seems getting bigger and broader every year. There may be a few men in America who shoot targets as well as our Barney, but they are decidedly scarce, while a more modest, quiet, unassuming shooter it would be quite impossible to find. May his shadow never grow less. Messrs. Peterman and Swann were also "in evidence," the former shooting a terrific clip, almost abreast of Barney, and the latter so full of vim and vigorous talk that an hour in his company is equal to a good rubdown or electric shock from a powerful battery. To properly appreciate and fully understand Mr. Swann you should be with him afloat; then and there he looms up like a pillar of fire at night, rendering the soft balmy atmosphere of his own sweet tropical clime aglow by his impressive, striking, and phosphorescent remarks.

Parker Brothers ad from February 19, 1898, issue of Forest and Stream, *showing AAH Pigeon Gun with Whitworth fluid steel barrels.*

Arthur sometimes laid it on a little thick, but I suspect the keepers of Parker Brothers' records will find guns sold and delivered to Messrs. Worthen, Peterman, and Swann during 1898. Further, du Bray wasn't just stroking good old Barney Worthen—he was a genuine good shot. The following blurb appeared a few years later (December 1903) in *Recreation* magazine:

> W. R. Crosby, one of the champion shots of the world, was treated to a surprise recently in Atlanta, Ga. Despite a heavy wind, amounting almost to a gale, Mr. Crosby broke 94 out of 100 clay birds, a remarkable record under such adverse circumstances, yet he was beaten by one bird, as Mr. Worthen smashed 95 of the clay flyers. The battle between these two men was a right royal one, and Mr. Worthen and the Parker gun achieved a triumph of no mean merit. Mr. Worthen used, as he always uses, the Old Reliable Parker gun.

Next stop: Savannah, Georgia, where things were quiet . . .

> . . . indeed since the most untimely end of the man whom all were proud to call their friend—of the man known and loved by all alike—of the incomparable late lamented George Cape. No man could lounge about a club room, or saunter more leisurely along a boulevard than George Cape; but be not deceived, he could wade in mud knee deep for hours and never turn a hair, or he could vault a fence like a college prize winner, carrying an eight-pound gun as though it was a feather, and shooting in that superbly easy, swinging manner which is just as natural to some men as it is for a duck to swim or a Spanish woman to walk. Be the rise where it may, or the angle ever so acute, he never lost his aplomb. Every shot looked easy when he fired it; and he never got twisted either in trying a backward shot at a darting snipe flushing from the rear, and we all know how hard that is when both legs are stuck fast in the mud, or when cutting down a pair of partridges going in opposite directions through

From turn-of-the-century stereo viewing card.

tangled vines and dense underbrush. He handled a gun in precisely the same manner as a finished billiard player does his cue, and I can still hear his merry gleeful laugh when he missed a shot, or more often still when he made a grandstand double; who goes next to join George and the millions and millions of billions though there be who have gone before? Mark me, predestined wanderer, be thou who thou wilt, seek these radiant souls and tell them we are impoverished by their loss, nor can we find others to take their places. Of mere shooters the land is full to overflowing, but the gap between a shooter and a sportsman is wider than the chasm separating a Landseer or even a Michel Angelo [*sic*] from a white-washer smearing a fence. So I say, and say it advisedly; *Brave soul, we miss thee, for of such clay as was thine is the true sportsman made!*

I suspect the Parker factory records will disclose that the late great George Cape had recently purchased a $400 AAH Pigeon Gun and was survived by a number of wealthy descendants poised and ready to follow suit. Captain du Bray had a way with words that went beyond lyrical, and he could sure sell

Parker guns—ten DHE 20s in one crack to the Widgeon Duck Club of California in 1913, according to Baer—and I suspect the good captain was also pretty handy with turnscrews and files. The best way to ensure his welcome as he traveled would have been the skillful "laying of hands" on guns of the rich and faithful. And on the issue of "Michel Angelo" versus Michelangelo, I'll give du Bray the benefit of the doubt. Gertrude Stein, the American expatriate writer and art patron living in France in the early 1900s, used the same "Michel Angelo" in her book *The Autobiography of Alice B. Toklas*. As a writer, Captain du Bray, was in good company.

Montgomery, Alabama:

> . . . I expected great things; tremendous bags of doves loomed up before me, and I went on from place to place attentive to my work, yet with mind far away in the dove field near Montgomery. I at last arrived, so had my shells (I won't say how many) and so had my incomparable Whitworth Steel gun. Furthermore, my afflicted hands and wrists were behaving pretty well, so all seemed to promise a great day at doves. Upon entering Mr. Westcott's store Tom Westcott came up with a sad long looking face and to my joyful pent-up exclamation of *semper paratus!* he simply threw up his hands and told me in his soft, sourful way that the doves had all left the baited field; that the shooting was knocked on the head. He further told me that our very good friend Mr. Julie had ridden a full one hundred miles on an engine to be sure that all was in readiness for the next day; to engage teams to take us from the little railroad station at 4 A.M. the next morning; to see to our luncheon, etc., etc., and that as a precautionary measure and to make assurance doubly sure he had driven out to the field itself "just to see how many thousands were there," he said. Well, he did not see any. The man who had baited and guarded the field told him that no doves had been seen there for several days so that settled it, and me and my most creamy, juicy, well

loaded factory shells and my gleaming, blue-barreled, double-barreled gun, and my erstwhile stiff though willing wrists and hands—and all was well, barring the doves, and they too were well—well out of it; and so it goes. So we must wait until some other time and trust to luck to have a better report to make of the great dove shoot that was to have been near Montgomery.

In other words, Captain du Bray didn't go dove hunting with Parker dealer Tom Westcott, although he did get to practice his Latin. Then it was on to New Orleans, where he could practice the French language mastered while a college student abroad. Du Bray was high on New Orleans and wrote:

> . . . I saw lots of things; one could always, if so inclined, see a good deal in New Orleans. Really, outside of New York, why isn't New Orleans No. 2? Or is it No. 1?"

Our hero's customer in New Orleans was John W. Phillips,

> . . . [a] . . . bred-in-the-bones sportsman . . . [who] . . . has the *feu sarcre'* to such an extent that were he deprived of shooting during the winter I think he would very soon be under the daisies. Indeed if he could not leave New Orleans methinks he would patrol those wide and deep ditches on either side of Canal Street hoping to flush a snipe or scorch on wheel in early morning along the river bank in the hope of tumbling down a duck on its *passé.*
> So we went to Abbeville, a splendid place generally, and one in which we have done well in other years. But it had rained a good deal and it continued to pour incessantly. The whole country was very soon under water, the snipe were banished, our fond hopes vanished, and we vamoosed the ranch, after being nearly swamped in our wagon several times or oftener. So the doves and the snipe have leagued against me, and nothing was left but to pull stakes and say adieu to dear old John. . . .

Captain du Bray moved on to visit

. . . a dear, kind and brainy friend, who sometime ago moved from Shreveport, La., to Lake Charles in the same state, and to him I promised time and time again that I would check my baggage and camp with him a day or two, knowing full well that for me the latch-string of his cheerful, hospitable and genuine Southern home is always hanging on the outside of the door. So I left my very comfortable seat on the Southern Pacific sleeper and got out at Lake Charles. I had no sooner reached the door than I saw my shooting companion, Mr. J. C. Elstner, elbowing his way through the throng. . . .

. . . driving along in his carriage we soon reached the hotel and there were met by Monsieur Pierre Theaux, of the Howard Hotel, who assigned me to about the only vacant room he had. We had supper, Jo and I, made still more palatable by a bottle of good white wine thoughtfully sent in by Mr. Theaux. Of course we talked dog and gun (what else could two such chaps converse on intelligently), and made our plans for an early start the next morning in quest of snipe—if any—partridges for sure.

Somehow we did not get a very early start, indeed we got a very late one; nevertheless we managed by dint of good shooting and splendid work by the dogs to bag forty-seven snipe and quail and return home long before 6:00 p.m. with the proverbial sportsman's appetite. On the way home we overtook a couple of men who had been out that day and killed some prairie chickens—I don't remember how many, eight or ten I think. Well, the sight of those big fine birds enthused me and carried me back many a day and over many a mile to the vast plains and prairies of the Northwest, where I have killed so many hundreds and hundreds of them. So I determined to give them a trial on the next day.

Piloted by a professional hunter, whose name is Love—a very good man by the way, who knows all about that country— we started at 5:00 A.M. and drove fifteen miles out to the prairie only to find the grass all burned off, so of course that squelched

all chances of game in that direction. However, I did get three having shot at four during the day, one unfortunate going off with a broken leg and flying so far that, although over a level, treeless country, neither of us could mark him down. On this occasion I used my Whitworth Steel Parker Pigeon Gun, full choke, and had it factory loaded with U.M.C. trap shells with 3¾ drs. DuPont and 1¼ Tatham chilled 7s, 3 in. cases.

I can safely assert that I did not get a shot at any of the chickens inside 40 yds., and as the gun is pretty light on right trigger— much too light for a field gun—I invariably pulled it off before I was on my bird, so had to do the business with the left barrel. It was blowing a very stiff breeze, and yet with this small shot in such a high wind and at such a distance, it was remarkable how that gun and those loads killed stone dead these big birds, two of which were over 70 yds. off. So I came back with my scant supply after a 30 to 35 mile drive, feeling all the better for the ozone.

Jo Elstner soon looked me up and we agreed to make one more day of it; this time starting early sure enough and going for quail principally, but snipe should we find any. So we put out at about 5:00 A.M., killed a few quail and were doing nicely when we saw an old rice fence which was a very likely place for snipe. We tried it, and before we got over the fence up went several wisps, wild as hawks, but nevertheless snipe. So we hammered away. Jo soon ran out of small shotloads, and as I was using a 16-gauge gun I could not help him, but he stuck to it manfully and made some surprising long kills with number 5 shot.

On this day Mr. Roberts, cashier at the Calcasieu Bank, accompanied us and used Jo's little 16 Parker, with which in his maiden effort he bagged seven snipe. When the bag was counted we found we had 107 quail and snipe, so as that was aplenty we drove home and all voted it a great day for us. For my part what pleased me most was that my foot, which has been very painful for a long time, held up well on that day and did not go back on the old man once [the "old man" was forty-nine].

I also had a splendid opportunity of testing my heavy (7½ lb.) full-choke 16-bore Parker gun, and a great shooter it certainly is. When we saw the snipe flushing in wisps and singly a way off we knew that meant plenty of shooting and not too many snipe, so we at once dispatched the wagon back to town for more ammunition.

As I had no more 16-gauge shells I had my hammer Parker Pigeon Gun sent out and some great loads, i.e., smokeless, factory-loaded shells, 3 in. long with 3½ drs. Du Pont and 1¼ Tatham no. 8½ chilled shot. That combination, take it all, guns and shells as so loaded, is hard, very hard, to beat for a snipe especially. It was delightful for me to know that though so abominable a shot as I certainly am at targets, yet I have a good account of myself on this extremely difficult, extra long-range shooting, which goes clearly to prove that my early training in the meadows in the north of France while at college there had not been forgotten; nor had the precepts of my beloved grandfather, than whom a better more thorough sportsman never lived.

Captain du Bray was a true renaissance man. He was born in England in 1849 and immigrated to the United States in 1870. He must have come from a family of some wealth as he was college educated, and on the continent at that. A. W. du Bray is somewhat of an enigma, a family man with a wife and three children (and a live-in servant), according to Ohio census records for 1900 and 1910, but he never owned his own home. The *Cincinnati City Directory* shows him as a traveling salesman in 1898, a saloon keeper in 1899, and with the occupation "Guns" in 1900. The $400 Parker AA Pigeon Gun du Bray used to hunt snipe in the swamps in 1898 cost more than the average salesman or saloon keeper earned all year.

Next stop was San Antonio, Texas, where Captain du Bray

> . . . met a lot of old friends, but was sorely
> disappointed when my partner down there

told me quail were scarce, and not in sufficient quantities to warrant going after them. But I could not leave the old town without having some kind of a shoot, so Mr. Geo. Chabot took upon himself the gathering of some pigeons. This he so successfully did that on the next day at Fort Sam Houston we had a splendid time shooting at as good pigeons as one could find anywhere. I was struck and amazed at the magnificent shooting of Lieut. P. Whitworth, U.S.A., who did as fine shooting and made as clean kills as I ever saw in my life. He shot a Parker trap gun, with which I don't remember how many deer, ducks, geese, quail, etc., etc. he has killed this season, using the full-choked and also the cylinder-bored sets of barrels.

Capt. Foster joined us late in the day and made some very pretty kills. Mr. Chabot, using a very small Parker 24-gauge gun, shot awfully well. But any man who has left the Army in good standing always feels homesick when he reaches an army post; there is a fascination about it that one can never outlive, and every bugle call left a mournful impression on my sensitive ears; every familiar army phrase kept ringing through my head, and I felt sad, for recollection instinctively carried me to that glorious old 2nd horse—Custer's regiment—with which I put in such happy memorable days!

At Dallas, Tex., I stayed but a very little while, still I was there long enough to shake hands with many of my friends, and to have a most pleasant shoot at 25 pigeons with Mr. Allen, of Allen and Glum, and he beat me at that. Just to show there is no ill feeling, I will get at him again and give him another chance.

That last paragraph reveals du Bray's forte—he didn't outshoot his customers. I don't believe he ever won a serious pigeon shoot. Parker Brothers published a brief biographical sketch in 1899 stating that "Mr. du Bray has always been an ardent supporter of the Parker Gun, and has been acting as a traveling salesman in its interests for the past nine years. He is a very fine live bird shot, and at inanimate targets has done excellent shooting with his trusted friend, 'The Old Reliable'." Other "amateur" Parker shooters in the same booklet had rather substantial and specific shooting credentials. Some trade professionals like Fred Gilbert and Harvey McMurchy actually made a living winning tournament prizes, while du Bray made a living losing tournaments and acting as a traveling salesman in the interests of the "Old Reliable" Parker gun.

This isn't to say that Captain du Bray, if given the chance, wouldn't have a go at one-upping the competition. According to a well-traveled story, du Bray goaded the shooting pro for Parker's arch-rival Hunter Arms (L. C. Smith) into a match of marksmanship on a dove hunt. Harvey McMurchy was one of the best live-bird shooters at the time. But trapshooting was one thing and dove shooting quite another, and du Bray laid a trap of his own. While du Bray may have been mediocre on trapped pigeons, he was an expert dove hunter, and apparently McMurchy didn't understand the difference. The bets and side bets were placed, and our good Captain ever so graciously steered his adversary to the "best" location. According to H. L. Betten in his 1940 book *Upland Game Shooting*:

> . . . [du Bray] put Mac on a stand where the shots were long range and where the birds came swinging through a low gap in the hills like dun-gray projectiles. There were cross currents also that made them cut all sorts of crazy capers—some of them would make a jacksnipe dizzy. The crack shot from Syracuse made an average of one bird to every six shells. With all his skill and reputation, Mac fell a victim to duplicity.

After having a little fun at McMurchy's expense, du Bray headed back east and stopped at Little Rock, where he met with

Harvey McMurchy was the shooting pro for L. C. Smith (Hunter Arms) at the turn of the century.

. . . Mr. Joe Irwin, and there we had a regular set-to talk—dogs, ducks, snipe, woodcock, etc., etc., and guns; and I verily believe Joe Irwin is one of the very best hunters I have ever met and that is saying a good deal, for my acquaintance in that field is legion.

At Memphis I struck the gang all eager and willing to shoot, and to know what a nice set of fellows shoot pigeons at Memphis one must go there and see for himself. Everyone was so bent on shooting that we went right at it hammer and tongs, and then some. Memphis among other very good things is the home of Mr. A. H. Frank, the man who captured the Memphis handicap first alone, and who since using his new Parker has scored 107 of 111 pigeons shot at all told, standing at 29 yds., and many at 30-34 yds. Mr. Frank Posten was unable to take part in the shoot on Feb. 22, owing to the severe illness of his aged mother. When

Posten and Frank cross their Parkers fur will fly, even if a few feathers fly out too. But that will be an interesting match to behold. Judge Walker, though, won't be far behind, if at all; and then Mr. Edrington will keep things very warm, while Dr. Saunders, who shoots quite as well as ever, will keep them all guessing. Leastwise don't forget Dr. D. Weaver, he clings to you so hard and works so awfully in dead earnest too—bad medicine that! Brother Allen will soon be at it again, so there's no telling what those Memphis men will do. And if any more of them improve like Irby Bennett and Abe Frank, anyone going down there to get their money will have to be Jim Dandy, or lose, and the chances are he'll lose.

So I drifted back to my old gun club at Louisville, KY., and there for the first time shot at some pigeons that seemed as fast, or nearly so as they do at Westminster Kennel Club; and that in my humble opinion is the end of the rope. It appears the Kentucky Gun Club has made permanent arrangements to hold its tournaments on a bicycle track in enclosed ground and when I know more about it I will forthwith enlighten my readers on this most interesting subject.

Tomorrow I leave for Boston where the old gun and I will stand together on the same platform, when I hope we may make a favorable impression. My part of the performance consists merely in telling people what they already know—i. e., that there are guns and guns, but that the Old Reliable just goes on forever.

Gaucho

Forest and Stream reported in the March 12, 1898, issue that

Capt. A. W. du Bray arrived in New York this week, taking a long flight from the far Southwest to be present at the Boston Exposition in the interest of his house, Parker Bros., and afterward he will be in attendance at the Grand American Handicap. He reports excellent upland shooting in Texas and Louisiana.

Du Bray cultivated the press. He was the consummate salesman, and, as one hand washes the other, it must have been extremely helpful to the editors of *Forest and Stream* and other weekly pulp sporting newspapers to receive du Bray's regular dispatches as they made good reading and filled the gaps between paid advertising. The fact that he was able to slip in "a few loving words anent the Parker gun" from time to time was simply the quid pro quo.

Captain du Bray shot live birds, but not to win. Before he left on his western trip, he sharpened his eye with some live-bird shooting at Indianapolis, Indiana, on December 13 through 15, 1897. The live-bird shoot was unique in that preliminary "races" used sparrows, rather than pigeons. There were special rules for shooting sparrows according to D. H. Eaton in his 1920 book, *Trap Shooting—The Patriotic Sport*:

English sparrows were often trapped on the grounds of the Limited Gun Club, of Indianapolis, Ind., and for quite a period of time around 1900, these little birds were used in place of pigeons by a number of gun clubs in the Midwest. The live bird rules of the American Shooting Association governed these contests, except that the rise was made 25 yards and the boundary 35 yards. No birds were retrieved, a bird once down within bounds being scored dead. Instead of 5 traps, 15 were used, a squad of 5 contestants going to the score at one time. This made it possible to accommodate a large number of shooters with all the shooting they desired, and the events progressed almost as rapidly as at inanimate targets. When a sparrow is liberated it generally takes flight at once; to avoid, therefore, any mechanical shooting, each contestant faced three traps, any one of which might be sprung on his command to *pull*. The traps closed automatically after being sprung, and as there were fifteen of them, it was practically impossible for a contestant, passing from one score to the next after each shot, to keep track of which traps had been emptied.

The first program at the Limited Gun Club was four races at sparrows, each of twenty birds, $6 entrance fee. Rolla O. Heikes killed seventy-six of eighty to win $10.20; Fred Gilbert, McMurchy, and Bartlett, each with seventy-five, divided second, third,

Charles W. Budd beat "Big Jim" Stice in 1889, for the American Field Cup, emblematic of the Championship of America, and was Parker's shooting pro through the 1890s.

and fourth monies, which paid them $6.80 each. Captain du Bray killed sixty-four of eighty, beating C. W. Budd's sixty-three. Budd was Parker Brothers' shooting professional, and du Bray was there to do a little itinerant gunsmithing, take orders for new guns, and hand out Parker trade cards.

The second day was a pigeon shoot. The program called for two events: the first in-

volved a $7 entrance fee for seven birds; the second a $10 entrance for ten birds. Twenty-three guns entered, and all shot from thirty yards. This was not a handicap event. Eight guns killed seven birds in the first race to split the money; du Bray killed six. Five guns killed ten birds in the second race to split the money, and du Bray killed nine. Then there was a miss-and-out for $5 with sixteen entries; three guns split the money with eight birds each, while du Bray was an early-out with four.

The third day was the Grand Central Handicap, twenty-five pigeons, entrance fee $25, birds extra—eight high guns split the purse. The birds were so good that everyone stayed outdoors to see what the next one would be like. As will happen in a twenty-five-bird race, some got the best of the drawing, and in this case Mr. Fanning, the winner, was a lucky man. Contestants kept shooting until they missed three birds and then dropped out. This was a handicap event, with Fred Gilbert the scratch shooter at thirty-two yards; McMurchy, Budd, and Fanning shot at thirty-one; and du Bray shot from twenty-nine yards.

Forest and Stream reported the results of the Grand Central Handicap and added that

> The trade was represented by R. O. Heikes and B. A. Bartlett of the Winchester Arms Co. . . . E. D. Fulford, with a Remington gun . . . Fred Gilbert . . . [and] . . . Harvey McMurchy, who was pleased to see four Smith guns placed in the main event . . . C. W. Budd, with Parker Gun and our oldest and best friend A. W. du Bray, of Parker Brothers.

Of all the high-powered professionals representing the trade, only Captain du Bray was referred to warmly as ". . . our oldest and best friend," perhaps as payback for having filed the report of the event.

I lost track of Captain du Bray after his "peregrinations" to the southern states, Texas, Indiana, and Boston in 1898. I found him

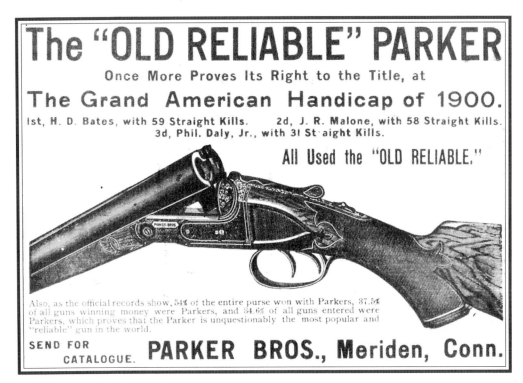

Parker Brothers ad from May 26, 1900 issue of Forest and Stream, *showing dominance of Parker guns at recent Grand American Handicap. More than a third of the competitors shot the "Old Reliable."*

again in Parker Brothers' order book after the Grand American Handicap at live birds in 1900. Although du Bray usually shot at live-bird tournaments he attended on behalf of Parker Brothers, his real job was to repair and sell Parker guns. The eighth Grand American Handicap (GAH) at Live Birds, with 211 starters, was held at Interstate Park, Queens, New York, April 4, 1900. The first, second, and third winners used the Parker gun. A contemporary ad says

> . . . as the official records show, 54 percent of the entire purse was won with Parkers, 37.5 percent of all guns winning money were Parkers, and 34.6 percent of all guns entered were Parkers, which proves that the Parker is unquestionably the most popular and "reliable" gun in the world.

Parker Brothers was riding the crest of unbridled popularity, and the factory order book for April 9, 1900, shows that Captain du Bray had sold quite a number of live-bird guns at the GAH. Fred Gilbert joined the Parker fold with s/n 95,821, a 12-gauge with 30-inch Titanic full-choked barrels, stocked 14¼-inch pull with only 1⅜-inch drop at the heel. The DH had no safety and weighed 7 pounds, 15 ounces (with pad), and was marked in the order book "consigned" (no doubt a reference to the fact that Gilbert didn't pay the $100 price but rather was given the use of the gun coincidentally with becoming Parker Brothers' shooting pro).

Another luminary showing up on the April 9, 1900, order-book page, published in the Spring 1996 *Double Gun Journal*, was Frank S. Parmelee, who ordered a 12-gauge with 30-inch Titanic barrels choked R.H. modified and L. H. close, s/n 95,820, with no safety and "no ext rib." The gun had 1¼-inch drop and 14½-inch pull, and was to weigh 7½ to 7¾ pounds with pistol grip and Hawkins pad.

Another "no safety" live-bird gun sold by du Bray at the GAH was shipped to Frank E. Butler, care of the Buffalo Bill Show, and marked "allowance $50." The gun was a 12-gauge with 30-inch Titanic barrels choked R.H. cylinder and L.H. full choke. The trigger pull was specified as R.H. 3½ and L.H. 4 pounds. Butler was married to Annie

Parker Brothers ad from October 19, 1901 issue of Forest and Stream. *Parker Guns continued to dominate by winning the Ninth Grand American Handicap at Live Birds and the Second Grand American Handicap at Targets. Parker's double-barreled trap gun was at its peak of trapshooting popularity in 1901, held its own in 1902, and began a downward trend starting in about 1903, as clay bird "trapshooting" with relatively inexpensive repeaters gained momentum.*

Oakley; however, the gun, s/n 95,819, was to weigh 7° pounds with 14⅛-inch pull, which seems outside the usual specifications for her guns. Parker Brothers wasn't making any money by consigning a DH to Gilbert and selling another for half price to Butler, but Pamelee did pay the $100 full price. Suffice it to say that Parker Brothers was flying high at the turn of the century and could afford to pass around some free guns for the free advertising. It was about 1900 when du Bray gave up his on-again, off-again employment as a saloon keeper to devote full time to selling the Parker gun.

I again lost track of A. W. du Bray until he and 455 other contestants signed up for the last Grand American Handicap at Live Birds at Blue Ridge Park in Kansas City, Missouri, March 31, 1902. He must have been pleased when he checked the entries and found that 162 of 456 starters (35.5 percent) were shooting Parker guns—no small number of which likely changed hands thanks to his own efforts. Two years prior, seventy-eight of 224 GAH entrants (34.6 percent) had shot the "Old Reliable" Parker gun. This, of course, was a sign of the times. Parker Brothers hunkered down with its production quota of roughly

4,000 hand-finished guns per year, while the smoothbore shooting sports took off like wildfire in the direction of everyman's machine-built repeater in the hands of amateurs. Meanwhile, back in Missouri:

The 1902 event began with the Kansas City Sweepstakes, a twelve-bird race, all shooters standing at thirty yards. Thirty-six men killed all twelve birds to claim $71.50 as their share of the pot. Captain du Bray was in his usual form, killing eleven birds from twenty-eight yards, in a 72-way tie for non-paying runner-up. The next day, 419 guns took part in another preliminary twelve-bird race, with eighty-one contestants making straight scores to collect $51.00 each, as against their $10.00 entrance fee. Captain du Bray didn't shoot up to his usual "also-ran" status and withdrew after missing three of eight birds. Then it was on to the Grand American Handicap, with 456 guns participating. W. R. Crosby, O'Fallon, Illinois; Fred Gilbert, Spirit Lake, Iowa; and J. A. R. Elliott of Kansas City were scratch shooters at thirty-two yards. Ansley Fox of Philadelphia stood at thirty-one yards; A. W. du Bray at twenty-eight yards (just as he is shown on Parker Brothers' circa 1893 trade card); and

Parker Brothers ad from March 1903 issue of Recreation *magazine. Fred Gilbert replaced C. W. Budd as shooting pro after the 1900 Grand American Handicap, and Gilbert had a long, successful career as Parker's "top gun."*

Mrs. Frank E. Butler (Annie Oakley) was at twenty-seven yards handicap.

The Grand American Handicap was twenty-five birds for a $25 entrance fee, birds extra, with sixty-three high guns splitting the $10,090 pot. Top gun paid $688.70, with a sliding scale through sixty-third place, which paid $138.70. The shooting progressed on 2, 3, and 4 April, with thirty-one men killing twenty-five birds straight. Fred Gilbert killed all his birds, and J. A. R. Elliott downed twenty-four; Annie Oakley and A. H. Fox had twenty-two; and A. W. du Bray killed five of eight and withdrew. Only sixteen contestants out of 456 missed more birds than our hero du Bray. When the feathers had settled or blown away, fourteen of thirty-one guns killing twenty-five pigeons straight carried the Parker Brothers name; L. C. Smith had nine; Winchester four; and Remington, Lefever, Cashmore, and Greener one each. Parker Brothers' pro Fred Gilbert used a seven-pound twelve-ounce, (plus pad) Parker with Winchester Leader shells loaded with 1¼ ounces of No. 7½ shot to win $438.70 for twelfth place. Gilbert's gun had to be the DH consigned to him in April 1900, and

the difference from the order-book weight was the three-ounce pad. Ansley Fox and Annie Oakley placed out of the money; Captain du Bray did well—"well out of it; and so it goes."

The 1902 Grand American Handicap was the best and last live-bird tournament sanctioned by the Interstate Association. The times were a-changin'. A few years before (March 19, 1898), *Forest and Stream* reported:

The following act has been read once in the New York State Assembly: ". . . [any person] . . . not being a member of a regularly incorporated shooting association, who enters into or trespasses upon the grounds of such association or comes within 200 yds. thereof for the purpose of shooting at pigeons or other birds, which may escape from the grounds of such association or who shall willfully injure any of the grounds, structures, buildings or other property of such association, shall be deemed guilty of a misdemeanor."

Three years later, the Interstate Association had to leave New York because the law had gone the other way—the gun clubs were no longer protected, but the pigeons were. Public sentiment was inflamed by the yellow press, and various states legislated against live-bird shooting. The Interstate Association left its home grounds at Interstate Park in Queens, New York, for Kansas City to avoid the acute angle. Meanwhile, the game had changed—clay-pigeon shooting became the mode and was more popular than anyone could have suspected when the nation's top live-bird shooters packed up their pigeon guns and headed home from Kansas City in April 1902. The golden age of shotgunning was rapidly coming to a close in the East and Midwest, while California seemed to be the

Mr. Perris's papers were letters back and forth representing informal contracts. The last letter was dated July 17, 1911, and referred to a three-year extension of the contract, for which Perris received a 28-gauge BHE, s/n 156,949, with Damascus barrels. Perris stayed on as the Parker factory representative for California until at least the summer of 1914. By then, A. W. du Bray was ranging far beyond his southern states and Texas territory to inspire a new generation of sportsmen to take up Parker Brothers' small-bore shotguns in the name

The "OLD RELIABLE"

"The Only Absolutely Reliable"

HAS NONE ITS EQUAL

BEST THAT CAN BE MADE

Fred Coleman's score of 47 straight, at live birds in England, as well as 24 out of 25 at 31 yards, shows how the Parker Gun shoots. See another column in this paper showing his marvelous records.

New York Salesrooms
32 WARREN ST.

PARKER BROS., 32 CHERRY ST., MERIDEN, CONN.

Parker Brothers ad from April 1906 issue of National Sportsman, *showing an early AAH Pigeon Gun without ejectors and the barrels have no engraving.*

land of golden opportunity, especially for Parker Brothers.

A. E. Perris was a manager with the Atchison, Topeka and Santa Fe Railway Company in and around San Bernardino, California, and had some influence with shotgunners in his part of the country. Perris cut a deal with Parker Brothers in 1902 to be a part-time representative on the West Coast. He would tout the Parker gun, take orders, or simply steer potential customers to the gun works, and was paid one BHE every thirty months or so. For details, the reader is referred to "Mr. Perris's Parker Papers" by Wayne Cowett in the *Double Gun Journal* 3-3.

of "conservation" and as the sportsmanlike thing to do.

Much had changed in the few years between Captain du Bray's grand tour through the Southwest in 1898 and the last Grand American Handicap at Live Birds in 1902. Between 1900 and 1902, Parker's share of the market represented by top guns at the GAH had increased from 34.6 to 35.5 percent, and the number of contestants had more than doubled, but the trend was toward less expensive guns and less expensive clay-pigeon shooting. Parker introduced the fifty-dollar VH grade with fluid-steel barrels in 1898, and had offered grades BH, CH, and DH with

Titanic fluid-steel barrels perhaps as early as 1897. A. W. du Bray's Quality AA Pigeon Gun with Whitworth fluid-steel barrels had first become available in 1894. By 1900 the country's top live-bird shooters adopted Parker's Titanic-barrel hundred-dollar gun to ply their trade. Two years later, the DH and higher-grade Parker guns had ejectors, and inanimate-target (clay-pigeon) shooting had taken off like wildfire, more than filling the void created by the rapidly declining popularity of shooting rapidly declining populations of wild pigeons.

wasn't likely to outshoot his customers with a small bore. The report of the Dayton, Kentucky, Live-Bird Shoot in *Forest and Stream* for January 9, 1909, says it all:

> Captain A. W. du Bray returned from a long trip to the northwest a few days ago, where he had been having great sport duck shooting with his favorite 20-gauge gun, and was using the same weapon here. He starts for New York in a day or two, and will make an extended trip through the south before getting back home again.

Parker Brothers ad from July 19, 1913 issue of American Field, *showing an A-1 Special "live-bird gun" with ejectors, but without safety. This ad is one of the first to mention A. W. du Bray as resident agent in San Francisco.*

As trapshooting became a more democratic pastime (D. H. Eaton called it "The Patriotic Sport"), the larger percentage of new gunners bought modern, less expensive repeating shotguns rather than going with the old iron—Parkers, Foxes, Smiths, etc. As the demand for double-barrel trap guns declined, Captain du Bray put down his AA Pigeon Gun and did the politic thing—he started touting and selling 20-gauge Parkers to West Coast duck hunters. His best customers were members of exclusive hunting clubs such as the Widgeon Duck Club of central California, where du Bray sold ten DHE 20s at one time.

Captain du Bray was never a top live-bird shooter with his 12-gauge Pigeon Gun, so he

The shoot took place at the Northern Kentucky Gun Club at Dayton, and du Bray, being from Cincinnati, was a qualified shooter. The first event, for a trophy emblematic of the live-bird championship of Ohio, Kentucky, and Indiana, was for residents of those states only. The purse was open to all amateurs, twenty-five birds in series of five, entrance fee $15—birds extra. Handicaps were twenty-eight to thirty-two yards; five straight kills and the shooter went back one yard; four of five, he stayed at the same handicap; three of five, he moved up one yard. The contest was won with twenty-four kills, and it took twenty-two birds to earn any money. Du Bray killed seventeen with his 20-gauge. No serious live-bird shooter would use a 20-gauge, but du Bray was not at Dayton to kill pigeons. He was there to demonstrate his small-bore Parker gun and perhaps take an order or two, just to make the trip pay.

The second race was fifteen birds, $15 entrance fee, and three guns killed fifteen birds; du Bray's small bore killed ten. The third race was ten birds, $10 entrance, with two ten-straight shooters; du Bray killed seven birds. As was usual in live-bird events, the pigeons remaining after the advertised races were used for miss-and-out competition. The first miss-and-out went six birds with du Bray dropping out at four; the second went five birds with du Bray dropping out at three; and the last race went four birds with du Bray in a three-way tie, but he was listed as "birds only." This meant he was in it only for the sport, did not put $2 in the pot, and won no money for his only winning effort. Captain du Bray paid $46 in entry fees and bought birds extra. At the same time, Parker Brothers was advertising a price reduction of VH grade from $50.00 to $37.50, and few could afford the least expensive Parker at either price. Live-bird shooting was and is an expensive sport.

There came a time when Captain du Bray's business on the West Coast became so attractive as to drag him away from Cincinnati to relocate in California. His son Ernest had finished medical school in 1913 and moved from Ohio to practice in San Francisco. Parker Brothers' advertising for 1913 listed A. W. du Bray as "Resident Agent" at a post-office box in San Francisco. Apparently one Parker Brothers resident agent on the West Coast was enough—a year later, A. E. Perris's contract was not renewed. Captain du Bray continued to go on the road selling Parker guns well into his seventies. A letter to the *American Field* dated February 26, 1921, from well-known trapshooter Benjamin Sherrod noted that:

Capt. A. W. du Bray, representing the Parker Gun Company, has just passed through El Paso, Tex., on his annual pilgrimage in the interest of his firm. The coming of the typical old sportsman is an event in the lives of the younger generation of outdoor lovers, and is a signal for the gathering of the clans who vie with each other in doing honor to this lovable example of "God's handiwork," a dignified courte-

"You could hit 'em, too, with a fast gun"

"Since I've had my Parker, seems as if I'm on my bird twice as quick. I'm bringing home nearly every one that gets up, and that's all a fellow can ask for. It isn't your eye, Jim; it's your gun. *Why don't you get a Parker?*"

The man that buys a Parker gets the finest gun for the money expended; long range, hard hitting and fast handling. Perfected design and skilled gunsmithing add to the pleasure of shooting a Parker.

The Parker D. H. E. for Field or Traps

The D. H. E. is used by many of the best known sportsmen the world over. Barrels of Titanic steel. Fancy figured walnut stock, finely checkered. Straight, full or half pistol grip, mounted with silver shield.

Beautifully engraved game scenes with scroll enrich its appearance. In 10, 12, 16, 20, 28 or .410-gauge. Weights, lengths and drops as desired.

Send for the Parker Catalog

PARKER BROS., *Master Gun Makers* 34 Cherry St., Meriden, Conn., U.S.A.

Pacific Coast Representative: A. W. du Bray Sutter Hotel, San Francisco, Calif.

THE "OLD RELIABLE" PARKER GUN

Parker Brothers ad from September 1926 issue of Outdoor Life. *Captain du Bray and his wife Pauline moved to the Sutter Hotel in 1926, to live closer to their son Dr. Ernest du Bray. This is the last ad in author's collection showing du Bray as Pacific coast representative for Parker Brothers. He died July 8, 1928, at age seventy-nine, while on a visit to Alameda, California.*

ous gentleman. There is never a dearth of listeners when Capt. du Bray is narrating one of his many interesting experiences. Of course, we all know that there are other just as good guns as the Parker, but when the captain lovingly handles and displays the many attractive features of the "Old Reliable Parker," for the life of you, you can't see how any other could possibly approach it, much less be superior. This kindly gentleman by his thorough knowledge, and convincing manner, has done more to put the Parker gun to the forefront all over the United States than any inherent superiority of the gun itself.

Some Parker magazine advertising started to omit reference to du Bray during 1925, and I last saw his name mentioned in a Parker ad in the September 1926 issue of *Outdoor Life:* "Pacific Coast Representative: A. W. du Bray, Sutter Hotel, San Francisco, Calif." At the time, the good captain was seventy-seven, and it's probably not coincidental that his son, Dr. Ernest S. du Bray, also resided at the Sutter Hotel. Captain du Bray had been showing signs of old age as early as his grand tour of 1898, when he wrote of dove hunting in Alabama and that ". . . my afflicted hands and wrists were behaving pretty well. . . ." Later, while snipe hunting in Louisiana: ". . . my foot, which has been very painful for a long time, held up well that day and did not go back on the old man once." It's quite remarkable that he was still selling Parker guns twenty-eight years later—and one thing's for sure, he hunted till the last.

H. L. Betten of Alameda, California, was a noted sportsman and field-trial judge in the 1920s, and du Bray's good friend. Betten wrote about sixty years of his own hunting exploits in his 1940 book, *Upland Game Shooting*, and told the story of a quail hunt with an aging Captain du Bray:

There was an occasion when I shot valley quail with Courtney Ford and Captain A. W. du Bray in Marin County . . . [just across the Golden Gate from San Francisco] . . . in a country which consisted of a series of gulches with very steep slopes. As the Captain was well up in years, we sought some birds lower down where the going was easier. [Then the younger men went uphill while] . . . the Captain had taken a stand at the base of the hill and the dogs were on point far above. Soon

From turn-of-the-century stereo card—part of the Sportsman's Series *by T. W. Ingersoll.*

chances came for the Captain, for some birds were flushed wild and Courtney and I missed several that we shot at. Here the quail were coming right down at the Captain from a very sharp angle. He missed a few shots, but finally, as the birds continued to come toward him, he got their number and dropped a swift incomer, holding far below the bird.

"Well, we learn something new every day," chuckled du Bray when we joined him. "I've shot all over the continent, but this is the first time the dogs have been good enough to dump quail in my lap from on high; this is something to write home about."

At this point the vibes are getting weak; my recollection is wearing thin.

Parker's display at the 1896 Sportsmen's Exposition at Madison Square Garden. Shooting and Fishing *reported that Arthur W. du Bray was in charge of this exposition and that he "is as popular as any 'knight of the trigger' that ever grasped a gun." Photo courtesy of Tom Broadfoot.*

Calls to the San Francisco Historical Society and Cincinnati Historical Society Library filled in a few gaps but were mostly unavailing. Parker Brothers' good ol' boy on the road died July 8, 1928, at age seventy-nine in Alameda, California, perhaps on a visit to his good friend H. L. Betten. He was survived by Pauline, his wife of forty-eight years. Captain du Bray's gunning life was well documented in the sporting press and stands as a prime example of a true gentleman mixing leisure pursuits with his life's work in a simpler time gone by.

Captain du Bray fairly characterized himself when he wrote of ". . . a set of men who loved sport for its own sake and who moreover are cosmopolitan enough to understand that we all can't be rich nor yet college bred men, yet we should at least be gentlemen . . ." Is there anyone reading this who wouldn't trade five Super Bowl Sundays for one chance to hunt prairie chickens, quail, and snipe with du Bray and Jo Elstner in Louisiana? Or a chance to hunt valley quail with Betten and du Bray in Marin County? The past is gone forever, but for me what lingers are my recollections of A. W. du Bray's exploits with America's finest sporting weapon—the Parker gun. I wish I could have been there. My friend Dave thinks I was.

GRADES OF QUALITY

Barrel quality was the most critical determinant of price, grade, and value throughout the seventy-five-year production of the Parker gun. Before Sir W. G. Armstrong Whitworth & Co., Ltd., pioneered the process for fluid-steel barrels for shotguns, Parker's various quality grades were self descriptive—finest Damascus, extra fine Damascus, fine Damascus, and finest Bernard twist. Lower grades were three-blade Damascus, English twist, plain twist, twist, laminated, and some of the early guns, from 1866 to 1873, had decarbonized steel or gun iron converted musket barrels. After Parker started to adopt fluid-steel ("black") barrels in 1894, the quality grades continued to be distinguished by the cost and perceived quality of barrels marked Whitworth (most expensive), Peerless, Acme, Titanic, Parker Special, Parker, Vulcan, and Trojan Steel (least expensive). While any gun could be ordered with a multitude of special features—custom engraving, better wood, and the like—stated barrel quality defined the grade for Damascus and fluid-steel Parker guns.

Forged iron-and-steel-composition barrels exhibiting any pattern are now generically called Damascus, even though twist and laminated barrels weren't considered to be Damascus when they were in common use. The pattern resulted from arrangement and manipulation of alternating bars or wires of iron and steel during the forging process. (Parker's description of Damascus barrelmaking is in Appendix B.) Rough barrel blanks were imported from England and Belgium as raw materials at relatively low tariffs, as compared to the punitive import duties levied on finished British and European guns. A letter written to *Forest and Stream* on August 27, 1885, explained the expense of importing a complete gun:

A Parker tells us that beauty of form and function has a place in a day-to-day world where beauty is too often obscured. For that reason alone, it has value beyond measure.

Michael McIntosh

> . . . It is true that thirty-five percent *advalorem* will be the duty, and a considerable additional sum for freight, insurance, counsel fees, port dues, and the like . . . [if you] . . . order from one of the old London establishments. . .

The Great Western Gun Works in Pennsylvania imported James Purdey's "Best" London guns priced from $500 to $600 in *gold*. Add thirty-five percent tax plus other expenses, and the attraction of Parker Brothers' finest-quality AH grade at $300 was readily apparent to all but robber barons.

The U. S. government protected its gunmakers, but there were few, if any, barrelmakers to protect. As Major Askins wrote in 1910,

> . . . strangely enough, while we turn out more shotguns than the remaining world put together, we are not and never have been a barrelmaking nation . . . [because] . . . the majority of our tubes are imported from Europe in rough form and then put together, filed, shaped, and bored in this country. Our manufacturers have various technical names to describe their different grades of steel barrels. The Krupp and Whitworth tubes, made in Germany and England respectively, have perhaps the greatest repute. Other grades of steel such as armor, nitro, high-pressure, titanic, homo-tensile, and vulcan mean nothing more to the outsider than that they are known to be placed upon certain grades of weapons by reliable manufacturers.

My survey of pre-1910 Parker catalogs offering Titanic-steel and Acme-steel barrels

Ed Muderlak Jr. with a very special A No. 1 Special. *Gun courtesy of Forrest Marshall.*

failed to disclose any reference to their origin as being domestic or imported. However, when the new Parker Trojan grade was announced in the February 8, 1913, issue of the *American Field*, the barrels were stated to be of ". . . imported Trojan steel, manufactured expressly for Parker Bros."

One of the imponderables of researching the Parker gun is why Parker Brothers considered it important to single out the Trojan as having imported barrels while the origin of Vulcan-, Titanic-, and Acme-steel barrels was left unstated. The firearms and sporting-goods catalog of Evans Brothers of Cincinnati for 1911 shows an interesting divergence of customer expectations between double-barrel shotguns and repeaters. Listings for five repeating shotguns (Stevens, Winchester, Marlin, and two Remingtons priced from $18 to $25.50) hardly mention the identity or type of barrels. Meanwhile, the double-barrel shotguns in the same price range feature "trademark" barrel identity (often in bold print) such as: Royal Steel, Blue Armory Steel, Tobalkan Steel, Homo-tensile Blued Steel, Smokeless Powder Steel, New Nitro Steel, Sterlingworth Fluid Compressed Steel, New "Armor" Steel, Ordinance Steel, Genuine Krupp Fluid Steel, and "Vulcan" Blue Steel Barrels. The interesting point is that the purchaser of a 1911 repeater bought a gun as a package deal and assumed the barrels to be of the proper quality. The double-gun customer, probably reflecting back on his experiences with Damascus-barrel guns, needed special assurances that his fluid-steel barrels were up to "grade." Meanwhile, Askins noted in 1910 that

> . . . It appears only a question of a short time now when America will forge her own barrels. The Stevens people are now making all the tubes used in their factory, and the Winchester and Remington factories [are using] those adapted to repeating shotguns.

Extra Set of Barrels.

We have numerous inquries from sportsmen, asking if we can build a set of 10-gauge barrels to fit the same stock used upon their 12-gauge, and *vice versa*. We can always supply 12-gauge barrels to fit a 10-gauge frame, but in order to make 10-gauge barrels fit a 12-gauge frame, the frame must be 2⅜ inches in width or over. Many parties having 10-bore guns write that they would like a pair of number 12 barrels fitted to the same stock, to be used for field purposes, thereby decreasing the weight and making a lighter gun.

To such we would say that the 12-gauge barrels will increase the weight instead of decreasing it, for the following reasons:—the inside of the 12-bore being two sizes smaller than the 10, and the outside of both being the same, there is of necessity more metal in the 12-gauge barrels than in the 10; consequently the 12-gauge pair will make the gun from one to two pounds heavier.

PRICE LIST.

Quality of Gun.	Extra Set of Barrels.	Quality of Gun.	Extra Set of Barrels.
A or A H	$150.00	I & K	$40.00
B or B H	100.00	L & M	37.50
C or C H	75.00	N & O or N H	37.50
D or D H	50.00	P & Q or P H	35.00
E & F or E H	45.00	R & S	32.50
G & H or G H	40.00	T & U	30.00

Replacement-barrel cost schedule from Parker's April 1, 1899 catalog. These prices are for Damascus (A through GH); Laminated (I, K, L, and M); and Twist (N through U). Note the omission of Whitworth replacement barrels for AAH Pigeon Gun. By 1906, extra Whitworth barrels were priced at $250 for A-1 Special, $200 for Quality AAH, and ejectors cost $25 extra. Fluid steel and Damascus barrels of the same grade cost the same in 1906, extra Vulcan steel barrels cost $30 for VH grade, and all extra barrel sets came with a new individually fitted fore-end.

Among the imports, English barrel tubes were generally considered to be the superior product; however, if the truth be told, many of the "English" barrel tubes were forged in Belgium.

Askins went on to say that

> . . . barrels cost in the rough as imported from two to twenty-five dollars a pair . . . [and] . . . usually our builders charge one-half the price of the arm for the extra pair of barrels of a grade similar to that of the gun.

This was true for Parker Brothers. Various Parker catalogs over the years show a second set of barrels with individual fitted fore-end cost 45 percent to 55 percent of a complete gun, depending on grade. Barrels were of first importance to quality and value; expensive barrels compelled an overall expensive gun. It was hard to justify common

walnut wood or an unembellished action when finest Damascus barrels alone cost $150 on a $300 AH grade. Damascus Parker guns were sold by barrel fineness, and the rest of the components were cost-matched to produce a gun of homogeneous overall quality.

After 1880 Parker Brothers went to letters to designate quality/grades (used interchangeably). Top-of-the-line in Parker's 1877 catalog was described as ". . . finest Damascus steel barrels, finest English walnut." In the 1882 catalog, guns of this description were called A Quality, and in 1895 Quality A. Guns with "fine Damascus, fine American walnut" in the 1877 catalog became Quality D; Quality B or B grade had "extra fine Damascus" and the C grade had "finest Bernard Twist." Qualities A-B-C-D were *fine* guns. The fineness had to do with the size of the Damascus or Bernard pattern; the smaller the pattern, the finer the pattern and the better the gun. Value was based on perceived quality of the barrels.

PRICE LIST

OF THE

PARKER HAMMER GUN.

TOP AND LIFTER ACTION.

Quality A. A. Pigeon Gun.—Whitworth Fluid Pressed Steel Barrels, Finest Imported Circassian Walnut Stock, Gold Shield, Finest Checking and Engraving, combined with finest workmanship and finish throughout, Skeleton Butt Plate; Straight or Pistol Grip; 12 Gauge. Weight, 7½ to 8½ pounds.. **$400 00**
    A certificate from Sir Joseph Whitworth & Co., guaranteeing the barrels to be Genuine Whitworth Fluid Pressed Steel, is furnished with every gun of this grade.

Quality A.—Finest Damascus Steel Barrels, Finest Imported Walnut Stock, Gold Shield, Finest Checking and Engraving, combined with finest workmanship and finish throughout, Skeleton Butt Plate. Straight or Pistol Grip; No. 10, 12, 14, 16 or 20 Gauge..................... **300 00**

Quality B.—Extra Fine Damascus or Titanic Steel Barrels, Extra Fine Imported Stock, Gold Shield, Extra Fine Checking and Engraving, Skeleton Butt Plate, Straight or Pistol Grip; No. 10, 12, 14, 16 or 20 Guage.. **200 00**

Quality C.—Fine Bernard or Titanic Steel Barrels, Fine Imported Walnut Stock, Silver Shield, Fine Checking and Engraving, Skeleton Butt Plate, Straight or Pistol Grip; No. 10, 12, 14, 16 or 20 Gauge............ **150 00**

Quality D.—Fine Damascus or Titanic Steel Barrels, Fine Imported Stock, Silver Shield, Fine Checking and Engraving, Skeleton Butt Plate, Straight or Pistol Grip; No. 10, 12, 14, 16 or 20 Gauge.............. **100 00**

Quality E.—Fine Damascus Steel Barrels, Fine Figured American or Imported Stock, Checked and Engraved, Pistol Grip, Hard Rubber Butt Plate; No. 10 Gauge.. **85 00**

Quality F.—Ditto, with Straight Grip........................ **80 00**

Quality G.—Fine Damascus Steel Barrels, Fine Figured American or Imported Stock, Checked and Engraved, Pistol Grip, Hard Rubber Butt Plate; No. 12, 14, 16 or 20 Gauge.................... **80 00**

Quality H.—Ditto, with Straight Grip........................ **75 00**

Quality I.—Fine Laminated Steel Barrels, Fine Figured American Stock, Checked and Engraved, Pistol Grip, Hard Rubber Butt Plate; No. 10 Guage........... **70 00**

Quality R.—Twist Barrels, American Stock, Checked and Engraved, Pistol Grip, Hard Rubber Butt Plate; No. 10 Gauge.................... **60 00**

Quality S.—Ditto, with Straight Grip........................ **55 00**

Quality T.—Twist Barrels, American Stock, Engraved and Checked, Pistol Grip, Hard Rubber Butt Plate; No. 12, 14, 16 or 20 Gauge............. **55 00**

Quality U.—Ditto, with Straight Grip........................ **50 00**

    No. 8, 10 and 12 Gauge Guns extra heavy when wanted.

    Length of Barrels from 28 to 32 inches, regular. Extra long to 40 inches, made only on Special orders, at extra price.

    Guns over specified weight, $10.00 extra. See page 16.

    For extra set of barrels, see page 18.

    All grades of Hammer Guns have the Improved Check Hook and Pin, Fore-End Lock, Straight or High Ribs, Solid Head Plungers, Extension Ribs and Rebounding Locks.

    No. 8 Bore Guns made to special order, and can be made to correspond with any of above grades at an advance of $35.00 above list for No. 10 Bore.

    The Parker Gun can be found in all the leading gun stores in the country, and is sold by dealers at factory prices. If your dealer does not keep them in stock, send your order direct to the factory.

Parker Brothers circa 1899 hammer guns price list. Compare descriptions and prices on this list to the price list of Parker hammerless guns which follows.

A letter to *Forest and Stream* on September 3, 1885, discussed state-of-the-art gunmaking:

> . . . If the barrels of a gun of, say $50 or under, are marked "fine Damascus Steel," or if a gun of such price is found described in a dealer's catalog as having such barrels, you need not put yourself to the trouble of making an examination; the barrels are counterfeits and frauds, and a good plain twist is much better. The best gun barrels in common use are the twist, the laminated and Damascus steel. On some of the finest English guns, barrels of Whitworth's fluid-compressed steel are used. These are by no means handsome, hardly presenting so neat an appearance as a good quality of stub-twist, but they are very strong and service-able, and the most expensive barrels with which I have any acquaintance.

Signed, *A. H.-P. E.*

Before the advent of fluid-steel barrels, when Damascus barrels were state-of-the-art, it was believed that tighter-twisted, smaller-patterned barrels had greater inherent strength than did less finely twisted Damascus, plain twist, or laminated barrels of the same dimensions. Whether this was the result of objective proof-testing or just prejudice in favor of the higher level of skilled workmanship required to produce finely twisted true-Damascus barrels is lost to history. However, the Board of Guardians of the Birmingham Proof House reported the results of destructive proof-tests performed in 1891, validating the superiority (and uniformity) of fluid-steel barrels while at the same time showing certain laminated barrels to be as strong as the finest Damascus, and no direct correlation of pattern fineness to overall strength among Damascus barrels in general. Parker Brothers had considered Damascus and laminated steel to be of equal quality and equal price in the circa 1869 catalog; then it omitted laminated-steel barrels altogether in the 1877 catalog and reintroduced "Fine Laminated Steel Barrels" as mid-grade I, K, L, and M in the early 1880s. The proof-house report showed a machine-forged laminated barrel topped the list, while barrels of fluid compressed steel (Whitworth process) were second in order of merit among thirty-nine groups of barrels tested, and cost about three times as much as other meritorious barrels tested. Whitworth no longer dominated the fluid-steel-barrel market in 1910, when Charles Askins wrote that ". . . barrels cost in the rough . . . [up] . . . to twenty-five dollars a pair," but I think we can fairly conclude that Parker Brothers paid much more than twenty-five dollars for a pair of Whitworth tubes prior to about 1897, when Titanic steel barrels came to be an option. But I digress; suffice it to say that a description of the Damascus barrelmaking process is in Appendix B. Now back to grades. Quality A or A grade was finest; B grade was extra fine; C grade, finest Bernard; and D grade, fine Damascus. Then there was a clear break.

Some authors have credited Parker Brothers with making an excessive number of grades by mistaking four letter designations within one grade as four separate grades. The laminated-steel-barrel guns designated Quality I-K-L-M are all of one *grade*; the various letters merely identified different features. Larry Baer wrote of the "rare" E and N grades when in fact these letter designations simply meant 10-gauge. The next grade

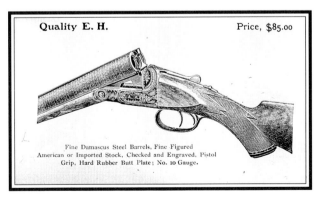

Quality E. H.   Price, $85.00

Fine Damascus Steel Barrels, Fine Figured
American or Imported Stock, Checked and Engraved, Pistol
Grip, Hard Rubber Butt Plate; No. 10 Gauge.

Parker Brothers Quality EH "grade" from the rare circa 1900 "Blue Ink" pocket catalog. This gun is nothing more than G grade with 10-gauge Damascus steel barrels.

below Quality D was letter series E-F-G-H, designating 10-gauge pistol and straight grips, and 12, 14, 16, and 20-gauge pistol and straight grips, respectively. The basic gun was a 12-gauge straight-grip G, and each option (10-gauge and pistol grip) cost five dollars extra. All four letter designations had Damascus barrels and in time were simply called Quality G or G grade.

The N "grade" was just part of the N-O-P-Q letter group, later called P grade. Parker's 1899, 1906, and 1908 catalogs don't list hammer guns in P grade; however, I own s/n 140,009 (circa 1906) and P is stamped on the water table. Parker catalogs are not necessarily definitive of the contemporary grades actually built and sold. Quality R-S-T-U was Parker's plainest grade, and this letter series was used only in connection with hammer guns. (See the color picture of my Quality S 10-gauge, s/n 9,385, with plain-twist barrels and straight grip.)

Concealed hammer or hammerless guns were introduced in 1888, and thus began the modern Parker grading story. Letter H was added to quality grades to identify the hammerless model. The new "H" guns were built to the same letter grades as hammer guns (with the exception of R-S-T-U) as, after all, the barrels made the difference. The finest Damascus hammerless model was Quality AH, extra fine was BH, finest Bernard

Parker Brothers Quality NH "grade" from the rare circa 1900 "Blue Ink" pocket catalog. This gun is nothing more than P grade with 10-gauge Fine English Twist barrels.

twist the CH, and DH grade had fine Damascus barrels.

As with the hammer guns, Qualities AH-BH-CH-DH were considered fine guns. Then came Quality GH, with a few 10-gauge guns stamped *E*; and PH grade, with a few 10-gauge guns stamped *N*. The GH shared fine or three-blade Damascus barrels with DH grade, and the PH had Fine English twist barrels. This was the line of hammerless guns from 1888 to about 1894, when Whitworth fluid-steel barrels were offered on Parker's then top-of-the-line gun. Only a few AA Pigeon-grade hammer guns were built with Whitworth barrels, and Captain du Bray either owned or was given the use of one of them.

Price levels for Parker guns were stable from after the Civil War until the early 1900s, as paper money was redeemable in gold. The finest Damascus Parker hammer gun sold for $300 in 1877; and remember, imported barrels controlled the cost. The finest Damascus hammerless cost $300 from 1888 through about 1908. Both the A (hammer) and the AH (hammerless) had the same finest-quality Damascus barrels and were top-of-the-line until 1894, when the same gun fitted with Whitworth fluid-steel barrels cost $100 more, and there was *no* credit for the finest Damascus barrels not used. The fluid-steel-barrel gun was called Quality AA or AAH Pigeon Gun and initially was offered only in 12-gauge to an exclusive clientele of live-bird shooters. Later, as fluid-steel barrels gained acceptance, the Pigeon Gun became the vanity grade, as did, in turn, the A-1 Special circa 1903 and the Invincible in 1923.

The first year of the twentieth century, Parker Brothers built hammerless guns in the following grades: AAH, AH, BH, CH, DH, GH, PH, and VH. Qualities AH, GH, and PH were exclusively Finest Damascus, Fine Damascus, and English twist respectively. AAH Pigeon Guns and Quality VHs were strictly fluid steel (with exceptions), BH and DH

PRICE LIST

OF THE

PARKER HAMMERLESS GUN.

Quality A. A. H. Pigeon Gun.—Whitworth Fluid Pressed Steel Barrels, Finest Imported Circassian Walnut Stock, Gold Shield, Finest Checking-and Engraving, combined with finest workmanship and finish throughout, Skeleton Butt Plate; Straight or Pistol Grip; 12 Gauge. Weight, 7½ to 8½ pounds.. **$400 00**
A certificate from Sir Joseph Whitworth & Co., guaranteeing the barrels to be Genuine Whitworth Fluid Pressed Steel is furnished with every gun of this grade.

Quality A. H.—Finest Damascus Steel Barrels, Finest Imported Walnut Stock, Gold Shield, Finest Checking and Engraving, combined with finest workmanship and finish throughout, Skeleton Butt Plate ; Straight or Pistol Grip ; No. 10, 12, 14, 16 or 20 Gauge **300 00**

Quality B. H.—Extra Fine Damascus or Titanic Steel Barrels, Extra Fine Imported Stock, Gold Shield, Extra Fine Checking and Engraving, Skeleton Butt Plate, Straight or Pistol Grip ; No. 10, 12, 14, 16, or 20 Gauge.. **200 00**

Quality C. H.—Fine Bernard or Titanic Steel Barrels, Fine Imported Walnut Stock, Silver Shield, Fine Checking and Engraving, Skeleton Butt Plate, Straight or Pistol Grip; No. 10, 12, 14, 16 or 20 Guage.............. **150 00**

Quality D. H.—Fine Damascus or Titanic Steel Barrels, Fine Imported Stock, Silver Shield, Fine Checking and Engraving, Skeleton Butt Plate, Straight or Pistol Grip; No. 10, 12, 14, 16 or 20 Guage..................... **100 00**

Quality E. H.—Fine Damascus Steel Barrels, Fine Figured American or Imported Stock, Checked and Engraved. Straight or Pistol Grip, Hard Rubber Butt Plate; No. 10 Gauge.. **85 00**

Quality G. H.—Fine Damascus Steel Barrels, Fine Figured American or Imported Stock, Checked and Engraved, Straight or Pistol Grip, Hard Rubber Butt Plate; No. 12, 14, 16 or 20 Gauge............................. **80 00**

Quality N. H.—Fine English Twist Barrels, Fine American Stock, Checked and Engraved, Straight or Pistol Grip, Hard Rubber Butt Plate; No. 10 Gauge.. **70 00**

Quality P. H.—Fine English Twist Barrels, Fine American Stock, Checked and Engraved, Straight or Pistol Grip, Hard Rubber Butt Plate; No. 12, 14, 16 or 20 Gauge **65 00**

Weight, 12 Bore, 7 to 9 pounds, 16 and 20 Bore, 5¾ to 7½ pounds; 10 Bore, 7¾ to 10½ pounds. Length Barrels, 28 to 32 inches. "Drop" of Stock, 2 to 3 inches. "Stocks" (measured from Center of Front Trigger to Center of Butt Plate), 14 to 14½ inches. We can make shorter or longer Barrels and different Stocks to special orders and prices, according to extra amount of labor.

For extra sets of Barrels, see page 18.

Eight Bore made to Special order and to correspond with any of the above grades at an advance of $35.00 above 10 Bore lists.

Parker Brothers circa 1899 price list for hammerless guns. Notice Quality EH is the same as Quality GH, except EH is 10-gauge at $5.00 extra. Quality NH and PH don't trace from the hammerless list to the hammer gun line, while Quality R, S, T, and U are "field grade" hammer guns with no equivalent on the hammerless price list. Quality VH was introduced April 1, 1899, by a "Special Announcement" insert, but doesn't yet appear on the catalog price list.

grades offered the option of Damascus or Titanic steel, and the CH could be had in Damascus, Bernard, or Titanic steel. A year later (1902), Parker Brothers added the letter E to the grading system to designate auto-ejectors. The 1906 Pine Cone catalog shows a fancy 28-gauge A-1 Special that topped the Parker line at $525, and AAH Pigeon Grade could be had with finest Damascus barrels in all the popular gauges.

A question that may forever go unanswered is whether one rough fluid-steel barrel tube was better than another. Ansley Fox claimed that his German Krupp barrels were better than sliced bread. Parker touted Whitworth, and then expanded to Titanic steel as an option on Qualities BH, CH, and DH. The irony is that Quality AH had $150 worth of finest Damascus barrels, which were forfeited with an additional $100 cash to have Whitworth fluid- steel barrels on a substantially equivalent AAH Pigeon Gun. Meanwhile, the $50 VH had $25 worth of indistinguishable Vulcan-steel barrels. Whitworth barrels for $250 or Vulcan barrels for $25: both were black, and there was no fine pattern to distinguish them! Ten times the money for different words on the barrel rib and a special stamp-mark on the barrel flats—who can figure? Major Askins (the father) described the conundrum:

> Probably there is quite a difference in the pressure that the cheaper and higher grades of compressed steel will sustain, but in its finished state the ordinary observer can not detect any difference in the appearance of the grades as he could with the Damascus and thus must rely solely upon the manufacturer's word and reputation for the quality of his gun barrels.

Put another way, why should the purchaser of a turn-of-the-century Parker BH pay $200 for a gun with Titanic steel when $100 bought Quality DH with the same barrels? The mindset had always been that guns were graded on barrel quality and that barrels cost half the value of the gun. The BH and CH were no longer good values with Titanic-steel barrels. What's a gunmaker to do? Parker put its word and reputation on the line and started roll-stamping *Acme Steel* on the ribs of BH and CH barrels. The firm carried unspecified barrel-quality distinctions to the extreme in its 1913 Flying Ducks catalog. The otherwise indistinguishable Acme-steel barrels for grades AH, BH, and CH were described as Quality AH ". . . of the *very best* grade;" Quality BH ". . . a *very high* grade;" and Quality CH had Acme barrels of only ". . .*high* grade." If anyone at this late date believes Acme barrel *tubes* were different among themselves, or were different from rough Titanic tubes (or Vulcan tubes for that matter), then I wonder why no objective proof has surfaced over the past hundred years.

Further, if anyone seriously thinks the circa 1895 Whitworth compressed-steel barrels were superior to 1930s Vulcan barrels, then his mind is made up, and all the advances in metallurgy from 1895 to the 1930s won't sway the "gun crank." For those with an open mind, consider the gasoline engine of 1895, the engine that powered the Wright Brothers at Kitty Hawk in 1903, the Ford Model T engine (with Vanadium-steel innards) in 1908, and the aluminum-alloy engine that powered Lindbergh across the Atlantic in 1927. If you were buying engine metallurgy and technology, which year would you prefer? The year a gun was built is an important consideration when buying a Parker to shoot.

If there was ever any difference in the suitability-for-purpose quotient of Vulcan versus Titanic or Acme versus Whitworth barrels, it could be argued that the lower grades were more likely to pass the test by being "ridden hard and put away wet." Colonel Charles Askins (the son) wrote of hunting ". . . with a Virginian who had laid a cool grand on the line for the one thousand dollar grade Parker. He would push the brush before that kingly fusee like he was clearing a path for Grandma Moses. He couldn't have been more solicitous had the smoothbore been made of Wedgwood China." My view is that high-grade Parkers are simply embellished Vulcans with better wood—essentially factory upgrades—but to be coveted (and pampered) nevertheless.

This is not to say that Whitworth and Peerless barrels aren't superior from the finish and collector's standpoints. However, Parker's sales pitch that Acme barrels were superior never addressed the flip side—that Titanic barrels must in some way be *inferior*. Parker Brothers told its customers what they wanted to hear. Acme on the barrel rib announced to the world that a particular gun cost so much, but no matter how fancy the special-order engraving, D grade couldn't be had at any price with *Acme Steel* on the barrel rib. Such were the class distinctions in the United States back then (and today)—mostly a matter of money and form over substance.

But class was *all* important back when Parker guns were in current production. Bank presidents owned fine-grade Parkers.

Bank clerks owned Trojans or Vulcans. I'll bet Mr. Roberts, cashier at the Calcasieu Bank in Louisiana, didn't use a borrowed Pigeon Gun to bag his seven snipe in 1898, when he hunted with Captain du Bray and Jo Elstner near Shreveport. To borrow a gun above his "station" would have been at best presumptuous, and potentially disastrous if he'd had to make good any damage to a gun that likely cost half a year's wages.

Once Parker offered the *finest* gun with the *best* Whitworth fluid-steel barrels and called it the AA Pigeon Gun, what more could it offer? Well, paint the lily, use some smoke and mirrors, and call it the A No. 1 Special at the next increment in price. And if someone could afford still more, blow a little more ego-smoke and call it the Invincible! Perhaps the Depression didn't kill Parker Brothers' prospects—maybe the firm just ran out of superlatives. Some writers have followed suit by calling the Parker gun "America's Finest" and "An Immortal American Classic." For my part, the "Old Reliable" will suffice. Essays follow for each of the quality grades, then the color pictures. Enjoy.

TROJAN, without Automatic Ejector.

A gun of merit, at a popular price, and carrying the name of "PARKER BROS." a guarantee of quality.

Barrels made of Trojan Steel, plain black finish. This steel is manufactured expressly for Parker Bros. Stock: American Black Walnut. Fore End and Stock neatly checkered. Cap Pistol Grip with plain finish. Hard Rubber Butt Plate. Drop about 2¾ inches. Length of stock, 14 inches.

Made to the following specifications only:
12 gauge 30 inch barrels, 7½ to 8 lbs., both barrels full choke.
12 gauge 28 inch barrels, 7½ to 8 lbs., right hand modified, left hand full choke.
16 gauge 28 inch barrels, 6¼ to 7 lbs., right hand modified, left hand full choke.
20 gauge 28 inch barrels, 6¼ to 6¾ lbs., right hand modified, left hand full choke.

(No deviation will be made from these dimensions, except they may be R. H. Cyl. and L. H. Mod. or Full Choke if desired).

TROJAN

Parker Brothers 1920 catalog description of Trojan grade. Trojans got lighter toward the end of the 1920s. Author's 12-gauge s/n 227,251 with 28-inch barrels is on a No. 2 frame and weighs 7 pounds 4 ounces.

When Larry Baer called the Parker gun "An Immortal American Classic," he probably wasn't referring to the Trojan. But in my book, the Trojan is the quintessential American shotgun—hands down—just as Henry Ford's Model T is a classic example of early twentieth-century American industrial genius.

The Trojan wasn't intended to be a "best gun," but today it stands as a fine example of the American gunmaker's art. The Trojan is perfectly suited for purpose, built in quantity to be affordable by many, and reliable, reliable, reliable. Parker Trojans are somewhat akin to the Lake Wobegon, Minnesota, school children who, according to their parents and Garrison Keillor, were "all above average." The Parker Trojan is that kind of gun.

Until the early 1900s, Parker Brothers advertised fine, finer, and finest guns for the top of the market while quietly offering less-fine barreled, less-finely engraved, less-finely finished, more-basic grades to the proletariat. My survey of Parker advertising from 1885 through 1910 shows an all but complete emphasis on A- and AA-grade live-bird guns. Parker Brothers solicited the top of the market, and the common gun customer was along for the ride. But the game began to change after the turn of the century with the ascendancy of the repeater. Ansley Fox was one of the first to fully grasp the true nature of the

change. He set aside his Parker in 1901 to use a $27 Winchester Model 97 for live-bird shooting, and in 1910 introduced his own $25 Philadelphia Sterlingworth. The handwriting was on the wall for makers of expensive double-barrel shotguns.

Parker Brothers got the message, and the $27.50 Trojan grade was introduced in February 1913. The switch in emphasis from top-of-the-line Pigeon guns for the shooting elite to semi-mass-produced knockabouts for the average Joe was a perfect example of the flexible American free-enterprise system, and likely helped keep Parker in the game until the Depression changed the game altogether.

In the final analysis, the Trojan is an A-1 Special without fine engraving or spun interior finish; a BHE without tight checking, skeleton steel buttplate, or *fleur-de-lis* drop points; a DHE without fore-end latch, metal fore-end tip, or ejectors; a VH without final machine cuts on the frame or the unnecessary doll's-head rib extension. The Trojan is a fine gun reduced to its most useful essence with common wood to minimize the mental reservations of use, a gun to be laid in the snow while the hunter climbs a fence, a gun without options. Standard chokes, weights, and measurements shifted such decisions from the Nimrod customer to fifty years of factory expertise. The Trojan is a classic of simplicity and function, a gun in working clothes for the working man: *An Immortal American Classic.*

"If I Only Had That New Parker"

"They've got just the one I want down at Greene's. Not very fancy, but looks and feels like a thoroughbred; balances like a feather and comes to my shoulder as if it was a part of me. And it costs but a few dollars more than any ordinary gun. That's the gun I'm going to have before the season opens."

Such thoughts come naturally to the sportsman once he has examined this gun. Step into your sporting goods store and see the Parker Trojan at $55.00. A plain gun, but it's every inch a Parker. The barrels are turned on a mandrel, insuring proper weight distribution and each is individually balanced; the stocks are practically hand made. Great care is used in the making of each part of the mechanism. If you prefer the automatic ejector type, ask to see a Vulcan Model.

Catalog of all grades sent upon request.

PARKER BROS., Master Gun Makers

32 Cherry St., MERIDEN, CONN.

Pacific Coast Agent: A. W. duBray, Box 102, San Francisco

The "Old Reliable"

PARKER GUN

Parker Brothers ad from September 1925 issue of Forest and Stream. *The push was on for Trojan grade and Parker was building approximately 2,000 per year. Parker's address at 32 Cherry Street was code for* Forest and Stream, *while other magazine ads solicited inquiries to different Cherry Street numbers.*

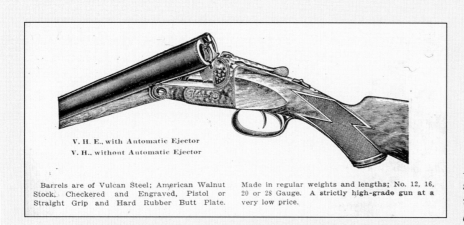

V. H. E., with Automatic Ejector
V. H., without Automatic Ejector

Barrels are of Vulcan Steel; American Walnut Stock, Checkered and Engraved, Pistol or Straight Grip and Hard Rubber Butt Plate.

Made in regular weights and lengths; No. 12, 16, 20 or 28 Gauge. A strictly high-grade gun at a very low price.

VULCAN

Parker Brothers 1920 catalog shows V grade was available with or without automatic ejectors, but not in 10-gauge.

We can now supply you with a 12 gauge "Vulcan" Steel (black barrel) Gun, . . . [also] . . . in 16 gauge and 20 gauge . . . catalog price, $50.00. This Gun, in material and workmanship, is first class, and will be kept up to our high standard in fitting, shooting and wearing qualities. It will fill the wants of persons desiring a genuine Parker gun at a medium outlay.

Special Notice dated April 1, 1899

Fifty dollars for an extractor double in 1899 wasn't cheap. The increasingly popular Winchester Model 1897 six-shot repeater cost $27 retail, and a large New York mail-order house offered new but possibly shopworn '97s for $17.82. When you consider that the '97 was, in effect, an ejector gun, the VH without ejectors was *real expensive*, and when ejectors became a $25 option on VH grade after 1906, the VHE was *real, real expensive*.

The Vulcan wasn't meant to be compared to the loose-as-a-goose, machine-made repeaters. Quality VH was a "fine gun" in its own right and a Parker in every way that mattered. Major Askins classified the VH as a "knockabout" and said this:

The principle to be observed by the purchaser of a knockabout is to buy all gun, unadorned. Every dollar which is placed in ornamentation must be subtracted from the fit, balance and soundness. The world has no better gun value for the money than the American knockabout guns. They are of such absolute utility, their merit so positive, that the owner must continually regret the lack of finish on his weapon.

"Knockabout" for sure, but why VH grade? Why Vulcan? Parker had used the letter series R-S-T-U for its low-end hammer guns, and letter V was of course next— but why Vulcan? Well, Vulcan is the Roman god of fire and metalworking, so there was a symbolic connection to the new black fluid-steel barrels. But I also see a connection to a series of ads run by Remington in *Forest and Stream* during 1898, showing Vulcan at his forge. Coincidence? Original thought? Who can say? However, if Remington had followed up on its own advertising and stamped *Vulcan* on an 1898 gun, then Parker Brothers would have had to find something other than *Vulcan Steel* to roll-stamp on its VH-grade barrel ribs. Perhaps the VH would have shared Titanic-

Remington ad from March 19, 1898, issue of Forest and Stream. *Pop quiz: Where did Parker get the idea to call VH grade "Vulcan" four months later?*

steel barrels with the BH, CH, and DH grades, or perhaps Parker steel would have been introduced earlier.

The price of a VH without ejectors was reduced in February 1908 to $37.50 retail, and mail-order discounters were letting them go for about $34. The price reduction made the VH an excellent value and probably anticipated the introduction, in 1910, of Ansley Fox's $25 Sterlingworth. It was unusual, however, for Parker Brothers to compete on the basis of low price when its forte was high quality, fine fit and finish, and extreme reliability at the top of the market. I suspect there was little or no profit in the VH at 1908 prices. Enter the Trojan in February 1913, to go head-to-head with the Fox-Sterlingworth as an under-$30 everyman's gun. Quality VH was considered a knockabout by Major Askins, and a knockabout it remains today as most Vulcans are sold as shooters to new collectors who want to whet their appetites without choking on price.

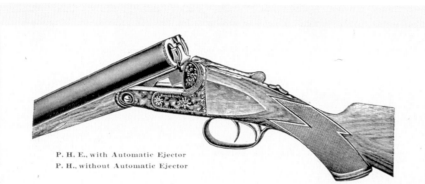

P. H. E., with Automatic Ejector
P. H., without Automatic Ejector

Parker Steel Barrels, Fine American Stock,   Hard Rubber Butt Plate; No. 10, 12, 16, 20 or
Checkered and Engraved, Straight or Pistol Grip,   28 Gauge.

QUALITY PH

*Parker Brothers 1920 catalog
description of P grade with or
without automatic ejectors and
the lowest grade available in
10-gauge.*

*Charles and Walter King were top gunmakers but apparently not good business-
men. Otherwise, how do we explain the existence of PH grade after the turn of the
century? Quality PH was the lowest-grade hammerless after the concealed-hammer
models were introduced in 1888, and with twist barrels and token engraving, it had its
greatest popularity in the ten years preceding the introduction of VH grade. Why Parker
Brothers created a new grade, rather than simply offering the PH with black Vulcan
fluid-steel barrels, is a puzzlement.*

Quality PH had Fine English twist barrels in 12- , 14- , 16- , and 20-gauges and cost
$65 in Parker's 1899 catalog. Quality NH was
the same gun in 10-gauge priced at $70, and
8-bores were made to special order for $35
above the 10-gauge price. The basic PH with
twist barrels was still priced at $65 in the
1908 Pine Cone catalog. There must have
been a significant number of gunners in love
with the patterned barrel to keep Quality
PH popular until German U-boats interrupted
the supply of barrel tubes from England
and Belgium.

Quality PH was offered with English
twist or Parker steel barrels in the circa 1913
Flying Ducks catalog for $48.75; a comparable
VH with Vulcan steel barrels was $11.25 less;
a GH with Parker Special steel barrels cost
$11.25 more. By 1920 Parker had exhausted
its prewar stockpile of twist barrel tubes, and
the fluid-steel-barrel PH lost its identity and
popularity. In 1926 a PH without ejectors was
only $6.50 less than a VHE. Parker Brothers'
1929 catalog pictures the PH grade with

"DISCONTINUED" hand-stamped over the
description, and "PH and PHE grades discontinued" is printed on the price list. The 1930
catalog omits PH grade altogether, except
for replacement barrels, retrofit ejectors,
and repairs.

Considering that fluid-steel barrels began
to dominate the market in the early 1900s, the
persistence of the PH with twist barrels is a
good example of how Parker Brothers could
make just a few guns to satisfy a niche market and presumably make it pay. Patterned
barrels were popular and had a life of their
own, even to the point that certain gun
manufacturers applied a Damascene finish
to fluid-steel barrels to trade on the aesthetic
appeal. But not Parker Brothers—at least not
after "laminated" musket barrels were
dropped from the line in the late 1860s.

Once Quality PH lost its Fine English
twist barrels in favor of Parker steel, there was
little to distinguish it from the Vulcan except
price and the fact that PH was the lowest-
grade 10-gauge. Parker Brothers' office

The rarest of the rare—Parker Brothers PH .410 s/n 218,476 with 26-inch barrels on No. 000 frame, weighing a handy 5 pounds, 11 ounces. This is a man-sized gun. Parker .410s weren't built for kids.

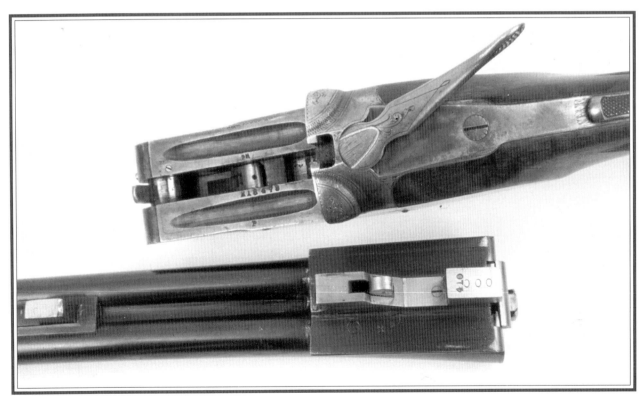

Parker Brothers PH .410 apart showing 000 frame size marked on barrel lump and characteristic weight removal grooves on water table.

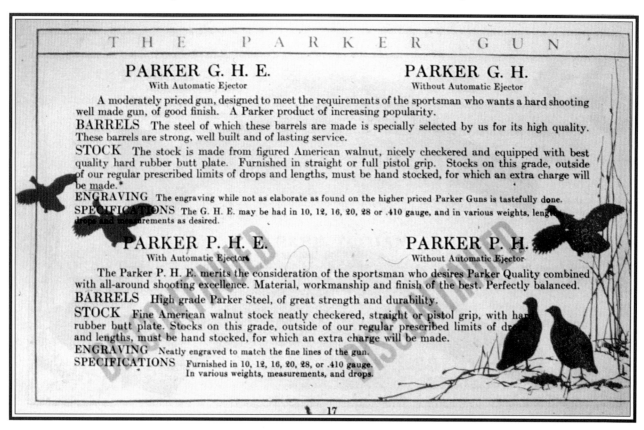

Quality PH was dropped from the line toward the end of 1928, and the grade was hand stamped "discontinued" in Parker's January 1, 1929 large Flying Geese catalog. Original catalogs have magenta or green ink stamp mark.

manager, H. L. Carpenter, wrote in a factory letter to William Meyers of Hampton, Iowa, on December 15, 1926, ". . . as you have noted, we do not make 10-gauges except in PH and higher grades, and therefore could not make you a VH at any price in 10-gauge." A short time later, VHs were built in 10-gauge, and sometime during 1928 the PH was dropped from the line.

Parker Brothers first offered the .410 bore size in its March 1, 1926, large Flying Geese catalog. Quality PH went the way of the passenger pigeon in 1928. During the short overlap of production, Parker Brothers built at least one PH .410, s/n 218,479, with twenty-six-inch barrels on a tiny 000 frame. There are reputed to be only one or two others, thus making the PH .410s at least as rare in numbers as the reclusive Invincibles.

QUALITY GH

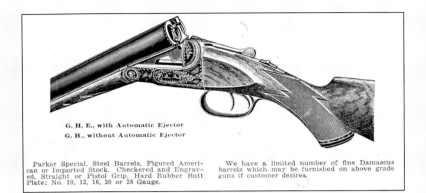

G. H. E., with Automatic Ejector
G. H., without Automatic Ejector

Parker Special, Steel Barrels, Figured American or Imported Stock. Checkered and Engraved, Straight or Pistol Grip, Hard Rubber Butt Plate; No. 10, 12, 16, 20 or 28 Gauge.

We have a limited number of fine Damascus barrels which may be furnished on above grade guns if customer desires.

Parker Brothers 1920 catalog description of G grade with or without automatic ejectors and available with fine Damascus barrels if customer desired.

My hunting gun is a Parker GH with thirty-inch modified- and full-choke barrels, straight grip, Miller single selective trigger, good dimensions, nice wood, and a Hawkins pad. Slight case color kept the price under $2,500 in 1993. The gun without a Miller SST cost $95 new in 1927. Quality GH had a comparable series of hammer guns (E-F-G-H, denoting 10- and 12-gauges, straight and pistol grips). In the early years of the hammerless, the GH-grade 10-gauge was stamped E and listed for $5 more than standard 12-, 14-, 16-, and 20-gauges. By the 1908 Pine Cone catalog, Quality GH could be ordered with ejectors, and 10- and 28-gauges were standard (8-gauge cost $120 but was only available with extractors). The GH was the lowest grade to have an engraved game scene, not nearly as elaborate as Parker's hundred-dollar DH, but in 1908 the GH cost only eighty bucks.

My GH is an all-purpose gun that has given me great pleasure in the field and at the traps. No small part of my enjoyment is the engraved game scene and better wood and checking, which serve as reminders that I own a threshold "fine gun." Major Askins lamented the owner of a favorite knockabout who, ". . . must constantly regret the lack of finish in his weapon . . . especially . . . when he grows to the arm with the passing of time. . . ." I know what he means, but my GH is no knockabout. I have grown to it, and the fit and finish suit me fine. I wouldn't trade the Miller trigger for any other, not even a factory Parker SST. The wood shows some nice pattern and color, the tighter checking is just right, and there are *no* ejectors—but that's another chapter.

Quality GH is my kind of gun. I don't *need* a DH or CH or BH or higher grade. I'm sure the situation was the same back in 1927, when my GH was built. The GH grade filled a real market need between the Trojan and VH "knockabouts" and the DH and CH "fine guns." The GH was the lowest-grade Damascus gun and shared fine Damascus barrels with DH grade. The PH, of course, had English twist. Although World War I ended the supply of twist barrels, three-blade Damascus became available after the war to supply a special market. Some of the early 1920s Parker catalogs offered ". . . a limited number of fine Damascus barrels which may be furnished on GH/GHE grade guns if customer desires." Although I've seen a mid-1920s VHE and DHE with seemingly original Damascus barrels stamped *OVERLOAD PROVED* on the flats, I have never seen a post-Great War GHE with anything but Parker Special steel barrels.

Current thought is that the last Parker built was a GH .410, s/n 242,387; Larry Baer wrote that it was s/n 242,385, a GHE 28-gauge. In either case, the G-grade hammerless demonstrated its popularity until the end. Quality PH fell by the wayside in 1928, and the Trojan grade ten years later. Quality GH was popular from beginning to end, yet to my knowledge no G grade was ever pictured or mentioned in any Parker advertising—I guess it sold itself.

Parker Brothers GH grade shared fine Damascus steel barrels with Quality DH, but lacked more extensive engraving and teardrop "drop point" on the side panel, which distinguished its more expensive cohort. Twenty-gauge courtesy of Pete Wall. "Tinnies" are Strater and Sohier 1874 patent shorebirds.

Parker Brothers 1933 catalog description of D grade with or without automatic ejectors.

The D grade was known to all as "Parker's hundred-dollar gun"—at least until the government started to disconnect the value of paper money from the gold hoard. If one Parker Brothers gun had to be selected as the dominant example, it would be the DHE. All of the higher grades—by way of wood, checking, engraving, and metal work—were a DHE and then some; D grades were fine guns, and the lower grades were not. There were price quibbles over slight differences in gauge and grip among qualities E-F-G-H hammer guns and the EH and GH hammerless. The DH buyer at the turn of the century didn't need to be bothered by extra charges for pistol grip or 10-gauge. The customer was always right when he bought Parker's hundred-dollar gun.

When Parker Brothers introduced the hammerless in 1888, the first picture ads showed a DH instead of Quality A as had been customary. This was the first indication that Parker might set its sights on the popular gun market rather than just touting the highest-grade live-bird guns to the rich and richer. However, the DH disappeared from Parker advertising by 1893, and A grades and Pigeon Guns were pictured almost exclusively for the next ten years.

Quality DH enjoyed a flush of popularity in 1897, when Parker Brothers first offered black barrels designated Titanic steel. Qualities DH, CH, and BH cost $100, $150, and $200 respectively, and for the first few years of the twentieth century, all could be had with Titanic steel barrels. For the customer who elected the black-barrel option, there was little incentive to pop 50 or 100 percent over DH price for slight incremental engraving, a few

more lines of checking, and the possibility of better wood. The DH was a bargain; the CH and BH were not.

Parker Brothers sold a large number of DHs and DHEs at $100 and up, and by dollar volume, D grade had to be Parker's highest-gross gun. As I write this, all previously published Parker production statistics are highly suspect, but in today's market, the DH and DHE constitute between 25 and 30 percent of collector guns. Parker Brothers introduced the Trojan in 1913, but had already been building DHs for twenty-four years (sixteen years with fluid-steel barrels). The DH had been in production for ten years before the introduction of the Vulcan-steel-barrel gun, and after 1913, the VH and Trojan split the knockabout market.

The D-grade hammerless was the dominant gun during current production, and as a collector's gun it dominates today. Collectors should have no problem finding a decent original DHE, but good DHs are relatively scarce. Imitation being the sincerest form of flattery, the DHE was reproduced during the 1980s in Japan. The Parker Reproduction seemed to do a steady trade for about ten years but ran out of popularity in 1995, when liquidators started dumping new guns priced below $2,000 on the market. The "investors" who had purchased similar guns for $3,000 or more were left holding the bag as market prices are driven by supply and demand. The long-term popularity of Parker Brothers' DHE is a two-edged sword; while it may seem sensible to imitate Parker's most popular gun, an abundant supply of original DHEs exists to satisfy collector-lust for a high-condition D grade. Why buy a copy when you can have the original?

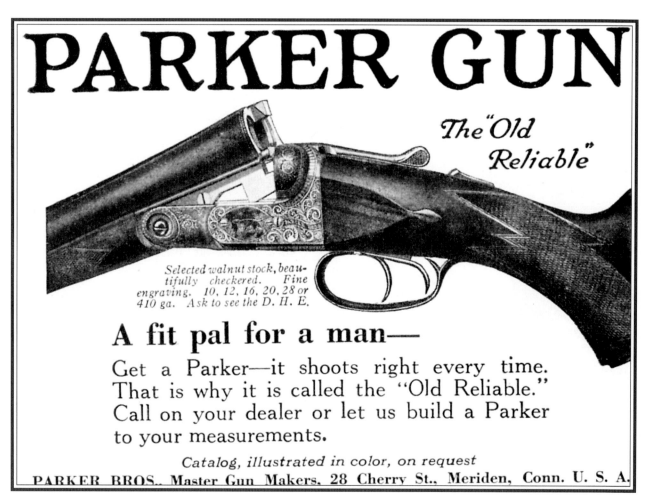

Parker Brothers ad from February 1927 issue of Field and Stream. *Quality DHE was a "fit pal," but a higher grade might be more analogous to an expensive mistress.*

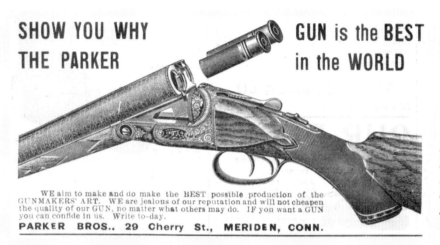

QUALITY CH

Parker Brothers ad from the November 26, 1904, issue of American Field. *This is the only ad of more than 150 in author's collection which shows CH/CHE grade.*

BERNARD WHO?

Parker's C grade had its origin as a barrel-pattern alternative to the more familiar Damascus offered in grades A, B, and D. Before letter grades were assigned in the 1880s, the "C" was simply described as having barrels of "finest Bernard steel." Leopold Bernard was a French barrelmaker and cannon maker from Paris who gave his name to a special grade of Damascus-type barrel with a bold chainlike twist pattern (in contrast to the fine, finer, and finest spirals of the various grades of true Damascus). Damascus guns were graded by perceived quality of the barrels, and the finer the pattern, the finer and more expensive the gun. Parker Brothers considered Quality C with finest Bernard steel to fit between guns with fine and extra-fine Damascus barrels, at least as to price. The C grade existed simply as a different barrel pattern until black Titanic steel barrels became available as a no-extra-charge option.

Parker Brothers offered Titanic steel barrels on the B, C, and D grades possibly as early as 1897. It must have been tough to convince a customer to part with an extra fifty dollars for a C grade with the same black barrels as the D grade. Remember, back at the turn of the century, barrels made the gun. Fancy wood, more extensive engraving, and tighter checking were justified only by the increased cost of rough barrel tubes in proportion to the overall cost of the gun. Any CH grade circa 1900 with original Titanic steel barrels ought to be a rare item.

By the 1906 Pine Cone catalog, a black-barrel Quality CH displayed *Acme Steel* on the rib and had an identity of its own. Acme barrels could be perceived as better than Titanic by customers with an extra fifty bucks to spend and couldn't be had on D grade at any

price. This sort of slight quality distinction coupled with a massive price increase persists to this day. Otherwise, why would anyone pay $10,000 for a gold Rolex when a Timex tells time just as well? Larry Del Grego Jr. told me about a special-order Acme-barrel CHE without any engraving at all. It seems strange that a Parker customer would pay CHE price for a plain gun, just for the *Acme Steel* roll-stamping on the barrel rib. However, the pecking order of Parker guns was mostly economic and superficial rather than a matter of inherent quality or suitability for purpose.

A Parker DH in the gun rack at the trap club is all but indistinguishable from a CH alongside. Quality CH typically has a hard-to-see engraved border around the frame while the DH grade typically does not. Quality CH checking is a little bit tighter and slightly more extensive. Parker guns were sold to a *want* rather than a *need* market. Apparently a fair number of Parker customers wanted "*Acme Steel*" on the barrel rib, thus the quality was apparent rather than implied, or, in the words of Major Askins:

> Probably there is quite a difference in the pressure that the cheaper and higher grades of compressed steel will sustain, but in its finished state the ordinary observer cannot detect any difference in the appearance of the grades as he could with Damascus and thus must rely solely on the manufacturer's word and reputation for the quality of his gun.

Put another way, the Quality CH customer wanted to believe his Acme-steel barrels were superior to the others in his price range, and was willing to pay a 50 percent increment based ". . . solely on the manufacturer's word and reputation." Every CH and CHE sold after the advent of black fluid-steel barrels must have been a source of constant amazement to the barrelmakers at Parker Brothers' gun works when they selected the correct roll-stamp to apply to the barrel rib based solely on the shop tag rather than any physical, aesthetic, or metallurgical characteristic of the barrels themselves. The CH grade was well-built but even more well-sold.

Parker Brothers CHE 12-gauge s/n 134,695 with 30-inch fine Damascus barrels choked mod and mod. This beauty left the gun works circa 1906, but has Hayes's 1910-patent wear insert. The No. 2 frame helps account for its 7 pound 12 ounce weight.

THE PARKER GUN 5

PARKER B. H. E.
With Automatic Ejector

Without a peer in the realm of fine quality guns offered at an attractive price.

BARRELS —A steel manufactured for PARKER BROS. under our trade name—Acme.

STOCK —Selected imported Walnut, highly checkered, gold shield, steel skeleton butt plate or rubber recoil pad. Monte Carlo or cheek piece, if desired.

ENGRAVING—Game scenes and Scroll, beautifully wrought.

SPECIFICATIONS
Straight or pistol grip, gauges, 10, 12, 16, 20, 28. Various weights, lengths, drops and measurements.

PRICES PAGE 15

BH GRADE

Parker Brothers 1933 catalog description of BHE with automatic ejectors standard.

At a simpler time, in a galaxy far away, Parker Brothers' second-best gun was designated extra-fine Quality B and cost two hundred bucks. An additional C-note bought the satisfaction of owning the finest Quality A, but relatively few elected to spend the extra money on A grade. One of these days the Parker factory records are going to be published, and if my analysis of 520 Parker guns offered for sale in the Double Gun Journal *can be extrapolated to impute the number of guns actually built, the ratio of BHs to AHs will be four to one or more in favor of the BH (more on this topic in Chapter 9).*

The *Blue Book of Gun Values* by S. P. Fjestad (fourteenth edition) shows Quality BH with 90 percent case colors to be valued at $6,375, and add 25 percent for ejectors. Meanwhile, a 90 percent AHE is valued at $12,250, and subtract 25 percent for extractors. My survey of Parker collector guns shows that thirty-seven of forty-one BHs and all twelve of the AHs offered for sale recently have ejectors. Valuing a BHE with extractors and then adding 25 percent for ejectors is like treating a heater as an add-on in the automotive *Red Book*. Adjusting BH for ejectors, a BHE is 65 percent of AHE price, condition being equal. However, adjusting AHE value for extractors, a BH is about 70 percent of AH value. The 5 percent difference is no big deal at the $10,000 mark (about $500); however, the 65 to 70 percent valuation ratio seems to be premised on Parker Brothers having made approximately 13,000 BHs and 5,500 AHs (according to Johnson, Baer, and the *Blue Book*.) I think these

numbers are pretty clearly wrong—especially as a ratio of one to the other.

So what's the point? Well, nothing is as it seems. For example, it's an article of faith that Parker Brothers operated at the highest personal level, working closely with a knowledgeable and fussy clientele to give every customer the benefit of every doubt. This is not true as a general statement but may be true in respect to BH grade and higher. Communication was not all that great at the turn of the century, so there was much incentive to buy a standard gun off the shelf rather than engage in a protracted letter-writing campaign with the gun works. Large sporting-goods dealers and distributors usually inventoried Parker guns with standard weights and measurements through DH grade. This may explain why so many DHs and DHEs have almost identical engraving after the style shown in Parker's various catalogs. Quality BH, however, was a special-order gun.

Parker Brothers BHE 16-gauge s/n 156,249 with 28-inch barrels weighing a "slight" 5 pounds 13 ounces. Light ⅞-ounce loads make this an ideal quail gun.

The Charles J. Godfrey 1900 sporting-goods catalog shows a CH as the highest inventory grade, and ". . . prices on higher grade Parker guns furnished upon application." In other words, Quality BH buyers dealt directly or indirectly with the New York salesroom, factory reps like A. W. du Bray, or the gun works. By the 1930s, Von Lengerke and Antoine cataloged Parkers from Trojan grade to BHE; however, it's doubtful VL&A actually inventoried more than a token few Trojans and VHs during the Depression. Anyone with a BHE on his mind was likely thinking about more than an off-the-shelf inventory gun (for example, the two-gun, four-barrel BHE set described in Chapter 15).

The fact that BHE grade was advertised in VL&A's 1933 fall and winter catalog must be taken in the context of Parker Brothers' 1933 production being less than 300 guns. Given the circumstances of the Depression, it's not likely any dealers were carrying much inventory at a time when some of their 1920s customers were selling apples on the street corner. BHEs in 1934 cost $300—about half the price of a new Chevrolet—and that's a whole lot of apples.

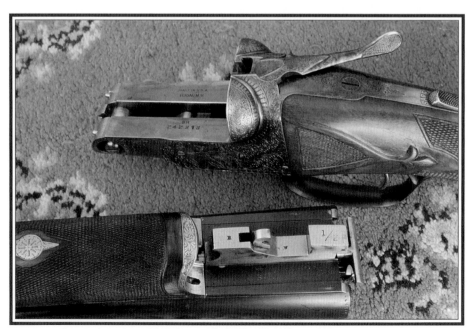

Rare Remington-Parker BHE half-frame in mint condition. Serial number 242,313 marks this as one of the last Parkers built at Ilion, New York. Number 1/2 frame and 26-inch barrels keep the weight down to 6 pounds 13 ounces, even with long pull and skeleton steel buttplate.

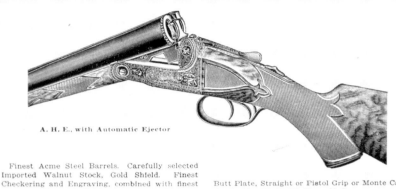

A. H. E., with Automatic Ejector

Finest Acme Steel Barrels. Carefully selected Imported Walnut Stock, Gold Shield. Finest Checkering and Engraving, combined with finest workmanship and finish throughout, Skeleton Butt Plate, Straight or Pistol Grip or Monte Carlo Stock; No. 10, 12, 16, 20 **or** 28 Gauge.

AH Grade

Parker Brothers 1920 catalog description of AHE with automatic ejectors standard.

HOLY GRAIL

Parker Bros. A.H. 12 ga., 30" M&F. Splinter fore-end, Miller SST, straight grip, skeleton buttplate, good dimensions. Perfect screws! Mint factory original condition—closet gun. Reasonable price.

Have you seen my Holy Grail? Not everyone lusts after an A-1 Special. I would be satisfied to find a real nice AH, and would not pass up an otherwise satisfactory AHE just because it has ejectors. A gun built after 1910 but before 1930 would be just fine. I prefer the style and execution of circa 1915 engraving. My post-1910 AH grade would have Acme-steel barrels, and if they should be thirty-two inch or twenty-eight inch, well, nothing's perfect. Number 1½ frame size would be expected, Number 1 standard 16-gauge would be a plus, and Number 2 heavy 12-gauge would be seriously considered. Any deviations from my ideal AH would be viewed in context. Thirty-two-inch barrels should not be fitted to a short-stocked gun. Twenty-six-inch barrels don't belong on a Number 2 frame. Wars have been fought over matters of less consequence than whether a Parker is 100 percent factory original or 100 percent "new" by a restoration artist. I would own an AH today at the $5,000 mark if restoration were an option—but I can wait.

When I think of AH grade, I think of Parker's *finest* gun. Until about 1895, Quality AH was described as having "... finest Damascus steel barrels, finest imported walnut stock, gold shield, finest checking and engraving, combined with finest workmanship and finish throughout, skeleton butt plate. Straight or pistol grip . . . 10, 12, 14, or 16 gauge . . . $300.00." After a gun is described as having the *finest* of everything, it would take some real advertising and marketing imagination to come up with something better. However, metallurgy upped the ante in 1894 when compressed-steel barrels became available. Whitworth-process barrels were

fitted on Parker's finest gun, thus creating the Quality AAH Pigeon Gun. At first, the AH and AAH were hardly distinguishable except for the black barrels. Parker's 1899 price list shows the stock to be of finest Circassian walnut on the Pigeon Gun, thus implying that the finest *imported* walnut stock on Quality AH was something different, even though the finest imported walnut *was* Circassian.

Quality AH cost $300 when the hammerless guns were introduced in 1888, and they held their price through feast and famine until about 1909. The price actually declined to $225 in the early teens but by 1917 was back up to $340, with auto-ejectors standard.

125

Parker's December 1, 1920, pocket catalog prices Quality AHE at $410. The last Parker Brothers AHE cost $467.50 in the January 1, 1934, pocket catalog, at the depth of the Depression. Six months later, Remington owned the Parker gun, and by the last dealer price list (February 16, 1940), a Remington-Parker AHE with double triggers cost $530 at retail. After being out of production for forty-one years, Remington revived the AHE in 1988, to be built by the Custom Shop on special order in 20-gauge only—suggested retail price $12,700. A Remington "reproduction" AHE sold for $21,700 at public auction, and in the best tradition of *deja vu* all over again," the "Old Reliable" Parker gun *again* went out of production.

My guess is that AHs and AHEs are scarce because they look so much like B grades but cost so much more. Vanity has its price. Before the turn of the century, $300 bought Parker's finest Quality AH while an extra-fine Quality BH cost a hundred bucks less. After the introduction of Whitworth compressed-steel barrels in 1894 and Titanic steel barrels shortly thereafter, the word "finest" became just another adjective. Money-conscious buyers could save $100 with B grade and get optional Titanic steel barrels free. The money-is-no-object buyer would opt for the AAH Pigeon Gun with the highly touted Whitworth fluid-steel barrels. By 1903 a vanity-gun customer could lay some more money down to own an A No. 1 Special. It's not surprising

that Quality AH and AHE slipped into the crack along with the CH-CHE and PH-PHE grades. The irony is that collector guns tend to be rare and coveted as an inverse proportion to their popularity during current production. My judgment is that A grades with original fluid-steel barrels are about as scarce in the collector market as Pigeon Guns and A-1 Specials. The Remington Custom Shop's one-off AHE 20-gauge may be the rarest of all, depending on how you define what constitutes an original Parker gun.

Quality AHs built after 1898 are rare for three reasons: first, they were offered only with finest Damascus steel for several years after fluid-steel barrels were available; second, the AH was neither fish nor fowl after 1894, when in a time of stable prices they still cost as much as Parker Brothers had ever charged for a Damascus gun but no longer had top-of-the-line *cachet* for the vanity-gun purchaser; and third, Quality AH shared Acme-steel barrels with the BH, so there was little incentive to pay $300 for a gun that was virtually identical to the $200 grade. Meanwhile, vanity-gun customers craved the incremental barrel engraving, three ribs or four behind the standing breech, more elaborate and distinctive checking, and the higher level of overall workmanship of the AAH Pigeon Gun and A-1 Special. Between 1894 and 1903, Parker Brothers created two new "best gun" grades that relegated its "finest" Quality AH to third-class citizenship—but my kind of gun nevertheless.

Parker Brothers circa 1930 Trojan 12-gauge s/n 232,052 has 30-inch barrels full and modified, No. 2 frame, and weighs four ounces less than eight pounds even.

(top) Parker Brothers circa 1928 GH 12-gauge—author's gun of choice for his bird of choice, the big-running, sneaking-away, low-flying ringneck of northern Illinois.

(bottom) Parker Brothers circa 1930 DHE 12-gauge Trap s/n 232,754. Duck call by Kent Bowers of Davenport, Iowa. Parker guns and Peters ammunition became "kissing cousins" in the early 1930s when both were acquired by Remington.

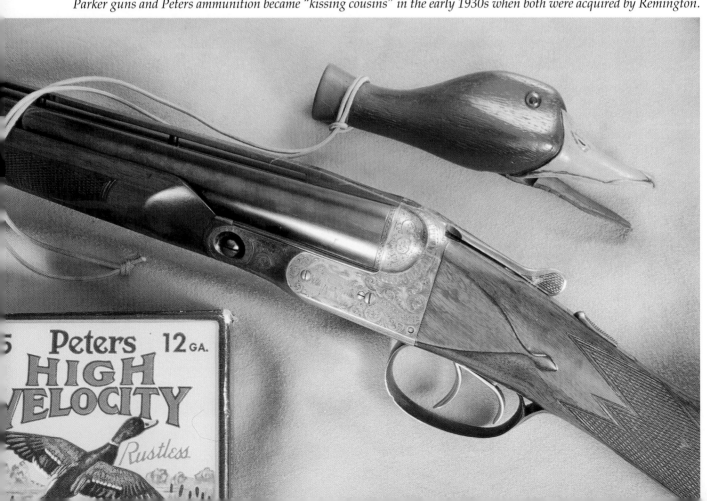

(top) Parker Brothers CHE 12-gauge Damascus "fowling piece," circa 1906.

(bottom) Parker Brothers circa 1896 BH(E) s/n 84,330 with retrofit Titanic steel barrels and non-factory automatic ejectors. Note the early-style checking pattern on fore-end.

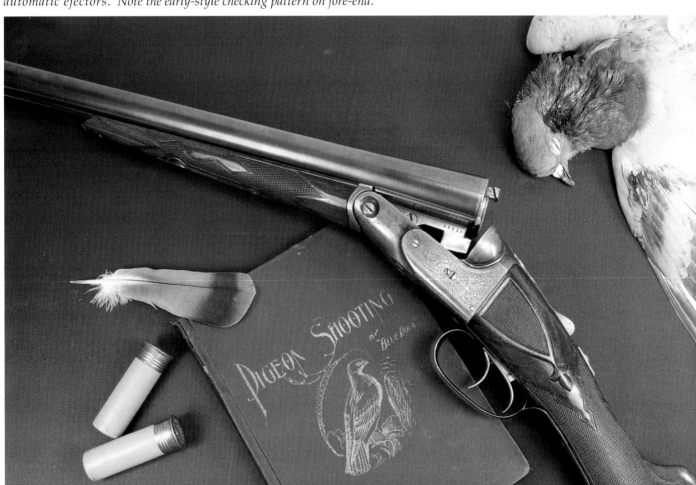

(top) Two very nice AHE 20-gauges for comparison. Both guns were built circa 1930, and have 28-inch barrels. On the top is s/n 231,263 with one game scene and one rib behind the breech. On the bottom is s/n 230,762 sans the rib, but with two game scenes, and is courtesy of Bill Nitchmann. Note late 1920s full cover checking on the fore-ends.

(bottom) Parker Brothers circa 1926 A No. 1 Special s/n 215,775 with 30-inch barrels on No. 1½ frame. Here's a gun that hasn't been laid on many logs in its lifetime.

(top right) Parker Brothers circa 1928 AAHE Pigeon Gun with Miller single trigger and vent rib. Rare look-back shorebird by Bill Spielman of Winnebago, Illinois.

(bottom) Parker Brothers AHE 20-gauge—weapon of choice for plantation quail.

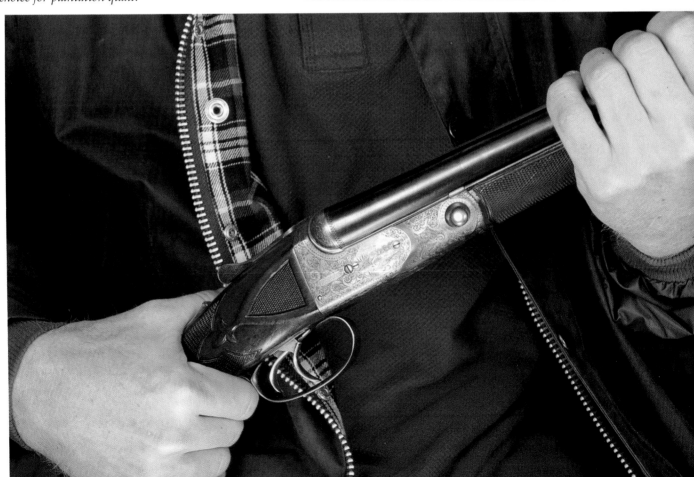

Three of Parker's top-end guns for comparison — AHE (circa 1930) with one rib behind the standing breech, AAHE (circa 1928) with three ribs, and A No. 1 Special (circa 1926) with four ribs. Late 1920s high-grade Parkers are the crème de la crème.

Parker Brothers A No. 1 Special s/n 180,178 ordered January 11, 1918, and delivered June 14, 1918, with 28-gauge and .410 barrels on No. 00 frame. This extremely rare two-barrel set illustrates that smaller bore size results in heavier barrels and a consequently heavier gun when frame size remains constant. Photo courtesy of J. C. Devine, Inc.

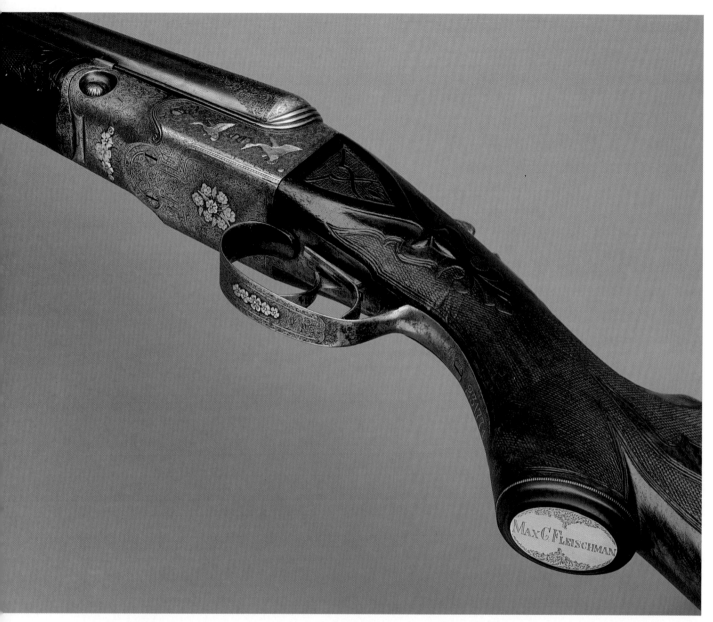

Max Fleischman's A No. 1 Special. He was chairman of the board of Standard Brands Corp., and gave away his entire fortune ($192 million) to charity after his death. Fleischman's gun was cataloged to sell between $80,000 and $120,000. The gavel price of $42,500 made the Parker point that original condition is everything and famous owners don't add much value to a high grade "Old Reliable." Photo courtesy of J. C. Devine, Inc.

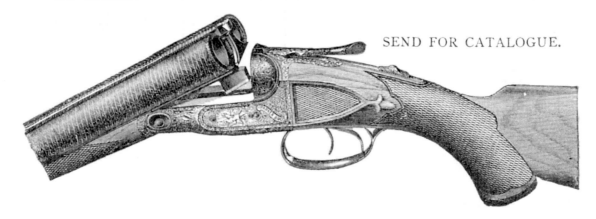
Parker Brothers ad from May 1893 issue of Outing Book. *Quality AH was top-of-the-line until the "Pigeon Gun" with Whitworth barrels was introduced in 1894.*

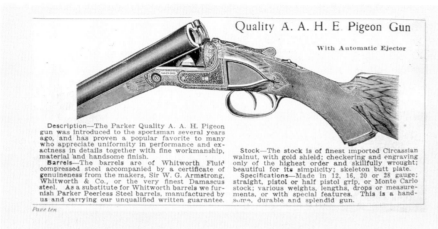

Description—The Parker Quality A. A. H. Pigeon gun was introduced to the sportsman several years ago, and has proven a popular favorite to many who appreciate uniformity in performance and exactness in details together with fine workmanship, material and handsome finish.
Barrels—The barrels are of Whitworth Fluid compressed steel accompanied by a certificate of genuineness from the makers, Sir W. G. Armstrong, Whitworth & Co., or the very finest Damascus steel. As a substitute for Whitworth barrels we furnish Parker Peerless Steel barrels, manufactured by us and carrying our unqualified written guarantee.

Stock—The stock is of finest imported Circassian walnut, with gold shield; checkering and engraving only of the highest order and skillfully wrought; beautiful for its simplicity; skeleton butt plate.
Specifications—Made in 12, 16, 20 or 28 gauge; straight, pistol or half pistol grip, or Monte Carlo stock; various weights, lengths, drops or measurements, or with special features. This is a handsome, durable and splendid gun.

Page ten

PIGEON GUN

Parker Brothers 1920 catalog description of Quality AAHE Pigeon Gun with automatic ejectors standard.

My first trip to Chadick's, Ltd., at Terrell, Texas, was in September 1993. I was like a kid in a candy shop. For the first time in my life, I had the opportunity to go through at my leisure a large number of high-grade Parker guns, many of which were beyond my threshold of financial pain. One AAHE really caught my eye and went up to my shoulder like a dream. Mental calculations of how a second mortgage might change my life were cut short when Herschel Chadick advised that the gun was sold. Even wife Nancy saw some merit in this particular AAHE Pigeon Gun, but I suspect that if the $19,500 issue had presented itself, serious discussions would have ensued.

A Pigeon Gun needs some working up to. Parker Brothers built guns to almost any reasonable specification and did a steady trade in replicating low-grade shooters with high-grade vanity guns after a customer, in the words of Major Askins, came to "... regret the lack of finish of his weapon. Especially ... when he grows to the arm with the passing of time and is unwilling to exchange his piece for another." Fortunately for Parker customers, guns could be built to special order. When through hard work, gift, inheritance, or blind luck a high-grade Parker

This 1934 Ford V8 sedan cost $695.00, while a Parker AAHE Pigeon Gun cost $687.50 the same year. My hunch is that Parker Pigeon Gun customers weren't driving Ford sedans.

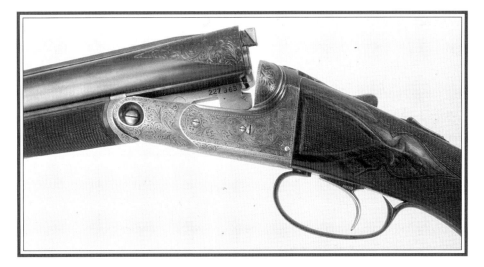

Parker Brothers AAHE 12-gauge with barrel engraving typical of Pigeon guns after say 1905.

became a real possibility, a low-grade Parker could be put into the closet with no compromise on the dimensions, fit, weight, and balance of a new gun.

No such luck for me. Finding an AH to match my GH could prove to be a life's work. Accordingly, if another AAHE comes my way, I guess I'll be back where I was in September of '93, concerned that a once-in-a-lifetime gun may slip away for failure to act, but cautious not to act impulsively. At the $20,000 mark, a Parker collector ought to have a pretty good grip on where he is and where he's going with his collection. It's a lot easier to buy a Pigeon Gun than to sell one. With the number of zeros involved, upgrades and artificial patina of age can cast real or imagined doubt, and when in doubt, the inclination is to do nothing.

Quality AAH Pigeon Guns with extractors cost $400 in 1899 and $425 in 1908, with standard automatic ejectors. Quality AAHE cost $610 in 1920 and $687.50 when Parker Brothers published its last price list on January 1, 1934. By comparison, a Ford V-8 Sedan cost $695 in 1934, when my grandfather was an out-of-work butcher selling apples for five cents each on a Chicago street corner. If an AAHE ever comes looking for me, I'll be reminded of grandpa Thomsen's apples—how many to a bushel, how many bushels to a truckload, and how many truckloads to earn $687.50 at the depth of the Depression. At today's prices, a Pigeon Gun still costs about as much as a midsize Ford, and at ten dollars per bushel for pick-your-own apples, I would be a long time picking the more than two semi-truckloads it would take to buy a $20,000 shooter—how do you like dem apples?

(left) Parker Brothers ad from October 1929 issue of The Sportsman. *Notice the AAHE is no longer referred to as "Pigeon Gun" in Parker Brothers late 1920s advertising.*

QUALITY A
No. 1 SPECIAL

Parker Brothers 1920 pocket catalog description of Quality A No. 1 Special

In my own many years of gun collecting I have only seen one Parker A-1 Special, and that was offered by Stoeger in New York at the beginning of the War, sometime in early 1942.

Peter H. Johnson

Peter Johnson saw an A-1 Special at Stoegers when he was sixteen years old and still had it in his mind's eye nineteen years later when he wrote *Parker—America's Finest Shotgun.* Larry Baer thought that "... the A-1 Special was Parker's finest effort, and ... the epitome of side-by-side shotguns." Baer's photographs of the first A-1 Special, a 28-gauge "miniature prototype experimental gun," s/n 120,404, leave little to the imagination. His description, however, reinforced the adage that a picture is worth a thousand words:

> ... the [A-1 Special's] execution is as fine and flawless as ... I have ever seen on any shotgun, ... the gun has no equal, and was made following the tradition of the very finest of English craftsmanship and design ... [and] ... many of the most astute Parker authorities consider the Thom A-1 Special the finest Parker ever created.

I don't mean to claim I'm "astute," but Thom's A-1 Special is a gun I wouldn't mind owning (subject, of course, to hitting it big in the lottery). However, I've seen a number of A-1 Specials that have not engaged my interest as much as some other guns. Perhaps I can't identify with a collector gun that cost as

much as a house—then and now. But I think the real reason is that many of the A-1 Specials strike me as being overdone. My tastes favor subtle engraving rather than Gothic gouging. The miniature 28-gauge pictured in Parker's Pine Cone catalogs, for example, seems awful busy, while Thom's A-1 Special with fine English scroll pleases my sense of aesthetics. The Thom gun is *engraved*—there is engraving on the miniature 28-gauge. There's a difference. I'm not going to waste words on the nuances of A-1 Specials when color pictures tell the better story.

Shortly before I wrote this, I had the opportunity to go through a well-known Parker collection and spent too much time with a real neat PH .410 and a rare BHE half-frame. Another collector had an interesting AHE 20-gauge with the Invincible ruffed grouse on the bottom and two game scenes on each side (one is usual), but without the characteristic single rib (or "fence") behind the standing breech. Time passed quickly, and all too soon Forrest and Bill had to leave for another engagement. As I packed up my camera and notes, I realized I hadn't closely examined three A-1 Specials and a Pigeon Gun. Was this a Freudian slip? A hint of some tiny flaw in my collector psyche? An omission that might cause my hosts to wonder if I could find my way home? The day was saved as I did shoot off a roll of film, but perhaps I'm the only Parker collector on the face of the Earth who doesn't lust after an A-1 Special.

When I think of A grade and above, I think of art—not just my alter-ego Art du Bray hunting snipe in the swamps with his $400 AA Pigeon Gun, but an *objet d'art* with symmetry, balance, fit, and functional elegance, a gun to both covet and shoot. Tom Selleck (*Magnum P.I.*) owns some fine British shotguns (a pair of H&Hs and three Purdeys), but his true love is his 1928 Bentley 4.5-litre British Le Mans racer—an open-cockpit, helmet-and-goggles kind of car with a little windscreen. Selleck isn't a collector or racer but says he gets his pleasure from owning the car and "... having the nerve to drive it. If you buy an expensive thing and you never use it, I don't think there's a point... I've even driven it on the [L.A.] freeway to my offices."

Selleck's "comfort level" is such that driving his expensive Le Mans racer on the freeways makes sense to him. My comfort level is more along the lines of shooting a nice AH 12-gauge infrequently—this makes sense to me. An A-1 Special at upwards of $50,000, however, would likely be just another possession, and possessions that transcend function often come to possess the possessor. That's why I drive a Volvo and not a Bentley, and most likely will never own a Quality A No. 1 Special.

art. Every line of this magnificent gun appeals strongly to the discriminating gun lover. We offer the Invincible made to your specifications with each detail perfectly executed. Price $1,250.

America's
Finest Gun

Confidence in each *Triple Tested* Parker Gun to give the utmost in service, is the result of eighty years of ceaseless effort in design and production of high grade sporting arms. Each Parker Gun reflects this long standing leadership. Each is a triumph of quality.

INVINCIBLE

Parker Brothers serial number 200,000. The absence of hinge-pin recess and the British-style clips on the side of the standing breech are features specific to the Invincible.

Let me pay lip service to the Invincible, lest the reader think I have missed something important and thus cast doubt on all I have written. Conventional wisdom is that there are three Invincibles. I've seen recent pictures of three, but speculation about others persists. The first Invincible—s/n 200,000—was actually designated "PP Super Fine" in Parker Brothers' 1922 stock book, and was offered for sale (but not priced) in the 1926 through 1930 large Flying Geese catalogs. The first Invincible was (and is) a big gun with thirty-two-inch barrels, full and full, 14°-inch pull, and left the factory at seven pounds fourteen ounces. Larry Baer's story of the mysterious disappearance of s/n 200,000 is itself a mystery now that the gun is present and accounted for. Also, speculation that s/n 200,001 was also an Invincible has been debunked by access to the factory records. All the Parkers with s/n 199,998 through 200,004 are Trojans with the exception of the "PP Super Fine."

The second Invincible—s/n 230,329—is known as the Middleton gun. The remarkable story of this 16-gauge, semi-pistol-grip skeet gun was told in *Guns & Ammo*, May 1971. Apparently the first owner, A. C. Middleton (founder of the Old Victor Talking Machine Company), took delivery a few weeks before the stock-market crash in 1929. This Invincible is the storied "closet gun" found by a young physician who had purchased the late Mr. and Mrs. Middleton's twenty-five-room mansion. Fortunately the young doctor knew something about guns and, after three years of nervous possession and cost-conscious deliberation, decided that if he couldn't hunt with the gun, he might as well realize some cash. The gun changed hands several times and as of May 1971 was

owned by a dealer in Connecticut and had a $100,000 price tag. One can only speculate what such a gun would be worth today.

The third Invincible is a straight-gripped 12-gauge with twenty-six-inch barrels—s/n 233,565—built during the Depression. To my knowledge this gun lacks a story. It wasn't found in a closet and did not mysteriously disappear while on display in Minnesota. But if you think about it, behind every Parker gun there must be stories about the proud first owner, exploits afield or at the traps, widows selling guns for pennies on the dollar, and even how it changed hands in a poker game, as did a certain high-grade 11-gauge hammer gun I came to know recently.

You will notice I haven't pictured any of the Invincibles, or any guns with forty-inch barrels or left-eye-dominant stocks. My view is that they are all extravagant curios and not particularly good examples of the gunmaker's art. It seems to me the Invincibles have about as much to do with shooting as Fabergé eggs have to do with chickens. But just in case you should ever run across a high-grade Parker in your deceased uncle's closet, be sure to check the hinge pin—the characteristic spherical recess around the hinge pin on the Invincible grade is filled flush with the frame so that no part of the metal would lack engraving. Hope springs eternal, and should your search of the nooks and crannies, closets, and attic avail you only an unfired .410, well, we can't all be so lucky as that young physician in Moorestown, New Jersey, back in 1959, when he stumbled upon his once-in-a-lifetime gun. As I write this thirty-seven years after the fact, I wonder if he has ever once regretted the decision to sell. Of all the Parker grades, an Invincible would likely be the only gun easier to sell than buy.

Parker Brothers never advertised Invincible grade in magazines until about the time of the stock market crash in 1929, although the s/n 200,000 Invincible was pictured (but not priced) in the 1926, 1929, and 1930 large Flying Geese catalogs. This ad from the October 1929 issue of The Sportsman *is a classic example of poor timing. Ad courtesy of Lou Razek.*

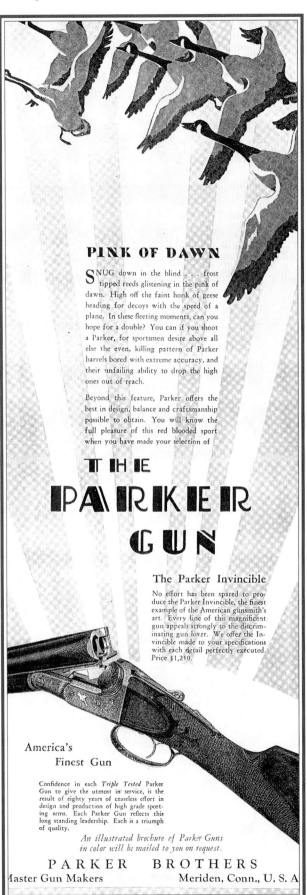

133

COLLECTING PARKER GUNS

The essence of gun collecting is the study and appreciation of fine guns. In other words, education is both the means and the end of collecting. With Parker shotguns, it also helps to have ample ready cash. Parker guns were never cheap, but in today's dollars, the "Old Reliable" is relatively underpriced. For example, at the turn of the century, Mason Premier Model decoys sold for twelve dollars a dozen while a Parker VH cost fifty dollars. Today it's not unusual for one Mason decoy in mint condition to cost as much as a mint Parker VH.

When it comes to collecting, Parker guns and Mason decoys have much in common. The rules of the game are the same, and most of the good ones are in the hands of collectors and dealers. The chance of finding a treasure-trove of original-paint Mason decoys in a boathouse or garage is about as likely as finding an unfired Parker Invincible in your deceased uncle's closet. In this context, education is not only desirable but mandatory. New Parker collectors will be buying from experienced collectors and dealers—and caveat emptor is the name of the game.

The chance of finding a decent collectible Parker at a sporting-goods store or local gun show is almost nil. Should you beat the odds and find a desirable gun, you will surely hear the plaintive cry of the casual and naive "dealer." "I've got more than that in it." Thus begins the education process; it's always easier to buy than sell. Get straight in your own mind whether you are building a collection or trying to buy below the market price to resell at a profit. If you think you have figured a way to buy Parkers low and sell them high, you can probably skip the rest of this chapter. My advice to a new *collector* is to keep reading and make the acquaintance of an established dealer who specializes in Parker guns, and the sooner the better. Also, try to find a mentor who isn't just trying to peddle his mistakes.

Buy low and sell high and if it doesn't go up don't buy.

Unknown

Parker Brothers "Benchmark" VHE 12-gauge Skeet showing 80% case colors and original barrel blue.

COLLECTING PHILOSOPHY: My wife was with me at a gun show last year, and she liked a Mason decoy on the table of a sports-memorabilia dealer. The asking price was seventy-five dollars. She didn't buy, but on the way home expressed second thoughts. I asked, "If you liked it, why didn't you buy it?" She said, "I don't know enough about decoys." And so the education process began, not with buying decoys but with reading books about decoy collecting in general and Mason decoys in particular. Reading books about decoy collecting helped us gain an educated point of view and develop a game plan. The pictures also helped with the philosophical and aesthetic issues of just what constitutes a genuine collector's item and folk art as contrasted to run-of-the-mill decoys. We

decided on quality rather than quantity, with an emphasis on Mason Factory birds.

At first we poked around antique malls and did our best to avoid the "fools-and-their-money-soon-parted" syndrome. Then we attended a large antique decoy show and sale at St. Charles, Illinois, and were amazed by the availability of excellent collectible decoys at reasonable prices, compared to what we had been seeing at the antique malls. We spent several days making the acquaintance of Mason dealers and met the authors of several books on Mason decoys. Meanwhile, we were scouting for the "benchmark bird" that would be as critical to our beginning collection of decoys as my "benchmark gun" was to Parker collecting.

BENCHMARK GUN: A hard fact of collecting is that it's always easier to buy than sell. The gun you buy at 80 percent case colors will invariably be appraised at 65 percent case colors, and the small scratch hardly noticed at buying time will take on the proportions of the Grand Canyon when your gun goes looking for a new home. Larry Baer, author of *The Parker Gun—An Immortal American Classic*, pronounced the first rule of Parker collecting: "It is always better to have one excellent gun than to have ten guns in average condition— original condition is most important. . . ."

Original condition is a beginning definition for what I call a "benchmark gun." Add good dimensions, unturned screws, and an original buttplate or pad, and we have a Parker that should increase in value over the years. Original *high* condition is the basic criterion for evaluating a collectible Parker. At a given price, it's always better to compromise grade rather than original condition. Good dimensions could be a tie-breaker. A Parker with thirteen-inch pull, four-inch drop, and thirty-four-inch barrels may be scarce but hardly qualifies as a desirable collector's item. High-grade engraving and high-percentage case colors will not redeem overall weirdness.

136

Anything short of a high-grade, original-condition gun with good dimensions is a compromise. The less you compromise on the purchase of your first Parker, the less likely you will make expensive compromises down the line. Remember, it's always easier to buy than sell.

My first benchmark gun was a circa 1908 VH 20-gauge. The gun was well cared for and had the appropriate patina of age and wear consistent with about 20 percent case colors. The screws were not visibly turned, and the gun appeared never to have been apart. This VH was a college education in what an original Parker should look like. I carried it to gun shows and gun dealers' showrooms to place alongside any prospective acquisition. I was like a bank teller using a worn but genuine $100 bill to search for counterfeits. Also, consider the pattern 3-D optical-illusion prints that are currently the vogue. If you look at them just the right way, you see dinosaurs or airplanes or whatever. My benchmark 20-gauge helped me to see other Parker guns in just the right way. Almost every gun I looked at turned out to be a trick on the eye or too good to be true or a "counterfeit" (i.e. refinished). I found it hard to buy another Parker. But it didn't matter; I had a Parker in absolutely original condition, and I could wait for a next gun that met my rather stringent test.

Another reason for a benchmark gun is that in the long run, the typical gun collection is not static. Early purchases are often sold or traded to finance later acquisitions, and original guns are always the better bargaining chip. However, almost every Parker collector I know regrets selling his first Parker. Larry Baer wrote about his regrets, and the occasional ad in the various gun publications gives a serial number and offers to buy back a "first Parker." One way to avoid selling your first gun is to have one that's worth keeping—that is, a benchmark gun in "drop-dead" original condition.

My benchmark 20-gauge more than paid for itself by keeping the fool and his money from being parted. As collecting progressed, my focus narrowed to straight-grip, good-dimension Parker twelves with high original condition. These guns are a pleasure to own and shoot, and my collecting dollars stretch farther with 12-gauge. The value of an original-condition gun was recently demonstrated when I easily traded my VH 20-gauge for an excellent CHE Damascus 12-gauge after I bought a benchmark VHE 12-gauge Skeet with much higher original condition. The VHE Skeet acquisition involved a bit of luck, as I was able to trade two common VHs plus some cash for one extremely desirable gun. From my standpoint, I wholesaled two shooters for about what I had in them, then added $1,000 to own a $3,500 collector's item. From the dealer's standpoint, he put $1,000 "profit" in the register and swapped a well-bought VHE Skeet for two VHs of roughly equivalent wholesale value—a good deal for all concerned.

Pᴀʀᴛɪɴɢ ᴡɪᴛʜ Cᴀsʜ: Money is almost always a limiting factor. It's better to stretch the budget once or a few times over a collecting career to buy a quality gun than to "bottom-feed" on every common Parker that comes along. Not all Parker guns are collector's items, and even the very best are poor collateral for a bank loan. A real question is how to finance your Parker collecting habit. You may need to talk to your banker about a ready line of credit as most dealers' "credit terms" are "cash on the barrel head." Some major dealers do offer a three-month layaway with 25 percent down; but if you can't pay cash, are unwilling or unable to borrow from your own bank, and don't expect to get possession of the gun 'til three months hence, then maybe you should adopt what I call the "sour-grapes defense" (see Chapter 7 *re:* the Quality A No. 1 Special). At any rate, you must make decisions about your likes and dislikes and concentrate effort in the direction of your real area of interest. The purchase of a mediocre gun today could impair your financial ability to acquire a once-in-a-lifetime Parker tomorrow. Study and shop around, buy selectively, and buy your benchmark gun.

Parker Brothers ad from October 1930 issue of Field and Stream. *Notice prices run from $55 for Trojan grade to $1,250 for Invincible.*

Don't consider your Parker gun collection as an "investment." If investment is your game, I suggest you talk to Merrill Lynch rather than Herschel Chadick. Quality Parker guns have appreciated over the years, but so has everything else. Also, the typical collector has reverse leverage in that he usually buys at retail and sells at wholesale. Case in point: Parker Brothers' Invincible grade sold for $1,250 in the early 1930s. Suppose your rich uncle had bought s/n 200,000, put it in his closet unfired, and you inherited the gun in 1996. Further assume it's worth $250,000 retail and that you could net $200,000 after the gun was brokered to one of the select few Parker collectors who could afford the price. This may be a windfall; but was it a good investment?

The Invincible would have been a good investment if your uncle's alternative was to put his money in bonds at 6.5 percent compound interest in 1933. This works out to an average of 2 percent above the inflation rate, and you would have inherited about $60,000 in principal and accrued interest. However, the same $1,250 invested in the S & P 500 would have a share value of about $70,000 in 1996, and your uncle could have spent dividends of $27,500 during his lifetime. That Invincible is still looking pretty good. But assume for a moment that your rich uncle didn't get rich by being unimaginative. Assume he put his $1,250 into well-known but somewhat speculative Coca-Cola stock. He could have spent the $150,000 of dividends and still passed on shares valued at $900,000 to his favorite nephew. But Coca-Cola was *speculative,* you say. Then assume he bought "blue chip" Standard Oil of New Jersey. If your rich uncle had put his money with the Rockefellers rather than with Parker Brothers and reinvested his dividends, your Exxon inheritance would be $3,125,000. Remember, those "investments" in the gun safe produce no product and pay no dividends or interest.

If, against all financial advice, a prospective collector decides to part with his hard-earned dollars, let me suggest this: buy the best original-condition, good-dimension, lower-grade Parker that you can get for the money you have. Save your money and be patient. Study and seek advice, particularly if that advice comes from one of the larger dealers specializing in Parker guns. Go to the dealer with pre-established parameters and a willingness to *not* buy unless you can find a gun to your liking. Established dealers have too much at stake to try to stick you with a bad gun. They want your repeat business.

Larry Baer wrote that ". . . It is best for the average fellow to start with a nice V grade, 12 gauge and work his way up to better guns. Most Parkers are expensive and a good VH 12 gauge is currently . . . [1974] . . . bringing from $150 to $450 for an excellent original gun." Moving ahead twenty years, the largest dealer in Parker guns is Chadick's, Ltd., and Herschel Chadick typically shows twenty to forty Parkers on his gun list, with high turnover. An example of what I call a benchmark gun appeared on Chadick's winter 1994 gun list, as follows:

Parker Bros. V.H. 12 ga., 28" F/F. Splinter fore-end, double triggers, P/G, dogshead buttplate. 95% orig. case colors, 99% orig. blue and stock finish. Beautiful!...................$2,450

By comparison, an ejector gun was offered on the same list for the same price:

Parker Bros. V.H.E. 12 ga., 30" F/F, 1½ frame. Splinter fore-end, double triggers, P/G, dogshead buttplate, 85% bright, orig. case colors, 99% blue. Perfect dimensions. A real gem in great condition $2,450

First, let's read between the lines. The VHE ad says "99% blue" but doesn't say *original*. Simply representing a gun as having 99 percent barrel-blue doesn't warrant the bluing to be original. This may account for the *ejector* VHE selling for the same price as the *extractor* VH. Notice that one gun is represented as having "original" blue and

stock finish and being "beautiful!" The other gun's description is less specific: "A real gem in great condition." These subtle differences have a considerable impact on price. My predisposition would be to "trade-up" 10 percent incremental case colors for extractors as I have no love affair with ejectors. However, a prudent buyer would be wise to inspect and compare both guns before making a decision. The UPS cost for two guns shipped and one gun returned is a drop in the bucket compared to not getting the better gun for your hard-earned cash.

Either gun could have been an excellent start to a collection. Both sold within ninety days. One might fairly conclude that the 1974 price of $450 for an excellent original 12-gauge VH (per Larry Baer) inflated to $2,450 by 1994. I think this is typical. However, guns haven't paid dividends or interest for twenty years, and a $450 investment made in 1974 ought to be worth $2,450 in 1995, just to break even. The rewards of collecting are not necessarily financial.

QUALITY OR QUANTITY: Better guns will usually increase in value, and even if you paid too much, you are less likely to lose money when you sell a quality gun. But what is quality? My definition of quality is a higher-grade Parker gun in original condition with good dimensions that looks as if it has never been apart. Higher grade is a relative term (VH versus Trojan, for example) but generally needs a deeper pocket; or it could involve tradeoffs in originality, condition, and dimensions. I'm not willing to compromise original condition and good dimensions simply to acquire a higher grade, but I don't consider 80 percent case colors to be much of a compromise. Opinions differ. Every collector needs to know his likes and dislikes. Define an area of interest and zero in, but don't be too restrictive. I passed up an excellent once-in-a-lifetime CHE twelve at a price I could afford simply because it had a pistol

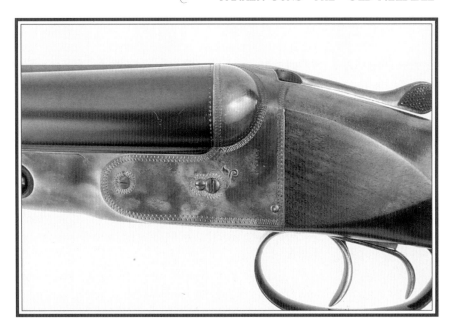

Parker VHE 12-gauge half-frame with 99% case colors going brown. Notice the extra little flourish behind the screws. Some would consider this a "Friday gun" (it was 4:00 PM and the engraver went a little overboard on the gun at hand, rather than start another project before the week-end). Maybe not, but it's small details like this that add collector interest and value.

grip. I allowed my straight-grip preference to let a good one get away. A collector should be flexible so that he is at once refining and expanding his collection.

The serious collector should set his sights on a particular category and begin to acquire a few choice guns. This would parallel Nancy's and my experience with Mason decoys. We decided we wanted a quality collection rather than a simple accumulation of numbers. We don't intend to keep everything forever, but we're not interested in buying simply to resell. As new collectors of Mason decoys, we reconciled ourselves to be retail purchasers, knowing that the most dollars spent seldom equate to the best investment. We began to educate ourselves by getting alongside knowledgeable Mason decoy people, and we gained valuable insight and firsthand experience by window-shopping at various antique decoy shows. We became "friends" with a number of knowledgeable and honest experts in the field. Decoy collecting thrives on new collectors, and we traded on our "new faces" to move ourselves along the learning curve.

The result of the process was a Mason Premier bluebill hen in original paint, minus some honest in-use wear and tear, and exhibiting the appropriate patina of age. This is our benchmark bird. We paid $625, and could have sold the bluebill the day we bought it for a slight profit. The real profit, however, has been that it sits at a conspicuous location in our home as a constant visual reminder of how an original-paint Mason decoy ought to look. Every future acquisition needs to pass the test of being as good as or better than our bluebill hen. This limits our opportunities to part with hard-earned cash, and we aren't likely to accumulate a room full of $300 mistakes. Using my own advice, I have never sold a Parker at a loss, although I probably have never beat the Consumer Price Index either.

UPGRADES: A new Parker enthusiast may zero in on high grade while compromising original condition. Many collectors don't mind buying restored guns, and the work of Del Grego, Runge, and Turnbull is beyond reproach. Certain high-grade guns are being advertised as upgrades while, sorry to say, there are guns that have been upgraded which are misrepresented as original. But in my opinion, the reproductions, upgrades, and fakes fall outside the definition of true collector guns. The jury is still out on the very subjective issue of Parkers that have been restored, refurbished, or refinished; and there is a quantum difference between re-blued barrels and recut checking or engraving.

I recently attended a gun show in a rather dimly lit armory. A dealer called my attention to an AHE with ventilated rib and did *not* represent it to be an upgrade, although, to be fair, he didn't certify it to be an untouched original either. Holding the gun to the best light available (bad light sells bad guns), I noticed a slight dip on the surface of the rib where *Acme* was engraved. Apparently vent ribs were not rigid enough to support the pressure from a roll-stamp. Most of the VRs I have seen have the Parker name, barrel steel, and "Meriden, Conn." engraved on the rib. It seemed to me the four-letter *Acme* was stretched to fill a gap that could have held seven letters (such as "Titanic"). This slight "defect" was a sufficient detraction from an expensive gun that no price reduction could have rekindled my interest. On the other hand, if the gun was in fact an upgrade and was honestly represented as such, I'm sure it would eventually find a happy new home at a fair price. It was beautiful—in a Michael Jackson sort of way.

Big Bore—Small Bore:
When Parker guns were in current production, a .410 or 28-gauge cost the same as a twelve. Not so today. Then, as now, there was small demand and little use for small bores, which are, in the immortal words of Colonel Charles Askins, ". . . A dread crippler, a toy and not a tool, . . . a scatter gun that does not pack enough powder to blow your nose." Nevertheless, small bores are a novelty and popular with some collectors.

If you are intent on playing the small-bore game, then the ordinary rules for collecting Parkers don't apply—just bring money. Small bores are expensive. Using DH grade at 90 percent case colors as an example, a 28-gauge will typically sell for twice and a .410 for seven times the price of a comparable 12-gauge.

Short supply is the reason for the high price. However, small bores are in short supply because they weren't popular when they were new. Now they are expensive because they were previously unpopular. Who can figure? I should mention that I do own a real nice Winchester Model 42, and the right Parker 28-gauge or 20-gauge will someday find its way to my gun safe. But for now, 12-gauge is my focus.

As an aside, my Model 42 has full choke, and when I'm shooting real good from sixteen yards at regulation trap, my .410 breaks sixteen or seventeen of twenty-five clay birds while my VHE Skeet breaks twenty-one or twenty-two; my GH hunting gun, twenty-two or twenty-three; and my DHE Trap, twenty-three or twenty-four, and once, but only once, twenty-five straight. More on small bores versus big bores in Chapter 13—"Figures Lie and Liars Figure."

Pitfalls: The average collector seldom has the short-term chance to buy low and sell high. On the other hand, the average collector doesn't have dealer overhead. Please be advised that people who make their living buying and selling expensive guns cannot acquire inventory at *blue book* prices and stay in business. I mean *Blue Book of Gun Values* by S. P. Fjestad (the seventeenth edition was current in 1996). Though other publications attempt to price Parker guns, the *Blue Book* is the most authoritative, with dated serial numbers to age guns and color pictures to help evaluate case colors. Although major dealers doing volume Parker business establish the published values, the new collector should be aware that *Blue Book* prices are not written on a tablet of stone.

My experience has been that a bona-fide dealer can pay 75 percent of *Blue Book* if he expects the gun to move out of inventory reasonably soon. Dealer profit is made at point of purchase. Occasionally the well-bought gun is reduced to improve cash flow, but a

Parker Brothers ad from June 1921 issue of Outdoor Life. *Parker built guns at the rate of about 4,000 per year during the 1920s, but gun works production peaked at approximately 7,000 annually just after the turn of the century. If there was a pinch, it was probably a shortage of skilled labor rather than plant facilities and machinery.*

dealer with an extremely high-condition Parker will try to bump the preestablished price upward. These are facts of life. A new collector who thinks he's going to build a collection by prying good guns loose from reputable and established dealers below *Blue Book* value is guilty of wishful thinking. On the other hand, I bought a mint, unfired Trojan 12-gauge with hanging tags and origi- nal box from a well-known dealer in June 1995 for $2,000. The *Blue Book* showed the gun alone to be a $2,200 item. *C'est la vie!*

The other side of the equation is that a small-time collector with a few good guns will find them difficult to sell at *Blue Book* value. Restrictive gun laws and a thin and scattered collector market are hard for the non-federally licensed (FFL) seller to over- come. The best advice for a small collector is to *minimize the need to sell.* Good lower- grade guns can be traded up for higher grades with cash to boot. Guns lacking high original condition are generally harder to sell or trade. This can be seen at gun shows, where someone is always trying to peddle the odd Parker at an exaggerated price.

Too many gun-show "dealers" are, in reality, retail purchasers trying to squeeze a profit out of a gun for which they paid too much. I recall a dealer from a southern state who traveled to a northern-Illinois gun show to try to sell Damascus Parkers. He had an inventory list showing he owned approximately 140 such guns. The twenty guns on his table were hopelessly over- priced. It should have been apparent to him that if he could acquire 140 Damascus Parkers, they weren't scarce. None of his "wall-hangers" could be called better than NRA Fair—most were "post-pounders" or worse. Nevertheless, his prices were out of sight. He commented that he had not received even one offer and was pretty fed up with the quality of the *buyers* at the show. I bit my lip to no avail. I tried to explain that Parker built almost a quarter-million shotguns and a Parker gun, *per se*, isn't rare. High original condition is rare, and con- dition is everything, particularly with wall-hanger Damascus guns. This dealer wasn't interested in an education and vowed to keep his guns forever rather than sell them at a loss. My recollection is that the gross price he had paid divided by all the guns on his inventory list equaled a cost of $585 for the only gun I could use. I felt I could pay no

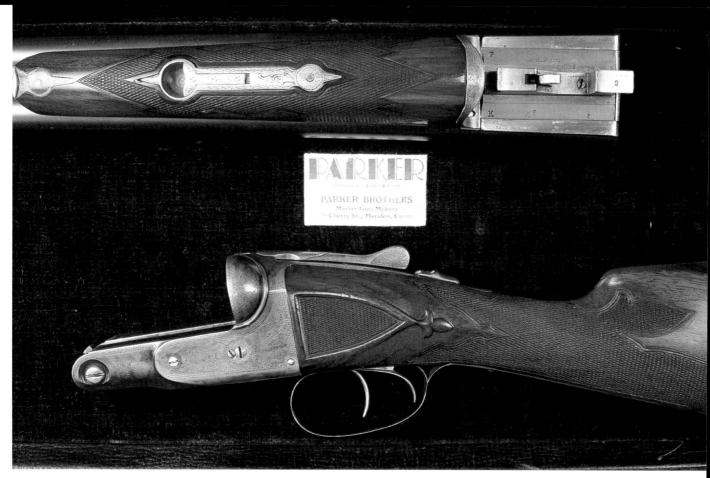

(top) Vintage Parker Brothers BH(E) with non-factory retrofit ejectors in black leather carrying case which adds collector value. Number 2 on the barrel lug denotes frame size. Case label is late 1920s style, while gun is circa 1896.

(bottom) Parker Brothers DHE 12-gauge Trap showing its 70% case colors in good company. The Mason Premier bluebill hen "benchmark bird" has original paint minus some in-use wear and tear.

Chadick's, Ltd. is the Parker venue of choice in Terrell, Texas. Herschel, America's best known Parker dealer, and his wife Bette are on the right. Tom Chapman is a former Browning gunsmith and can cure what ails wood or metal. Tricia Wilson keeps things running smoothly while Herschel's buying and selling and Tom's a fixin'. Author has spent up to three full days at Chadick's absorbing the ambiance — and I've bought a few guns. Photo by Charlie Jandrew Photography.

Checkered (or "checked") butt on author's VHE skeet gun. Rare special features like this add value from the collector's point of view. Less than 5 percent of collector guns have this special-order buttstock treatment.

(top) As the leaves start to turn, a serious hunter's thoughts turn to . . . what do you do with a four-ten? Well, this particular Parker PH .410 is handled with respect due a collector's item, which until just recently was believed not to exist. Rumor has it there may be two others, but for now, this neat little gun may be the rarest Parker of all.

Author's bargain wall-hanger. This field-grade gun has twist barrels and the engraving looks to be roll stamped rather than cut by an engraver. Collecting Parker hammer guns is a special area of interest. Excellent Damascus guns sometimes command prices approaching modern hammerless guns of comparable grade and finish, but are still a chancy investment compared to a high original condition, good dimension shooter.

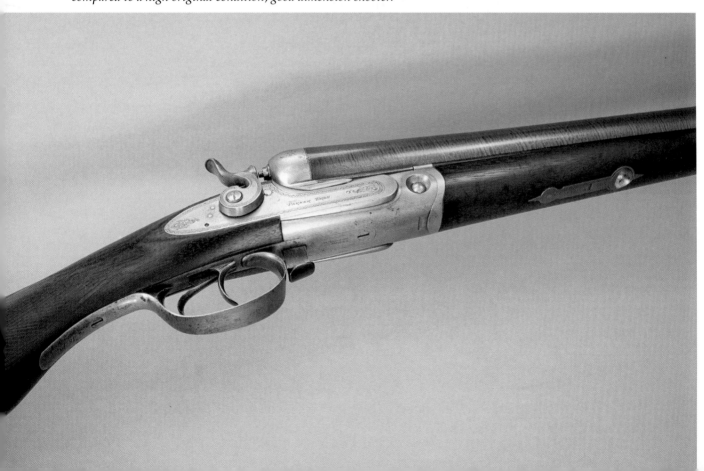

Parker Brothers circa 1881 12-gauge hammer gun s/n 18,110. The "wall-hanger" was purchased by author at a major gun show from a well-known dealer for $225 and cleaned up. Keith Kearcher "browned" the barrels back to 100 percent, and, all things considered, the author's out-of-pocket expenses for this gun are under $400. Not all Parker collector guns cost a small fortune.

more than $400 for the gun, and then only because it was a straight-grip, fishtail PH twelve that I could clean up to fill a niche in my collection. When I offered $400, he predictably said, "I've got more than that in it," and I caught a few bits and pieces about my ancestors as I made my getaway.

It can be as much a pitfall of collecting to fail to buy a good gun as to buy a bad gun. However, it's one thing to lament a missed opportunity and quite another to own a gun that is an ever-present reminder of past mistakes. The way to avoid such pitfalls is to get smarter sooner. Have a collecting philosophy with established goals, and buy only what you like within pre-established (but not inflexible) parameters. And remember, one high-grade collector gun is more appreciated and is easier to care for, store, and ultimately sell than are ten "yes buts." Get on the mailing list of dealers specializing in Parker guns; attend quality gun shows; and periodically check the ads in the *Gun List, Gun Journal*, and the *Double Gun Journal*. With forbearance and perseverance, you may assemble a significant collection of high-grade Parkers that will someday find a ready market at 75 percent of *Blue Book*—and your widow will appreciate your diligence.

SUPPLY-SIDE ECONOMICS

In the summer of '94, I spent three hot days in Terrell, Texas, sorting through Parker shotguns at Chadick's, Ltd. I bought a DHE 12-gauge Trap with good dimensions, 70 percent case colors, and 99 percent barrel-blue. Herschel Chadick described the gun on his list as ". . . excellent condition and *very* rare!" We discussed just what constitutes a rare Parker gun. Apparently my new acquisition achieved "rare" status because of a factory ventilated rib. High condition, beavertail fore-end, and straight grip also set this gun apart, but not every Parker is a rare collector's item. After all, Parker Brothers and Remington built at least 242,387 Parker guns over approximately seventy-five years.

As I wrote my check, Herschel volunteered that my DHE was the kind most collectors are looking for—a good-dimension, shootable, original gun in excellent condition. He believes, however, that *real* collectors look for the scarce gun. I guess a real collector would have spent the same money as 25 percent down on a three-month layaway for a VHE .410 in comparable condition. Different strokes for different folks!

After returning home and running twenty-five birds at trap with my new DHE, I decided to do some research into just what constitutes a rare Parker collector's item. If the true measure of collectibility is escalating prices, then forget about Parker guns. Parker catalogs were giveaway items when published and are now selling for hundreds of dollars (more about "Parker Paper" in Chapter 10). Meanwhile, most Parker guns have had a hard time keeping pace with inflation.

The beginning point in my quest for enlightenment as to the supply (and imputed scarcity) of Parker guns was Peter Johnson's book, *Parker—America's Finest Shotgun*. This book has been the first and basic source of Parker knowledge since the early 1960s. Unfortunately, Johnson was an enthusiast rather than an experienced Parker researcher and collector. Johnson lists the percentage of a normal year's production occupied by each grade—for example, Trojan, 40 percent, and Vulcan, 25

If all of the world's economists were placed end to end, they would never reach a conclusion.

Common Knowledge

The PARKER GUN

Ruffed Grouse

As full of tricks as a barrel of monkeys, this bird. Study its habits and feeding places and, above all, learn to be fast with your gun. Breaking the clay birds on the rise at close range is good practice for this.

Photo from Keystone Co.

The "Old Reliable"

Spiral Top Lever Springs

A strong spiral spring set snugly in a housing. Positive lever action always assured.

PERFECT BALANCE and quick, sure-firing mechanism make the Parker an especially desirable gun for fast work in the field or at the traps.

Parker Guns have earned the name "Old Reliable" by fifty years of unfailing performance.

This is because, from rough forging and stock block to final pattern test, every detail of Parker manufacture receives the individual attention of master workmen.

Send for the Parker Booklet

PARKER BROTHERS
Master Gun Makers
32 Cherry Street, Meriden, Conn., U. S. A.

Parker Brothers ad from August 1924 issue of National Sportsman. *Notice the spiral top-lever spring fits in a capsule. This way, if the spring breaks it will continue to be effective until a gunsmith can make it right.*

percent—and claimed that ". . . in normal years, about 4,000 guns were made." Johnson was long on stated facts and conjecture but short on footnotes and attribution, so we need an educated guess as to which years were "normal."

A close reading of Johnson's book shows he interviewed Charles S. Parker, who, according to Johnson, was in the shop in 1926 and president in 1928. (According to contemporary news accounts, Charles S. actually became president of The Charles Parker Company in 1932.) Johnson also spoke to H. L. Carpenter, Parker's long-time office manager until the move to Ilion, New York, in 1938. The serialization of Parker shotguns in Baer's book, *The Parker Gun—An Immortal American Classic*, and Fjestad's *Blue Book of Gun Values* (seventeenth edition), shows that Parker Brothers built roughly 40,000 guns during the 1920s or about 4,000 per year—right on, Mr. Johnson!

However, the production percentages cited by Johnson are likely those that prevailed *only* during the 1920s. It should be obvious that Trojan grade wasn't 40 percent of production prior to 1913. Likewise, before the Trojan was introduced in 1913, the Vulcan grade's percent of production must have been considerably higher than its 25 percent of production during the 1920s. Johnson hedged his production figures with the *caveat* that ". . . it should be emphasized . . . [my] . . . figures are only estimates and may, in some cases, be wide of the mark." Unfortunately, most writers didn't take Johnson's warning seriously, and his highly suspect figures are often quoted as the Gospel truth in efforts to impute relative scarcity of Parker collector guns.

For example, add up the hammerless production as shown in a recent *Blue Book*, and you might conclude that over 217,000 hammerless Parkers were built. Wrong! Factory records show that approximately 56,000 Parker hammer guns were built before the

Parker Brothers circa 1912 D grade hammer gun s/n 156,982 with Titanic fluid steel barrels.

1888 introduction of the H models. Simple arithmetic shows that a maximum of 186,000 Parker guns (not 217,000) were made after the first hammerless. A significant number would have been post-1888 hammer guns, of which Johnson claims roughly 10,000 were built. Also, there were Single Barrel Trap Guns beginning in 1916, and a significant number of hammerless Damascus-barrel guns built after 1888 and as late as 1927. Parker catalogs of the early 1920s offered Damascus barrels on grades GH-DH-CH, and a Damascus VHE, s/n 227,XXX, with "overload proved" on the barrel flats, was recently offered for sale by Chadick's, Ltd. The highest-serial-number hammer gun I have seen is 156,XXX, a circa 1912 DH grade with Titanic steel barrels.

In the final analysis, Parker guns are rare if you can't find what you're looking for. I distinguish *rare* from *scarce*. The easiest way to create a scarce gun is to build one that nobody wants. A Damascus VHE wasn't popular in 1927, and there doesn't seem to be any catalog evidence that Parker ever built the Vulcan grade with Damascus barrels. This gun is scarce and unquestionably original, but the jury is out on whether it's a *rare collector's item*. Small-bore Parkers weren't popular when they were in production, even though .410s and 28s were priced the same as 12-gauge models. Now the sky is the limit on high- grade small-bore "rare" guns. I would rather pay $15,000 for an excellent AHE twelve as a genuine example of high gunmaker art than marvel at the absence of embellishments on a scaled-down VHE for the same money. Again, different strokes for different folks!

My research into just what constitutes a rare collectible Parker abandoned published but obviously suspect production figures and focused instead on current market availability. (The soon-to-be-published production records won't change my analysis as present-day availability doesn't necessarily correlate to built-gun figures.) The first step in my search for a nice DHE was to go through all the back issues of the *Double Gun Journal* (*DGJ*) to get a feel for the type of guns that had been available over the prior five years. This disclosed a threshold issue—just how complete and accurate are the descriptions of the guns offered for sale? A person could spend much time and money shipping guns back and forth when one man's "99 percent blue" is another man's "reblued." Likewise, a seller's "90 percent overall condition" could be a "trace of case colors" to the buyer, with obvious difficulties in agreeing which percent-of-condition column in the *Blue Book* serves as a beginning point to properly value the gun. Much can be said for going in person to see a significant number of sale guns rather than passively waiting for one or two to arrive by UPS.

Probably the biggest help in the search for my DHE was advice from the immortal Willie Sutton. Mr. Sutton would be long forgotten had he not responded to a news reporter's question, "Mr. Sutton, why do you rob banks?" with, "Because that's where the money is!" My *DGJ* research listed 145 DH and DHE Parkers that had been advertised over the prior five years. Twenty guns caught my eye. Of these, Chadick's had offered eleven. Accordingly, I took Willie Sutton's advice and headed for Texas—with good results.

Later I decided to do a comprehensive study of recent Parker ads for all the grades. I thought that ads in the *DGJ* should be representative of the universe of better Parker guns currently available. To test this premise, I reviewed all the advertising in issues 1-1 (winter 1989) through 5-2 (summer 1994), and prepared a detailed list of 520 Parker side-by-sides for sale over the prior five years. I could have expanded my universe by using the *Gun List* and *Gun Journal* (*Shotgun News* is a misnomer and of little or no interest to Parker collectors); however, I wanted to avoid duplications that would tend to overstate the number of guns available. The cost and delay of quarterly advertising in the *DGJ* tend to exclude ads for less-expensive, lower-grade shooters. The *Gun List* with its relatively inexpensive biweekly classified advertising tends to attract more VHs and Trojans. My methodology, in effect, drew a line under the "collector market" at about $1,000 for Trojans; $1,500 for VHs, PHs, and GHs; and $2,000 for DHs. I did my best to exclude guns that showed up repeatedly in certain dealers' advertising. In doing so, I was enlightened as to how rapidly some dealers turn inventory by reducing the price on slow-moving guns while other dealers hang on to obviously overpriced guns forever.

The following chart shows the results of my bean-counting. The surprise *rarest* Parker is the PH with Parker-steel barrels. According to my research, a wealthy collector would find it

520 PARKER GUNS OFFERED FOR SALE IN THE DOUBLE GUN JOURNAL
1989-1994

	T	VH	PH	GH	DH	CH	BH	AH	AAH	AIS
Guns[1]	29	176	6	61	145	21	41	12	19	10
Percent[2]	5.6	33.8	1.2	11.7	27.9	4.0	7.9	2.3	3.7	1.9
Ejector(%)	0	65	67	77	95	86	90	100	100	100
Extractor	100[3]	35	33	23	5	14	10	0	0	0
12 Ga. (%)	38[4]	40	66	40	43	43	53	33	58	70
16 Ga. (%)	28	15	0	13	16	10	15	17	10	10
20 Ga. (%)	34	22	34	23	26	24	20	42	32	20
28 Ga. (%)	0	15	0	16	12	19	10	8	0	0
410 (%)	0	8	0	8	3	4	2	0	0	0
SST (%)	0	24	0	25	30	33	29	75	26	60
DHBP (%)	0	50	50	44	0	0	0	0	0	0
SSBP (%)	0	0	0	0	31	48	46	50	63	70
CK (%)	0	6	0	8	4	5	2	0	0	0
BTFE (%)	0	20	17	25	24	24	22	33	11	20
SG (%)	0	19	33	15	23	24	39	33	21	0
VR (%)	0	1	0	3	10	0	10	25	5	20
BBL 32 (%)	0	3	16	8	13	16	24	0	13	13
BBL 30 (%)	16	16	50	28	36	26	32	15	48	75
BBL 28 (%)	68	38	16	33	29	21	30	31	22	12
BBL 26 (%)	16	41	16	28	22	37	11	46	17	0

NOTES: (1) Total of 520 Parker Guns offered for sale.
(2) Totals 100% of 520 guns.
(3) All Trojans have extractors—100% = 29 guns.
(4) Eleven Trojans were 12-gauge = 38%.

Note: Three guns were 10-gauge, one gun an 8-gauge. Two guns had 24" barrels, three guns had 34" barrels, one had 36" barrels, and one had 38" barrels. None of these are shown on the chart.

Guns advertised as "made" or "upgrade" are not included on this chart.

easier to acquire an A-1 Special than to find *any* collectible PH grade. The rarest of the rare is a PH .410, s/n 218,479, reputed to be but one of three .410s in PH grade. The introduction of the .410 and the discontinuation of PH grade were almost simultaneous. A-1 Specials were expensive, well-owned, and well-cared-for, so high condition is assumed, while PH grade typically suffered heavy use associated with a low-grade shooter. Although it's unlikely that first owners considered their PH "shooters" to be family heirlooms, this grade with fluid-steel barrels now appears to be the rarest of all Parkers—Invincibles being beyond the scope of this discussion.

The chart of 520 Parker guns offered for sale in the *Double Gun Journal* could lead an inquiring mind to the following conclusions:

Collector-quality Trojans are grossly under-represented relative to the number produced. However, from a buyer's standpoint, there seems to be no real scarcity of high-condition guns, so it doesn't matter which of the conflicting claims about the number of Trojans built is correct. Johnson claims 50,000, while Baer and the *Blue Book* claim 48,000. If you apply Johnson's 40 percent production percentage to Baer's post-1913 serialization, the number is more like 32,000. Parker advertised that 2,000 Trojans were to be built in 1926, about half of the year's production. Even assuming Trojans were built at the rate of 2,000 per year from introduction in 1913 until the last year of full production in 1930, the number of Trojans built could certainly not exceed 35,000, but few are now in truly collectible condition.

The chart shows that VH and DH grades constitute over 60 percent of collector guns on the market. My recent purchase of a DHE Trap and a VHE Skeet—at prices approximating new reproduction guns—leads me to believe that good-dimension, high-condition examples of these grades are not scarce if you follow Willie Sutton's advice.

Tracking down a good GH or GHE Parker is relatively difficult, but if you have a decent D grade, the issue could be moot. Likewise, CH and CHE Parkers are genuinely scarce, but it takes a practiced eye to distinguish a C from a D grade. Apparently this lack of identity has prevailed since the

Parker Brothers ad from February 1923 issue of Hunter-Trader-Trapper, showing a Trojan grade with "false" doll's head rib extension.

days of manufacture and accounted for the relatively few fluid-steel-barrel C grades built. Quality BH and BHE Parkers are easy enough to find, but restoration of higher grades starts to be a problem for purist collectors. My chart includes restorations but excludes stated upgrades. Parker collector and restoration artist Oscar Gaddy discovered recently that the arrows on the barrel ribs correlate to grade and thus generated a flurry of rib checking by owners of "restored" high-grade guns.

Quality AH and AHE Parkers are nowhere near as prevalent as Pigeon Guns and not much more available than A-1 Specials. To be fair, we're talking about a nominal number of guns on the market over five years. However, my numbers are difficult to reconcile with the *Blue Book* claim that 5,500 AHEs were produced as against 340 AAHEs. I believe the number of post-fluid-steel-barrel A grades may be overstated by a factor of as much as ten. Perhaps the issue will be clarified if and when the Parker production records at the Remington Arms Museum in Ilion, New York, are published.

About half of the collector-quality VH-PH-GH guns have the dog's-head buttplate. Roughly one-third of the DH grade and half of CH-BH-AH grades have skeleton steel buttplates, which show up in escalating percentages on the AAHEs and A-1 Specials. Approximately 5 percent of grades VH through BH have a checkered (checked) butt. My focus is English-style guns, and it seems the straight grip is advertised about 25 percent of the time. Beavertail fore-ends are found on 20 to 25 percent of grades VH and above. Ventilated ribs are extremely rare as they were introduced late in Parker Brothers' production. A limitation to my statistics is that some of the advertising is overly brief and may fail to mention all the value-added features. For example, the ad for one of the A-1 Specials on my chart adds nothing but 12-gauge to the data.

A high percentage of Parker guns were built with twenty-eight-inch and thirty-inch barrels. However, the most available barrel length for the Vulcans in my sample is twenty-six inches. It's hard to understand why a collector should pay the *Blue Book-* suggested 20 percent premium for a VH or VHE with twenty-six-inch barrels. Scanning the data on other grades, it seems twenty-six-inch barrels are no less available than twenty-eight- or thirty-inch barrels. After my statistics were published in the *DGJ*, some collectors rationalized that the twenty-six-inch barrel results were skewed by post-manufacture hacksawing. I don't think so. I went back over my original data, and most (if not all) of the ad text and prices seemed consistent with original, unaltered guns. A few may have slipped by, but certainly not enough to distort the results of my survey.

It should be no surprise that 12-gauge dominates and 20s are a distant second. However, 16-gauge and 28-gauge are almost equally available. If scarcity is the test, it would seem prices for 16s and 28s should be about the same. Obviously this isn't the case. Colonel Askins explained the disparity when he equated the popularity of the 16-gauge with death and taxes. Also, the 28-gauge owes some of its cachet to the "Skeeters" and the rumor that it mysteriously shoots better than a peashooter should. Although .410s are truly scarce, any collector who really wants one usually has no problem finding a decent VH grade as these micro-bore guns seem to have a high turnover. However, the one known PH .410 is well-owned and not likely to come on the market soon. Higher-grade .410s have collector interest that transcends the small holes in the barrel tubes, but soon after collector-friends of mine have been amazed by the dollars paid for a diminutive under-embellished Parker VH, these smallest of the small bores often have gone back on the market. After you've savored a one-of-a-kind

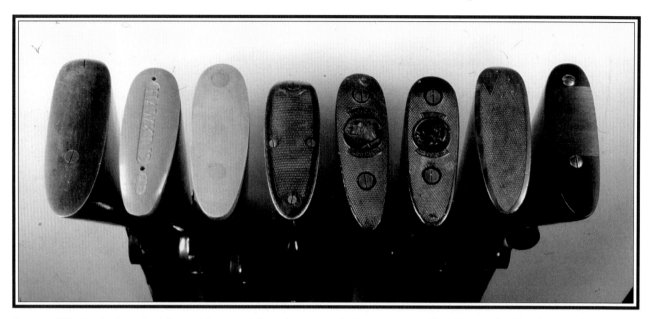

Range of Parker buttstocks left to right: steel buttplate on early hammer gun; Hawkins pad; Silver's pad; skelton steel buttplate (early version); dog's head buttplate (early and late version); checked butt, and Trojan buttplate.

PH .410, BHE half-frame twelve, AHE 20-gauge, or AAHE Pigeon Gun, you'll tend to put it back in the gun safe to be enjoyed another day.

One final observation: a disproportionate number of Parker shotguns (with the exception of the Trojan) came with automatic ejectors. Of 176 lowly Vulcans in my survey, roughly two-thirds have AEs. (Note—that figure would be more like 50/50 had I included the *Gun List* classifieds in my sample.) Ninety-five percent of the DH grade have ejectors. I question why ejectors are a value add-on (*Blue Book* adds 40 percent for a DHE), when a DH with

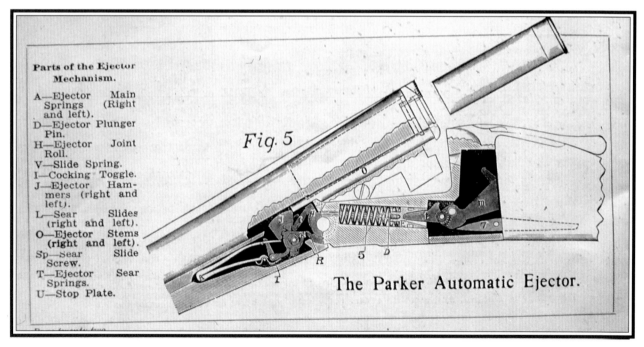

Parker Brothers was the last of the makers of premium doubles to offer automatic ejectors. This cross section from Parker's 1920 pocket catalog shows the relative complexity and numerous small, fragile parts of this popular but troublesome special feature.

extractors is the genuine rare item. The price disparity between 28s and 16s can be ratio-nalized in part because the 16- and 12-gauges tend to be considered "alike," thus making the small-bore 28 rare when compared to large bores in general. Similar analysis might explain the popularity premium paid for twenty-six inch barrels as the twenty-eight-inch, thirty-inch, and even thirty-two-inch barrel lengths are considered functionally "equal," thus making the twenty-six inch rare when compared to *all* longer barrels taken as a group. Nevertheless, ejectors aren't rare, but they seem to command a premium price through inertia—they *always* cost more—rather than for any rational reason. (More on this topic in Chapter 16, "Doves and Extractors.")

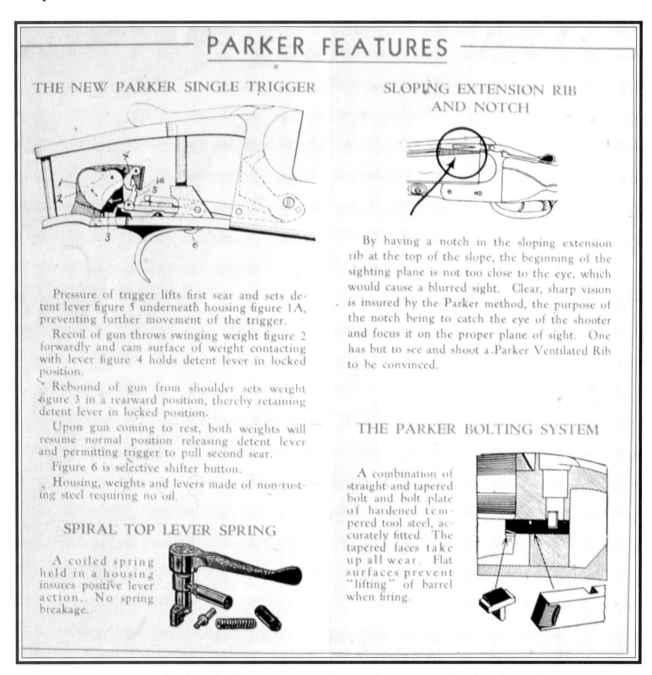

Late 1920s Parker Brothers brochure (with cover picture of hunter shooting over dog) describes Parker special features.

Much information about the Parker gun is becoming available through networking directly attributable to the existence of the *Double Gun Journal* and the Parker Gun Collectors Association. Ron Kirby, secretary of the association, set the tone for Parker research when he wrote in the member newsletter, *Parker Pages*, that "As new information becomes available, incorrect generalizations and speculations must be addressed. The intent is not to ridicule or condemn, but to merely set the record straight. However, the record cannot be corrected with more speculation." I hope my statistical analysis of recently available Parker collector guns meets the non-speculation test. Facts are where you find them. I found mine in the *Double Gun Journal*. Time and availability of the factory records may prove previously published production figures to be close to or wide of the mark. Meanwhile, a few dollars will get you various dealers' gun lists. Forty-nine percent of the Parker guns in my survey were offered by Chadick's, Ltd. This is the kind of information that puts guns in the hands of collectors.

When I wrote this chapter as an article for the *Double Gun Journal*, I was looking for an honest, good-dimension, straight-grip PH or PHE 12-gauge in high original condition. My survey of 520 Parker ads wasn't encouraging, but I persevered and eventually found a nice *rare* P-grade 16-gauge hammer gun to suffice. Now I'm having the devil of a time trying to find a high-condition, good-dimension, straight-grip BH or AH to add to my collection. However, collecting should be a challenge, with success measured by quality and interest rather than simple accumulation of numbers. Quality is what keeps us in the hunt as we search for that "rare" Parker gun.

PARKER PAPER CHASE

Simply stated, a shotgun is a killing device used to reduce small game to possession. Using this definition for the Parker gun, however, would be like referring to Michelangelo as a ceiling painter. Parker guns are a rare combination of apparent quality and strong provenance. The guns stand on their own merit as fine sporting arms. The books, articles, catalogs, hanging tags, factory letters, and related memorabilia make the Parker gun a true collector's item.

Nobody owns a Parker by accident or default—at least not for long. Even the inherited gun comes with knowledge that dad or granddad made a conscious special effort to own the very best his money could buy. A little knowledge and a touch of curiosity must lead to at least a cursory inquiry into the Parker heritage and mystique. A book is purchased, read, and put on the shelf, and Peter H. Johnson's efforts are rewarded with still another printing of *Parker—America's Finest Shotgun*. Since it was first published in 1961, most Parker collectors have cut their teeth on Johnson's pioneering book.

When I bought my first Parker in the mid-1970s, there wasn't much information available other than Johnson's book and *The Parker Gun—An Immortal American Classic*, by Larry Baer. The Parker factory records weren't available, and these two books, almost by default, became the basic information for a whole generation of Parker collectors. Baer's book was first published in two volumes: Volume I in 1974 and Volume II in 1976. The two volumes were combined in 1980, with some slight changes to the text and a few pictures shuffled around between chapters. Most Parker collectors are familiar with the 1980 single-volume edition, which is still available at gun shows and through mail-order sporting-book dealers. Neither book has been updated or revised. Johnson's first edition tends to sell for twice the cost of the current printing—if you can find one in decent condition. Likewise, Baer's two-volume set has itself reached "classic" status and sells for $100 and up.

Paper at these prices could lead a person to adopt the lifestyle of a packrat and never throw anything away.

Author

Norm Flayderman is universally known to gun collectors for his *Flayderman's Guide to Antique American Firearms . . . and Their Values*, now in its sixth edition. The most recent editions of *Flayderman's Guide* have a section devoted to "American Shotguns and Fowling Pieces," which sheds some light on Parker's nineteenth-century lifter and top-lever hammer guns and Damascus-barrel hammerless. Flayderman's annotated bibliography leads the wall-hanger *aficionado* to the right books to expand his consciousness about the early Parker guns, and pretty well summarizes the consensus of present-day collectors about the merits and demerits of the various books listed. For example, Flayderman considers Baer's book to be a

> . . . compilation of uncorrelated and often unsubstantiated information without given sources; more or less a scrapbook of the author's collecting experiences and gripes. Liberally illustrated but much of the uncaptioned material [is] difficult to identify. Information on Damascus doubles meager.

Flayderman considers Johnson's book to be

> . . . basic information but lacking definitive detail for the collector; some unsubstantiated facts.

Flayderman may have been generous when he used the word "some." However, it is a substantiated fact that Johnson literally invented the Parker gun as a collector's item with his typewriter and carbon paper. Johnson's and Baer's books have errors and omissions in view of what has become known about the Parker gun in the past thirty-five and twenty-two years respectively; but nevertheless, *Parker—America's Finest Shotgun* and *The Parker Gun—An Immortal American Classic* are essential reading for anyone with even the slightest interest in the "Old Reliable" Parker gun.

Late 1920s "The Parker Gun" four-page brochure showing Parker special features.

After a collector gets oriented by reading what various gun authors have had to say about the Parker gun, it's time for some original information—that is, some first-hand experience with what Parker Brothers itself put in print about the Parker gun. While most Parker people would rather put their money in guns, original catalogs are popular collector's items for some, though they require special effort to get into the

The Triple Tested Parker Trojan
a gun you will be proud to own.

When you buy your gun this Fall consider this finely made, triple tested Parker Trojan. Here is a gun that you will prize for years to come. Made like all Parkers, it is accurate, hard hitting, perfectly balanced and will never shoot loose. The Trojan is a remarkable value at the popular price of $55.00. See your dealer. Send for the Parker Catalog.

America's Finest Gun

PARKER

Parker Brothers, Master Gun Makers
30 Cherry St., Meriden, Conn. U.S.A.

Parker Brothers ad from September 1928 combined issue of Outdoor Life *and* Outdoor Recreation.

loop. Gun shows are not the proper venue for most paper collectors. I've had better luck at sports-memorabilia shows, decoy shows, cartridge collectors' get-togethers, and with mail-order dealers.

There are various paper dealers who keep an inventory of sporting collectibles and publish lists on a regular basis. At the risk of making this book dated, I'll mention some 1996 sources for Parker paper. Pat McKune usually has a good list of original Parker catalogs and related memorabilia for sale by mail-order, and he sets up at some of the bigger gun shows. My unfired in-the-box Parker Trojan 12-gauge was purchased from Pat at the June 1995 CADA gun show. As part of the deal, I tried to spend $600 for an original circa 1908 Pine Cone catalog with order-form insert (used by R & R Books for its reprint) plus an 1889 half-page invoice with the Parker open hammer-gun logo. Pat wanted

$700, and we weren't able to compromise. Such is the perceived sound value of original Parker catalogs and other paper in good to excellent condition.

Another source for Parker paper is Bruce Johnson, a dealer who travels to many of the larger gun shows. During 1994, Bruce had a nice circa 1915 *Balancing Clown* pocket-size catalog, asking price $1,200. A short time later, our paths crossed at another gun show and the catalog was sold. Meanwhile, a paper collector from California offered another copy of the same catalog for $1,600, and I've since heard from paper dealer Ron Willoughby that three others changed hands recently at the $900 mark. Paper at these prices could lead a person to adopt the lifestyle of a packrat and never throw anything away. A sometime source of Parker paper is James Alley, I.S.D.A. Books; and John Delph, author of *Firearms and Tackle Memorabilia*, usually has a few of the

157

rarest of the rare at correspondingly rarefied prices (for example, an original 1922 Bert Sharkey squirrel poster for $4,000 and an unfired Parker *paper* shotshell for $1,500). Many of the special-interest dealers are regular advertisers in the "Books and Magazines For Sale" and "Prints, Stamps, and Collectibles For Sale" sections of the *Gun List*. Some general-interest paper and memorabilia dealers advertise on a sporadic basis, and often a collector sells out by placing a classified ad. A prudent Parker paper person peruses the *Gun List* on a regular basis. A dollar or two plus large SASE to the right dealers should produce some interesting opportunities to enrich a Parker paper collection. The following are some representative paper prices based on my research during 1994, 1995, and 1996:

Parker letterhead circa 1889	excellent condition	$235
Circa 1888 40-page catalog	average condition	$300–$600
Circa 1893 trade card	excellent condition	$325–$375
Circa 1906-1908 32-page Pine Cone catalogs		$400–$475
Circa 1914-1922 Small Bore brochure		$100–$165
Circa 1915 24-page Balancing Clown pocket catalog		$900–$1,200
1918-34 pocket catalogs, various covers, 15 to 24 pages		$100–$225
1926-1929-1930 large Flying Geese catalogs		$200–$335
Circa 1934 Parker Joins Remington brochure		$125–$190
1937 large spiral-bound catalog		$200–$425
1936-1940 Dealer, Jobber, Retail price lists		$75–$125

Over the years, I've accumulated reprint catalogs to help me understand and appreciate the Parker gun. From the standpoint of research, a reprint or photocopy will do as well as the original, and some state-of-the-art color copiers produce enhanced sharper images. Many reprint catalogs printed in the 1970s or earlier lack quality based on 1996 expectations. According to Larry Baer, ". . . several publishers have offered reprints of Parker catalogs. Some are of excellent quality, but I'm afraid most of them are cheaply and hurriedly made with profit the main objective." I disagree. I can't think of anything less profit-motivated than creating or republishing Parker-gun literature. Clifford Potter incurred the expense of publishing 500 reprint 1899 catalogs, and after twenty years he still had ninety catalogs in inventory. The Potter April 1, 1899, reprint has the best non-photograph production qualities

Parker Brothers reprint catalogs clockwise from 1926 large Flying Geese; 1906 Pine Cone; 1927 Man and Dog pocket catalog; "Congratulations on Your Parker Gun" brochure; author's circa 1913 Flying Ducks reprint by Old Reliable Publishing; and 1933 small Flying Geese pocket catalog in the center.

Parker Brothers circa 1906 CHE 12-gauge Damascus and the book that started the collector-ball rollin'—Parker—America's Finest Shotgun, by Peter Johnson.

(top) Parker Brothers circa 1927 PH .410 — the rarest of the rare.

(bottom) Parker Brothers circa 1928 GH 12-gauge in excellent condition, but with case colors removed. Books are the two volume set of Larry Baer's "Classic."

(top) Parker Brothers A No. 1 Special s/n 231,774 with gold inlays. Parker avoided gold inlay unless the customer insisted, and even then used gold sparingly as with these two flying pheasants. Courtesy of J. C. Devine, Inc.

(bottom) Parker Brothers Trojan s/n 227,251 in mint "unfired" condition with hanging tags. This gun was purchased by author in the original cardboard box with Parker tag on the end and the barrels were still wrapped in corrugated cardboard — a real collector's item.

Parker Brothers original paper, including 1930 large Flying Geese catalog (lower left) and clockwise: the envelope it came in and October 23, 1930 cover letter; late 1920 "The Parker Gun" special features brochure; 1920 pocket catalog; 1933 pocket catalog; late 1930s Remington-Parker skeet gun brochure; 1919 pocket catalog; and circa 1923 "Parker Bros Gun" pocket catalog in center.

of any I've seen. However, Parker catalogs illustrated with line drawings and etchings are easier to republish than catalogs with halftone photos and colors.

In 1996 I published a limited edition of Parker's rare circa 1913 Flying Ducks catalog, using state-of-the-art color separations and computer-enhanced imaging. The process isn't cheap, but the results are spectacular—the reprints are deceptively similar to the original. Whether quality sells and reprint publishing pays remains to be seen.

Books of limited interest are "out of print" the day they first become available. Press runs are short and the published material goes to a small but scattered audience, so the market is pretty much catch-as-catch-can. Current 1996 dealer sources for some Parker catalog reprints are Galazan, Gunnerman Books, and Rutgers Book Center. Reprint publishers advertising recently include R & R Books and my own Old Reliable Publishing. My research file contains the following Parker catalog reprints acquired over the past several years:

Circa 1869-70 catalog, 14 pages, two versions, reprint publisher unknown.

April 1, 1899, catalog, 24 pages, light yellow cover, reprinted by Clifford Potter, original has light yellow cover with impression.

Circa 1900 pocket catalog, 16 pages, blue ink throughout, BH on cover, reprint publisher Old Reliable Publishing. First catalog to picture full line of hammerless guns.

Circa 1906 catalog (refers to 140,000 guns—page 19), light brown Pine Cone, 32 pages, reprint publisher unknown, dated by page 21 reference to 1905-patent hardened steel wear insert.

Circa 1908 catalog (refers to 150,000 guns—page 19), multi-color Pine Cone, 32 pages plus order blank, 1995 reprint publisher R & R Books. The reprint itself claims to be circa 1910, but my research shows it to be early 1908. Better quality than Moulton reprint—costs more.

Circa 1908 catalog (refers to 150,000 guns—page 19), light green Pine Cone, 32 pages, reprinted by R & A Moulton. Identical to R & R Books' reprint but is poorer quality and costs less.

Circa 1913-catalog (refers to 170,000 guns—introduces Trojan grade), tan, green, and black Flying Ducks, 36 pages, reprint publisher Old Reliable Publishing.

March 1, 1926, catalog, 32 pages, large red Flying Geese, reprinted by R & A Moulton (original catalog has green cover).

January 1, 1927, pocket catalog, 16 pages, hunter sitting with dog, reprint publisher PRP Americana.

January 1, 1929, catalog, 32 pages, large green Flying Geese, reprint publisher unknown. (Original has "discontinued" hand-stamped in color on page 17.)

January 1, 1930, catalog, 32 pages, large brown Flying Geese, reprint publisher unknown. (Original catalog has green cover.)

April 1, 1933, pocket catalog, 16 pages plus January 8, 1934, price insert, brown Flying Geese, reprinted by Lightner Library Collection. (Original has red cover.)

1937 wire-bound (spiral) catalog by Remington, 36 pages, reprint publisher R & A Moulton (available from Gunnerman Books).

February 16, 1940, Dealers Price List, 8 pages, reprinted by Lightner Library Collection.

Reprints and photocopies are important research tools as they save wear and tear on original catalogs and other collectible Parker paper, but not every piece of Parker paper is worthy of reprinting. The market can digest only so much in the way of reprints, and many

Parker catalogs are simply redundant. Various Parker booklets—*The Small Bore Shotgun*, for example—aren't illustrated and thus can be duplicated on a photocopy machine as well as by reprint publishing. Hanging tags and factory letters also photocopy well, and some of the newfangled color copiers seem to reproduce better than the originals. The color separations of my circa 1893 Parker trade card, pictured in the *Double Gun Journal's* autumn 1995 issue, were made from a color photocopy and not the original. Other research materials worthy of acquiring include all of the available back issues of the *Double Gun Journal* and back issues of *Parker Pages,* the newsletter of the Parker Gun Collectors Association.

A low-cost way to assemble a Parker collector's file of background information is to buy old outdoor magazines at gun shows and clip Parker ads. Scattered throughout this book are the results of my ad-clipping efforts. Editorials, letters to the editor, stories, and technical articles can be scanned for Parker-related information. (Much of the nostalgic factual information in this book was obtained from old magazines, newspapers, and out-of-print books.) From the 1880s to early 1920s, the *American Field* was published as a weekly newspaper. *Forest and Stream* and *Shooting and Fishing* were late 1800s weekly pulp newspapers that eventually went to a monthly magazine format. My advertising file contains Parker ad copy from 1885 through 1935 from the *Outer's Book, Field and Stream, American Field, National Sportsman, Hunter-Trader-Trapper, Outdoor Life, Forest and Stream, Shooting and Fishing, Outdoor Recreation, Rod and Gun in Canada, Outdoor America, Hunting and Fishing, Harpers,* and *Town and Country.* Whew! Peter Johnson complained back in 1961 that ". . . the amount of ordinary magazine advertising in even the most respected sporting journals was so small that a search for it in the world's largest library turned up almost nothing of value and precious little of any

sort at all." Apparently he just wasn't looking in the right places.

I don't really consider my Parker advertising file to be research as such. I simply bought and sold old magazines—sometimes at a profit and sometimes at a loss but never for much more than current newsstand prices for comparable magazines. I don't mind dwelling in the past as there's nothing particularly timely about my interest in fine double-barrel shotguns and hunting upland game and migratory birds. There's increasing interest in pre-1940s magazines such as *Field and Stream, Outdoor Life, Sports Afield,* and the like, but copies with good covers still sell in the two- to eight-dollar range. Because magazine prices are usually based on the condition and interest of the cover, careful removal of one interior page with a Parker ad is of little or no consequence.

Some of the turn-of-the-century sporting newspapers I mentioned were sold as hard-bound editions each six months to libraries. I have *Forest and Stream* for the first six months of 1909, hard-bound with better paper but in a slightly smaller format than the original pulp. My hardcover was at one time owned by the University of Illinois Library, according to a stamp inside the front cover. My assumption is that the U of I ran out of space and sold or gave away the bulky, seemingly *passé*, hard-bound periodicals to make room for more current reading material. If I'm correct, there may be any number of university and big-city libraries with hard-bound sporting magazines on the shelves or in storage. A real collector *coup* would be to acquire complete sets of *Forest and Stream, Shooting and Fishing,* and *The American Field* at dumpster prices.

Some paper collectors are into old sporting-goods catalogs such as Abercrombie & Fitch, Stoeger, Sears & Roebuck, and others. While some mail-order firms sold Parker guns, the pictures and ad text are of limited

Old original photographs of Parker guns can sometimes be found at sports memorabilia shows, flea markets, etc., etc. Check with postcard dealers who have a section devoted to guns and/or hunting. This postcard cost $7.50 after author spotted the telltale recessed hinge pin on the squirrel hunter's shotgun. Parker paper is where you find it and this postcard was found at a flea market.

interest because they usually do nothing more than restate Parker's own catalog information, but there are exceptions. The Chas. J. Godfrey illustrated trade catalog for 1900 tipped me off to the discounting of Parker guns, contrary to the protestations of contemporary Parker catalogs that guns are ". . . sold by dealers at factory prices." The Evans Brothers, Cincinnati, 1911 catalog offered the Philadelphia Sterlingworth discounted to $22 and the Parker VH discounted to $34.50, which perhaps explains why Parker Brothers introduced Trojan grade in 1913 at $27.50 list. Another point of interest is the 1946 edition of the *Shooter's Bible* (Stoeger Number 37), which offered a full line of Parker shotguns as an exercise in postwar wishful thinking. The "Old Reliable" even found its way into a 1986 award-winning short story by well-known mystery writer Sue Grafton, titled—you guessed it—"The Parker Shotgun."

The Parker Gun Collectors Association, the *Double Gun Journal*, and this book should generate a continuing level of collector interest to justify reprinting various Parker catalogs. It seems to me that a Parker collector who owns a yet-unreprinted original catalog could publish it and at least break even. This is especially true now that Parker collectors have their own association newsletter. Sporting-book dealers (such as Galazan, Gunnerman, and Rutgers) purchase quantities of good-quality reprint catalogs, typically at half the price they think the retail market will bear. Some evidence of demand is that during 1994, Gunnerman Books sold out its inventory of 1908, 1926, and 1934 Parker reprint catalogs. Remember, reprints are again out of print the day they

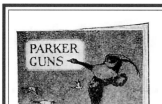

Yours
If you shoot
send for it
PARKER BROTHERS, *Master Gun Makers*
31 Cherry St., Meriden, Conn., U.S.A.

PARKER GUNS
The "Old Reliable"

Parker Brothers ad from October 1927 issue of Hunting & Fishing, *showing large Flying Geese catalog of the type issued in 1926, 1929, and 1930.*

are published, due to the small press run and limited interest. After Moulton's Pine Cone catalog reprint sold out, R & R Books immediately took up the slack, reprinted the circa 1908 Pine Cone catalog, and started advertising in the *Gun List*. There is currently much interest in reprint catalogs, and—surprise, surprise—the reprints are adding interest and value to the originals.

My catalog reprint library was acquired for prices ranging from $2.50 for the 1940 Dealer's List to $17 for the 1937 spiral-bound catalog. It will cost $20 to add the recent R & R Pine Cone catalog reprint to my collection. By comparison, original 1936-40 Remington-Parker price lists cost $100 or more, and original 1937 spiral-bound catalogs have been offered in the $400 range.

Considering that Parker Brothers catalogs were free handouts, it would be hard to compute the rate of investment return to the first owner of the 1915 Balancing Clown catalog, now that $1,000 to seems to be the approximate value set by the market (depending on condition). However, it's likely all the first owners have gone to their final reward. The real issue is whether a new collector can own original Parker catalogs at today's prices and stand an even chance of laying them off on someone else for a fair price at a future date. This depends on the level of interest in Parker collectibles. I'm an optimist. My feeling is that Parker guns and related provenance have

a bright future as an increasing proportion of Americans take up the avocation of dwelling in the past. Witness the exponential increase in the number of antique malls, where a high concept is that everything not new is old and therefore collectible.

In a society where almost everyone is interested in collecting something, genuine collector's items such as Parker guns and related memorabilia are sure to have better-than-average investment potential. However, be mindful of where you are in the pecking order of dealers and collectors. A dealer cannot front the money to acquire inventory, publish a list, answer phone inquiries, travel and set up at shows, and spend time away from other pursuits, only to turn a catalog, hanging tag, or factory letter over to a collector with little or no profit. In the final analysis, there are retailers and wholesalers, collectors and dealers. A Parker paper person needs to decide at which level he intends to operate. A collector who wants to buy paper at wholesale is going to have a problem building a collection. A dealer who acquires inventory at close to retail will likewise have a problem—the "I've got more than that in it" problem.

There was a time when I considered $17 for a reprint copy of the 1937 spiral-bound catalog to be a chancy investment, but one thing led to another and now I own an original. Be careful when you buy that first reprint or relatively inexpensive piece of original Parker paper—it could be addictive.

Boxlocks and Case Colors

Certain gunwriters wax enthusiastic about sidelocks, with the stated or unstated implication that boxlocks are an inferior framework upon which to build a fine gun

Lock plates may be more aesthetically pleasing to some, and can be an aid to better-quality engraving, but the boxlock is simply a next step in the evolution of firearms. Lock plates were necessary when hammers were on the outside of the frame; however, as makers one-by-one adopted Anson & Deeley's concealed-hammer (hammerless) boxlock action, lockplates came to be a cosmetic add-on with no real function. Of *The Best Shotguns Ever Made in America*, according to Michael McIntosh, only the L. C. Smith is a true sidelock with lock parts attached to the sideplates. Early Lefevers had sideplates, but weren't true sidelocks because the hammers, springs, etc. were attached to the frame—just like a Parker boxlock. Fox, Ithaca, Lefever, Winchester 21, and Parker hammerless guns were all built exclusively on boxlock frames. Most London "best guns" kept the sidelock, but Birmingham makers in general and

Contrary to general belief, Parker guns are not what is popularly known as machine made. While the frames and other component parts are accurately produced from machines, the various parts are so designed and produced as to require their being entirely fitted by hand, equally as much so as if each frame and its parts were to be specially jobbed out for the particular gun of which they are to be a part.

Walter A. King

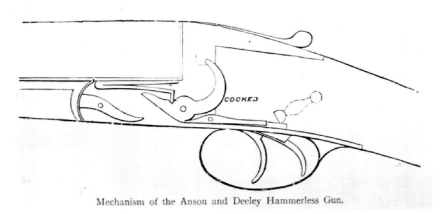

Mechanism of the Anson and Deeley Hammerless Gun.

Anson & Deeley were British gunmakers who devised the boxlock action, whereby concealed hammers were cocked by barrel leverage when the gun tipped open. This picture shows Anson & Deeley's circa 1875 action in its simplest form, which is the basis for C. A. King's series of 1887-89 boxlock patents for the Parker hammerless gun.

W. W. Greener in particular saw the merits of attaching action parts to the frame. According to Greener:

> The Anson & Deeley type lock gives quicker ignition than the ordinary lock, for the blow is much shorter and the mainspring stronger. The sidelock hammerless guns have not this advantage. The advantage they possess is the ease with which the locks may be removed and the lockwork inspected. This is not a matter of importance, since a well-made "boxlock" is so placed as to be efficiently protected from the intrusion of dust, dirt, or wet, and will work well for years without attention. The great advantages the [boxlock guns possess] over those in which sidelocks are used should determine the sportsman in his choice, for, in addition to the disadvantages already mentioned, sidelock guns are found to be more liable to accidental discharge. . . .

American manufacturers built double-gun frames from either steel forgings or semi-steel (malleable iron) castings, depending on the expected selling price of finished guns. Higher-priced guns (including the Parker) were built with drop-forged frames. Lower-priced guns used sand-cast frames poured around a core to minimize expensive internal metal removal. The initial cost of a raw forging or sand casting was about equal when Parker guns were in production. However, the incremental cost of removing internal metal from forged frames made the Parker gun a premium product from the beginning of the manufacturing process. Parkers were extremely expensive, due in part to the wide variety of frame sizes, each with its own special forging dies, jigs, gauges, and tooling. When a Parker customer bought his 20-gauge on a size 0 frame, the gun had the aesthetic appeal and proper balance of being scaled down in total, rather than just having small-bore barrels affixed to an otherwise 12-gauge boxlock. (See Appendix F, "Parker Frame Sizes".)

Drop-forging was first adapted to firearm manufacture in 1853 by Samuel Colt. The process involves forming the hot end of a steel bar by machine hammering between dies (essentially female molds)—one-half of the die being attached to the bed of the drop-forge anvil and the other fastened to a ram that pounds and compresses the hot metal until it fills both sides. After the forging cools, surplus metal is trimmed away and scale is removed by pickling in a hot acid bath. The forging is then ready for metal-removal operations, which, in the case of the Parker gun, totaled more than 100. With the exception of pins and screws, almost every component of the Parker frame and action was forged. The process was expensive, and as a consequence, Parker guns were expensive—and reliable.

The first step in building a forged Parker frame and action was the purchase of special-order steel of a specified tensile strength, transverse strength, malleability, and elongation percentage. Parker used both chemical and physical tests to verify the specifications. Certain metals had to pass a special "memory test" done at the Parker gun works. Steel samples of consistent size and shape were bent in progressive stages to determine their ability to spring back to original contour and the point at which the metal would lose "memory" and stay bent. Forgings were clearly superior for gunmaking, and the component raw steel kept getting better and better.

An example of the advances in metallurgy over the years of the Parker gun is that malleable iron circa 1868 had a *high* tensile strength of 35,000 pounds while by 1938 malleable iron had a *low* tensile strength of 70,000 pounds (a 100 percent increase). The tensile strength for forged steel circa 1938 was 60,000 pounds, but the real differences between forged steel and malleable casting were the yield point and elongation percentage.

Forged steel would yield at approximately 35,000 pounds in 1938, more than sufficient for gunmaking but only about half that of malleable iron. Castings, however, were brittle, having an elongation percentage of only 5 to 10 percent, while forgings could be bent and stretched in the range of 25 to 30 percent. This is what Parker Brothers checked with its bending test. The result was a forged-steel boxlock frame that could be bent back into shape after case-hardening. Cheaper guns with cast frames were built to tolerances and simply went together slightly crooked. Parker guns were bent, scraped, filed, and fit to what could be fairly called "zero tolerance."

In the early years, Parker Brothers did its own forging—probably because Charles

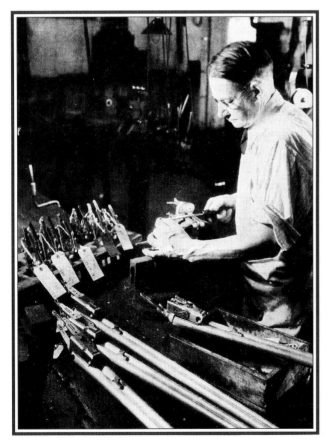

Parker Brothers gun mechanic removing that last enth of metal from the water table to achieve "zero tolerance" fit with barrel flats. Kerosene soot was mixed with oil and painted on the surfaces as a marker to establish high spots needing perhaps another "close look" with the finest file available.

Parker's company manufactured special-order punch presses and die-press machinery and was forging a full line of hardware items. Parker Brothers' circa 1869 gun catalog also advertised "Drop Presses to Work by Hand or Power." In time, forging techniques improved and the process became more specialized. According to Peter Johnson's interviews with various Parker officials: ". . . In the latter years of the company's existence . . . forgings were . . . to a large extent made by outside forge plants with Parker Brothers furnishing the steel." Whatever the source, forgings went to the machining department to be processed in frame-size batches of 100 or more. The raw forgings underwent machining procedures such as milling, drilling, reaming, shaving, broaching, profiling, and nibbling. W. A. King wrote "Step by Step in Building a Gun," published in the September 1924 issue of *National Sportsman* magazine. He discussed the frame-making process as follows:

It is interesting to watch a frame progressing through the machining department and observe its changing appearance from a rough forging to a completely machined, skeletonized product. There are over 100 different machine operations on the frame alone, and each and every operation must have a jig, a fixture specially designed to hold the work in an exact position while the operation is being done, and every operation must have its particular gauge in order that the accuracy of the operation be checked. Contrary to general belief, Parker guns are not what is popularly known as machine made. While the frames and other component parts are accurately produced from machines, the various parts are so designed and produced as to require their being entirely fitted by hand, equally as much so as if each frame and its parts were to be specially jobbed out for the particular gun of which they are to be a part.

After the frames and other component parts were machined to close tolerances

Parker Brothers gun works in the early years of the twentieth century.

(about plus .005-inch), they were inventoried in the stockroom until selected to build a particular gun. Upon selection for a work order, the frame and action components entered the soft-fitting process in which skilled gun mechanics—through judicious removal of metal using hand tools, the trained eye, and a feel more delicate than the thinnest feeler gauge—entirely hand-fitted the components to the boxlock frame and, in turn, the frame to the barrels, fore-end piece, and stock.

Parker Brothers published a six-page brochure, *A Trip Through Parker Bros*, which like so much Parker literature is undated. However, the reference to barrel-proofing and that ". . . the proofmark is put on the flats of each tube . . ." dates the brochure to the late 1920s. The brochure states that ". . . raw

material . . . [was] . . . checked by chemical and physical tests . . . [and] . . . with the exception of pins and screws, practically every other component part of the gun frame and action is a forging." The section "Action Fitting" describes the following procedures:

Action, or soft fitting, is the accurate fitting and assembling of all component parts of the gun in the soft state. The action fitter receives the parts from the machining department, where they have been prepared with suitable allowances provided for proper fitting. The fitter must be an expert with file and scraper, accustomed to working to extreme accuracy and capable of presenting for inspection, parts so perfectly fitted as to shut out even daylight. The fitter uses very thin mixtures of oil and lamp-black [kerosene soot], painting the parts, putting them together and filing or scraping until the bearing points are in exact and perfect relation. When a gun is fully action fitted, it is a completely fitted gun with every part assembled, all in the soft state. It will function, although very stiffly, because the action fitters purposely leave very tight joints so that the second or hard fitters may have a very small amount of material to work upon in their part of the final assembling.

According to Peter Johnson in the gunbuilding chapter of his book, *Parker-America's Finest Shotgun*:

> ... The soft-fitted and shoe-filed parts of the gun were polished, engraved and given a bone-black case hardening before going to the hard fitters. During the case hardening operations it was not unusual for some of the parts to warp slightly. Although the soft fitting operation consisted almost entirely of filing, the hard fitting operation was one of bending, springing and stretching the parts of the gun to the point that they once again fitted properly.

Hard-fitting procedures were dependent on Parker Brothers' use of drop-forged frames with elongation percentages of 25 to 30 percent, as contrasted to the relatively brittle malleable steel sand-castings with elongation percentages of 5 to 10 percent. Forged steel could be bent back into shape after case-hardening consistent with Parker's "hand-fit and finish" process.

Case-hardening is heat-treatment that adds carbon to metal to a certain depth, resulting in a glass-hard surface and Parker's distinctive blue and brown *case colors*, considered by most to enhance the appearance of a finished gun. *Carbonizing* (sometimes called *carburizing*) is case-hardening that generally involves packing the parts in crucibles with a mixture of carbon sources such as animal charcoal, vegetable charcoal, and powdered cyanide of potassium. The crucible is then baked in an oven at approximately 1800 degrees for the prescribed time; the red-hot gun components are then quenched (dumped into cold, agitated water), thus fixing the carbon to the metal and organizing the surface structure to a hardness greatly exceeding that of the interior metal. The relative hardness of the exterior minimizes impact damage and wear; the relative softness of the interior strengthens the frame by preserving malleability and memory while avoiding overall brittleness.

According to Parker collector Richard B. Hoover, writing in *Parker Pages*, the newsletter of the Parker Gun Collectors Association, the concept of tempering steel by heating and quenching was well known to ancient Syrians. Hoover described a "... parchment recovered from an armorers' shop [that] revealed the cruel details of how the Damascus blades were quenched in flesh of an Ethiopian slave: '... then let the master-workman, having cold-hammered the blade to smooth and thin edge, thrust it into the fire of the cedarwood charcoals, in and out ... until the steel be the color of the rising sun ... and with a quick motion pass the same from the heel thereof to the point, six times through the fleshy portion of the slave's back and thighs, when it shall become the color of the purple of the King. Then, if with one swing and one stroke of the master-workman, it severs the head of the slave from his body and displays no nick or crack along the edge ... it shall be accepted as a perfect weapon....'" Apparently the famous swords of Damascus were quenched in a carbon-rich environment at the controlled temperature of 98.6 degrees. Ouch!

Parker Brothers' more conventional (and less fatal) carbonizing and heat-treating processes were described by W. A. King in his 1924 *National Sportsman* article:

After the engraving is completed, the parts are cleaned and prepared for case-hardening or other heat treatments necessary. All case-hardening done in the Parker factory is accomplished by packing the parts in a mixture of charcoal and raw bone, finely ground, subjecting the iron pots in which the packed parts are placed to a certain heat for a definite period of time and then immersing the heated parts in water or oil, dependent on the nature of the material and upon the character of the work the part is called upon to perform.

The frames, fore-end irons and trigger plates are all immersed in a water-bath, which produces the beautiful blue and gold effects so much admired. Parts such as sears, hammers, cocking links and cranks are given a different treatment, as some of these parts must be extremely hard in order to resist wear, and others must be so treated as to ensure the maximum of strength. After hardening, the gun goes to the second or hard fitters and final assemblers.

Parker's boxlock case colors—or Syrian armorers' purple Damascus blade, as the case may be—are simply the cosmetic result of the carbonizing process. Loss of case colors through wear or removal doesn't affect hardness. Reestablishing case colors, however, may affect hardness and may cause the parts to warp. Whether the distortions are insignificant or can be *normalized* away or need hard-fitting operations such as bending, springing, and stretching parts of the gun to the point where they once again fit properly is beyond the scope of this book. But if you collect restorations or upgrades, be sure to check the metal-to-metal fit.

Donald F. Carpenter was one of the DuPont executives transferred to manage the Remington Arms Co. at the time the assets of Parker Brothers were acquired. His 1972 article, "A Short History of the Remington Arms Company—1933-1940," gave Remington's view of the hand fit and finish essential to the prestige of the Parker gun:

Parker was a "double fit" gun. Many guns in Europe were double fit, but Parker was probably the only one produced in the United States. Since most people don't know what double fit means, we had to explain it to many. There are no tolerances, but the gun is fit tight, then hardened, and then the unhardened parts are honed down to fit. The result is a gun which has as close to a perfect fit as possible. Guns made to tolerances, however, may have adjacent parts with openings between them which are as much as the combined tolerances of the two parts. This double fit procedure leads to very high manufacturing costs, and since it was hardly appreciated, it was very questionable whether it was worth it. The same applied to the outside finish which was mottled by the very special ingredients used in a high-cost, casehardening procedure. [After the war] . . . several studies had shown that there was no way that the Parker operations could be conducted profitably, [and] the line was dropped.

Toward the end of production, Remington adopted the cyanide process to case-harden Parkers, thus late Remington guns have a more definite case-colors finish. Larry Del Grego Sr. took the process with him when he left Remington to start his own gunsmithing business specializing in Remington Model 32s and the Parker gun. Del Grego restorations are easy to spot with their darker and seemingly thicker case colors, while most other restoration experts have pursued the less-definite, seemingly thinner, almost ethereal colors ". . . mottled by the very special ingredients used in [Parker Brothers'] high-cost, casehardening procedure . . ." As an addendum to Parker Brothers' process of building forged and case-hardened frames and action parts as described by King, Johnson, and Carpenter, an article, "Shotgun Manufacture—The Smaller Parts," by A. P. Curtis appeared in the September 1938 issue of the *American Rifleman*. The author discussed "modern-improved" Winchester frame-building methods as follows:

> The Winchester Repeating Arms Company do no surface hardening by the [Parker Brothers] method. They forge their frames, trigger-plates, and other parts from alloy steel, and heat-treat them *before* machining. This heat-treatment consists of heating and quenching, and then drawing or annealing by reheating to from 1000 degrees to 1100 degrees F. This treatment increases the tensile strength of the metal nearly twofold. At the same time it renders it soft and malleable enough to be drilled, machined, etc., for the reception of the lock parts and other mechanisms. This is a new [circa 1930s] method of constructing guns in America, although used by some European gunmakers. This system of heat-treating before machining produces a nearer approach to the interchangeability of all parts than any before used. Any warping, shrinking, or expanding of the metal takes place before any of the machining cuts are made, which means only one action-fitting operation instead of two. Undoubtedly alloy steel and its early heat-treatment will be employed by other American producers of quality guns in the near future, as it is a radical departure from the old methods, and a forward step in the construction of double shotguns.

Curtis's article was written contemporaneous with Remington's 1938 move of the Parker gun works to Ilion, New York. The Remington Model 32 is considered a fine gun worthy of inclusion in *Best Guns* by Michael McIntosh, but typically has roll-stamped "engraving" on a blued frame. The Model 32 was introduced in March 1932, and a reasonable person could conclude that the absence of case colors indicates heat-treating according to the one-step Winchester process rather than the two-step (double-fit) Parker process. It's possible that Remington built fewer than 1,800 Parkers after moving the gun works to Ilion because the "improved" but abbreviated manufacturing process was inconsistent with producing double-fit, zero-tolerance Parker guns with the hand-finished appearance and characteristic case colors at a profit. The Winchester Model 21 is blued (rather than case-colored), likely because of the Winchester process described above, and has the same Remington Model 32 blued frame and machine-finished look. If you have ever seen a Parker with a blued frame, you'll understand why the "Old Reliable" was quietly put to rest by Remington after the war.

The various methods of heat-treating, case-hardening, annealing, stress relief, and the like were and are proprietary trade secrets. The recipes for mixing animal charcoal, vegetable charcoal, cyanide of potassium, and other carbon sources, and the baking temperatures, oven times, and quenching mediums (water, oil, slave, etc.) are as closely guarded as the formula for Coca-Cola syrup. Nevertheless, a number of modern-day restoration experts are achieving case colors deceptively similar to those on original Parker guns. For the time being, patina of age is the saving distinction.

Accompanying this brief dissertation on boxlock frame-building and case-hardening are color photographs showing original Parker case colors at various percentages and some of the best efforts of restoration experts. Two caveats: the photographs don't do justice to the guns in real life, and *do not* buy a gun based on a photograph unless you are accustomed to disappointment. Case colors don't tell the whole

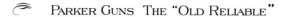

story. The only way to properly evaluate a Parker is to examine it in person, side-by-side with your "benchmark" gun and as many other comparable Parkers as you can get your hands on. When I bought my DHE Trap at Chadick's Ltd. in 1994, I selected from eleven D-grades all lined up on the same table with my benchmark VH 20-gauge. A picture may be worth a thousand words, but with Parker guns, a million words is no substitute for hands-on experience.

12

Pounds and Ounces

No one ever accused Colonel Askins of lacking an opinion. But as to the fact that the perfect shotgun has a bore to fit a lead ball weighing one-twelfth of a pound, he was clearly right, in my opinion. The typical Parker 12-gauge is intended to safely and comfortably launch 1¼ ounces of lead shot and as a consequence typically weighs seven to eight pounds or more. Charts showing standard Parker Brothers gun weights for the early 1920s, and Remington-Parker late-1930s gun weights, barrel lengths, and chambers are shown below.

The perfect shotgun is the 12. If, man or boy, a gent isn't stud enough to shoot a 12, then he should take up ping pong.

Colonel Charles Askins

THE PARKER GUN

CHOICE OF BORING OF BARRELS

The barrels of PARKER guns, including the "TROJAN," are furnished with any combination of borings desired—from true cylinder to extreme full choke. When no other boring is specified, barrels of all guns, except those for Skeet and trap shooting, will be furnished with the right barrel bored modified choke and the left barrel bored full choke.

EXTRA LONG RANGE GUNS

12 Gauge, 3-inch Chamber; 10 Gauge, 3½-inch Chamber

PARKER double barrel guns, with the exception of the "TROJAN," will be furnished in 12 gauge with 3-inch chambers and in 10 gauge with 3½-inch chambers for use with maximum long range heavy loaded shells. PARKER guns so chambered are guaranteed to handle these shells properly, and will give unsurpassed performance at extreme ranges. There is no extra charge.

CHAMBER LENGTHS, BARREL LENGTHS, AND WEIGHTS

The following table shows the chamber lengths, barrel lengths, and weight limits of PARKER shotguns, in all grades, with the exception of the "TROJAN." All PARKER shotguns are manufactured as light in weight as possible, consistent with strength and durability, as well as maximum shooting qualities and minimum recoil. PARKER methods of manufacturing and hand fitting permit holding the weight of a gun to within one ounce of any weight specified in the brackets indicated below, and at the same time to maintain perfect balance. Each PARKER gun is guaranteed to handle properly any standard factory loaded shell for which it is chambered.

Gauge	Chamber	26-Inch Barrels	28-Inch Barrels	30-Inch Barrels	32-Inch Barrels	34-Inch Barrels
Double Barrel Shotguns, with regular fore-end and two triggers:						
10	3½ in.			10½ to 10¾ lbs.	10¾ to 11 lbs.	
	2⅞ in.			9 to 9¼ lbs.	9¼ to 9½ lbs.	
12	3 in.			7¾ to 8 lbs.	8¼ to 8½ lbs.	
	2¾ in.	6⅞ to 7⅛ lbs.	7 to 7¼ lbs.	7¼ to 7½ lbs.	7½ to 7¾ lbs.	
16	2¾ in.	6⅝ to 6⅞ lbs.	6⅞ to 7⅛ lbs.	7⅛ to 7⅜ lbs.		
20	2¾ in.	6⅛ to 6⅜ lbs.	6⅜ to 6⅝ lbs.	6⅝ to 6⅞ lbs.		
28	2⅞ in.	5¾ to 6 lbs.	5⅞ to 6⅛ lbs.			
.410	3 in.	5⅝ to 5⅞ lbs.	5¾ to 6 lbs.			
Double Barrel Trap Guns, with ventilated rib, beavertail fore-end, recoil pad, and single trigger:						
12	2¾ in.			7⅞ to 8⅛ lbs.	8 to 8¼ lbs.	
Single Barrel Trap Guns:						
12	2¾ in.			7¾ to 8 lbs.	8 to 8¼ lbs.	8¼ to 8½ lbs.
Skeet Guns, with beavertail fore-end and single trigger:						
12	2¾ in.	7¼ to 7½ lbs.	7⅜ to 7⅝ lbs.			
16	2¾ in.	7 to 7¼ lbs.	7¼ to 7½ lbs.			
20	2¾ in.	6½ to 6¾ lbs.	6⅝ to 6⅞ lbs.			
28	2⅞ in.	6 to 6¼ lbs.	6⅛ to 6⅜ lbs.			
.410	3 in.	5⅞ to 6⅛ lbs.	6 to 6¼ lbs.			

Guns exceeding tabulated weights, extra $24.00
Barrel lengths other than shown above (24-inch minimum, 34-inch maximum), extra 24.00

Chart from Remington-Parker 1936 price list showing 12-gauge gun weights from 6⅞ to 8½ pounds.

IS THERE ONE "BEST" GUN?

THIS question is a pertinent one that is constantly being asked and we answer it as follows:
The best gun combines the greatest number of good qualities, built with regard to its safety, continuity of balance, durability, unsurpassed shooting qualities, superior workmanship, beauty of outline, and greatest general excellence of its performance under all conditions.

Under the most strenuous conditions the Parker Gun has never failed to withstand the test, has always done its work satisfactorily, earning for itself the unbounded confidence of its owner, and ever reflecting credit on its makers. Because of this it has become universally and familiarly known as "The Old Reliable."

Thousands of testimonials have been received during the last half century. They stand as irrefutable proof of its soundness and sterling worth, and fully substantiate our claim that for general excellence the Parker Gun will be found, dollar for dollar and grade for grade, the best gun produced, as even Time, the relentless leveler of all things, has failed to dim its fame.

Our terms are Cash. Where parties ordering guns have no commercial rating, or are unknown to us, the order must be accompanied by 20% of the purchase price, the balance C. O. D.

Styles. We make any style of gun desired, in our action as illustrated, but deviation from regular weights and measurements compels us to make extra charge. Prices cheerfully furnished on application.

Weights and Lengths. Regular weights and lengths furnished on all our guns.
No. 10 gauge guns ....7¾ to 10	pounds; barrels...........28 to 32 inches.
No. 12 gauge guns ....6½ to 9	pounds; barrels...........26 to 32 inches.
No. 16 gauge guns ....6 to 8	pounds; barrels...........26 to 32 inches.
No. 20 gauge guns ....5¾ to 7½	pounds; barrels...........26 to 32 inches.
No. 28 gauge guns ....5¼ to 6	pounds; barrels...........24 to 30 inches.

Regular stocks, 2 to 3¼ inches drop, 13½ to 14½ inches long.

Extra Weights and Lengths.—An extra charge will be made for 10 or 12 gauge guns, made extra heavy, or for barrels exceeding 32 inches in length—made to order only. We shall be pleased to furnish full information and prices.

Chart from Parker Brothers 1920 pocket catalog showing 12-gauge gun weights from 6½ to 9 pounds.

Parker Brothers published a 1922 booklet, *Parker Guns—The Double Barrel Game and Trap Guns—Single Trap Guns*, which spoke highly of its own 12-gauge models:

By the consensus of universal opinion it has been decreed for an all around shotgun, one that can be used at any kind of game, in any climate and under all conditions, the twelve-gauge double gun is without doubt the first choice. Be it understood the gun in hand [seven pounds with 28- or 30-inch barrels] is as near an all around game gun as it is possible to find; portable, handy, easily carried and mounted to the shoulder, and when bored . . . [modified and full choke] . . . you have a most serviceable fowling piece; one that can be used successfully at all kinds of upland game and still be a good companion when duck shooting from blinds . . . [up to] . . . thirty-five yards . . . [with] . . . it chambered for 2⅝ inch to 2¾ inch shells. The usual game loads of 3 drams of bulk nitro powder and 1 to 1⅛ ounces of shot would be used . . . [and] . . . either 30 inch or 32 inch barrels, chambered for 2⅞ to 3 inch shells, in which can be properly loaded 3¼ to 3½ drams bulk nitro powder and 1⅛ to 1¼ ounces of shot . . . [and patterned three-quarters modified (65 percent) and full (75 percent)

for long-range duck shooting]. As guns of this kind [duck guns] are not meant to be carried long distances, the increased weight will not be detrimental and will help in a great measure to absorb the recoil.

Sir Isaac Newton taught that a body at rest tends to stay at rest and every action has an equal and opposite reaction. Parker Brothers learned the lesson well. The action of accelerating 1¼ ounces of lead shot from at rest to maximum velocity in the length of a shotgun barrel will cause an equal and opposite reaction that can be mitigated by gun weight. You don't need to be a rocket scientist to know that a light six-pound gun will kick more than a heavy eight-pound gun. Of course a lighter load has less kick, but there's more to the equation. A Parker 16-gauge (typically pushing one ounce of shot) is usually between two ounces and sixteen ounces lighter than a Parker twelve of comparable dimensions. The "heavy" 16-gauge used by Captain du Bray on his Grand tour of 1898 weighed 7½ pounds. Colonel Askins, however, thought ". . . the popularity of the 16 is about on a par with death and taxes." As to 28-gauge and .410, he wrote that

. . . the more narrow bore of the .410 is a veritable grinding mill. When you funnel ¾ of an ounce of soft, leaden pellets . . . through a bore measuring only .410-inch, a fantastic number of tiny spheres are hammered out of round—these flat sided pellets will not kill.

He was willing to allow the 28-gauge to be better than the .410, as it

. . . does not mutilate the shot nearly so badly . . . but, it's another dread crippler, a toy and not a tool, . . . a scatter gun that does not pack enough powder to blow your nose.

When comparing 12- and 20-gauges, Colonel Askins was somewhat less critical, but critical nevertheless:

. . . there isn't anything you can do with the 20 that cannot be accomplished with twice the efficiency swinging a 12. If you want to argue the matter of weight, I'll produce a 6 pound 12; the average 20 these days runs 6½ pounds. And on the score of cartridge I'll find a 12-gauge cartridge, that runs a mere 2 inches for length and poops out a trifling 1 ounce of shot.

Following the Colonel's analysis of the 28-gauge and .410 as grinding mills, it's clear that a 12-gauge would flatten and deflect fewer shot than a 20 or 16, assuming an equal one-ounce load. The various shot-tower companies went to great heights to achieve near-perfect spherical shot in consistent sizes. Colonel Askins's thesis is that larger bore size preserves spherical correctness with consequent improvement in pattern. If Newton were alive today, he might add a fourth law of physics to the effect that "the perfect shotgun is a seven- to eight-pound 12-gauge that can handle a proportioned load of 1¼ ounces of hard shot."

At the lightweight end of the spectrum is a 12-gauge as light as 5¼ pounds, advertised by D. M. Lefever, Sons & Co. in 1903.

Keith Keacher wrote an article in the *Double Gun Journal* (5-3) about such a gun: "The Lightest 12-Bore Made in America?" It featured a 1903 Lefever 12-gauge with twenty-six-inch barrels that weighed exactly six pounds. By comparison, a more conventional same-grade Lefever with thirty-inch barrels weighed seven pounds fourteen ounces. The thirty-ounce weight difference is mostly in the lighter twenty-one-ounce barrels. Here's a pop quiz: Which gun do you think is more useful? Fact: The only way to achieve significant weight reduction at a given gauge is to thin and shorten the barrels.

Keacher's article mentions that the right barrel of his six-pound gun developed a slight bulge ten inches from the breech. Are you surprised? Is a bulge acceptable if it's "slight?" One must question the usefulness of an ultra-light and consequently delicate shotgun. Certainly Uncle Dan must have known something about Newton's laws of physics. A six-pound 12-bore pushing 1⅛-ounce of shot would kick like a horse, and I wouldn't want to be around if the trigger were pulled on a 1¼-ounce load. No wonder this gun is rare. The way to make a rare gun is to build one with excessive recoil that isn't safe to shoot. Maybe it was built for export to England. A six-pound 12-gauge for the American market is a rare item and rightfully so.

Parker Brothers' April 1, 1899, catalog shows standard 12-gauge weights from seven to nine pounds (depending on twenty-eight- to thirty-two-inch barrel lengths, frame size, pull, etc.) while recommending 1⅛ ounces of shot. The 1908 Pine Cone catalog has 12-gauge weights from seven to nine pounds with barrel lengths from twenty-six to thirty-two inches. Parker's circa 1913 Flying Ducks catalog through early 1920s pocket catalogs show twelves as light as 6½ pounds with twenty-six-inch barrels. The 1926 through 1929 large Flying Geese catalogs offered regular 12-gauge guns from 6¾ to nine pounds with barrel lengths of twenty-six to thirty-two inches, and any factory-approved deviation from regular lengths and weights would have cost extra. Parker guns began to get heavier at the same time the gun works started to memorialize proof-testing by stamping *OVERLOAD PROVED* on the barrel flats (circa 1925-26, between s/n 211,XXX and 216,XXX). A six-pound twelve-ounce circa 1920s Parker twelve is a rare item—probably built on a Number 1 frame with twenty-six-inch barrels and a short straight-grip stock. A 6½-pound 12-gauge Parker may exist, but I've never seen or heard of one.

The low weights shown on the charts, and quoted in various 1910s and early 1920s Parker catalogs, may have been hard to achieve in the lower grades after 2¾- and three-inch chambers came to be the norm. I have a factory letter dated March 17, 1927, from Parker Brothers to Mr. William Meyers of Hampton, Iowa, signed by Parker's long-time office manager H. L. Carpenter. The following should give the reader a feel for Parker's policy in respect to gun weights:

> Factory, in checking up the specifications, advises us that the weight you have given is somewhat too light for a gun to be used with the 2¾-inch shells. Our light weight limit for this length in a 12/30 is 7 pounds, 10 ounces and the addition of the recoil pad and the ¼-inch length of stock would increase that weight probably 4 to 6 ounces. The fact you have specified a heavy comb would also tend to make the gun slightly heavier. It is impossible for us to accept an order for a gun lighter than as described above, and we trust it will be satisfactory to you to allow us to increase the weight as stated. A gun as light as you have ordered, would be unsafe in our opinion to handle the 2¾ inch loads, in which as you know, the heavy Super-X and similar powders are loaded.

Parker's 1926 catalog shows regular stock dimensions of 13½ to 14½ inches, so it's likely

Meyers wanted a 14¾-inch pull. Other letters from December 1926 show that he considered a 10-gauge with thirty-four-inch barrels; apparently he was looking for a big gun. H. L. Carpenter recommended against overly long barrels, writing that "... it is our opinion that you would gain practically nothing in the thirty-four-inch barrels over the thirty-two-inch except by a little more perfect alignment . . . [i.e. longer sighting plane] . . . it is our opinion that thirty-two inches would give you equally as good satisfaction." Put another way, any Parker gun with thirty-four-inch or longer barrels was probably purchased contrary to factory advice. William Meyers was considering a VH 12-gauge with thirty-inch barrels and long pull, likely weighing right on eight pounds. In fact, it seems eight pounds was the magic number for 12-gauge shotguns. Beginning in 1893, the Interstate Association held its annual Grand American Handicap at Live Birds, and contestants' guns could weigh *no more* than eight pounds (excluding the recoil pad).

Parker guns were always well represented at the Grand American Handicap, and in 1902, at the last GAH at live birds, 162 (36 percent) of the 456 starters shot Parkers. Of the top thirty-one shooters killing twenty-five birds straight, fourteen had Parkers. By comparison, L. C. Smiths were used by 105 (23 percent) of the 456 shooters and accounted for nine of the thirty-one guns killing twenty-five birds.

The weekly edition of *Shooting and Fishing* for April 10, 1902, lists all 456 GAH contestants, giving names of shooters, make and weight of his or her gun, maker of shells, charge and kind of powder, and weight and size of shot. With few exceptions, the guns weighed from seven pounds twelve ounces to eight pounds even. A. W. du Bray shot a Parker weighing seven pounds fifteen ounces, C. W. Budd's Parker weighed seven pounds fourteen ounces, and Fred Gilbert's Parker weighed seven pounds twelve

(right) *Parker restoration artist Oscar Gaddy lifts a red-hot crucible packed with carbon sources and Parker parts from his case hardening oven. The next step is to spill the contents into his cold water quenching tank to fix carbon near the surface of the metal and establish case colors.*

(left) *Oscar Gaddy dumping red hot gun parts into his quenching tank to fix carbon and establish case colors.*

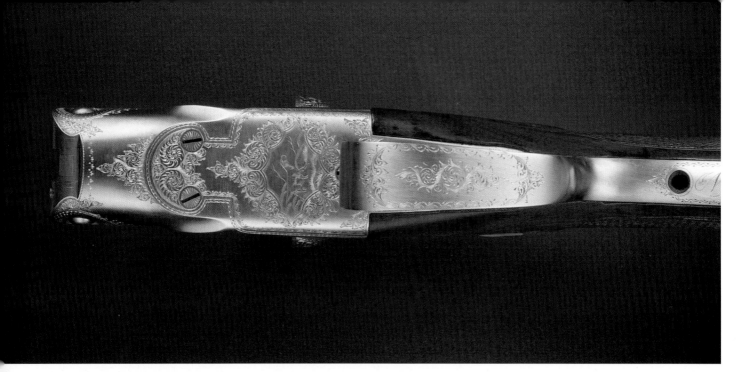

(top) Bottom view of Parker "C" upgrade with engraving complete. Oscar's next step is to pack the raw metal parts in a crucible with carbon sources and bake in his oven at a secret temperature for the right length of time.

(bottom) Side view of Parker "C" upgrade in the works with engraving complete. After heat treating by the carbonizing process, Oscar will quench the red hot boxlock to fix carbon at the surface and create Parker-like case colors.

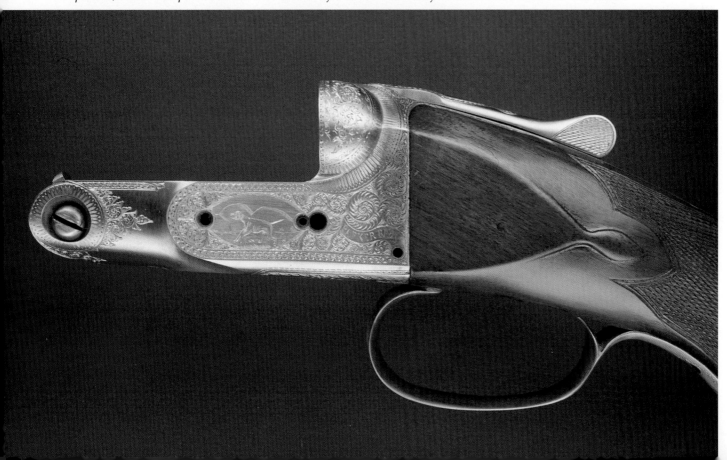

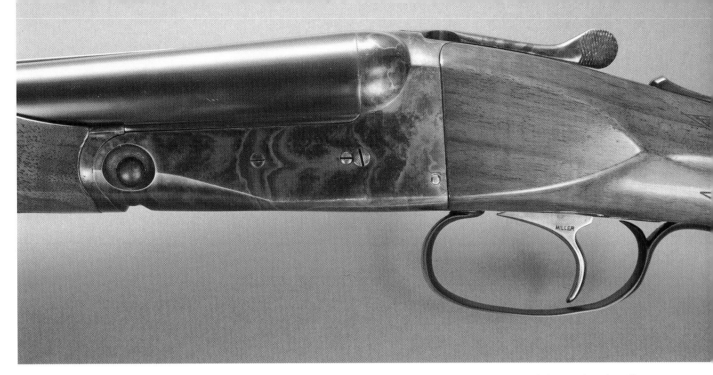

(top) *Here is one exceptional Trojan displaying classic Del Grego case colors. Notice the beavertail fore-end and Miller single trigger. This gun was built from parts by Larry Del Grego Sr. in 1975, for Lawrence's tenth birthday. Some people believe the last Parker was made in 1947, but this Trojan 20-gauge s/n 240,543 was built from a raw Remington-Parker serial numbered frame by a Parker Brothers gunmaker—it's not a restoration, certainly not an upgrade—it's a* Del Grego!

(bottom) *Oscar Gaddy's case colors are deceptively similar to Parker Brothers originals. One of these VHs is original—which one? Oscar has come as close as anyone to replicating Parker's "trademark" case colors. For the time being, patina of age will distinguish the restoration below from the original above.*

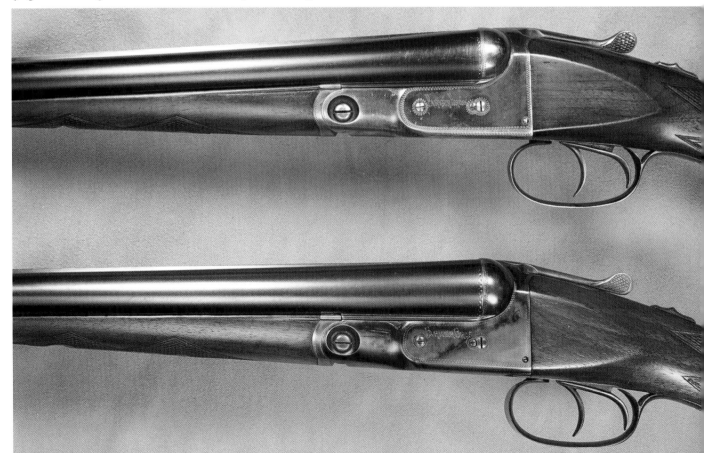

(top) *Parker Brothers circa 1928 Trojan shows 100 percent case colors. Look at the wood fit!*

(bottom) *Parker Brothers 100 percent case colors Trojan. Notice original sealant is still present where it oozed out from between the bottom plate and the frame. This gun is not only* **mint-unfired**, *but has been handled hardly at all.*

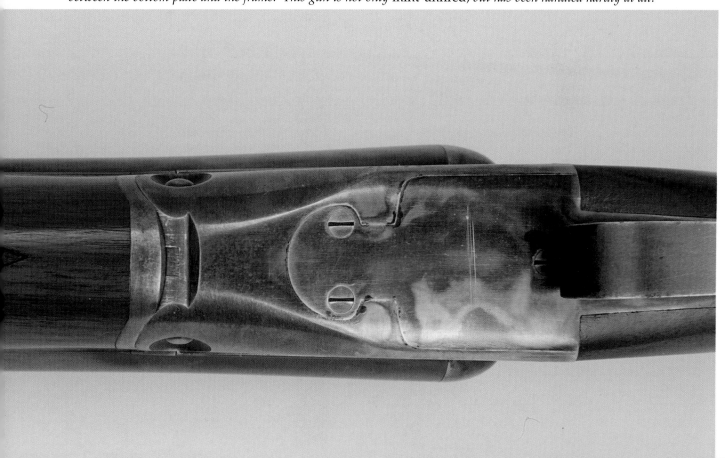

(top) Remington-Parker VHE half-frame showing darker 99 percent case colors characteristic of late Remingtons. This gun is immaculate.

(bottom) Remington-Parker 99 percent case colors VHE half-frame with simply "Parker" on the bottom. Remington purchased the Parker Gun—not Parker Brothers. Remington-built Parkers of all grades are typically marked PARKER on the bottom of the frame. Look at the trigger guard—almost zero wear!

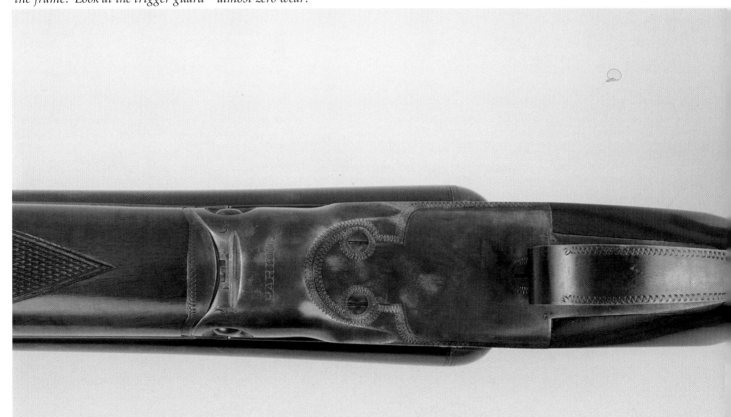

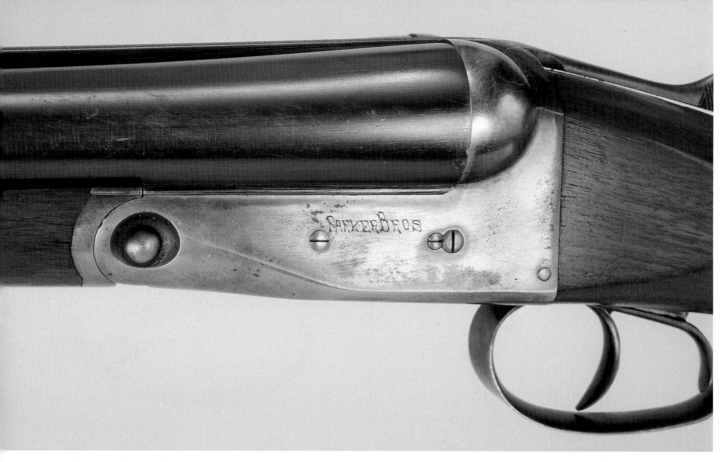

(top) *Parker Brothers circa 1930 Trojan showing about 90 percent case colors coverage, but thinning in areas of wear. Note the wood fit, unturned screws, and original barrel blue.*

(bottom) *Parker Brothers Trojan showing 90 percent case colors, perfect unturned screws, and encroachment of slight wear on the edges of the browned trigger guard. Compare the screw slots to the VHE that follows.*

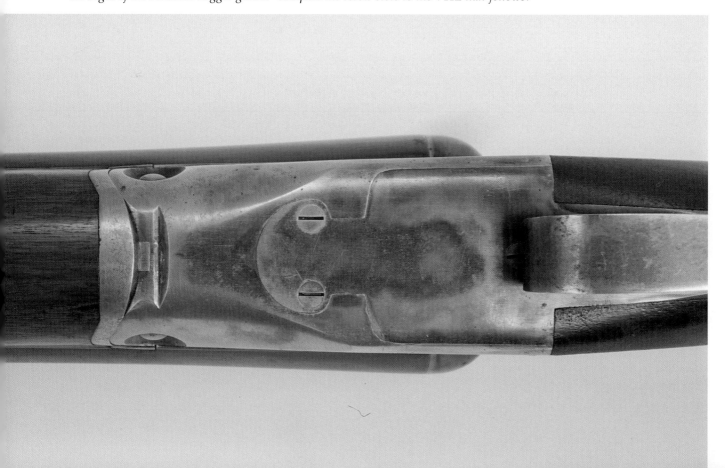

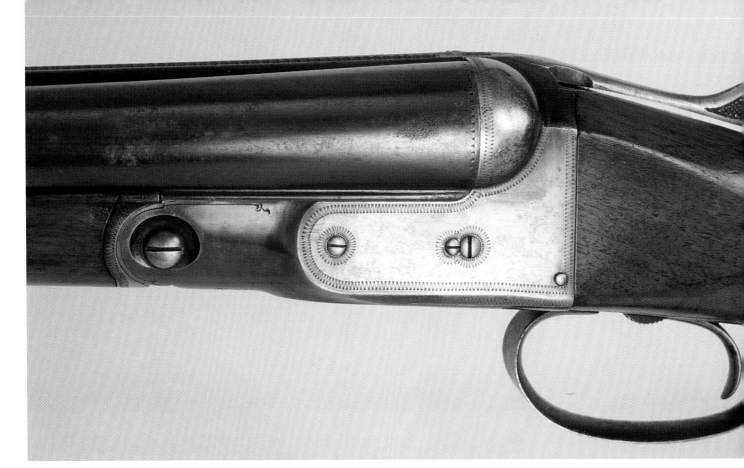

(top) *Remington-Parker VHE date stamped XE (December 1936), showing 80 percent case colors with original barrel blue, slightly pitted upon closest examination.*

(bottom) *Remington-Parker VHE built December 1936, showing 80 percent case colors with characteristic* PARKER *engraved on bottom of the frame. Compare these screws to the Trojan's and you'll notice they have been turned, but not boogered. This gun was twice sent back to Remington for repairs, according to date stamps on the barrel flats.*

(top) Parker Brothers circa 1930 DHE Trap showing 70 percent case colors going brown. This gun has been used but not abused. The magnifying lens and special lighting tend to bring out scratches and dings not ordinarily visible to the naked eye.

(bottom) Parker Brothers DHE Trap showing 70 percent case colors and less than perfect screws. The bottom plate has been off more than once.

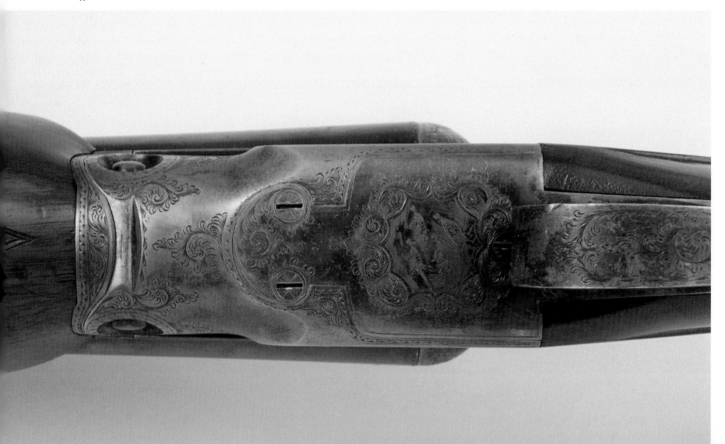

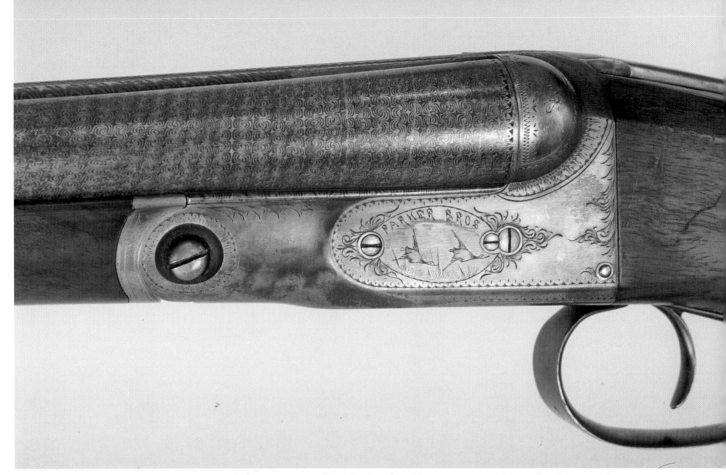

(top) *Parker Brothers circa 1903 GH with fine Damascus barrels showing 60 percent case colors going brown. The screws have been turned by a turnscrew not fat enough to fill the slot.*

(bottom) *Parker Brothers 60 percent case colors GH going brown, but with a fair amount of bluing on the trigger guard.*

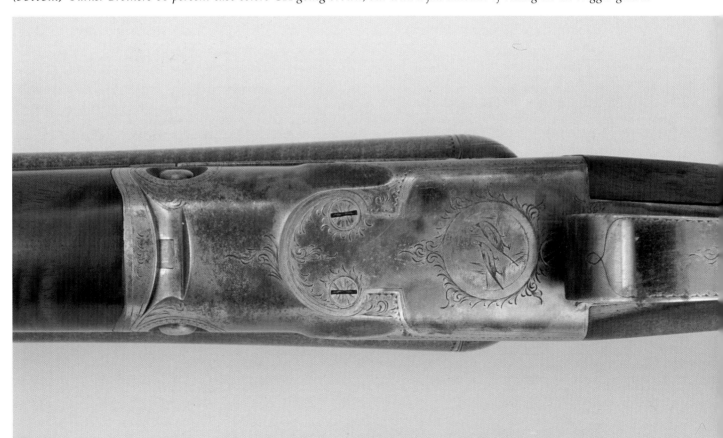

(top) Parker Brothers circa 1928 PH .410 showing 50 percent case colors. Given the "one-of-a-kind" rarity of this particular gun, higher condition would probably not result in much increased value.

(bottom) Parker Brothers PH .410 showing 50 percent case colors going brown and appropriate patina of age on trigger guard.

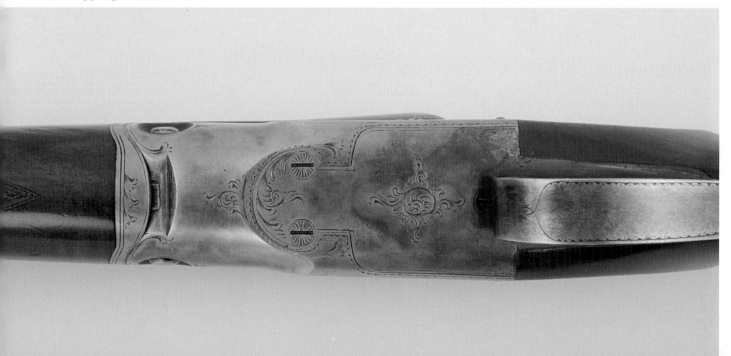

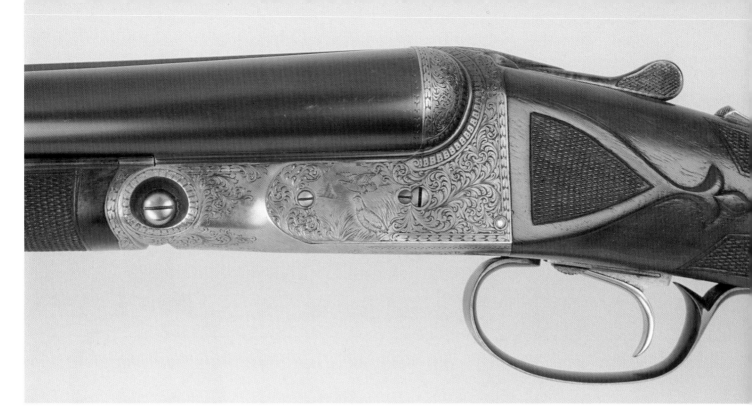

(top) *Remington-Parker circa 1930 AHE showing 20 percent case colors, but higher overall condition than case colors alone would indicate. Apparently the higher grades with their more elaborate engraving had thinner colors to start with and simply lost colors with passage of time rather than as a function of wear.*

(bottom) *Remington-Parker AHE showing 20 percent case colors, but as much as 95 percent blue on the trigger guard. With a gun like this, percentage of case colors doesn't even begin to describe condition.*

(Top) Parker Brothers circa 1906 fine Damascus barreled CHE with case colors removed. This appearance is often called "clean and sharp" by sellers. Notice the screws have been turned with a less than adequate turnscrew. Also note the engraved border where frame joins the stock—then go back and compare to the DHE Trap with 70 percent case colors. See the difference?

(bottom) Parker Brothers "clean and sharp" CHE with a high proportion of bluing on trigger guard. My guess is the gun was sent in for refurbishing many years ago and the barrels were rebrowned, trigger guard reblued, and case colors removed at the owner's request.

(top) *Parker Brothers circa 1896 BH with more case colors than it ought to have. The less-than-sharp engraving shows the gun was buffed down and recase-colored. Compare this gun's engraving to the "clean and sharp" CHE. Note the factory engraving on the retrofit Titanic barrels.*

(bottom) *Parker Brothers BH showing too much blue on the trigger guard for a gun 100 years old. My guess is this gun was refinished by Remington or Del Grego Sr. long, long ago.*

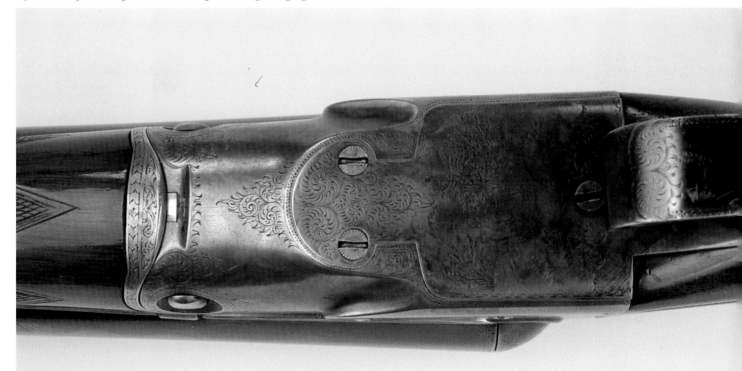

This gun doesn't fit with the case colors examples — why?

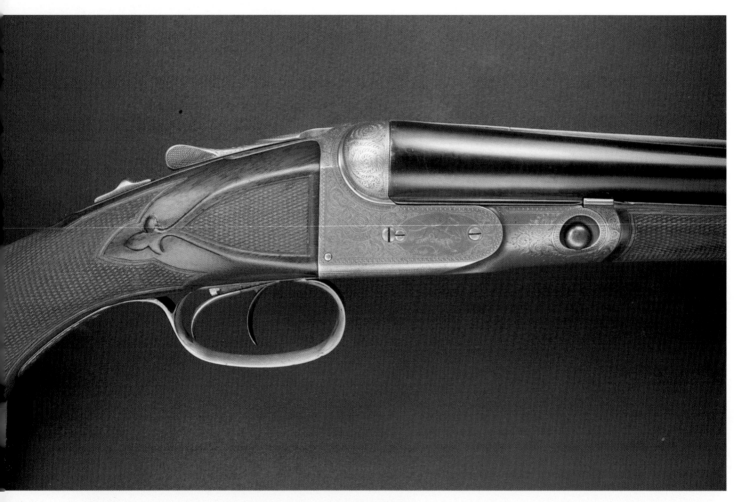

It should be obvious this vintage BH has been restored, but did you notice the lack of an engraved margin under the barrel blue at the breech? Poor barrel fit? Uncharacteristic full-cover checking on the fore-end? Many restorations just don't ring true, but all of the case colors examples are factory originals.

(right) *BH 12-gauge 100 years old and lookin' good.*

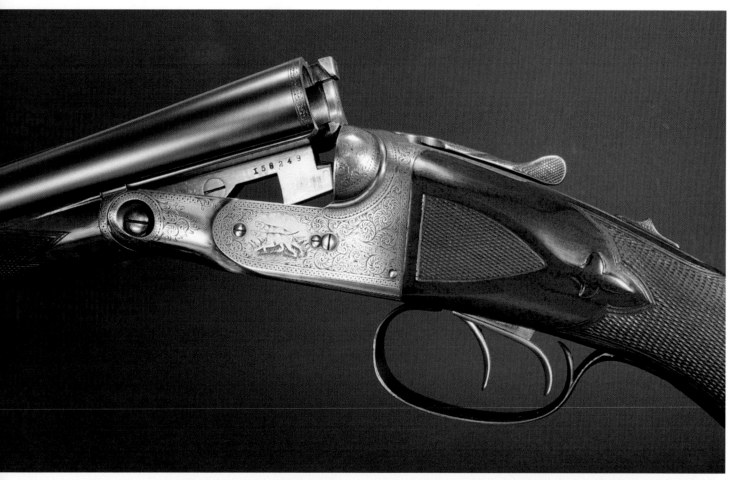

Parker Brothers circa 1910 BHE 16-gauge with 28-inch barrels on No. 0 (standard 20-gauge) frame weighing in at a "feather-lite" 5 pounds, 13 ounces. This gun has been refinished/refurbished/restored—or whatever you want to call it. Some purist collectors would walk away from a nonoriginal-condition gun. But when it comes to BH-grade and above, my records show that only one or two high-condition originals are offered for sale each year. What to do? I made the mistake of mentioning this gun to a friend—and he bought it! I was disappointed, but then I acquired the BH 12-gauge on the preceding page. I guess there are enough decent Parkers to go around. Now if only I can find a high-condition, original AH 12-gauge—my "Holy Grail"—with good dimensions and at a reasonable price.

NEW YORK SALESROOM
25 MURRAY ST.

THE PARKER GUN

PARKER BROTHERS

MASTER GUN MAKERS

MERIDEN, CONN.

March 17, 1927.

IN REPLY REFER TO

HLC

Mr. William Meyers,
Box 722,
Hampton, Iowa.

Dear Sir:

We received your order of the 3rd several days ago. It has
been entered and the $15.00 credited to your account, for
which we thank you.   Factory, in checking up the specifications, advises us that the weight you have given is somewhat
too light for a gun to be used with the 2 3/4" shells.

Our light weight limit for this length in a 12/30 is 7 lbs.
10 oz., and the addition of the recoil pad and the 1/4 " extra
length of stock would increase that weight probably four to
six ounces.

The fact that you have specified a heavy comb would also tend
to make the gun slightly heavier.

It is impossible for us to accept an order for a gun lighter
than as described above, and we trust it will be satisfactory
to you to allow us to increase the weight as stated.

A gun as light as you have ordered, would be unsafe in our
opinion to handle the 2 3/4" loads, in which as you know, the
heavy Super-X and similar powders are loaded.

It is quite possible you would never use them, but there is
always a chance that if the gun is chambered for them, either
you or someone else may use these shells, and we have therefore
established what we have found to be proper light weight limits.
These weights are controlled by wall thicknesses of course,
and these vary from the breech toward the muzzle.

We have entered the order for a full pistol grip stock, which
we trust is satisfactory, and believe we can make up a gun which
will please you in every way, even though the weight is greater
than you desire, because it will be properly balanced, and will
handle most satisfactorily.

We are holding up the order awaiting your reply.

Yours very truly,
PARKER BROTHERS

HLC.B

William Meyers was a prolific letter-writer during the 1920s, and every one of his "gun crank" inquiries drew a lengthy response from the gun works. Contrast this Parker Brothers factory letter (one of more than twenty to VH customer Meyers) to the form letter sent by Remington to the recent purchaser of the expensive BHE half-frame pictured on the title page of "On the Skids" in Chapter 5.

It's interesting that in 1927 Parker Brothers considered it a challenge to build William Meyers a 12-gauge with thirty-inch barrels to weigh much under eight pounds when, back in 1902, Parker couldn't have sold a twelve with thirty- or thirty-two-inch barrels weighing more than eight pounds to a competitive shooter. What happened? Did Parker guns get heavier after World War I? Sure they did, as the nitro loads started to pack more punch.

Turn-of-the-century Parker guns have a finer, sleeker look as compared to the Remington guns made at Ilion, New York, in the late '30s. Part of it is that earlier guns have less wood. The later Remington guns are war clubs by comparison. This isn't to say late Remington-Parkers aren't desirable, but they seem to lack the fineness of guns made prior to World War I. I've weighed a few guns in my time, and the following may illuminate this point:

I took some guns along when I went shopping for a nice D grade in Terrell, Texas. My circa 1908 benchmark VH 20-gauge with size 0 frame, thirty-inch barrels, splinter fore-end, and Hawkins pad tipped Chadick's scale at six pounds one ounce. Herschel Chadick had an identical circa 1929 VHE 20 that weighed six pounds fifteen ounces, and a circa 1940 late Remington VHE 20 with twenty-six-inch barrels that weighed six pounds four ounces. Gun for gun, my 20-gauge was fourteen ounces lighter than the same gun built by Parker Brothers twenty years later. The same gun with four-inch-shorter barrels, built by Remington in 1940, weighed three ounces more. My twenty was not only lighter on the scale but also was visibly lighter and couldn't be mistaken for the later models. Some people like late Remingtons, and others like turn-of-the-century guns. I'm not taking sides, but Parker guns put on weight toward the end of production.

Some of the weight gain resulted from options like beavertail fore-end and ventilated

Annie Oakley—sometimes called "Little Miss Sure-shot"— favored a Parker gun for live-bird shooting at the 1902 Grand American Handicap.

ounces. Du Bray, Budd, and Gilbert were at the GAH on business, as they were all employed by Parker Brothers.

One of the lightest twelves at the Grand American was Annie Oakley's seven-pound two-ounce Parker. The dominant weight was seven pounds fourteen ounces, with very few guns lighter than seven pounds ten ounces. The consensus of the top live-bird shooters of the day was that a seven-pound fourteen-ounce 12-gauge using a proportioned load of 1¼ ounces of Number 7 chilled shot was most effective. In this context, it's hard to understand why Uncle Dan built a six-pound 12-gauge. However, one wouldn't need to take off his shoes to count the number of Lefever guns represented at the Grand American.

rib, but gun for gun, less hand-finishing was the culprit. There are exceptions. Parker collectors are likely aware of the 12-gauge A-1 Special with gold, s/n 241,000, offered for sale by Chadick's recently. This gun was built on the very rare half-frame and has a beavertail fore-end, single selective trigger, auto ejectors, capped pistol grip, and skeleton steel buttplate. I called Herschel, and he put the gun on his scale; it weighs eight pounds even. This A-1 Special is relatively heavy when you

Here's one solution to the "heavy gun" problem which hasn't occurred to many 6-pound 12-gauge evangelists — simply give the dogs a break.

consider that turn-of-the-century Parker live-bird guns were built on size 1½ or size 2 frames and could weigh no more than eight pounds (without pad) under the Interstate Association rules. The late 1930s chart shows that a double-barrel 12-gauge trap gun with ventilated rib, beavertail fore-end, recoil pad, and single trigger should weigh between seven pounds fourteen ounces and eight pounds two ounces with thirty-inch barrels. Herschel says his A-1-S is a "big gun specially ordered for trapshooting." The skeleton steel buttplate added weight over a recoil pad. This gun cost $1,004 in 1940. Adjusted for inflation, the 1995 price of $79,500 was lots higher but down from $125,000 in 1994.

If Annie Oakley at age thirty-six could heft a seven-pound two-ounce Parker 12-gauge, then a grown man should be able to handle a comparable all-purpose twelve in the seven- to eight-pound range. Short-barrel twelves purpose-built for skeet, quail, woodcock, and thick brush could weigh slightly less than seven pounds, and light spreader loads would naturally minimize recoil while compensating for close-range shooting. Colonel Askins was a fan of the light twelve chambered for two-inch shells with one ounce or less of shot for short-range shooting, the less physically adept, and children; but he had this to say about small bores:

> . . . The reader may leap to the conclusion, judging from these comments of mine, that I am somewhat prejudiced against the dinky, two-bit small bores. If he has gotten this impression, I am delighted to know that the salvo hasn't missed the mark.

The Colonel and I might be accused of prejudice in favor of twelves; however, one's lifetime experiences often add up to an educated judgment that is tantamount to fact. The operative *fact* in my situation is that the big, healthy, wild, running-away pheasants on my place in northern Illinois will not surrender to a small bore. It takes a 12-gauge with at least $1^1/_8$ ounces of hard sixes to get any respect around here. One of these days, Bismuth or some other miracle substitute for steel shot will allow my favorite Parker to once again realize its potential as a duck gun. And though I'm not a regular at "Plug and Pellet," I usually get down there a few times before hunting season to show the trick-gun specialists what my "old iron" will do to clay birds. My all-purpose GH fowling piece weighs a perfect all-round seven pounds eight ounces. Should I ever go where the quail are thick, my VHE 12-gauge Skeet at six pounds fifteen ounces with one-ounce loads would be the gun of choice. If the day comes when I consider a shotgun weighing seven to eight pounds to be an undue burden, I can heed Colonel Askins's advice and take up ping-pong.

Figures Lie and Liars Figure

Parker small bores were a market success because the gun works found it much easier to sell high-margin second guns to preexisting 10- and 12-gauge customers than to actively compete with the Winchester 97 and other relatively inexpensive repeaters for a share of the "popular priced" 12-bore market. Parker Bothers thrived on repeat customers in the early years of the twentieth century. The last Grand American Handicap at Live Birds was held in 1902, and Parker accounted for 35.5 percent of the competitors' guns, up slightly from two years before when 34.6 percent of all entrants used the "Old Reliable" Parker gun. The Winchester 97 and other slide-action shotguns were still highly suspect, and it was then an article of faith that no repeater could ever balance or point like a double. But the times they were a-changin': by 1910 a double was the rare gun at trap competition, almost as rare as the repeater in 1902. The Parker gun became a *want* rather than a *need* item by 1905, so it was up to S. A. Tucker, A. E. Perris, Captain du Bray, and other factory reps to convince their customers to "heighten charm of game shooting" by retiring a perfectly good Parker 12-gauge in favor of a new "more-efficient" small bore.

Back in 1975, when I was buying into the cattle business in a small way, my neighbors, Johnson Brothers Angus, were in the cattle business in a big way. I needed some advice and got to talking across the fence to Glen "Putter" Johnson about some performance-tested Angus heifers soon to be sold at auction in South Dakota. Putter looked at the sale catalog, which was full of very compelling statistics, took it all in, paused, and then divulged one of life's great truths: "Figures lie and liars figure." I went to South Dakota anyway and bought a draft of heifers. But, ever mindful of Putter's advice, I had a cautious respect for the numbers, and my eyes made all the final decisions. As I wrote this chapter, it occurred to me that Putter's advice is true in spades when applied to the ongoing 12-gauge versus small bore controversy.

In view of the many inquiries that are constantly being received by us relative to the merits of small bore shotguns—particularly the 20-gauge, we feel that some information on this interesting subject may appeal to sportsmen who would like to heighten charm of game shooting, and at the same time place no material handicap as to actual results achieved, when using light gun of small caliber.

The Small Bore Shotgun
by Parker Bros.

Parker Brothers ad from August 1911 issue of Outer's Book, *bragging up the success of Parker's double barreled shotgun. Repeaters had pretty much taken over by 1911, so when a double did well it was news.*

My intention is not to disparage small-bore guns. The 20-gauge, 28-gauge, and .410 "bore" all stand on their own objective ballistics. Much has been written about the merits and demerits of small-bore shotguns. Half-truths, convoluted logic, wishful thinking, flights of fancy, and downright foolishness are the stock-in-trade of those who cannot simply take a small-bore shotgun at face value. Many small-bore true believers are "less is more" evangelists, and for them, anyone who does not pick up a 20-gauge in the name of "conservation;" anyone who does not abandon his slow, inefficient twelve in favor of a smaller, "faster" bore size; anyone who doesn't also believe the world is flat—well, such a person is a regrettably bad shot, a game hog, and just not privy to all the compelling arguments and proofs of the Flat Earth Society.

My thesis is that the real recipe for Parker's 20-gauge popularity in the early 1900s was the repeating 12-gauge and snake-oil in equal parts. Parker Brothers was at the top of the market in 1900, selling what the top competitive live-bird and clay-target shooters wanted and needed. In a few short years thereafter, Parker Brothers was selling only the *want* side of the equation. The repeater had swamped the 12-bore market—a perfect opportunity for "doctor" du Bray and his elixir of 20-bore to cure what ails.

Parker Brothers' response to the increasing popularity of repeaters was to protect its average annual production of 4,000 guns by convincing a sufficient number of its existing clientele to buy arms that were less effective by design. The market for high-quality side-by-side double-barrel twelves was thin and getting thinner by 1905, but the market for twenties and twenty-eights was mostly unexplored.

At the turn of the century, the 12-gauge had pretty well displaced the 10-gauge in the field and at the traps. Tens were heavy to hunt with and competitive live-bird loads were limited to 1¼ ounces of shot, so there wasn't any advantage to the larger bore size. The maximum gun weight allowed by the Interstate Association was eight pounds even plus pad. A Parker 10-gauge with size 3 frame wasn't even close. So the logic was in place, the precedent was set, and if you didn't look too closely at the underlying facts, the "small-bore" twelve could do the job as well as the "big-bore" ten. This was progress. Likewise, why shouldn't the miracles of bulk smokeless powder, nitro loads, and repeatable choke boring allow the 16-gauge (and in turn the 20-gauge) to supersede the twelve? This was the modern way—science over common sense.

H. L. Betten as a youngster in the early 1880s hunted band-tailed pigeons with a

10-bore muzzleloader. He was the consummate sportsman and hunted with Charles Askins (both father and son) and Captain A. W. du Bray. Betten wrote *Upland Game Shooting* in 1940, summarizing the high points of his sixty-odd years afield. For example, he participated in the first pheasant season in Oregon in 1892 (sixty-seven birds in three days). But every shotgunner has his prejudices. Betten liked the sixteen. I'll let him explain:

> Knowing something of the great popularity of the 10-gauge at its peak, and being in at its death, I would not be surprised if the 16-gauge, in turn, supplanted the 12-gauge as the popular all-around gun. The modern sixteen has been stepped up until it is now capable of handling $1\,{}^3/_{16}$ oz. of shot in high velocity loads. In other words, it has advanced beyond the ballistic capabilities of the 12-gauge during the period when it was making history and supplanting the now obsolete ten.

A. W. du Bray, Parker Brothers' good ol' boy on the road, had been operating out of Cincinnati, hunting with his Parker hammerless sixteen and Pigeon-grade twelve hammer gun throughout the Southwest in 1898, about the same time A. E. Perris was freelancing for Parker Brothers in San Bernardino, California. Captain du Bray sold Parker guns on commission, while Perris was paid in guns—one BHE 12-gauge with thirty-inch barrels, s/n 134,749, in 1906; a BHE 16-gauge with twenty-eight-inch barrels, s/n 148,780, in 1908; and a BHE 28-gauge with twenty-six-inch barrels, s/n 156,949, in 1911. All Perris's commission guns followed the contemporary trend away from 12-gauge to progressively smaller bore sizes, but his guns also reflected the status quo as they all were ordered with Damascus barrels.

The trend was toward small bores in 1908, and A. W. du Bray had long been the nation's leading proponent of the 20-gauge. This was a sign of the times and evidence that Parker Brothers was doing the hard sell on small bores. Captain du Bray headed to the Northwest in fall 1908, and returned home to Cincinnati in January 1909 by way of the Dayton, Kentucky, Grand Central Handicap live-bird shoot. Du Bray had been on the road pushing the 20-gauge as the salvation of duck hunting, and he no doubt spent some time in the duck blind with none other than well-known writer-sportsman Edwin L. Hedderly. The proper duck-hunting venue for the well-to-do was the members-only duck club. If and when du Bray and Hedderly got together, it probably went something like this:

> Du Bray: Good to see ya, Ed, ol' friend. Thanks for inviting me to your very exclusive and private northern California duck club for a day of sport. What's our self-imposed daily limit this year? Thirty? Forty? Fifty?
>
> Hedderly: Glad you could make it, Arthur, but sorry to say, ducks are in short numbers, so we only shoot mornings and quit when we each have twenty. By the way, is that a new gun?
>
> Du Bray: Sure is . . . glad you asked. It's my new 20-gauge duck-club gun with three-inch chambers. Faster than a downwind teal and weighs only six pounds fourteen ounces. Kills ducks like a twelve—*if you're good enough*. It will take a real crack shot to get twenty ducks by noon with this baby.
>
> Hedderly: Wow! It just happens I have vast amounts of money burning holes in my hunting-coat pockets, and I deem myself a real sportsman and a crack duck shot. Would you possibly take an order for a high-grade 20-gauge duck gun for me?
>
> Du Bray: Sure, Ed, no problem. The factory's a little backed up right now, given the big demand for small bores, but I'll write your order and wire it right away. If you want to try my twenty today, we can switch guns; I'll shoot your sixteen. If you like my twenty, we'll expedite your order.

By the way, why don't you trade on your image as a well-known sportsman to spread the word about small-bore guns being the modern way? You don't need to mention Parker Brothers. Just write *Forest and Stream* about your decision to go to a 20-gauge in the name of good sportsmanship and conservation.

Hedderly: Sure will, Arthur. Now let's go kill our forty ducks.

And so it came to pass that *Forest and Stream* noted Captain du Bray was back in Kentucky for the Grand Central Handicap in January 1909, after a duck-hunting trip to the Northwest with his favorite 20-gauge. At the same time, Edwin Hedderly began a letter-writing campaign in favor of the 20-gauge and, in turn, was "flamed" by a nemesis who signed himself "Twelve Gauge." What follows is a sample of what passed for shotgun science in 1909. Meet small-bore expert and famous sportsman of the early 1900s Edwin L. Hedderly, made semi-famous again by Larry Baer's picturing Hedderly's A-1 Special in his book, *Parker Guns—An Immortal American Classic*. In the words of Edwin (the italics are mine):

Since my last letter I have been doing considerable experimenting with a 20-bore in the matter of loads. It is this use of a heavier proportionate load without greatly increasing the weight of the gun, but rather lightening it and facilitating its handling, that, in my judgment, makes the *small-bores so deadly in capable hands*. My 16 weighs 6 pounds 5 ounces; the 20s I have been shooting are about 3 ounces lighter, and have 28-inch barrels, bored full choke.

The trouble is, *the average man is afraid to tax his skill* with the small-bore's smaller killing circle, and wants to rely on the 12's slop-over margin, which, like charity, covers a multitude of sins. *Every test* conducted in this or any other country has shown that the proportioned loads of the *small-bores excel the large in velocity*. Velocity is penetration; penetration is shock. Shock is

clean killing power. Now, if this is true of proportioned loads, how much truer is it of increases in power that are possible with smaller bores? These hold the shot together better than the larger, else the killing circles would be smaller. There can be no question that the smaller bores *call for closer holding*, nor that they have a tendency to *kill clean or miss clean* that endears them to their users. Size of shot must be considered. Sixes work splendidly in the 16s; 7s in the 20, although some of these handle sixes very well. I consider myself *no great sharp as a duck shot*; never a day goes by that I cannot look back on a dozen birds that I ought to have got, and slop-shot or otherwise missed, but I believe I can kill ducks as far and *about* as regularly with a 16 as anything else, and am now taking up a 20 in earnest. . . . If one loads his ammunition, there is enough savings to pay interest on the cost of a new gun, if an *average amount of shooting* is done. The saving all comes in quantities, however; empties, wads, all cost about alike. Shot is the big item, and ¾-ounce against 1⅛ mounts up in *5,000 or 6,000 shells* to quite a sum.

Hedderly deemed himself "no great sharp as a duck shot," so he decided to tax his skill by taking up a 20-gauge in earnest, perhaps because small bores are "so deadly in capable hands"—"less is more," and there's *more* to the story. Hedderly was going to make his new 20-gauge pay by the shot savings of using ¾-ounce rather than his standard one-ounce 16-gauge load. He was going to save ¼ ounce times 5,000 to 6,000 shells per year, or 80 to 90 pounds of shot at $1.65 per 25-pound bag—less than $6 per year. Hedderly's A-1 Special pictured in Baer's book listed for $525 in 1909. I have a hunch that Hedderly didn't pay for his A-1 Special with the money he saved by hunting ducks with a 20-gauge, although if his wife believed the story, then maybe there was some "profit."

Meanwhile, Mr. "Twelve Gauge" wrote to *Forest and Stream* to dispute some of the

Parker Brothers ad from November 1922 issue of Field *and* Stream. *Pacific coast agent A. W. du Bray was a strong advocate of the 20-gauge. Capt. du Bray's biography in the Christmas 1905 issue of Shooting and Fishing said that "He is regarded as the leading exponent of small bores for upland-game shooting." Parker Brothers rediscovered the 12-gauge as the ideal fowling piece after the enactment of the Migratory Bird Treaty Act of 1918, and the small-bore craze fizzled for lack of a "grand passage" of ducks.*

anecdotal evidence and self-aggrandizing statements made by Hedderly. "Twelve Gauge" stated his case and concluded:

> On the whole, I think Mr. Hedderly will have difficulty in persuading duck hunters generally that it would be wise for them to discard their 12-gauge guns in favor of 16s or 20s or that the 12s will not kill further than the smaller bores.

Hedderly was quick to write back to *Forest and Stream*, shoring up his arguments in favor of the 20-gauge by invoking the alleged consensus of duck clubs with 1,000 members, and claiming:

> . . . It is a fact that the *crack shots*, almost without exception, have adopted small-bore guns . . . [and] . . . here we think *any good shot who sticks to his 12 wants to rake flocks for extra birds.* [italics mine]

Aha—Hedderly tips his hand! He's going to take up a 20-gauge so he can join the ranks of "crack shots." I don't think anyone really believed him when he described himself in his first letter as ". . . no great sharp as a duck shot." But the readers of *Forest and Stream* no doubt waited with bated breath to read his further pronouncements on "less is more," and the veiled attacks on Twelve Gauge, who, according to Hedderly, could only be a bad shot or a bad sport for using his namesake. Hedderly wasn't pulling punches when he wrote that 12-gauge shooters ". . . rely on slop-over margin, which, like charity, covers a multitude of sins . . . [and] . . . any good shot who sticks to his 12 wants to rake flocks for extra birds." The letter-writing campaign degenerated from name-calling to name-dropping as Hedderly and Twelve Gauge lined up "experts," quoted to support their respective positions. Meanwhile, R. E. Stratton of Mississippi wrote to join the fray, although he missed the point completely; Stratton agreed with Twelve Gauge simply

because he was unable to buy 20-gauge shotshells near home. By 1916, however, the 20-gauge was so well established that even those in Mississippi could enjoy the benefits of the small bore if that was their pleasure (or affliction). Probably the most deadly shot made in the 12-gauge versus 20-gauge war of words was a direct hit by the writer of an August 1916 letter to the *Outer's Book*:

> Editor, gun department: I have a 20-gauge in my head and would like to ask a few questions. I use a Parker 12 at present, and do you think the extra shots in a 20-gauge pump would offset it?
>
> Answer: The extra shots in a 20-gauge pump would quite offset the 12-gauge Parker, except for long range work, where a heavy load of shot was demanded for say duck and goose shooting.

So there it is—the owner of a perfectly useful 12-gauge Parker was advised to put it in the closet and go buy a 20-gauge repeater to blaze away. Five or six shots from a 20-gauge repeater should "offset" two from a Parker twelve. The game had changed, birds were getting scarce in 1916, and *less* gun meant *more* shooting—less *was* more!

The real key to effectiveness of the small bore (then and now) isn't nitro powder or choke-boring or magnum loads or straight shooting; it's the clever use of adjectives, omissions, and exculpatory statements. Friends brag up hunting pheasants with their 20s and 28s, but if the truth be told, they are shooting pen-raised birds, which might be had as easily with a tennis racket or baseball bat. Parker Brothers' booklet, *The Small Bore Shotgun*, has to be read closely to notice that the twelve and twenty are never really compared at standard range. The 20-gauge is said to be ". . . no material handicap . . . [or] . . . almost as effective . . . [and of course] . . . the average man . . . [must] . . . tax his skill," but the apples are never really compared to the oranges.

The "Old Reliable"

PARKER GUN

FOR small game, like rail, snipe, woodcock and plover, we recommend a 20-bore Parker. It is lighter and easier to handle than a larger gun would be, and usually makes a cleaner kill.

Of course, a Parker is a Parker in any gauge; same sturdy construction, perfect balance and unfailing action.

The Parker Bolting System

typifies Parker simplicity and reliability. It is a combination straight and tapered bolt. The tapered faces take up all wear; the flat surfaces prevent any lifting of the barrel when firing.

PARKER BROS.
Master Gun Makers
34 Cherry Street, MERIDEN, CONN.

Parker Brothers ad from February 1924 issue of Outdoor Life, *touting the 20-bore for small game like rail, snipe, woodcock, and plover; but notice brandt and mallard were no longer recommended smallbore targets. Waterfowl had become too scarce and protected for the luxury of "bragging rights" smallbores.*

According to Colonel Askins, ". . . a shotgun is made primarily to kill game and not to save it—the more effective it is, the better adapted to its purpose." Shotguns aren't for conservation and shouldn't be ineffective. The small-bore fans needed to paint over or rationalize away the relative ineffectiveness of the 20-gauge when compared to the 12-gauge. Parker Brothers was up to the task. *The Small Bore Shotgun* booklet was published after the twenty-versus-twelve debate had pretty well wound down. Characteristic of Parker Brothers, once everyone had reached a consensus, the gun works jumped in front of the parade. Parker Brothers had been making 20-gauges since the late 1870s, so the *Small Bore* booklet was not exactly on the cutting edge of technology, and the topic of small-bore velocity was an old but resurrected debate. In a letter to *Forest and Stream* dated October 31, 1889, a small-bore fan stated his case:

> If the 16 and 20-gauge are not powerful enough, how is it that such scores are made with them? For instance: Miss Oakley, at Gloucester, N. J., used a 20-gauge with a charge of ¾ ounce of shot, weight of gun 5½ lbs. and killed 49 out of 50 birds. Was it an accident? No. They get there every time.

This is what I call the "Small-bore Superman Theory"—faster than a speeding bullet, "They get there every time." The proponents of small bores verily believe that speed is the name of the game. Forget good pattern; forget the inertia of larger shot; forget the proportionate number of pellets rubbing against the grinding mill of the forcing cone, bore, and choke of a 20-gauge versus a 12-gauge; and forget the shot count in a thirty-inch circle at forty yards. None of this matters to small-bore true believers. But where did they get the idea that bore size controls velocity?

Some insight into Parker Brothers' philosophy of "lightweight" guns can be gleaned from *The Small Bore Shotgun*. This booklet extols the virtues of 20-gauges weighing 5¾ to 6⅛ pounds using ¾ ounce of shot; 6¼ to 6½ pounds using ⅞ ounce of shot; and a purpose-built 6¾- to seven-pound, 3-inch-chambered duck gun for nitro powder and ⅞ ounce of shot. Note that the 3-inch duck gun was made to be *faster* (i.e. room for more powder) but still used ⅞ ounce of shot.

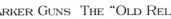

TABLE SHOWING SIZE OF SPREAD OF SHOT AT 25 YARDS FROM PARKER GUNS OF DIFFERENT GAUGES AND DEGREE OF CHOKE

Make of Gun	Gauge.	Drams of Powder.	Quantity of No. 9 Shot in Ounces.	Killing Circles in Inches of Cylinder Barrels at 25 Yards.	Average in Inches of Cylinder Barrels.	Killing Circles in Inches of Modified Choke Barrels.	Average in Inches of Modified Barrels.	Killing Circles in Inches of Full Choke Barrels at 25 Yards.	Average in Inches of Choke Barrels.
Parker	12	3	1⅛	29, 30	30	22, 22, 22, 23	22	16, 16, 17, 18	17
Parker	16	2¾	1	28, 28, 28	28	. . . .	. . . .	18, 19, 17	18
Parker	20	2¼	⅞	28, 30, 28	29	. . . .	. . . .	20, 19, 21	20
Parker	28	2	¾	24, 26, 26	25	. . . .	. . . .	20, 19, 18	19

Table from early 1920s small-bore booklet showing a Parker 28-gauge with ¾ ounce load had a killing circle of 19 inches at 25 yards as compared to a Parker 12-gauge with 1¹/₈ ounce shot having a 17-inch killing circle. Say what?

The booklet shows interesting ballistic information available to Parker customers if they knew enough to ask. For example, a Parker 12-gauge with 1⅛ ounces of shot had a "killing circle" of thirty inches at twenty-five yards for cylinder bore, twenty-two inches at twenty-five yards for modified choke, and seventeen inches at twenty-five yards for full choke. By comparison, a 20-gauge with ⅞ ounce of shot had a twenty-inch killing circle at twenty-five yards with full choke. My conclusion is that Parker Brothers compared apples to oranges. However, Parker Brothers concluded that a full-choke twenty with ⅞ ounce of shot had the same twenty-five-yard *killing power* as a twelve using 1⅛ ounces of shot; Parker just glossed over the smaller *killing circle* as "crack shots" like Hedderly were willing to *tax their skill by closer holding*. According to *The Small Bore Shotgun* booklet:

It is quite apparent therefore that the gauge of the gun does not operate against the shooter by handicapping him in his shooting, because by having his 20 gauge built and bored according to his special requirements, he can be supplied with a most useful and highly serviceable weapon, whether he use it at quail when shooting from 15-25 yards or at snipe up to 45 yards.

Parker Brothers patterned all gauges by test-firing at a standard thirty-inch circle at forty yards and tagged guns with shot-count results. An exception occurred in the 1870s and 1880s, when some guns were patterned at forty-five yards, but conversion factors were stated on the 1880s hanging tags to adjust to thirty inches at forty yards. Parker's use of ill-defined "killing circles" and "killing power" in *The Small Bore Shotgun* booklet was just plain hocus-pocus; or, in the sage words of Putter Johnson, "Figures lie and liars figure."

Bob Brister seemed to beat Hedderly's Small-bore Superman Theory to death, or at least into submission, in his 1976 book, *Shotgunning—The Art and The Science*. Edwin Hedderly believed that ". . . there can be no question . . . small bores have a tendency to kill clean or miss clean that endears them to users." Hedderly also liked Number 7s in his 20-gauge for ducks because of his mistaken belief that a speedy Number 7 could penetrate, shock, and kill better than a laggard load of Number 4s. Parker Brothers' own velocity tests show that Hedderly's 20-gauge wasn't any faster than his 16- or 12-gauges. Parker's velocity tests and Brister's penetration tests put the double whammy on Hedderly's Small-bore Superman Theory by showing killing energy to be a function of mass rather than speed—E=MC², according to Einstein—but, velocity being equal, pellet weight (mass) controlled killing power. Brister concluded that:

> Retained energy figures will help explain to those who favor 7½s for ducks why virtually every scientific test made on live ducks indicates 4s kill further and cleaner. The retained energy difference of a No. 4 shot at 50 yards is 3.11 foot pounds while a 7½ shot fired at the same high velocity (1330 fps) retained only .93 foot pounds. Obviously very few hits with No. 4s at 50 yards will put more energy into the bird than a swarm of 7½s . . . [which] . . . become vital area cripplers rather than killers.

If circa 1910 loads with velocities of 925 to 975 feet per second (fps) are plugged into Brister's equation, the same disparity of "killing power" would simply move closer to the muzzle—say thirty-five yards rather than fifty yards. Hedderly's observation that "small bores killed clean or missed clean" could have been based simply on the fact that ducks he dusted with Number 7s flew away to die "out of sight—out of mind," while Mr. Twelve Gauge was breaking wings and downing birds with Number 4s. Those latter birds may have given the dog fits, but they were ultimately retrieved and counted toward the 12-gauge's bag.

Parker Brothers' 1899 catalog has a chart that shows Tatham Number 7 chilled shot to have 299 pellets to the ounce. The ⅞-ounce 20-gauge *heavy* load would be 261 count against a *moderate* 1⅛-ounce, 336-count, 12-gauge load. When 261 pellets leave a 20-gauge shell, more shot (by count and percentage) will come into contact with the bore than would 336 shot traveling a 12-gauge barrel. Every pellet that comes into contact with the forcing cone, bore, and choke loses spherical correctness and is likely to go spinning off like a curve ball rather than hit the center of the target. Parker Brothers never defined "killing circle," but if you think 261

Number 7s in a twenty-inch circle are going to do as much damage as 336 in a seventeen-inch circle, then you are likely to own a small-bore shotgun for the wrong reasons. The pattern density of a 12-gauge can be opened up for close shooting (quail, for example), and light loads may be used to reduce recoil, but the 20-gauge has no such flexibility. Colonel Askins touched this base and came down on the side of the lightweight twelve being the more effective purveyor of ⅞ ounce of shot. Parker Brothers addressed the same issue in *The Small Bore Shotgun* booklet but drew various different conclusions:

> A small-bore gun, if of sufficient weight and properly bored to withstand full charges with perfect safety, is a tremendously hard shooter, giving greater velocity to the shot than can be obtained with any featherweight of wider bore, which, owing to its lightness can never be loaded up to the capacity of its gauge. Hence, a 12-gauge weighing 6 pounds is merely a 12-gauge in name, but not by any means any representative of the 12-gauge class, whereas a 20-gauge weighing 6 pounds is a very serviceable gun and quite capable of withstanding a moderately heavy charge. A 12-gauge of 6½ pounds weight is still of dwarf type as compared to the full size, but a 20-gauge at that weight is a very powerful shooter and unless needed for exceptionally hard shooting that is the full weight limit for guns of that caliber.

Enter the 3-inch-magnum duck-club gun—exit common sense and a healthy respect for wild game as a capable adversary. Parker Brothers' 3-inch-chambered duck gun was built to weigh 6¾ to seven pounds and push ⅞ ounce of shot. The goal was speed, and speed (in theory) meant penetration. However, penetration could also be enhanced by using Number 4 rather than Number 7 shot, except that a larger proportion of the bigger pellets would come into contact with the small-bore grinding mill, only to become "curve balls" once they left the muzzle. Put another way, Hedderly didn't use Number 4s in his 20-gauge duck gun for obvious reasons—Number 7s worked better for him but certainly not better than Number 4s in a 12-gauge, which he deemed beneath contempt, given his self-proclaimed "crack shot" status.

The 3-inch-magnum duck gun is the "Small-bore Superman Theory" put to practice. It's hard to fault Edwin Hedderly for some of his just plain wrong "expert advice," when Parker Brothers was confused and on both sides of the same issue (and building 3-inch-magnum 20s to boot). *The Small Bore Shotgun* booklet, published by Parker in at least four versions from 1914 to 1922, left no room for doubt that

> A small-bore gun . . . [gives] . . . greater velocity to the shot than can be obtained from any featherweight of wider bore. . . .

The gist of Hedderly's letter-writing campaign to *Forest and Stream* in 1909 was that

> Every test conducted in this or any other country has shown the proportioned loads of the small-bores to excel the large in velocity . . . penetration . . . shock . . . [and] . . . killing power.

However, Parker Brothers published another booklet in 1922, *Parker Guns—Double Barrel Game and Trap Guns—Single Trap Guns*, which should have put the "Small-Bore Superman Theory" to rest for all time. Parker's own tests showed that contemporary *heavy* (7/8-ounce Number 7) 20-gauge loads had *exactly* the same 973-fps muzzle velocity as *light* (one ounce No. 7) 12-gauge loads. The only difference was chamber pressure—6.1 tons per square inch for the twenty and 4.0 tons for the twelve. When Parker increased the 12-gauge load to standard 1⅛ ounce, velocity dropped to 930 fps; when the 20-gauge load was reduced to a proportioned ¾ ounce,

the velocity dropped to 922 fps. If you don't believe it, check it out on Parker Brothers' chart at right. And if you think the issue was put to rest in the 1920s, read farther.

Michael McIntosh's new book, *Shotguns and Shooting*, hit the ground running in 1995, and none can call a spade a spade better than Mike. I'm going to let him have the parting shot on the 20-gauge magnum:

> In theory and in fact the 3-inch 20-gauge cartridge is the worst abortion foisted upon the gunning world. Here's why. The only way to get more shot into any given bore is to stack the pellets. The longer the shot column in relation to bore diameter, the less efficient the performance, for several reasons. First, the longer column places more pellets in contact with the barrel wall, which scrapes them out of round and turns them into useless fliers. The longer and heavier the shot charge, the more it resists thrust from the powder gases, in part because of increased friction and in part simply because a heavier object is harder to move. This increases chamber pressure and also means more crushed pellets at the bottom of the column; these string out behind the main swarm, rapidly shedding velocity and contributing nothing to pattern efficiency.

Hedderly was long on bold-stated facts and short on attribution. His velocity theory was just plain wrong—a luxury indulged in, surprisingly, by a sportsman of his stature, writing ability, and access to all the popular sports media in the early years of the twentieth century. As a member of a private duck club, he also had the luxury of access to both spring and fall hunts, great rafts of flyway ducks drawn to massive baiting and live decoys, and ample opportunity to blow off 5,000 or 6,000 shells in an "average season." Given today's two-, three-, or four-duck limits, steel shot (or bismuth at two bucks each), diminished wetlands, and short federally mandated seasons, to "heighten charm" of waterfowl hunting by using an ineffective weapon is not only a lost art but a lost cause.

Lead Crossing Birds Well.

When shooting at flying birds, most hunters do not make sufficient lead allowance, because they fail to take into consideration the speed of the birds. The following table will help impress hunters with the necessity of giving plenty of lead, especially on crossing shots.

Ft. per Second	=	Miles per Hour	Ft. per Second	=	Miles per Hour
40		27.2	100		68.1
45		30.7	105		71.5
50		34.1	110		75
55		37.5	115		78.4
60		40.9	120		81.8
65		44.3	125		85.2
70		47.7	130		88.6
75		51.1	135		92
80		54.5	140		95.4
85		58	145		98.8
90		61.4	150		102.2
95		64.7			

Facts About Shot

In the old days before arms were rifled, missiles were round and shot from the barrel that was always smooth bore like a shotgun; the gauge or calbre was numbered according to the quanity of a perfect sphere of lead there was contained in a pound. Thus, 50 gauge gun was bored for a ball that took 50 of them to weigh a pound, 20 gauge twenty to the pound, 16, 14, 12, 10, etc. The areas of various bores as calculated from the nominal calibres is as follows:

Gauge or bore	Diameter decimals of in.	Diameter Milim'rs	Sq. Inch Area
8	.835	21.8	.548
10	.775	20.0	.472
12	.729	18.6	.417
14	.693	17.8	.377
16	.662	16.8	.344
20	.615	15.6	.297
28	.550		.238

10

TABLE OF BALLISTICS

Tests of 10 rounds each, to determine pressures and velocities over a 120 foot range of various loads of bulk nitro powders in 12, 16, 20 and 28 gauge Parker guns.

Gauge of Gun.	Charge of Powder, Drams	Charge of Shot, Ounces.	Mean Pressure, Tons.	Velocity Feet, Seconds.
12	3½	1 No. 7	4.00	973
12	3½	1¼ " 7	4.42	959
12	3¼	1 " 7	3.17	940
12	3¼	1⅛ " 7	4.00	930
12	3	1⅛ " 7	3.62	900
16	2¾	⅞ " 7	3.14	929
16	3	1 " 7	4.01	924
16	2½	⅞ " 7	2.56	885
20	2¾	⅞ " 7	6.10	973
20	2½	¾ " 7	4.73	922
20	2½	⅞ " 7	5.65	920
20	2¼	¾ " 7	4.41	887
28	2⅛	⅝ " 7	5.39	934
28	2	⅝ " 7	5.10	910

STANDARD 12-GAUGE SHOTGUN LOADS

We are fully convinced—and our convictions are based on scientifically determined facts—that these standard loads will serve every purpose and meet every requirement of the most exacting sportsman. Our selection of the best standard 12-gauge shotgun loads s shown below:

Species of Game	Order of Choice	Powder Drams	Shot Ounces	Shot Size No.
Large Ducks	First	3¼	1⅛	6
	Second	3	1	6
	Third	3¼	1⅛	4
Grouse, Medium Ducks	First	3¼	1⅛	7
	Second	3	1	7
	Third	3¼	1⅛	6
Quail, Upland Birds	First	3	1	8
	Second	3¼	1⅛	8
	Third	3	1	7
Reed Birds	First	3	1	10
	Second	3	1	8
Large Geese, Turkeys	First	3½	1¼	2
	Second	3¼	1⅛	4
Medium Geese, Brant, Etc.	First	3¼	1⅛	4
	Second	3	1⅛	4

11

Various charts from Parker Brothers 1922 big-bore booklet recommending 12-gauge for everything from reed birds to large geese and turkeys. Notice the comparative velocities on the "Table of Ballistics" which according to Parker's own tests negate the "Smallbore Superman Theory."

All the preceding isn't to say the 20-gauge should be abandoned in favor of the twelve or that the 28-gauge and .410 are hopeless cases. Nothing could be further from the truth. My thesis is that the 12-gauge is the most flexible, near-perfect, all-round gun, and small bores are simply a compromise. Live and let live; different strokes for different folks! Anyone who disagrees will have no trouble finding vast amounts of slightly oblique literature extolling the virtues of small bores. Just don't tell me "less is more."

CHOKE BORING—PURE ACCIDENT

Choke-boring, or bore-choking, had long existed in theory and was mentioned in sporting literature of the late 1700s. The theory, however, was never put to repeatable practice until the 1870s. Fred Kimbell of Peoria, Illinois, is generally credited with having built the first effective American choke-bored shotgun in 1868, even though Roper's revolving shotgun, patented in 1866 and first produced in 1867, featured a variable choke ring threaded on the muzzle. Choke-boring was a common-sense application of a concept known to gunsmiths at least as early as the 1780s, but state-of-the-art *repeatable* tolerance for barrel boring in the 1860s was .010-inch. While mid-nineteenth-century gunmakers could measure to the ten-thousandths of an inch (.0001), boring machinery was accurate only to .010-inch, and the difference between cylinder and modified choke on a 12-bore is about .012-inch. Bore diameters were easy to measure but hard to control with nineteenth-century equipment. Hand-honing to more precise tolerances was often counterproductive at a time when experimentation with different size wads could be the better solution to the tradeoff between pattern and penetration.

Repeatable choke-boring was a hot topic in the sporting press during the 1870s, but didn't become a fact of life for most shooters until the 1880s. Meanwhile, Fred Kimbell, perhaps unjustly, claimed most of the credit. W. W. Greener, in his tome *The Gun and Its Development* (Ninth edition, 1910), mentioned Kimbell but credited Roper: "The invention of choke-boring has been claimed by many, and is usually attributed to American gunsmiths . . . [based on] . . . the first patent for choke-boring granted to Roper, an American gunsmith, on April 10, 1866, thus preceding Pape, the English claimant, by about six weeks." However, Bob Hinman, in his book, *The Golden Age of Shotgunning*, points out that Roper's April 10, 1866, patent didn't seem to cover the choking device, and Roper belatedly (July 14, 1868) obtained patent number 79,861 for the detachable choke-muzzle ring. If Hinman is right, then Greener is wrong, but at this late

You may wonder how I happen to be the one to discover choke-boring when other men, for centuries indeed, had been working on the same problem. It was luck, blind luck; and more than luck, it was pure accident.

Fred Kimbell (1936)

This proud owner of a Parker hammer gun went to the trouble of having his image recorded for posterity. Too bad he didn't write his name, address, and particulars of his Parker fowling piece on the back of the picture.

date who cares? Well, yours truly, the "Parker Trivia Detective," cared enough to go back to the archives and do a little basic research. What follows may shed some light on the issue of who's on first—and what's on second.

Fred Kimbell probably deserved *none* of the credit for actually inventing bore-choking. However, the proof of the pudding is often in the making, and by the late 1860s, Kimbell had made a name for himself in shooting circles. He was also considered to be a crack duck shot along the Illinois River, but no small part of his success at live-bird shooting was the choked bore of his early 1870s muzzleloaders.

Kimbell's first recorded competitive shoot was the Championship of Illinois in 1872. He shot the first ten-bird race with his choked 9-gauge muzzleloader, while most of his 150 fellow competitors used cylinder-bore breechloaders. Kimbell and fourteen others killed ten birds at twenty-one yards and moved back to twenty-six yards for a miss-and-out shootoff. When the pigeon feathers and black-powder smoke had settled, Captain A. H. Bogardus—the then self-declared "champion of the world"—and Fred Kimbell were tied. They shot even for three more rounds until they ran short of good birds, and the promoter divided the purse.

Adam H. Bogardus wrote and self-published *Field, Cover, and Trap Shooting* in fall 1874. (Note—the reprint is of the revised 1878 edition.) Bogardus devoted his life to shooting and promoting his shooting abilities. He was the consummate hustler and name-dropper, and could spin tales *ad nauseam* about championships won and records set. He lived along the Sangamon River at Petersburg, Illinois, less than fifty miles from Fred Kimbell's home at Peoria. Guns were the

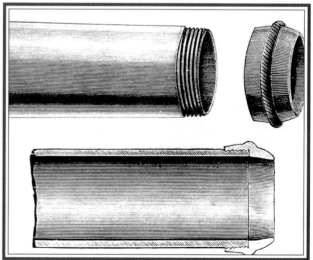

Roper's detachable choke-muzzle seems conceptually sound, but wasn't particularly effective when put to the test by W. W. Greener.

It is no more essential to the marksman or young sportsman that he should understand the mechanism and mode of manufacturing guns, than it is that he should determine whether the Chinese or Roger Bacon first invented gunpowder before he shall fire a shot off. Sportsmen may safely leave such matters to the gunmakers, who are nearly everywhere a very ingenious, painstaking, trustworthy class of men.

Captain Adam H. Bogardus — self-proclaimed champion wing shot of America. Captain Bogardus and his friend W. F. ("Doc") Carver — self-proclaimed champion rifle shot of the world — once shot a contest involving 60,000 moving targets each, at the rate of 10,000 per day for six days. "Doc" Carver won with 58,892 hits using a rifle — Bogardus lost with a shotgun. Assuming they were shooting twelve hours a day, each would have had to fire 833 shots per hour, 14 shots per minute, or one shot every 4.3 seconds. Not my idea of fun with a gun.

tools of Bogardus's trade, so it's surprising his position on the fine points of gunmaking was that:

> I could never see any use to the shooter in a long theoretical or practical description of the principles and details of guns as they are made. All such knowledge is necessary to the gunmaker, but of no practical use at all to the shooter, for which reason I shall say next to nothing about it.

Bogardus's book sheds little light on 1868-78 methods of gunmaking other than to point out that muzzleloaders had given way to breechloaders. Accordingly, it's not too surprising that no mention was made of choke-bored guns. What is remarkable, however, is that Bogardus authored and self-published 443 pages with no mention of his close neighbor and co-winner of the 1872 Championship of Illinois, Fred Kimbell. Bogardus's book lends no support to Kimbell's claim to have invented choke-boring in 1868 or any other year. Bogardus seldom mentioned his losses, except in the context of getting even in spades the next time, and considered gunmaking something best left to the gunmakers. The fact that he ignored Fred Kimbell's first use of close-shooting guns so essential to his trade can only lead to the conclusion that Kimbell was not receiving any credit for "inventing" or "developing" the choke-bore gun back when recollections were clear and knowledge was firsthand. Nevertheless, the Championship of Illinois and the "Kimbell edge" built into the bore of his gun (by whomever) had as profound an impact on the future development of shotguns as the news of gold had on the settling of California. The rush was on, and several years later, Captain du Bray, writing as *Gaucho*, had this to say about shotgun chokes:

> When choke-boring first came out, the man who had nothing better than cylinder was unhappy in the extreme, for the man with the choke gun was relentless, cruel

"Stalking Horse" from an 1884 hand-colored etching.

and so selfish, that he lost no opportunity for displaying the marvelous performance of his improved weapon. The superiority of the choke-bore was simply squelching.

Fred Kimbell's real claim to fame was that he was the first to squelch the competition with a muzzle restriction that could keep shot clustered a bit longer than preexisting shotguns with variations of cylinder bore. In 1936 the accomplishments of Kimbell, then ninety, were still of such interest to sportsmen that interview articles were published in *Sports Afield* and *The American Rifleman*. Bob Hinman, in *The Golden Age of Shotgunning*, quoted Kimbell from *The American Rifleman*:

I shot the first choke bore gun, so far as I know, in history. The gun which I had bored myself. It would outshoot any other gun in Illinois by 30 yards. In those days the greatest range any shooter could expect from his shotgun was 40 yards. Mine would kill at 60 or 70 and I don't know how the idea came to me, for I had never heard of these early experiments in choke boring; but one day I thought if I could constrict the muzzle of a gun—make it smaller than the rest of the bore, the shot wouldn't spread over so great an area. So I found a musket with a good heavy barrel and began experimenting with it.

Kimbell disclaimed being a gunsmith, but he apparently had watched gun-borers at work and claimed to know their business. His alleged experiments supposedly began with barrels bored *true* cylinder, and he patterned the gun with a spread over a five-foot area. Then he tried relieving the muzzle just a little, consistent with what he believed to be the contemporary English gunmakers' experiments. The relieving reduced the spread from five feet to four feet. Kimbell thought he was on the right track, so he rebored the gun (a muzzleloader) from the breech end, leaving about one inch of choke at the muzzle. The

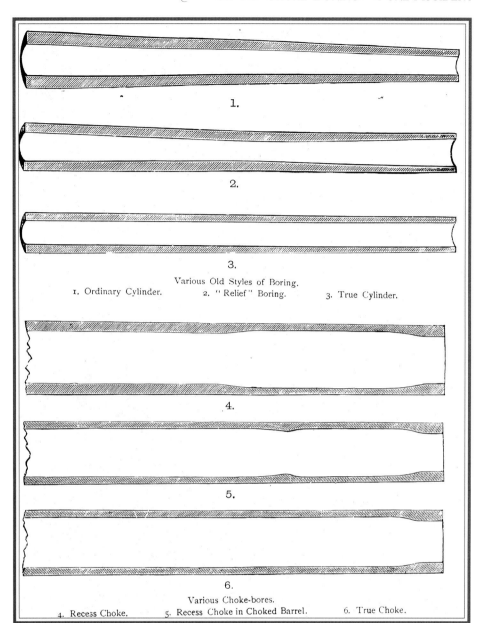

Various Old Styles of Boring.
1. Ordinary Cylinder.   2. "Relief" Boring.   3. True Cylinder.

Various Choke-bores.
4. Recess Choke.   5. Recess Choke in Choked Barrel.   6. True Choke.

W. W. Greener pictures these choke-bore configurations in his tome The Gun and its Development. *The examples are simply to demonstrate nineteenth century jargon and don't necessarily represent state-of-the-art choke-boring then or now.*

gun scattered shot up to seven feet, and Kimbell decided he was "... an excellent failure." He cut the choke section off the gun, intending to go back to cylinder bore, and tried it again at forty yards. The entire shot charge clustered in a thirty-inch circle—a 100 percent pattern! Thus began choke-boring in the United States, according to Fred Kimbell.

Kimbell discovered that he hadn't quite cut off all the choke. The part remaining was arrived at strictly by accident, but test results showed it to be exactly what generations of gunmakers had been seeking. Kimbell wrote

to his friend Joe Long in Boston about the discovery, and Long is said to have had a gun built by Joseph Tonks according to Kimbell's specifications. Then Kimbell ordered a Tonks gun—a single-barrel 9-gauge—which proved to be an extremely close shooter. Once Kimbell mastered his new gun, he was in a class by himself with a gun that could reach out farther than any other shotgun in Illinois. The next step was to enter the Championship of Illinois and make Captain Bogardus a believer.

The preceding paragraphs are representative of the "invention of choke-boring" scenario generally attributed to Kimbell by most authors. I disagree. Just as Johnson's ".14-gauge with 29-inch barrel" misinformation was kept alive by gunwriters for more than thirty-five years, Kimbell's "enhanced recollection" has been elevated to Gospel-truth status by being quoted again and again and again. Remember, it's always easier to paraphrase a recent article or quote from the last book written than to go back to contemporary writings for firsthand verification of an important fact. Based on my reading of contemporary writings, Kimbell was a bystander and true bore-choking was "invented" and developed by others.

The Gun and Its Development by W. W. Greener traces the evolution of firearms through the end of the nineteenth century. In typical pre-WWI British fashion, Greener, in over 800 pages, hardly mentioned anything American and managed to ignore Parker guns completely. Fred Kimbell is credited with slight success as the *owner* of a choked shotgun, and this has been stretched to add credibility to Kimbell's 1936 claim to fame. According to Greener:

> An American 6-bore muzzleloading gun, the property of Fred Kimbell, a companion of Long's, was sent over to England for trial, and while it shot well with large shot it did not give regular results, making but one really good pattern out of every three shots, which would point to the conclusion that although the Americans were undoubtedly the pioneers of the choke-boring system, they had not really progressed far beyond the elementary stage, and their guns still continued to lead, threw irregular patterns, and did not shoot straight.

Fred Kimbell's 6-bore muzzleloader was a "trick" live-bird gun. Though competitive loads were limited to 1¼ ounces of shot and Kimbell complied, the gun ran afoul of some new rules that cropped up after he showed himself unbeatable with his Tonks gun. The 6-bore, having been declared "illegal," was

shipped to England for the trials referred to by Greener. However, Greener never credited Kimbell with anything more than *owning* the choke-bored gun, and wrote that ". . . the invention of choke-boring has been claimed by many, and is usually attributed to American gunsmiths." Kimbell wasn't a gunsmith, but Greener did credit the Americans, so let's go to his source.

Greener's reference to ". . . Kimbell, a companion of Long's . . ." pinpoints Joseph W. Long, who wrote *American Wild-fowl Shooting*, first published in 1874. Long's book is dedicated "To my friend Fred Kimbell of Peoria, Illinois, a crack duck-shot and an honest man. . . ." The first edition makes no mention of choke-boring (although Kimbell is featured in the context of killing a lot of ducks during an Illinois River hunt). The 1879 revised edition added Chapter XXXI, "Choke-bores—Their True History, Form, and Manner of Construction." Perhaps Kimbell should have refreshed his recollection by reading Long's book before giving his 1936 interviews. What follows is Long's 1870s version of the "invention" of the choke-bored shotgun:

> Just when choke-boring was first practiced, or who is rightfully entitled to the honor of its invention, will probably never be known. There have been scores of claimants, however, and one, Mr. Pape, of Newcastle, England, so far made good his claim as to receive recognition as the inventor. Mr. Pape, however, is *not* the original inventor, for he dates his discovery back only to the year 1866; and though he may have found out its peculiarities by personal effort and without knowing it to have been previously practiced, yet he put his revelation to little use, and, it would seem, hardly appreciated its value. Choke-boring is, without a reasonable doubt, an American invention. I have most positive and reliable proof of its having been practiced in this country, according to the most approved manner of the present day, over fifty years ago; the earliest person I have

been able to trace a knowledge of it to being Jeremiah Smith, a gunsmith of Smithfield, Rhode Island, who discovered its merits in 1827.

Long goes on to say that choke-boring was kept a secret in the United States because of the unique American experience: "With the American gunsmith, in the rural districts especially, doing a comparatively small business . . . it was an especial advantage to him to keep all such processes a secret . . . [so as to] . . . gain the reputation of superiority in some branch of his business . . . thus was the knowledge of the system so long kept hidden, and the *true* history of its general dissemination, never before published, is [paraphrased] as follows:"

During the winter of 1869-70, Long and Fred Kimbell hunted ducks in Illinois with their 11-gauge muzzleloaders, ". . . bored on the old plan. . . ." Both agreed that a gun which could reach out farther would be more effective on ducks and, ". . . as a consequence we determined to have made for the next season's shooting two heavier guns, bored to shoot as close as possible. Fred gave his order to Mr. O. P. Secor, of Peoria . . . and wanted me [Long] to do likewise; but I, residing in Boston, Mass., made choice of Mr. Joseph Tonks, of that city. It was a matter of considerable rivalry between us as to who would get the best shooting-gun . . ." Both Long and Kimbell intended to have muzzleloaders built to order, ". . . but to my surprise, Mr. Tonks absolutely refused to make me one, and would have it that I didn't want a muzzleloader, but a breechloader." Long goes into the pros and cons of muzzleloaders versus breechloaders and his reluctance to own a newfangled gun. Tonks insisted, and offered to give him the breechloader free if he wasn't pleased. Tonks's offer was, ". . . I'll first make you a breechloader, and if it doesn't shoot as well as any muzzleloader you can bring against it, I'll make you a present of it, and then build a muzzleloader for you afterward." Long agreed to accept the breechloader,

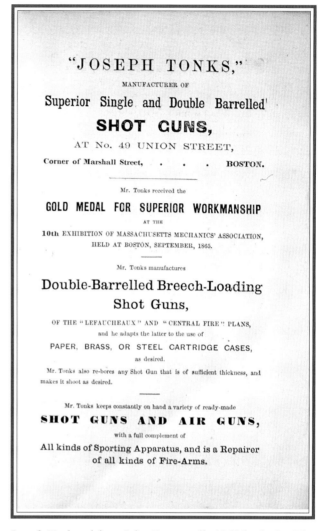

Joseph Tonks ad from John Bumstead's 1869 book, On The Wing. *Tonks gravitated from manufacture and repair in the late 1860s, to be a Parker dealer in the early 1870s.*

thinking that Kimbell's muzzleloader would surely be the closer shooter, and said, "Mr. Tonks, you'll be one breechloader out."

While Long's breechloading double was being built, he borrowed a Tonks 10-gauge single-barrel muzzleloader and targeted it with a *half*-ounce of shot on a target one foot square at forty yards. I should mention that guns of the 1870s were typically patterned in a thirty-inch circle at forty yards; however, one-foot-square paper targets were used for mailing back and forth to compare the close shooting propensities of experimental guns. Long was amazed by the pattern of the borrowed Tonks 10-gauge and declared, ". . . Tonks was safe; I was satisfied; sent Fred the targets and their history; back came his answer by return mail, 'Buy that gun, and send it to me sure.' I did so, and that same act was a means of causing choke-bores to spread, as they never had spread before, even throughout the civilized world."

All the preceding transpired when Long returned home to Boston in early 1870, immediately after hunting ducks with Fred Kimbell—"a crack duck-shot and an honest man"—who was then using an apparently unsatisfactory 11-gauge muzzleloader "bored on the old plan." Kimbell may have been an honest man and a crack duck shot in the 1870s, but he was clearly the victim of enhanced recollection in 1936, when at ninety years of age he claimed to be the inventor of choke-boring. He may have been the first to skillfully demonstrate the close shooting of Tonks-built guns, but the invention of choke-boring, by accident or otherwise, wasn't one of Kimbell's accomplishments.

Long wasn't able to hunt with Kimbell during the 1870-71 season, but he had several close-shooting guns built by Tonks and another Boston gunsmith, William R. Shaefer, and he ". . . sent them to Fred and others, shooting friends in the west. Their shooting qualities were very similar to the first one sent. Two were single-barreled muzzleloaders, pigeon guns—one of them made by Tonks and known among eastern match-shooters as 'the old referee'." Kimbell used "the old referee" to shoot to a tie with Captain Bogardus at the Championship of Illinois in 1872.

Meanwhile, Long, Kimbell, and all concerned ". . . kept [the] secret, as far as possible, partly out of a sense of regard for Tonks and Shaefer, and in greater part perhaps through selfishness the plan upon which our guns were bored; confiding only in a few particular friends. [But word of Fred Kimbell's] . . . shooting soon spread, and his gun became the wonder of sportsmen in that neighborhood." During 1872, J. L. Johnson, a gunsmith

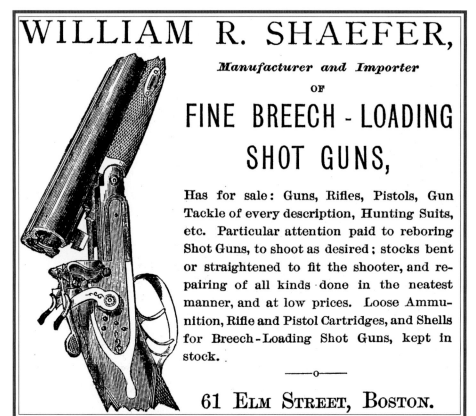

William R. Shaefer was a gunmaker privy to Tonks' method of choke-boring. Joe Long bought some close-shooting Shaefer and Tonks breechloaders in 1870 and 1871, sent them back to his friends in Illinois, and the rush was on for choke bored guns.

198

from Young America (now Monmouth), Illinois, took measurements of Fred Kimbell's "old referee" pigeon gun and began experimenting on some old musket barrels with favorable results. (Kimbell probably recalled Johnson's experiments and appropriated them as his own when he was interviewed in 1936, much like the sports-bar recollections of those who claim winning touchdowns at high-school championships even though their yearbooks show they weren't even on the team.) In 1872-73 Johnson issued circulars that Long considered to be the first public advertisements of choke-boring. As was the custom at the time, Johnson's circulars gave references that included N. Carr of Monmouth, Illinois, who owned a Parker breechloader, and Fred Kimbell with two muzzleloaders.

Captain A. H. Bogardus was conspicuously absent from Johnson's list of references, and according to Long, ". . . when these circulars came to the notice of gunmakers in Chicago and St. Louis, they ridiculed the idea that a gunsmith in the little burgh of Young America could do what the oldest and best gunmakers of the world had been unable to accomplish; but sportsmen took a different view of the matter, and very many sent their guns to Johnson to have them rebored."

Long's failure to mention Fred Kimbell's tie with Captain Bogardus at the Championship of Illinois is surprising. However, Bogardus was considered a blowhard and not quite a gentleman by many, including some of his own backers. The reciprocal omissions of both Long's and Bogardus's books could be taken in the context of not wanting to give the nemesis any free press. For example, after a long-winded discussion of a match with Abraham Kleinman, constituting the Championship of Illinois at Chicago in 1868—which Bogardus won by one bird— he found it necessary to mention that ". . . soon after, I shot with another man two or three times, and won, but I shall not men-

tion his name [Kimbell] in this book for sufficient reasons." It's likely that much history of the choke-bore went unrecorded simply due to such petty and unspecified rivalries. The fact that Long never mentioned Bogardus must be taken in the context of Bogardus never mentioning Long, Kimbell, or Johnson. Considering how Bogardus and Long could devote pages to the most trivial shooting experience, the mutual failure to mention the other couldn't have been an accident.

In my book, Joseph Tonks of Boston gets credit for the invention of choke-boring. Tonks may have purchased his barrel blanks from J. H. Johnston's Great Western Gun Works of Pittsburgh, Pennsylvania, (not to be confused with J. L. Johnson of Monmouth, Illinois). Great Western began as a firm in 1866, selling guns, shooting materials, and gunmaking parts by mail order. No mention is made of choke-boring in Great Western's 1871 or 1873 catalogs, but by 1881 Johnston was as busy choke-boring as anyone in the trade, and Great Western's 1881 catalog announced:

> We choke guns to order, and only charge $2.00. Guns, choke-bored to order, for special target $3.00 to $5.00. Choke-boring improves the force of penetration, and makes the gun throw shot closer and harder at long range, than ordinary boring at short range. Old guns choke-bored costs from $3.00 to $5.00.

Just how Great Western was able to choke-bore old guns will never be known for sure, but I have my opinion. Tonks developed a choke restriction; Long bought some Tonks guns and sent them to Illinois; J. L. Johnson of Monmouth, Illinois, discovered the secret by examining Kimbell's Tonks gun; and according to Greener:

> While Johnson was at work in his shop a man named Faburn endeavored

to discover the secret. He was not allowed to get the breech pin out of the gun, and from his observations of the muzzle end of the barrels he concluded that a short recess had been cut out just at the back of the muzzle; he therefore contrived an expanding bit to do this boring, and on June 25, 1872, secured a patent for it. This bit, which ostensibly carried with it the right to "choke-bore" barrels, had a large sale throughout the United States, and every gunsmith claimed the knowledge of choke-boring, but endeavored to keep the method of boring a secret.

My guess is that Great Western used Faburn's patent bit (or reamer) to relieve the bores slightly, just inside the muzzle. Gun trials showed such relief choking to be not particularly effective, but back in the 1870s, anything was better than nothing, and Great Western only charged three to five dollars. Suffice it to say that Joe Long's and Fred Kimbell's duck hunt on the Illinois River during winter 1869-70 was the catalyst for a chain reaction of choke-boring experiments, refinements, and tinkering that, as I write this, are not yet complete.

Bob Hinman wrote in his book, *The Golden Age of Shotgunning*, that ". . . by the mid-seventies, no matter who invented it, the choke had taken hold in the public's mind and gunsmiths and makers were all busy." One would assume that Parker Brothers was choke-boring its shotguns at least as early as the middle 1870s. Remember that N. Carr of Monmouth, Illinois, was a Parker owner and was given as a reference by J. L. Johnson in his first circular advertising choke-boring. Rest assured that Mr. Carr's letter describing Johnson's pattern trials was received by Parker Brothers within a few days of the event. My cursory review of Parker Brothers' summer 1873 order book disclosed no reference to close shooting or choke-boring or shot count as specifications for guns ordered at that time. Early 1870s ads touted

the Parker as ". . . the best and hardest shooting gun in the world." Reference to "hardest shooting" was an effort to debunk the belief of those resistant to change that muzzleloaders shot harder than breechloaders; "hardest shooting" wasn't a claim for the close-shooting ability of the Parker gun. Cylinder bore was the name of the game at Parker Brothers in 1873; and the 1874 and 1877 catalogs are devoid of any mention of choking for close shooting: "All we have to say about the shooting of the Parker Gun is that every one of our guns is thoroughly tested as to distribution and penetration before it leaves the factory, and if properly loaded and handled, we know they cannot fail to please any sportsman . . . [and Parker guns were claimed to be] . . . at a point so near perfection that we see no chance for further improvement."

No one ever accused Parker Brothers of holding back on hyperbole or soft-selling its guns. If choke-boring had been part of Parker's manufacturing process in the early 1870s, rest assured the announcement would have been in bold type. However, Parker's circa 1872-73 catalogs did explain self-help methods to alter and improve pattern and penetration:

Parties using our Guns are recommended to use "pink edge" wads, larger than their shells, always putting them down in place flat and square; otherwise the shooting qualities of the Gun will be greatly impaired . . . [and as a guide for charges of powder and shot] . . . we submit the following as a basis, although "the distribution" can be increased either by decreasing the quantity of powder or increasing the quantity of shot. And to produce better "penetration," increase the quantity of powder used or decrease the amount of shot. The exact amount of ammunition required to be used with each Gun to give satisfactory results to parties owning the Gun can only be ascertained by repeated trials at a target.

Parker Brothers' 1878 catalog had no explicit reference to choke-boring, but continued to suggest that ". . . satisfactory results to parties owning [Parker guns] can only be ascertained by repeated trials at a target." However, by the late 1870s, Parker Brothers started to distinguish "close shooting" from the tradeoff between pattern and penetration. According to Parker's 1878 catalog, "We were fortunate in the beginning in adopting a system of boring that secured the best results in both pattern and penetration, and the Parker Gun has made a remarkable record for *close*, hard shooting. All of our guns are thoroughly tested, and each one bears a tag when it leaves the factory giving its record at the target." Before the advent of choke-boring, Parker guns could be made to shoot closer by manipulating bore dimensions, but state-of-the-art was "hit or miss," so there was always the risk of opening rather than closing the pattern. The fact that each late 1870s gun had a tag ". . . giving its record at the target" must be considered in the context of the customer being expected to conduct his own ". . . repeated trials at a target." Early hanging tags provided the customer with a performance baseline rather than certifying the gun to be of a particular choke. Close shooting was factored into the pattern and penetration equation with the advent of factory choke-boring in the late 1870s, while the prior focus had been on the customer's self-help trials with variations of powder, shot, and wads.

Guns that predated actual choke-boring were made to shoot closer than a *true* cylinder bore (i.e., the same bore diameter from breech to muzzle) by honing the bore to a taper from breech to muzzle (called ordinary cylinder). The gradual decrease in diameter from breech to muzzle was intended to help the wads seal, thereby mitigating blow-by and making a harder-shooting gun. Reducing blow-by with an ordinary cylinder (tapered bore) often mini-

mized blown patterns, but close shooting before the advent of true choke-boring was simply the random hit-or-miss result of attempts to keep the pellets ahead of the rapidly expanding gases. By the turn of the century, improved machinery had made barrel-boring a science—perhaps even to the ten-thousandths of an inch—but choke-boring was still an art in 1910, according to Major Askins:

> Close shooting or density of pattern is a mere matter of correct mechanics, but with our present skill in gunboring uniformity is in a degree dependent on luck, for the most skilled gun-borer, cutting his tube to the exact thousandth of an inch, cannot foresee with any certainty that his barrel is going to make an even spread. He can, however, usually much improve the shooting of a barrel by carefully retouching it, but no matter what the experience of the mechanic he can never make two barrels that will pattern exactly alike, and it follows that only on rare occasions is a perfect shooting barrel turned out. This explains why our great trapshots may try fifty guns before finding one that patterns up to the standard they require, and why when such a piece is obtained it is considered invaluable.

Early hard evidence of Parker choke-boring is the circa 1885 hanging tag for s/n 45,973 (pictured in Baer's book), which shows that a 12-gauge with thirty-inch barrels was targeted at forty-five yards on a twenty-four-inch circle and ". . . if targeted at 40 yards on 30-inch circle there will be *one-half more* pellets on target. We use no. 8 Tatham Shot having 399 pellets in an ounce. Shot made by different makers vary from 375 to 600 pellets in an ounce, and target will vary according to number of pellets in an ounce." The hanging tag shows that 175 pellets of number 8 *soft* shot hit the twenty-four-inch circle from both right and left barrels. The load was $1\frac{1}{8}$ ounces, so the total shot count would have been 449 pellets. Adjusted to a thirty-inch circle using the

Comparative Sizes of Drop Shot.

To give a general list of all the manufactures we find takes up too much space, and as some of the manufacturers write us that "such a table is unreliable anyway—two bags of shot made by any manufacturer will vary more or less, and a table of pellets per ounce is not therefore thoroughly reliable," we will only try to compare a few leading manufacturers, showing the extremes, and to show no injustice, will add the names of all the manufacturers in the United States that we know, and no doubt they will give inquiries such information as they desire:

Le Roy Shot and Lead Works,
New York.

Sportsmen Shot Works,
Cincinnati, Ohio.

Raymond Lead Co.,
Chicago, Ill.

Collier Shot Tower Works,
St. Louis, Mo.

Merchants Shot Works,
Baltimore, Md.

Thos. W. Sparks,
Philadelphia, Pa.

Gulf Shot and Lead Works,
New Orleans, La.

Chicago Shot Tower Works,
Chicago, Ill.

Jas. Robertson Manufacturing Co.,
Baltimore, Md.

Caldwell Lead Co.,
New York.

Markle Lead Works,
St. Louis, Mo.

Bailey & Farrill Shot Works,
Pittsburg, Pa.

Thatham & Bros , 82 Beekman Street, N. Y.			Omaha Shot and Lead Works, Omaha.		Selby Smelting and Lead Co., San Francisco, Cal.		
Size	Soft	Chilled	Size	Soft	Size	Soft	Chilled
	NO. TO OUNCE.	NO. TO OUNCE.		NO. TO OUNCE.		NO. TO OUNCE.	NO. TO OUNCE.
F F	24		O O O	30	T	41	
F	27		O O	37	B B B	48	
T T	31		O	42	B B	55	
T	36		B B B	48	B	66	
B B B	42		B B	56	1	75	
B B	50		B	65	2	92	
B	59		1	81	3	111	120
1	71	73	2	100	4	137	142
2	86	88	3	128	5	189	194
3	106	109	4	143	6	210	220
4	132	136	5	187	7	280	285
5	168	172	6	248	7½	324	330
6	218	223	7	338	8	373	385
7	291	299	8	456	8½	460	478
7½	338	345	9	680	9	549	580
8	399	409	10	896	10	812	870
8½	472	495	11	1540	11	1350	
9	568	585	12	3248	12	2260	
9½	688	716	Dust.	9000			
10	848	868					
10½	1056	1130					
11	1346	1380					
12	2326	2385					
Dust.	4565						
FineD't.	10784						

Chart showing circa 1893 comparative sizes of drop-shot. Notice No. 7 soft shot had a count of 280 or 291 or 338 pellets to the ounce depending on manufacturer. Turn-of-the-century shooters had to have this information as they were expected to conduct their own trials to fine tune their Parkers for maximum pattern and penetration.

factor of 150 percent (one-half more), 262 of 449 pellets would have been counted for an approximate 58 percent pattern or, in modern terms, at the low end of improved-modified (three-quarters) choke. The gun with Damascus barrels might have been considered tight-shooting, borderline full-choke, as it would have patterned higher with chilled shot. The whole idea of bore-choking in its infancy was to tighten up the pattern of an otherwise true cylinder bore. Accordingly, the tighter the better, and full choke was best. Remember, choking for close shooting was originated, developed, and refined in the context of duck shooting and live-bird competition, but was of no particular concern to quail and grouse hunters, to whom open pattern distribution was the name of the game.

Peter Johnson discussed Parker's 1920s choke-boring in his book, *Parker—America's Finest Shotgun*:

> . . . The barrels are then counter bored from the butt end to a point 6 inches from the muzzle by pulling through them rotating cutters called nut augers. This process is the beginning of the choke in the barrels. The barrels are next bored and the choke cut into them. All barrels are full choke until the gun goes to final boring after it is practically completed. The Parker full choke is in the form of an ogive curve starting 6 inches from the muzzle and going to a point about ¾ inch from the muzzle, from which point on to the muzzle there is a straight section without curve or taper . . . after both tubes have been bored the barrels go to the stock room. Each pair of barrels has the weight stamped thereon. [After a gun was built, it was] . . . sent to the shooting room where a range and other devices were kept to test accuracy and patterns. In this room the barrels were locked in a fixed rest from which they were aimed at the center of a thirty-inch steel plate standing forty yards away. This steel plate was mounted on a small car which traveled in either direction. The plate itself was painted white but had a bolt head

in the center which was painted black. After each shot fired at it, the plate received a fresh coat of white paint, then was rolled back and the shots were counted by painting them out with a paintbrush. In this way the distribution of shot was noted and the percentage pattern was calculated. In the so-called shooting room there were two barrel boring lathes, and also a barrel straightening press. If the barrels did not shoot properly as to shot distribution and percentage of pattern, they were immediately rebored or straightened until they would fire dead center and produce the proper pattern. In this room also all barrels were proof tested for strength of the steel and single trigger guns were tested to make sure that they would not hook up or double. It was in this room that the final judgment was passed on the shooting qualities of the Parker gun. It was thus a very important room in the Parker plant.

Parker Brothers ad from October 1923 issue of National Sportsman, *showing the fixed firing rest used to proof test and pattern the "Old Reliable."*

Parker Brothers never really advertised choke-boring or touted pattern results until the 1913 Flying Ducks catalog, in which an absolutely meaningless two pages were devoted to the subject. The fact that Parker guns shot top patterns for accuracy and distribution went almost without saying. Parker Brothers didn't need to preach to the choir, so overly specific choke-bore advertising was abandoned in favor of the more generalized "article of faith" approach. Parker's ad copy from the October 1923 *National Sportsman* shows the fixed firing rest used in the gun-works target room (see picture). W. A. King wrote about Parker choke-boring to a "standard of pattern" in his 1924 article, "Step-By-Step in Building a Gun," and generally described the process but didn't divulge any secrets:

> . . . The barrels are sent to the testing and targeting room, where they are finally bored for pattern and or shot. Every gun is tested and each barrel must shoot to a certain standard of pattern, otherwise the barrel is not passed by the inspector. Each gun is shot in a fixed test, carefully aligned at the center of a 30-inch metal target at various distances. Each barrel must place its loads centrally and must handle standard loads, showing proper distribution and showing percentage of pattern.

The often-quoted Colonel Askins, it turns out, wasn't infallible. He claimed in his article, "The Classic Parker Shotgun" (*Gun Digest*, 1973), that ". . . the Parker was made with any combination of borings the buyer might suggest, but unless otherwise specified he got a gun which was bored modified in the right tube and full choke in the left." Not true, or at least not completely true. Parker Brothers' 1899 catalog states that ". . . all our guns are made to use either paper or metal shells, and both barrels to shoot alike, unless otherwise ordered." A survey of the circa 1906-08 Pine Cone catalogs, 1920 Pocket catalog, 1926 through 1930 large Flying Geese

catalogs, and 1934 small Flying Geese catalog didn't disclose any policy change, although the 1913 Flying Ducks catalog says, ". . . we can furnish you any degree of choke from cylinder to full choke . . . and we are prepared to bore special orders to meet the requirements of our patrons." W. A. King wrote that the barrels were "bored for pattern" in the targeting room, and Johnson wrote that ". . . all barrels are full choke until the gun goes to final boring after it is practically complete." It makes sense that barrels were tentatively bored full choke, and those test-fired full choke would have been left "full and full." A too-tight pattern could be opened up by using soft shot, and it was relatively easy to degrade pattern count by opening the chokes, but it was almost impossible to make a gun shoot closer by adding back choke after it left the factory (even with Faburn's patent reamer).

It was usual for Parker Brothers guns to have both barrels choked the same unless a customer special-ordered something different. Exceptions would have been short-barrel Skeet guns (skeet in/skeet out) and Trojans with twenty-eight-inch barrels (modified and full). Colonel Askins was probably looking at the Remington-Parker 1937 spiral-bound catalog, which says:

> CHOICE OF BORING BARRELS—the barrels of PARKER guns, including the *TROJAN*, are furnished with any combination of borings desired—from true cylinder to extreme full choke. When no other boring is specified, barrels of all guns, except those for Skeet and Trap shooting, will be furnished with the right barrel bored modified choke and the left barrel bored full choke.

The preceding is a good example of why it's prudent never to say "never" or make a strong general statement about Parker guns. Juxtaposition of Parker Brothers-era and Remington-era facts often leads one down the primrose path of misappre-

Parker hanging tags. The three on the left are a full set which accompanied author's s/n 227,251 Trojan 12-gauge. Tag s/n 206,278 is a "shop tag" which accompanied a gun through production, but was replaced by a set of hanging tags after pattern and proof testing. Apparently Abercrombie & Fitch had its own special "house" tags for their used Parker inventory guns.

The "Old Reliable"

PARKER GUN

FOR turkeys, ducks and geese, there is no better gun made than the Parker. It has the long range killing power necessary to bring down these big birds at a distance, and is balanced so nicely that even the heavier guns can be brought to the shoulder with surprising ease and quickness.

The perfection of Parker performance is due to the painstaking workmanship employed in every detail of manufacture.

The Parker Cocking Hook

is of chrome vanadium steel, strong enough to lift half a ton and tempered to a hardness that shows no perceptible wear after years of use.

PARKER BROS.
Master Gun Makers
4 Cherry Street, MERIDEN, CONN.

Pacific Coast Agent:
A. W. du Bray, Box 102, San Francisco

Parker Brothers ad from April 1924 issue of Outdoor Life. *Notice reference to the Parker cocking hook of chrome vanadium steel. This alloy first became available in the United States in 1905, and was the forerunner of other metallurgical advances which would be hidden improvements to the Parker Gun.*

hension. When "Babe" Del Grego tells about the Parker guns he's seen in almost fifty years of gunsmithing, the listener goes away with the distinct impression that everything was the exception and nothing was the rule at Parker Brothers. For example, Parker guns traveled through the manufacturing process with a "shop tag" showing the order number, serial number, and required specifications. Shop tags in the s/n 206,XXX series variously refer to chokes as "close" or "close-close" or "mod-full," rather than by expected pattern count. However, the hanging tag that accompanied a s/n 206,XXX gun to its first owner "always" showed the minimum number of a specified size and hardness of shot that would penetrate a thirty-inch circle at forty yards (except that 28-gauges were *sometimes* and .410s *always* targeted at thirty yards). So Parker Brothers shop tags referred to "choke," but the customer tags didn't. You'd think it would have been the other way around.

Choke-boring advanced from Fred Kimbell's faulty recollections of "blind luck" and "pure accident" of the 1860s and 1870s to somewhere between art and science by 1910, when Major Askins (father of Colonel Askins) wrote about state-of-the-art gun boring in his book, *The American Shotgun*; and my guess is that choke-boring was still pretty much of an art at Parker Brothers through the end of production. Choking early Parker

Damascus guns was no simple matter, and keeping the choke was a problem as the relatively soft barrels shot themselves thin, especially at the muzzle. The writer of a letter to *Forest and Stream* dated October 31, 1889, claimed that

> Two of my friends . . . have Parker guns. One, a light 12-gauge, has been used from Florida to Maine, and has been shot until the barrels are as thin as paper at the muzzles. The locks and breech mechanism are as good as new. . . .

Prospective Parker owners circa 1900 were, as a rule, more gun-savvy than the larger number of collectors and shooters today. Shooting was more of a hands-on sport at the turn of the century. When placing an order for a new Parker gun, a customer had to know the shot count of his desired load and the number of pellets expected to pattern in a thirty-inch circle at forty yards. Parker choke-boring was by shot-count percentages, but the number of pellets rather than the percentage was stated. A tight-shooting barrel would place 75 percent of the shot in a thirty-inch circle. A 12-gauge typically patterned with $1\frac{1}{8}$ ounces of number 7 Tatham chilled shot at 299 to the ounce would put 252 of 336 pellets into the thirty-inch metal target in Parker

	Choke Diameter According to			Percent Reduction	Percent of Shot in 30-Inch Circle at 40 Yards	Trojan s/n 227,251		* Choke Diameter According to SAAMI
Choke	Larry Baer	David Butler	Ithaca Gun			** Left Barrel	*** Right Barrel	
Full	.690	.694	.693	10%	65%–75%	.695		.694
Imp. Mod.	——	.708	.702	6%	55%–65%			——
Mod.	.707	.718	.711	3%	45%–55%	51%	.712	.710
Imp. Cyl.	.719	.723	.720	2%	35%–45%		40%	.720
Cyl.	——	.730	.729	BORE	25%–35%			.729

SCHEDULE OF BORE AND CHOKE DIMENSIONS FOR 12-GAUGE ACCORDING TO VARIOUS AUTHORITIES

Conclusion — Simple choke measurements will not define how a Parker shotgun will pattern in a 30-inch circle at 40 yards. The "Dime Test" does not work.

Note — Trojan s/n 227,251 has 28-inch barrels and was built by Parker Brothers circa 1928, when any combination of chokes could be special ordered.

* * SAAMI — Small Arms and Ammunition Manufacturers Institute.*

* ** Left Barrel Measures .695-inch full choke, but patterned 51% modified.*

* *** Right barrel measures .712-inch modified, but patterned 40% improved cylinder.*

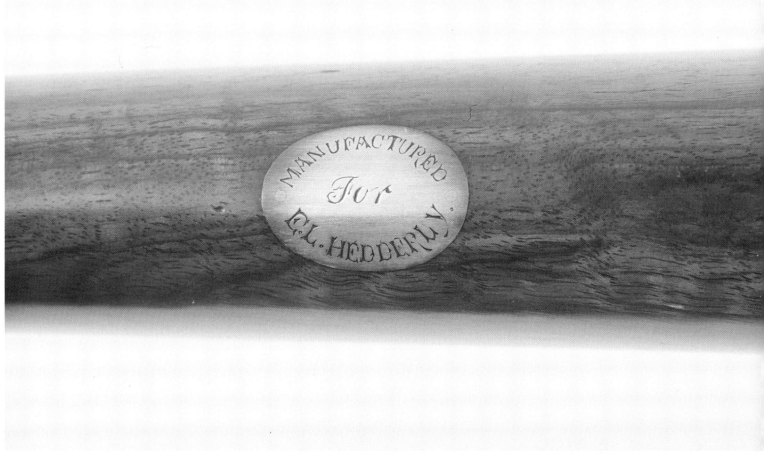

(top) Edwin L. Hedderly had a special-order engraved medallion placed in the stock of his 28-gauge DHE. It's surprising more proud Parker owners didn't incur the slight extra expense to have their "Old Reliable" personalized.

(bottom) Edwin L. Hedderly was one of Parker's best and most loyal customers. He bought this DHE 28-gauge s/n 156,717 in 1911, perhaps at the behest of Captain du Bray.

Remington-Parker VHE 12-gauge on rare No. $^1/_2$ frame, weighing in at 6 pounds, 12 ounces. Photo by William W. Headrick.

(top) Parker Brothers A No. 1 Special 20-gauge two-barrel set s/n 231,774 on size 0 frame with seven magnificent factory gold inlays. Condition was described as "... sound, original, and well used ..." when the gun sold at public auction in August 1995. Photo courtesy of J. C. Devine, Inc., Firearm Auctioneers & Appraisers.

(bottom) LIMIT!—To "heighten charm" of waterfowl hunting by use of an ineffective weapon in the 1990s is not only a lost art, but a lost cause. This circa 1896 BH has seen 100 hunting seasons.

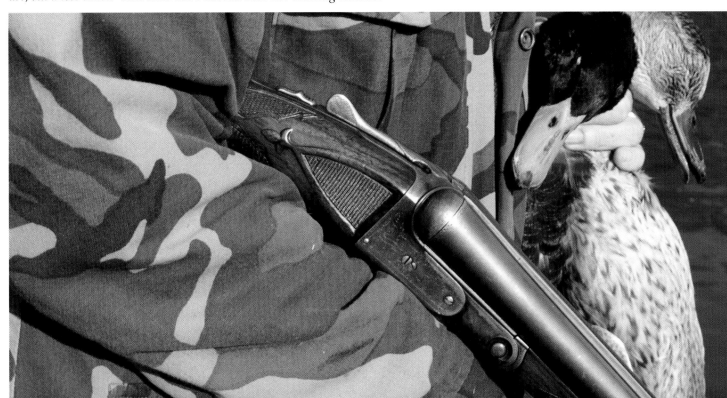

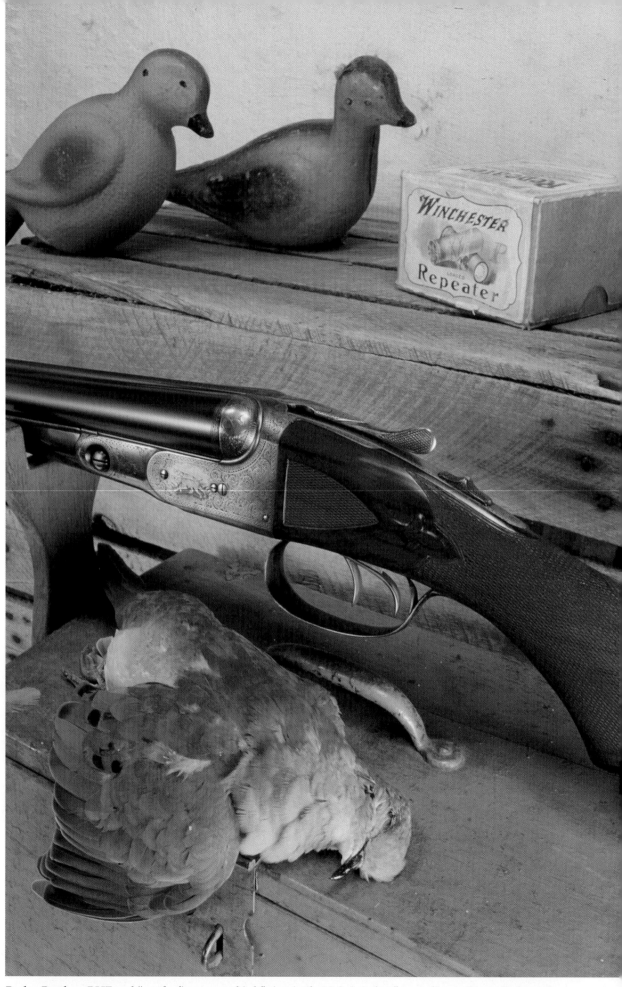

Parker Brothers BHE and "... the finest game bird flying in the U.S.A. today," according to Bryon Dalrymple,
but the dun-gray projectiles were scarce during the 1996 season in northern Illinois. Maybe next fall. . . .

Brothers' testing and targeting room. If the barrels didn't achieve the standard count (percentage), they would be worked on until they did. Most Parker hanging tags seem to register standard shot counts, and I believe they usually aren't specific to individual test-fired guns. In other words, most 12-gauge full-choke barrels would be marked at 252 pellets if they achieved at least a 75 percent average pattern during test firing, but never say "always," because there are exceptions.

On the preceeding page is a chart showing 12-gauge choke information gleaned from various sources that justifies the *caveat* of certain Parker catalogs that "... the so called dime test is no indication of the shooting qualities of our gun. Pattern and penetration are determined by the form of choking and not the exact muzzle diameter." The fact that an inside micrometer measures .694-inch at the muzzle is no assurance the barrel will pattern 75 percent (full choke), and modern shotshells are capable of improving pattern percentages over those originally counted for a particular gun. On the other hand, patterns are easily opened with the use of soft shot or a modern spreader load. Even measured choke diameters seem to be somewhat subjective. Note that Baer shows full choke to be .690-inch while Butler used .694 inch in his book. Nevertheless, shot count in a thirty-inch circle at forty yards is definitive (except that Parker Brothers used thirty-yard fixed tests to more fairly show the capabilities of .410 and 28-gauge).

The far right columns on the chart show the bore sizes of my mint, in-the-box, *unfired* Trojan 12-gauge, s/n 227,251 with twenty-eight-inch barrels, compared to the industry standard. The hanging tag calls the gun L.H. 171 pellets (51 percent—modified) and R.H. 135 pellets (40 percent—improved cylinder). My inside calipers measured full choke and slight improved-modified. I don't believe I could reconcile the apparent difference or satisfy my curiosity by test firing, as I'm not about to put together a circa 1927 load of $1\frac{1}{8}$ ounces of number 7 Tatham chilled shot and three drams Bulk Smokeless Powder in a contemporary paper shotshell. I guess I'll just keep that Trojan unfired.

A parting shot: I think it's self-evident that if a gun is represented to be *original* and turns out to be an upgrade or a restoration, then the buyer should get his money back. But what about a gun represented to have full and modified chokes based solely on measurements of bore diameter? This is contrary to the *caveat* of various Parker catalogs that "... the shooting qualities of our guns ... pattern and penetration are determined by the form of the choking and not the exact muzzle diameter." Should a prospective mail-order purchaser get to shoot a collector gun to determine if the chokes are fairly represented? I don't think so. My opinion is that chokes as represented should, of necessity, be considered as measured rather than as actually patterned, given the vagaries of shot hardness, powder characteristics, wads, cups, etc. But rest assured that opinions will differ in direct proportion to the amount of money involved. While *caveat emptor* may be the name of the gun-collecting game, sellers should be wary of contentious buyers in the land of the free and the home of the litigious. *Caveat vendor!*

CIRCUMSTANTIAL EVIDENCE

Much of what passes for serious Parker research amounts simply to articles summarizing what has been written before. As the story is told and retold, shuffled upside-down and backwards, many "facts" have gained a life of their own with no basis other than repetition. As you read this, see if you can separate the wheat from the chaff.

When Parker collectors talk guns, they often sound like a bunch of medieval monks debating the number of angels that could dance on the head of a pin. One of the angels often found dancing on the head of a Parker screw is the half-frame. After all, does anyone really care that Remington produced a small number of 12-gauge shotguns with ½ stamped on the barrel lump shortly before Parker production ceased? Sure, some advanced collectors do, so let's look at the facts.

Parker never advertised frame size as an option. Numbered frames were used by the factory as a gauge to size the barrels and fore-end metal in order to build a gun of proper scale and balance. Some Parker "monks" seem to think Remington built the half-frames simply to titillate collector interest sixty years after the fact. My theory is the half-frame was used to compensate for extra weight resulting from increased reliance on machine fit and finish in the late 1930s. The number ½ tooling may have been slightly altered dies, jigs, and gauges for the Number 1 standard 16-gauge frame and was first used to produce a special one-off BHE 12- and 20-gauge two-barrel set. Absent hard facts, my theory is as good as another until some new facts come along (which is doubtful at this late date).

I'm a great fan of Michael McIntosh, but sometimes I think he writes over Parker subjects by relying too much on 1960s and 1970s authors who, in turn, were long on conjecture and short on facts. Life is too short and the checks are too small for gunwriters to go to original sources to verify every fact for every article. Reliance on previously published books, magazine articles, and the like is natural and essential, but too often the casually printed word becomes an article of faith simply

Cha. Parker

Parkers were never really light guns.

Stephen J. Bodio

because it's published (Peter Johnson's ".14-gauge with 29-inch barrel" first Parker, for example).

As an avid Parker collector, I'm always searching out Parker-related articles to glean for factual information to annotate Baer's and Johnson's books and to bring my research file up to speed. I picked up the May-June 1992 issue of *Sporting Classics* magazine at a gun show recently and was pleased to see an article by McIntosh about Remington's 12-gauge Parkers with the rare half-size frame. Mike's book, *A. H. Fox: "The Finest Gun in the World,"* is definitive for those interested in Ansley Fox's gun. On the other hand, much of what has heretofore defined the Parker gun ranges from slightly wide of the mark to just plain wrong. Mike's article about the Parker half-frame appeared in his regular "Shotguns" column, and though his facts represent some excellent original research, I believe his conclusions are slightly off the mark. His Parker half-frame facts and conclusions are as follows:

> There's no question that . . . [the half-frame] . . . was introduced after Remington Arms purchased the Parker Brothers guns works in June 1934. . . .
>
> In a letter of August 1966, Larry Del Grego Sr.—who had worked in the Parker division at Remington and later established his own gun shop specializing in Parker repair and restoration—had this to say: "When Remington took over the Parker gun in 1934, we did design a ½ size frame as we eliminated the #1 size frame which was a 16-gauge and we did hundreds of guns on the ½ size 12-gauge frame."
>
> . . . the No. ½ frame was in production at least as early as the fall of 1937. A Parker news release of September 1937 describes a special-order pair of B.H.E. grades, each with two sets of barrels; one gun, fitted with barrels of both 12 and 20-gauge, is built on a No. ½ frame, which the release describes as "a size ordinarily used by Parker on 12-gauge guns of lighter weight." According to the best information I have, Remington

made a total of 7,287 Parkers, of all gauges, between mid-1934 and 1947, when the last guns were shipped. The frame itself was available for any grade, and specimens have now turned up reaching all the way from V.H.E. to A-1 Special; the highest grade I've seen is a B.H.E.

> Generally speaking, the overall quality of American guns noticeably declined during the 1930s . . . [and] . . . depression-era American guns look rougher than those of earlier times simply because the makers couldn't afford as much hand-work in fit and finish.

The best fact of all is an excellent photograph by photo-artist William W. Headrick showing a high-condition VHE 12-gauge with a rare half-frame. Headrick's picture is worth a thousand words. The half-frame gun belongs to Bill's father and weighs just six pounds twelve ounces. (See color section.)

McIntosh parlayed several pictures and the above-quoted facts (including questionable production information from Johnson's book, *Parker—America's Finest Shotgun*) into an extremely interesting article with the thesis that " . . . there's no sweeter gun than a 12-bore that weighs between six and 6¾ pounds . . . [and] . . . the No. ½ frame Parkers are about as close as the American trade ever came to adopting British principles of tailoring guns to certain classes of ammunition." The implication is that Remington used the half-frame to build short-chambered, light-weight 12-bores for light loads. I respectfully disagree. Parker half-frame twelves were built to weigh 6¾ to eight pounds and were typically patterned with 1¼-ounce *heavy loads*. We can quibble about whether 6¾-pound 12-gauges are "lightweight," but the fact remains that the Parker half-frames were built no lighter than comparable guns with standard-size frames.

At this late date, reader interest is perhaps more important than documentation or accuracy as the well-told story is often constructed of preconceived opinion applied to conflicting facts. But gunwriters cannot be held to the same evidentiary standards as trial lawyers. To paraphrase the jury instruction having to do with circumstantial evidence: *If the jury is to find O. J. Simpson guilty based on circumstantial evidence, then the same circumstantial evidence must exclude all reasonable possibilities of his innocence.* In other words, if the half-size frame is the circumstance used to impute the existence of lightweight 12-bore Parkers, then I wonder why the VHE pictured with McIntosh's article weighs six pounds twelve ounces—a standard weight offered by Parker

Brothers in its 1926 catalog, eleven years before the first half-frame 12-gauge was built. Further, Parker offered twelves as light as 6½ pounds beginning with the circa 1913 Flying Ducks catalog (about s/n 170,XXX), and this low-end standard weight persisted until 1926 (about s/n 215,XXX), when, for some unstated reason, the minimum standard weight reverted to 6¾ pounds. Parker's circa 1926 brochure, *A Trip Through Parker Bros*, refers to "... the race between ammunition and guns ..." and it was 1925 or 1926 when the company started stamping OVERLOAD

THE PARKER GUN

HOW TO ORDER A GUN

Our Terms are cash. We find it unavoidable to ship other than C. O. D., and orders from parties not known to us must be accompanied by 20 per cent of purchase price.

Styles. We are prepared to make *any style of gun desired*, in our action as illustrated, but deviation from regular weights and measurements compels us to make extra charge. Prices cheerfully furnished on application.

Weights and Lengths. Regular weights and lengths furnished on all our guns.

No. 8 gauge guns	11 to 14	pounds; barrels		32 to 38 inches
No. 10 gauge guns	7¾ to 10	pounds; barrels		28 to 32 inches
No. 12 gauge guns	6½ to 9	pounds; barrels		26 to 32 inches
No. 14 gauge guns	6¾ to 8¼	pounds; barrels		26 to 30 inches
No. 16 gauge guns	6 to 8	pounds; barrels		26 to 32 inches
No. 20 gauge guns	5¾ to 7½	pounds; barrels		26 to 32 inches
No. 28 gauge guns	5¼ to 6	pounds; barrels		24 to 30 inches

Regular stocks, 2 to 3¼ inches drop, 13½ to 14½ inches long. Eight gauge guns to special order to correspond to any grade except Vulcan and Trojan. Eight gauge not made with automatic ejector. Nos. 8, 10 or 12 gauge guns made extra heavy, or extra long to 40 inches, when desired, only on special orders and at an advance of $10.00 for extra weight and $10.00 for extra length above regular lists.

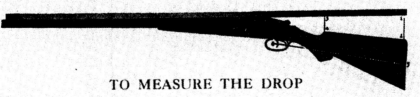

TO MEASURE THE DROP

Take a straight-edge, narrow enough to lay along the rib of the gun and long enough to reach from the sight of the gun over and beyond the butt. After being particular that the straight-edge lies along the rib and touches it at muzzle and breech, take the measurement from 1 to 2 and 3 to 4, which will give what is called the "drop." Length of stock always measured from center of front trigger to center of butt plate.

Parker Brothers weight and barrel length chart from circa 1913 Flying Ducks catalog. Notice 12-gauge guns were built as light as 6½ pounds with 26-inch barrels.

PROVED on the barrel flats. Perhaps nitro-proofing showed the guns to need a little more weight up front.

Headrick's VHE 12-gauge, s/n 241,886, has ° stamped on the barrel lump, *ILION N.Y.* stamped on the water table, *OVER-LOAD PROVED* stamped on the barrel flats, and the rib has no markings, as is the case with Remington-built Parkers. If the gun had weighed in at less than 6° pounds, this would be a fact in support of McIntosh's thesis. However, the pictures show "fat wood" typical of late Remington Parkers, and McIntosh correctly observed that "...depression-era American guns look rougher than those of earlier times simply because the makers couldn't afford as much handwork in fit and finish." Remington was acutely aware of this "rougher look" problem with Parker's fit and finish in the late 1930s. Donald F. Carpenter was one of the executives who managed Remington after the acquisition by DuPont in 1933, and he was in the loop when Remington bought Parker in 1934. Carpenter wrote a 1972 article, "A Short History of the Remington

Arms Company—1933-1940," which addressed the issue of the perhaps false perception that Remington had "cheapened" the Parker gun. According to Carpenter, "... we took steps to offset this reaction. They were only partially effective. Although the quality of the wood was upgraded, the ejector problems which had bedeviled Parker for years were largely overcome, the finish was brought back to earlier standards, and the fitting was improved, still the trade had a hard time trying to understand that Parker was actually improved and not deteriorating." While the "rougher look" may be true of American-made guns in general, I think it's fairer to say the Parker gun maintained its quality of fit and finish through the 1930s, but that Remington-built guns have a less slim and trim profile and appear to have a slightly different finish than those built by Parker Brothers before the Depression.

The half-frame A-1 Special referred to by McIntosh is Remington-Parker, s/n 241,000, manufactured at Ilion, New York. It is described as a "big gun" by Herschel Chadick. It has thirty-inch barrels, long pull, beavertail

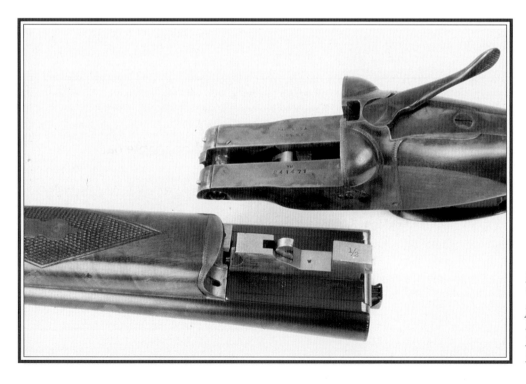

Remington-Parker VHE 12-gauge half-frame built after the late 1937 move from Meriden, Conn., to Ilion, New York.

fore-end, and ventilated rib. The frame, however, is half size, and the gun weighs eight pounds even. This is hardly a lightweight of the British genre. Also, I have photographed and weighed a half-frame BHE and three half-frame VHEs, all with serial numbers above 241,000; all four weighed between six pounds thirteen ounces and seven pounds two ounces, and the heavier guns had twenty-eight-inch barrels.

The BHE and all the VHEs are full-size short-barrel guns chambered to use *heavy* American loads and, notwithstanding their half-frames, are *not* ". . . about as close as the American trade ever came to adopting British principles of tailoring guns to certain classes of ammunition." The BHE, for example, has hanging tags that show the gun was patterned with 3¼ drams of bulk smokeless powder and 1¼ ounces of Tatham No. 7 chilled shot. If there was any tailoring of Parker half-frames to certain classes of ammunition, it was to cope with the American inclination toward extremely heavy loads.

According to the best facts available, Remington tooled up for the half-size frame shortly before moving the Parker operation to Ilion, New York, in late 1937. Larry Del Grego Sr. wrote his August 1966 letter twenty-nine years after the fact. I think his somewhat ambiguous quotation should mean: "Remington took over the Parker gun in 1934 . . . [and during 1937] . . . we did design a ½-size frame." The part about ". . . we eliminated the #1 size frame which was a 16-gauge" is contradicted by the existence of a late Remington-Parker VHE 16-gauge, s/n 241,665, built on a size 1 frame stamped *ILION, N.Y.* While this frame may have been old inventory, recollection reduced to paper long after the fact is still weak circumstantial evidence. Perhaps Del Grego Sr. meant the 16-gauge *tooling* was eliminated, possibly by retooling in January 1937, to reduce the frame

size for a special-order BHE two-gun four-barrel set. (The critical interior dimensions of the half-size frame are the same as the size 1 frame; some of the "cosmetic" exterior dimensions are slightly smaller.)

McIntosh correctly stated that ". . . the No. ½ frame was in production at least as early as the fall of 1937. A Parker news release of September 1937 describes a special-order pair of B.H.E. Grades, each with two sets of barrels: one gun, fitted with barrels of both 12 and 20 gauge, is built on a No. ½ frame." The complete news release—actually a letter from Parker to the National Rifle Association dated September 15, 1937—doesn't mention a frame size number. However, Chadick's ad for the special-order BHEs claimed: "The *half-frame* gun is the only one made with both 12 and 20-gauge twenty-four-inch barrels." The BHE set is quite the collector's item and was offered by Chadick's, Ltd. for $250,000 in 1991, up from an estimated $1,400 when the guns were new. The Parker-NRA letter says that ". . . the guns were finely engraved and finished, almost five months being required before they were ready for delivery. Because of overweights and special barrel lengths, there were some extra costs in the manufacture, and the cost of such a gun would approximate $700.00." My original Remington-Parker retail price list for January 2, 1936, shows that the BHE grade with selective single trigger cost $385.80; beavertail fore-end $26.73; and an extra set of interchangeable barrels, including regular fore-end, $154. Add a second beavertail fore-end at $26.73, and we have roughly $600 per gun, before the extra work occasioned by matching different gauge barrels and the cost of the obviously expensive special case.

The reference in Parker's letter to "overweights" doesn't fit Mike's "lightweight" premise. The letter goes on to paint a picture of guns weighing six

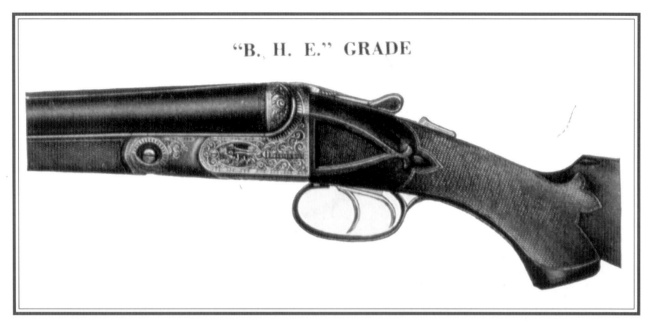

"B. H. E." GRADE

Remington-Parker BHE from 1936 price list. Note full cover fore-end checking.

pounds fourteen ounces for the 28/.410 combination and seven pounds three ounces for the 12- and 20-gauges:

> . . . the combination 12 and 20 gauge gun was required to weigh from 7 pounds to 7 pounds 3 ounces . . . [and] . . . the frame used on the 12-20 combination was a size ordinarily used by Parker on 12 gauge guns of lighter weight, and the 20 gauge barrels were of necessity somewhat wider across the chamber centers and had heavier breeches than are commonly used.

My first question is whether the Meriden-built 12- and 20-gauge BHE actually has a half-size frame of the same dimensions as the Ilion-built half-frame guns. The letter simply refers to ". . . a size ordinarily used by Parker on 12-gauge guns of lighter weight." This would not exclude the Number 1 standard 16-gauge frame, a size that had previously been used for heavy 20s and light 12-gauges. However, the buyer didn't want an extremely heavy 20-gauge.

Let's take a sidebar for a moment to put some dimensions on frame sizes. The definitive measurement is the distance between firing-pin centers, which, in turn, defines

chamber centers. The distance between firing-pin centers plus one chamber diameter, plus outside thickness of barrels at the breech, defines the width of the metal parts of a particular gun. The length from the hinge pin to the standing breech, and the width of the barrel-lump slot in the frame, are identical for all Parker frame sizes. The essential difference is the space between the firing pins: standard 20-gauge Number 0 is one inch, standard 16-gauge Number 1 is $1^1/_{16}$ inch, and standard 12-gauge No. $1\frac{1}{2}$ and heavy No. 2 are both $1^1/_8$ inch between firing-pin centers. Lightweight Parker 12s and heavyweight 20s used Number 1 frames, but the mating of interchangeable barrels of the two gauges on one frame entailed a special compromise. The rare half-size frame has $1^1/_{16}$ inch between the pins and other inside dimensions of the standard 16-gauge frame, while the outside dimensions split the difference between 16- and 20-gauge. The buyer of the special-order BHE didn't want a heavy 20-gauge built on a 16-gauge frame, but the standard 20-gauge frame had insufficient distance between the firing pins for 12-gauge barrels. (See Appendix F for more information on frame sizes.) Now back to the situation at hand.

The Remington-Parker spiral-bound 1937 catalog shows that a standard 12-gauge Skeet with beavertail fore-end and single trigger should weigh between seven pounds four ounces and seven pounds eight ounces with twenty-six-inch barrels. Shorten the barrels to twenty-four inches and the 12-gauge BHE wouldn't have needed a light frame to weigh seven pounds three ounces. However, a size 0 frame Skeet gun in 20-gauge with beavertail fore-end and single trigger had standard weights of six pounds eight ounces to six pounds twelve ounces with twenty-six-inch barrels. The consideration of *overweight* had to do with overly thick 20-gauge barrels rather than the 12-gauge barrels of ordinary outside diameter. Parker Brothers explained this in the April 1, 1899, catalog:

> Many parties having 10 bore guns write that they would like a pair of number 12 barrels fitted to the same stock, to be used for field purposes, thereby decreasing the weight and making a lighter gun. To such we would say that the 12-gauge barrels will increase the weight instead of decreasing it, for the following reasons: the inside of the 12-bore being two sizes smaller than the 10, and the outside of both being the same, there is of necessity more metal in the 12-gauge barrels than in the 10; consequently the 12-gauge pair will make the gun from 1 to 2 pounds heavier.

Go back and reread the catalog quote, substituting *12* for *10* and *20* for *12*—then visualize how fat and heavy the 20-gauge barrels would have been compared to the relatively thin and light twelves if Parker hadn't narrowed the 12-gauge frame to split the distance between 12- and 20-gauge firing-pin centers. One could speculate that Parker actually had to add weight to the 12-gauge barrels to achieve balance. The special-order BHEs were for skeet, and competitive Skeeters weren't using 2-inch to 2½-inch 12-gauge

shells with ⅞ or one ounce of shot in the 1930s. Likewise, the half-frame A-1 Special was built to a specification weight of eight pounds for trap competition. The American trend was away from light 12-bores of the British type and toward guns that could handle magnum loads. Firepower has always been the name of the game on the west side of the big pond. Strike two for McIntosh's theory that ". . . the No. ½ frame Parkers are about as close as the American trade ever came to adopting British principles of tailoring guns to certain classes of ammunition."

The September 15, 1937, Parker-NRA letter goes on to say that ". . . the story of Mr. Green's unusual guns begins in January of this year when an order for them was received . . . [and] . . . 5 months being required before they were ready for delivery." This clearly dates the BHE special set as being built at Meriden before the late-1937 to early-1938 move to Ilion, New York. The two-gun set has s/n 240,656 and 240,657. However, serial numbers alone aren't necessarily definitive of where or when a certain Parker gun was built. For example, s/n 239,746 is the first Ilion-stamped gun that shows up in my records. I own a VHE 12-gauge Skeet, s/n 239,826, that is definitely a Meriden gun date-stamped December 1936 by Remington (see Appendix D for Remington date codes). I've handled s/n 240,807, a VH .410 with twenty-six-inch barrels and rib marked *PARKER, MERIDEN, CONN.*, but no Ilion, N.Y., stamp on the frame. This .410 was built by Remington at Meriden and shipped July 31, 1937, to Abercrombie & Fitch in New York. Note that the roll-stamping on the rib is transitional as it omits "Bro's" and "Vulcan Steel" and soon became *passé* with the move to Ilion, when Remington eliminated identifying marks on the rib altogether.

The last Remington-Parker gun is said to be a GH .410, s/n 242,387, built from odds-and-ends inventory and delivered in 1947. The authority for the "last Parker" is none other than Mike McIntosh, who wrote: ". . . I've had the privilege of holding No. 242,387— a GH grade .410 assembled in 1947. . . ." My records show that more than 1,000 serial numbers overlap between Meriden (s/n 240,807) and Ilion (s/n 239,746) guns. According to Peter Johnson, Remington built only 1,723 Parkers in New York. He interviewed at least five Remington management-level employees, and they should know. By using s/n 239,746 as the *first Ilion gun*, New York production was more like 2,600. By using s/n 240,807 as the *last Meriden gun*, Ilion production would have been about 1,580. Special-order BHE s/n 240,657, subtracted from the total Parker production of 242,387, would compute to 1,730 against Johnson's claim of 1,723 guns. Although there was no definite last Meriden or first Ilion serial number, I think it's pretty clear that the VH .410 shipped to A & F and Mr. Green's special-order BHEs were close to the last guns out the door at Meriden. Most, if not all, half-frame guns were Ilion production, stamped as such, and had serial numbers of 241,000 or higher. (More on dated serial numbers in Appendix C.)

Walter King ran the Parker Gun Works from 1910 until shortly before the sale to Remington in 1934. He wrote an article, "Step By Step In Building A Gun," for *National Sportsman* magazine in 1924, and had this to say about frame building:

It is interesting to watch a frame progressing through the machining department and observe its changing appearance from a rough forging to a completely machined, skeletonized product. There are over 100 different machine operations on the frame alone, and each and every operation must have a jig, a fixture specially designed to hold the work in exact position while the operation is being done and every operation must have its particular gauge in order that the accuracy of the operation be checked. All component parts

Parker Brothers ad from August 1923 issue of National Sportsman. *This special "stop" feature was patented by C. A. King in 1875, and with the vanadium steel check hook keeps the "Old Reliable" from being broken open beyond repair.*

are produced to gauge, with certain allowances permitted. . . .

Let me speculate on a scenario that may account for the half-frame. According to the serialization of Parker shotguns in the *Blue Book of Gun Values* (seventeenth edition), Parker Brothers was building fewer than 300 guns per year during 1932, 1933, and 1934, until Remington bought the company. (According to "Babe" Del Grego, many of the depression-era guns were built for inventory just to keep the core group of skilled gunmakers working.) Parker had averaged 4,000 guns per year over the prior fifty years. Remington picked up the pace after the acquisition and produced about 1,300 Parkers per year for 1935, 1936, and 1937. However, this hardly justified maintaining a separate plant in Connecticut, especially since the size of the leased Parker Brothers gun works had an estimated annual capacity of 7,000 guns or more. The manufacture of the Parker gun was moved to Ilion, New York, in late 1937 and early 1938, and Remington's production was a scant 430 guns per year for 1938 through 1941.

Consider this: Parker Brothers' average annual production exceeded 4,000 guns for the fifty years between 1880 and 1930, and approximately 46,000 guns were built in the "heyday" years of 1900 to 1906. This would suggest that the gun works' annual capacity was at least 7,000 guns, to make up for seasonal demand, bad years, and World War I. The entire Ilion production (1,800 Parkers from 1938 to 1947) was about one-quarter of the Meriden capacity for one year. Work-in-process was three to six months or more depending on grade. (The BHE special-order set took five months.) Peter Johnson wrote about frame-making economies of scale in his book, *Parker—America's Finest Shotgun*: ". . . Frames . . . travel through this [machining] operation in batches of generally 100 at a time of one size and gauge." Parker guns were built using a minimum of eight frame sizes for the different gauges. One or two thousand frame forgings of different sizes in inventory at the time of the move to Ilion is not beyond the realm of possibility.

The special-order BHE set kept a few skilled gunmakers and engravers busy until the summer of 1937. The somewhat oddball configurations of 12-20 and 28-.410 required extensive special handwork on the barrels. W. A. King described over 100 different machining operations with special jigs and gauges on the frame alone. My guess is the BHE 12- and 20-gauge frame is a retooled size 1 frame. Remington ". . . eliminated the #1 frame," according to Larry Del Grego Sr., but to be more precise, he likely meant the *tooling*

was eliminated by changing it to half-size. Once the factory set up to run the half-size frame, they might as well have run a couple hundred or more. This is consistent with Peter Johnson's description of production whereby ". . . frames thus processed travel through this operation in batches of generally 100 at a time of one size and one gauge," and dovetails with Del Grego Sr.'s August 1966 letter claiming ". . . we did hundreds of guns on the ½ size 12-gauge frame." Further, Remington stockpiled inventory at Meriden so gunmaking wouldn't be interrupted any more than necessary by the breakdown, ship-

Fourth-generation Parker gunsmith Lawrence Del Grego puts the final master's touch on a repair project at America's most famous Parker Gun venue — Larry Del Grego & Son, of Ilion, New York.

ping, and setup of the Parker machinery over the several months it took to move the gun works "lock, stock, and barrel" to Ilion. Anyone who has seen the volume of Parker parts at Del Grego's shop has to believe that Remington inventoried a whole lot of half-size frame forgings back in the late '30s.

After the move to Ilion, Parker guns were built to more standard dimensions with more uniform finish, and the manufacturing process may have been streamlined by eliminating some frame sizes. Remington adopted the half-size frame to build lighter (but not lightweight) twelves, perhaps to compensate for weight-additive features such as beavertail fore-end, ventilated rib, and the "war club" wood dimensions typical of late Remington-Parkers. The various frame sizes have been measured and documented, and the basic dimensions have persisted since the early 1880s. It's not surprising, however, that advances in metallurgy from the 1880s to 1930s could result in some scaling down of outside dimensions, but gauge for gauge, the distance between the firing pins had to remain constant. The slightly smaller dimensions of a half-frame, when compared to a standard 1½ frame, accounts for metal removal about equal to the volume of one silver dollar—one ounce. Unless the smaller frame was used as a gauge to build an overall scaled-down gun with finer lines, thinner barrels, and less cross-sectional wood in the stock, the half-frame alone was not going to lighten up a 12-gauge. I've had my hands on a number of Parker half-frames, and in weight, handling, balance, and appearance they are all but indistinguishable from my more typical Number 1½-frame VHE Skeet. In short, the half-frame Parkers don't contradict Stephen Bodio's observation that "Parkers were never really light guns."

There are certain facts about the half-size frame that ought to be repeated. The

half-frame was first used to mitigate the extra weight of 20-gauge barrels on a special-order BHE 12- and 20-gauge two-barrel set. The half-frame didn't result in truly lightweight twelves—none I have handled weigh less than 6¾ pounds. Chadick's Remington-Parker A-1 Special, s/n 241,000, has a half-frame but weighs eight pounds even. The work lavished on an A-1-S and the dollars involved certainly would have resulted in a lighter gun if the half-frame were so intended.

The half-frame VHE 12-gauge pictured with McIntosh's article seems to have too much wood for the author to wax enthusiastic about ". . . no sweeter gun than a 12-bore that weighs between six and 6¾ pounds," even though it weighs 6¾ pounds. Headrick's VHE is a Parker collector's treasure, but you wouldn't want a 12-gauge any lighter. My VHE Skeet weighs but three ounces more, is built on a standard 1½ frame, and has a 14 ⁵/₈-inch pull with checked butt; Headrick's half-frame VHE has a Silvers pad. Finally, Parker Brothers offered twelves as light as 6½ pounds as early as 1913, long before the advent of the "rare" half-frame. Strike three! Case closed. The jury is instructed to retire to the kitchen, grab a beer from the fridge, take all the preceding with a grain of salt, and be mindful of the *caveat* that evidence of a 6¾-pound half-frame 12-gauge isn't necessarily a circumstance proving that Remington was trying to build lightweight light-load 12-bores of the British genre.

The fact is, nobody knows what Remington had on its corporate mind when it retooled for the half-frame in 1937. It earned $925,000 on gross sales of $14.5 million for 1936. Assuming Remington sold 1,723 Ilion-Parkers at an average price of $133 (jobber's price for a DHE on the February 16, 1940 price list), the gross sales of Remington-Parker guns for 1938 through 1941 would have been less than $60,000 per year (four-tenths of 1 percent of Remington's 1936 gross sales). Remember that DuPont controlled Remington, and DuPont executives were calling the shots. Half-frame Parkers at best would have been a speck of dust on DuPont's year-end operating statements. After the war, when resumption of normal production was being considered, the cost accountants determined that to revive the "Old Reliable" Parker gun would be a money-losing proposition. The Parker gun died unceremoniously at age eighty-two, a victim of the bottom line.

If there exists a 6½-pound or lighter 12-gauge Parker, it would be a rare item indeed, much the same as the 5½- to six-pound Lefever 12-gauge offered at the turn of the century. However, the six-pound Lefever that I know about has thin barrels to the extreme, with one bulged—certainly not built to the standard of the "Old Reliable" Parker gun.

DOVES AND EXTRACTORS

Dove season opens the first of September in my part of northern Illinois. Each year high hopes for an opening-day limit are fueled by an abundance of birds shoulder to shoulder on the electric wires during the last week of August. For me this is the beginning of the fall hunt. As I walk down the road to my killing spot by the old windmill, I notice that doves have good instincts. They take flight well out of shooting range. If I were driving my truck, they'd sit tight and watch me go by.

At my stand I tie a clothesline to the old windmill and string the other end through the crotch of a nearby tree. Decoys are hung on the line, and when I pull it taut, my stool looks like doves on a wire. Birds of a feather flock together—I hope.

One advantage of this lying-in-wait type of hunting is time to think. Doves are scarce, and my mind wanders back to 1992, when I killed my limit over a sunflower patch at a neighbor's place. However, the essence is dove shooting rather than dove killing, and shooting a Parker enhances this link in the chain of lifetime outdoor experiences.

The mourning dove, without question, is one of the finest, if not the finest game bird flying in the U. S. today!

Byron W. Dalrymple

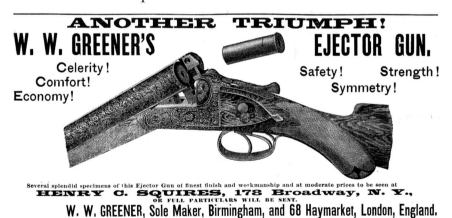

W. W. Greener advertised this ejector gun in an 1885 issue of Forest and Stream. *The automatic ejector gimmick was an instant success and most American manufacturers were on the bandwagon by the mid-1890s, but not Parker Brothers. The "Old Reliable" achieved ejector-gun status in 1902, but only as a $25 option on D grade and above. Ejectors were offered on the lower grades by 1908, but were never an option on Trojan grade.*

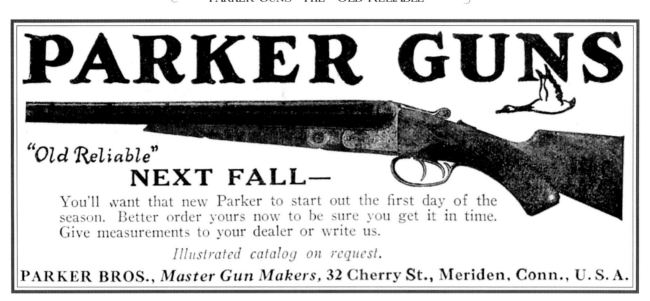

Parker Brothers ad from April 1927 issue of National Sportsman.

Birds are few and far between. Quite a few are flying in the distance, but they all seem to roost in trees well out of range. I wish I had a few shooting buddies to keep them moving—and I should have planted some sunflowers. Then three incoming doves flare at my decoys. I defend myself and double. The third dove leaves to spread the warning to his entire species that the season is open.

Time passes with more thinking and less shooting. I think about the Parker GH in my hands. It has a straight grip with good dimensions, and I particularly like the extractors. I own this farm, and I don't want plastic shell casings scattered all over. Automatic ejectors are fine for driven-bird shooting in Great Britain and Europe, as they somehow help enhance the experience when passing your pair of matched doubles back and forth with your loader. One stuffy Londoner at a Twelfth of August grouse drive, when asked whether his matched Purdeys had ejectors, reportedly said, "I don't know. I don't load my own guns." But the American experience is quite different. I doubt whether anyone on this side of the Atlantic ever got off two shots at a duck, pheasant, quail, or grouse, then automatically ejected the spent shells and reloaded to make a *good* third or fourth shot. Meanwhile, ejected plastic shells with a half-life of hundreds of

years litter the countryside. Pardon me if I like extractors.

Doves are better than ducks for thought-gathering. When the doves are out of range, I can resolve in my mind the larger issue of extractors versus ejectors, or perhaps try to figure out what this world's coming to. In a similar situation, the duck hunter would feel compelled to destroy his concentration by blowing his duck call.

A single surprises me from behind. Two shots but no bird. Now I'm shooting 50 percent. It will get worse. I lift the spent shells from the chambers, put them in my pocket, and wonder why anybody would pay extra for automatic ejectors. In Chapter 9, "Supply-Side Economics," there's an analysis of 520 Parker guns offered for sale over five recent years. My survey shows that automatic-ejector guns dominate. Roughly two-thirds of the VH and PH grades, three-quarters of GH grade, and 95 percent of the DH and higher grades have ejectors.

While I prefer extractors, there are too few collector-quality Parkers offered for sale to pass up an otherwise desirable gun just because it has ejectors. If a good gun has extractors, so much the better. If it's a shooter, I don't scatter shells on the farm, and any shell that hits the ground at the trap range usually belongs to the club. Parker guns regarded as too good to shoot will never have occasion to eject shells. In either case, shooter or collector's item, I'll be pleased to take the extractor price discount. For those of my persuasion, this is a win-win situation.

The weird squeaking of dove wings brings me back. A small flock zips past, but I don't get off a shot. My opening double was the kind of shooting that makes a dove hunter proud. However, twenty shots later I've added only four more dun-gray projectiles to my bag, and it's time to quit. On my way home, I recall that my alter-ego, Captain du Bray, had once put champion shot Harvey McMurchy in a position to kill but one dove with each six shells. I'm consoled (but not satisfied) with my one-of-four shooting.

Dove season was short this year. Six birds reduced to possession on opening day, one the second day, one the third, and then nothing. I killed eight birds with thirty-one shots—not a particularly efficient way to feed the family. However, my GH cost $1,000 less than a comparable gun with automatic ejectors. I can buy groceries with the savings. And I didn't need to crawl around on my hands and knees looking for ejected shells in the high grass.

EPILOGUE

FALL OF '96

This book could as well have been titled *Parker Guns—The Never-Ending Story*. However, at some point the edited manuscript had to be considered complete, and once the type is set, there will be no changes. So for all intents and purposes, this book is a tablet of stone. This makes me a little nervous, as every day I find something to contradict or expand on what I have written. And it has tempered my opinion of other books that can stand some revision but can't stand the expense of doing so.

Some authors may deem parts of my book insensitive to their professional ego. Sometimes no amount of praise or exculpatory statements can make up for even one small instance of calling attention to another's errors or omissions. On the other hand, the greater good is served by continuing to zero in on what is true and accurate, as the process would be sure to fail if researchers didn't go back to correct the record. Meanwhile, the record continues to change with each newly discovered or correlated tidbit about the "Old Reliable" Parker gun.

One example of an eleventh-hour correction of my own record follows. My manuscript had been edited by Craig Boddington and was being typeset during September 1996, when I slipped away to Nashville for the NRA National Gun Collectors Show and Conference held at Opryland. The Parker Gun Collectors Association designated the NRA/Opryland show as the venue for our annual get-together, and Parker collectors from throughout the country had tables or just stopped by to visit. After dinner one evening, I made the acquaintance of Louis C. Parker III, great-great grandson of the Connecticut industrialist who gave his name to the Parker gun. Louis and I found a quiet place and ordered up some beers, and he kindly offered to take a look at my Chapter 2—"Charles Parker's Company"—to ensure that things were as right as they could be. The next day, I received back my manuscript with two very substantial corrections involving his great-grandfather, Wilbur Fisk Parker. I called the publisher first thing Monday morning, and fortunately we were able to make the changes

"Clipper" and his first 1996 retrieve. Lookin' good at eleven years old!

without serious disruption of the publishing process. The additional information and subtle changes make this book more accurate and complete; but it could be that almost everything I've written will be subject to expansion, correction, refinement, or change soon after this book is published, as every stated fact is an open invitation for others to enter the fray.

It must seem quite remarkable to Peter Johnson that his Parker book has been printed and reprinted for over thirty-five years. Likewise, Larry Baer has been in print and reprint for over twenty years. I hope I'm around twenty years from now to see how much of what I've written has continuing validity. This is my best effort to pass along the best quality of information available to me through the last possible moment before publication. The ball is now in someone else's court. I'm putting down my tape recorder, and Nancy will have a well-earned vacation far away from the word processor. My chocolate Lab, "Clipper," seems interested in the pheasants we hear squawking down on the Conservation Reserve land. Birds are abundant this year. There will be ample opportunity to prove some of my Parker twelves worthy of all the attention given them in *Parker Guns—The "Old Reliable."*

Patents and Patent Models

The U.S. Constitution provides for establishment of a patent office to encourage innovation by allowing the exclusive use of a novel idea for a limited period of time. Until 1836, the patent office merely registered patents, but took no steps to examine the application for originality or patentability. Multiple patent claims for the same invention, innovation, or refinement were simply filed away; every dispute had to be resolved in the courts. After 1836, the patent office examined applications and granted *letters patent* for unique ideas, thus screening out duplications and claims to "innovations" that were in the public domain.

From 1836 to about 1880, the U. S. Patent Office required an applicant to submit a working model—not larger than a twelve-inch cube—to document claims of novelty, innovation, or improvement. It's possible that a fully functional patent model of the first Parker gun exists somewhere. The years of patent models were the years of the Industrial Revolution; by 1879 almost 200,000 models were on display or in storage at the U. S. Patent Office. Then in 1880, fire destroyed 60,000 to 70,000 of the models, and the law was changed so that models were no longer required to document patent applications. The models that survived the fire were put into dead storage in 1893, but some inventors failed to get the message, and models continued to trickle in until as late as 1907.

The patent office began to clean house in the 1920s, and the Smithsonian selected historically significant models for display. Also, most large manufacturers were notified to come and get their patent models, so it's likely The Charles Parker Company sent a representative to regain possession of the various Parker Brothers' circa 1866-80 models. If William Miller's Lifter-T-Latch model survived the 1877 fire, it could be in storage at the Smithsonian, or possibly it is in possession of the Parker family, the Remington Museum, or in the hands of a private collector. Other Parker patents that would have been documented by models were Wilbur Parker's 1869 shotshell and 1875 taper-bolt breechlock mechanism, as well as C. A. King's 1875 spherical-recess hinge pin, 1876 barrel-boring fixture, 1876 one-piece lifter, and 1878 Deeley & Edge fore-end latch. Perhaps someday one of these patent models will be identified and offered for sale in the collector market.

The U. S. Patent Office has a valuable service for collectors interested in researching Parker shotguns, cartridges, and related equipment. General information about patents, trademarks, and copyrights can be had by calling 1-800-786-9199 (or directory assistance as area codes and numbers have the habit of changing). The Patent Office copy-order department, currently at 703-305-4350, will send you a crisp, clean copy of any patent you request by *number*, while charging a relatively nominal copy fee (three dollars in 1996) to your credit card. The only catch is that you do need the patent number. For example, William H. Miller's name and the date he patented his improvement in breechloading firearms will not penetrate the system at the copy-order level—you need number 59,723. Parker Brothers stamped patent dates rather than patent numbers on its various guns. Dates can be traced to numbers through microfilm records and indexes at the library of any good engineering school, but to save you duplication of my effort, I've included a synopsis and schedule of dates and numbers for all patents date-stamped on Parker guns. Also, there are selected letters patent and patent drawings for certain gun improvements, plus cartridge patents by Berdan, Milbank, and Wilbur Parker. This book could pay for itself in savings of microfilm access and copy-order fees for the truly curious.

LIST OF PATENTS OF INTEREST TO PARKER OWNERS

Bold indicates patent drawings pictured in Appendix

No. 46,292—February 7, 1865—Hiram Berdan's basic patent for a brass center-fire cartridge having its own offset anvil. Berdan's patent **No. 82,587** of September 29, 1868 (reissue No. 4,491, August 1, 1871) modified the design to be a center anvil with two flash holes, as commonly seen on Parker metallic Berdan-primed shotshells.

No. 59,723—November 13, 1866—W. H. Miller's breechloading firearm. Miller's T-Latch, *Meriden Man'fg Co., for Cha's Parker* shotgun patent drawings are pictured and discussed in Chapter 4, "First Parker Shotgun." His letters patent are in this Appendix.

No. 62,283—February 19, 1867 (reissue August 6, 1867)—I. M. Milbank's innovation was simply a soldered strengthener inside the base of a brass cartridge, so as to take the impact of repeated blows from the hammer and mitigate damage to the base from capping and removing primers repeatedly in self-primed reloadable cartridges. Milbank's interior strengthener was used by Union Metallic Cartridge Company in conjunction with Berdan's patent anvil to strengthen the base of Berdan-primed shotshells. Berdan's and Milbank's patent dates are seen on early Parker metallic central-fire shotshell boxes.

No. 84,314—November 24, 1868—John Stokes's rebounding locks adopted by Parker Brothers in the early 1870s. Although back-action locks are shown on the patent drawing, the rebounding feature was equally applicable to front- or bar-action locks. Parker Brothers' 1872-73 catalog stated that Stokes's patent rebounding locks could be installed only on front-action guns, and back-action guns were soon dropped from the line.

No. 88,202—March 23, 1869—Wilbur F. Parker's shotshell patent for a slot-head feature to allow removal of the primer by using a pick, penknife, or similar pointed object. Wilbur's cross-section drawing shows a two-piece shotshell with a thick base soldered to a thin brass tube. The patent drawing should serve to define circa 1869 shotshells, used in Parker shotguns until the adoption of the Berdan-Milbank patent, Berdan-primed shotshells in the early 1870s.

No. 124,939—March 26, 1872—J. C. Dane's rebounding locks for front action guns super-seded Stokes's rebounding locks in the mid-1870s. Parker Brothers stopped charging for rebounding locks during 1873, as the feature was considered essential to safety.

No. 130,984—September 3, 1872—F. S. Dangerfield's patent for a doll's-head rib exten-sion gripped by a sliding bolt, and a check-hook feature to take the strain off the hinge pin. Dangerfield assigned his patent to Daniel M. Lefever, who, in turn, refined and repatented the doll's-head and check-hook features in 1878, and assigned them to Parker Brothers in March 1881.

No. 160,915—March 16, 1875—Charles A. King's first patent after joining Parker Brothers. Most visible is the recessed hinge pin that lies flush without needing a spline for orientation. The second part of his patent is a sleeve that fits over the hinge pin and serves to stop the barrels when the gun is opened, thus relieving *some* of the pressure on the hinge pin. (Adoption of the Dangerfield-Lefever check-hook in 1881 solved the problem completely.) Note that King's patent was filed February 6, 1875, and shows Wilbur Parker's patent im-provements per his application filed the day prior—thus the application date, rather than the date of letters patent, is definitive.

No. 161,267—March 23, 1875—Wilbur F. Parker's taper-bolt improvement, whereby a sliding bolt with a tapered lower surface engages a slot with matching tapered surface at the back of the barrel lump. Wilbur also eliminated the pin protruding through the top of the breech, evident on earlier Miller-patent guns.

No. 175,862—April 11, 1876—C. A. King's barrel-boring jig, whereby joined barrels were packed in a box filled with plaster of Paris, which, upon hardening, would make them rigid during the boring process.

No. 184,716—November 28, 1876—C. A. King's one-piece lifter. At this point, the only vestige of Miller's lifter T-Latch remaining was the basic concept of lifter-opener. Miller didn't seem to claim the lifter-opener in his letters patent, and this basic feature may not have been patentable. Nevertheless, Parker Brothers stamped Miller's *Nov. 13, 1866,* patent date on lifter guns for the seventeen-year duration of his patent, while actually building post-1868 guns with the toggle-bolt breechlock mechanism as improved by Wilbur's March 23, 1875, (taper-bolt) patent and King's November 28, 1876, (one-piece lifter) patent.

No. 201,618—March 26, 1878—C. A. King's version of the Deeley & Edge fore-end latch.

No. 205,193—June 25, 1878—D. M. Lefever's doll's-head rib extension was essentially Dangerfield's doll's head, cut with square shoulders and matched to a recess in the breech. Lefever's improvement was to cut the square shoulders of the rib extension on a radius from the hinge pin. The second element of Lefever's patent was refinement of Dangerfield's check-hook, which was adopted by Parker Brothers after March 1881 on all hammer guns. Display of Dangerfield's 1872 patent date on post-1881 doll's-head and check-hook hammer guns may have been through an abundance of caution, as Lefever's refinements might not have stood a test in patent court. On the other hand, doubling up with Lefever's 1878 date stamp could have stretched the patent monopoly an additional six years.

No. 356,321—January 18, 1887; No. 368,401—August 16, 1887; No. 402,675—May 7, 1889; and No. 412,340—October 8, 1889, are a series of patents by Charles A. King for mechanical features of the Parker Brothers boxlock concealed-hammer (hammerless) action. Anson & Deeley's circa 1875 patent is a boxlock action with hammers cocked by leverage from the barrels when the gun is opened. King's refinements of the basic Anson & Deeley patent were: spiral mainsprings instead of leaf springs and a single slide to cock both hammers at once (356,321); refinements to relieve friction and withdraw the firing pins as the gun was opened (368,401); internal sleeve over hinge pin as a barrel stop, to achieve in hammerless guns what Lefever's check-hook was doing in hammer guns (402,675); and rebounding hammers to withdraw firing pins from the chambers by release of the trigger after firing (412,340).

No. 673,641—May 7, 1901—C. A. King and J. P. Hayes collaborated on a complex ejector mechanism that has provided Parker gunsmiths with a steady source of income ever since.

No. 797,123—August 15, 1905—Charles King's hardened replaceable wear insert. Note the patent drawing shows the old-style connection between the top lever and the taper bolt.

No. 973,655—October 25, 1910—J. P. Hayes improved the hardened wear insert by cutting a flat surface on either side of the tapered surface, so the taper bolt slides over the top and grips the barrel lump "hand in glove" with two different bearing surfaces. Also note that the 1910 patent drawing shows the top lever operating the taper bolt directly as a cam, thus eliminating some interior mechanical parts. At this point, the Parker hammerless gun achieved final mechanical form.

No. 1,219,964—March 20, 1917—Frank C. Lefler's single selective trigger, which provided Parker gun mechanic Frank Fama with a long-term employment opportunity. Lefler's patent left much to be desired, and Fama gets credit for refinements that made it adequate.

United States Patent Office

WM. H. MILLLER, OF WEST MERIDEN, CONNECTICUT, ASSIGNOR TO MERIDEN MANUFACTURING COMPANY.

IMPROVEMENT IN BREECH-LOADING FIRE-ARMS.
(Specifications forming part of letters patent No. 59,723, dated November 13, 1866)

To all whom it may concern:

Be it known that I, W. H. Miller, of West Meriden, in the county of New Haven and State of Connecticut, have invented a new Improvement in Breech-Loading Fire-Arms; and I do hereby declare the following, when taken in connection with the accompanying drawings and the letters of reference marked thereon, to be a full, clear, and exact description of the same, and which said drawings constitute part of this specification, and represent, in——

Figure 1, a side view; Fig. 2, a sectional side view, the several parts in a home position as for discharge; Fig. 3, a central section, the parts in position for charging; and in Fig. 4, a top view.

My invention relates more particularly to an improvement in double-barrel shotguns, yet it is applicable to other arms and other purposes, and is designed for the use of the "Maynard" cartridge, which has the rear centrally pierced; and consists in the peculiar manner of opening and closing the breech, and locking the same when closed.

To enable others to construct and use my improvement, I will proceed to describe the same as illustrated in the accompanying drawings.

A is the barrel, represented as double, (see Fig. 4;) B, the stock; C, the lock; D, the trigger-guard, and E E the triggers, of the usual form and construction; G, the breech-piece, which is formed upon a tail-plate, H, and into which the tubes I are set, communicating directly with the barrel, as denoted by broken lines, Fig. 1. The said breech-piece G extends forward, forming a frame for the support of the barrel, (see Figs. 2 and 3,) and to which the barrel is hinged, as at K, so as to be raised from the position in Fig. 2 to that in Fig. 3, or returned.

L is a latch formed upon a lever, M, pivoted to the tail-piece H at a, and formed to enter a recess in the top of the barrel, as denoted by broken lines, Fig. 4, when the barrel is in its home position, and so as to secure it in that position. The said latch is returned by the reaction of a spring, c, and in order to make the security of the latch L more certain projections d are formed upon the sides of the lever M, which, when the lever M descends, fall into notches f in the breech-piece G, as seen in Figs. 3 and 4, which said projections d relieve the pivot a from the strain of discharge which would otherwise be brought up on it, and makes the security doubly sure.

In addition to the security of the latch L, I form a projection, h, upon the under side of the barrels, (see Fig. 3,) which, as the barrels descend, falls into a corresponding notch, i, on the frame J.

P, Fig. 3, is a bolt passing through the breech-piece G, so as to enter a hole in the rear of the barrel, as denoted in broken lines, Fig. 2, when the barrel is at rest, as in the position in said Fig. 2, which prevents the barrel from being accidentally opened.

To operate the bolt P and the lever M to release the barrel—that is, to move them from the position denoted in Fig. 2 to that denoted in Fig. 3—I place centrally in the rear of the barrels and sliding bar, R, extending up to the under side of the lever M and down through the trigger-guard plate to receive a finger-plate, S. The upper end of the bar R is forked, so that one leg passes up either side of the flattened portion of the bolt P, and the rear side of the said forked portion is inclined, so that a head, r, on the said bolt will rest upon the incline of the two legs of the fork, so that the movement of the bar R upward from the position in Fig. 2 to that in Fig. 3 will withdraw the bolt, as denoted in said figures, and when the said bar has returned a plate, l, attached to the bar R, and correspondingly inclined, bears against the head r of the bolt and returns the bolt, as denoted in Fig. 2. The upward movement of the bar R at the same time raises the lever M, as denoted in Fig. 3, and thus raised the rear end of the barrel rises from the position in Fig.2 to that in Fig. 3, in which position the cartridge is inserted in the usual manner.

In order to retain the bolt P and the lever M in the position seen in Fig. 3 until the barrel is again returned, a lever, N, (see Fig. 2, and denoted in red, Fig. 3,) is hung to the frame at *m*, which, when the barrel is raised, is forced by a spring, *t*, from the position seen in Fig. 2 to that in Fig. 3, the shorter arm extending out, so as to catch under a pin, *s*, on the bar R, as seen in Fig. 3. This retains the bar R in its upward position, and consequently the bolt P and lever M; but when the barrel is again returned, as in Fig. 2, it strikes the longer arm of the lever N, forcing it down, as in Fig. 2, and, releasing the bar R, the lever M and bolt P return by the action of the spring *c*, and securely lock the barrel in its home position.

To start the discharged shell from the barrel, I place a slide, T, beneath the barrel, its rear end extending up so as to come in front of the flange of the cartridge, as seen in Fig. 3. The said slide extends forward to a pin, *u*, on the frame J, near the bearing K, so that as the barrel rises from the position in Fig. 2 to that in Fig. 3, the slide T strikes the pin *u* and starts the shell from the barrel, as denoted in Fig. 3. Returning the barrel to the position in Fig. 2 the slide strikes the breech-piece G, and returns as denoted in Fig. 2.

To charge my arm, press the finger-plate S from the position in Fig.2 to that in Fig. 3, when the barrel will freely rise, as denoted in Fig. 3; then insert the cartridge and return to the position denoted in Fig. 2, the central perforation of the cartridge corresponding to the passage of the tubes I. A percussion-cap or other equivalent placed upon the said tubes and discharged will, through the said passage, ignite and discharge the cartridge in the barrel.

That part of the stock U forward of the joint K, I fix to the barrel, and form the joint between the two parts of the stock, so that the space between the two necessary to permit the movement of the barrel will be closed when the barrel is in its home position, as seen in Fig. 2.

I have thus far described my arm as for two barrels; yet the same arrangement may be equally well adapted to a single barrel, as those skilled in the art will readily understand.

I have also described my arm as specially adapted to the use of the Maynard or other similar central-fire cartridge; yet the common fulminate-cartridge may be used, it only being required that the hammers so communicate with the cartridge that the blow of the hammer will explode the fulminate.

If occasion requires that the arm should be used as a muzzle-loader it is only necessary that a cartridge-shell should remain in the barrel, so as to prevent the escape of gas at the joint between the rear of the barrel and the breech-piece.

I am aware that a latch upon the upper side of the frame has often been used to lock the barrel in its home position. I do not, therefore, broadly claim a latch so constructed; but,

Having thus fully described my invention, what I do claim as new and useful, and desire to secure by Letters Patent, is—

1. The lever M, constructed and arranged with the projections *d*, in combination with a corresponding recess, *f*, and the latch L, so as to operate substantially in the manner herein set forth.

2. The vertical bar R, in combination with the bolt P and the lever M, constructed and arranged to operate substantially in the manner and for the purpose herein set forth.

3. The combination and arrangement described of the lever N with the bar R and the barrel of the arm, substantially as and for the purpose described.

WM. H. MILLLER.

Witnesses:
GEORGE A. FAY,
ALFRED P. CURTISS.

I. M. MILBANK.

Cartridge.

No. 62,283.   Patented Feb. 19, 1867.

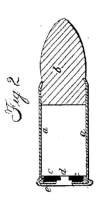

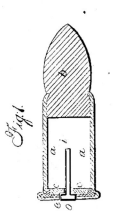

Witnesses.

Geo. D. Walker

Chas. H. Smith

I. M. Milbank
per S. N. Snell
Atty

H. BERDAN.

Metallic Cartridge.

No. 82,587.

Patented Sept. 29, 1868.

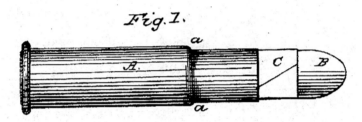

Fig. 1.

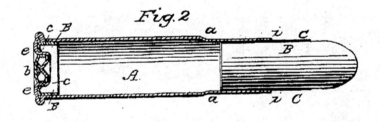

Fig. 2

Inventor;

H. Berdan

Witnesses
A. Lellere

J. STOKES.

Gun Lock.

No. 84,314.

Patented Nov 24, 1868.

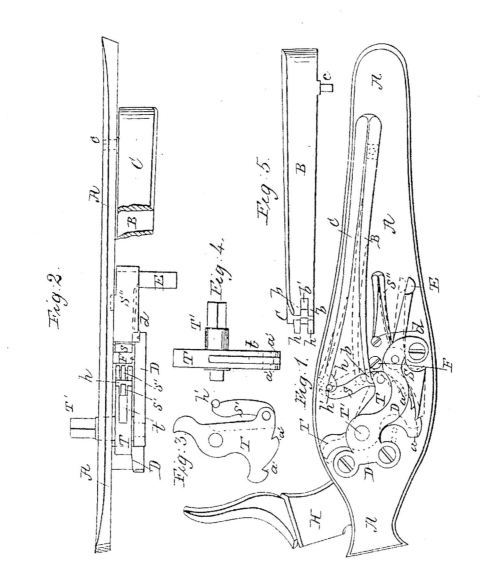

Witnesses.
C.E.Buckland
J.P.Buckland.

Inventor.
John Stokes

W. F. PARKER.

Cartridge.

No. 88,202.

Patented March 23, 1869.

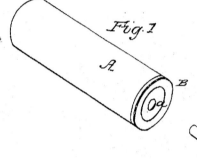

Fig. 1

Fig. 2

Fig. 3

Fig. 4

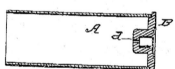

Fig. 5

Fig. 6

Fig. 7

WITNESSES

Jo. H. Shumway

a. J. Libbey

W. F. Parker
INVENTOR
By his Attorney,
John C. Earle,

J. C. DANE.

Improvement in Gun Locks.

No. 124,939.   Patented March 26, 1872.

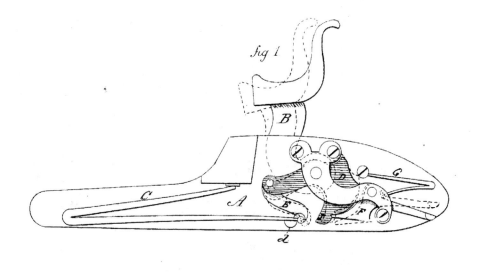

fig 1

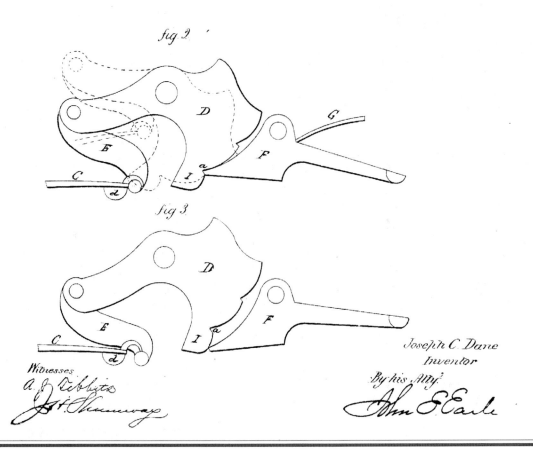

fig 2

fig 3

Witnesses
A. J. Dibbits
J. H. Shumway

Joseph C. Dane
Inventor
By his Atty.
John E. Earle

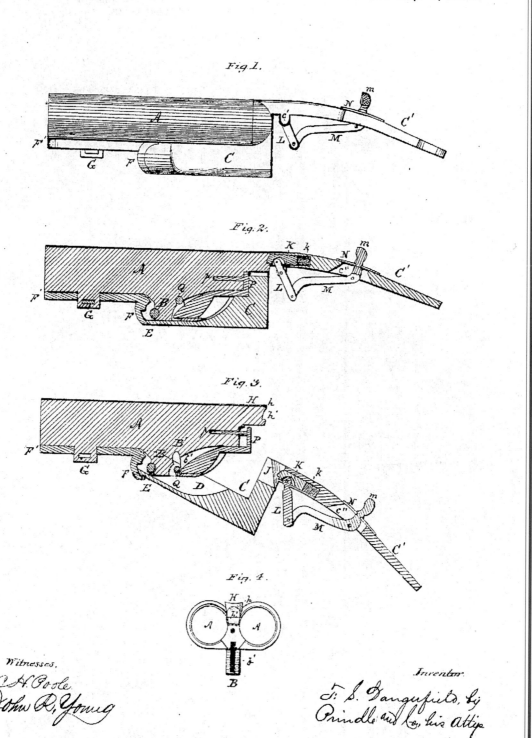

2 Sheets--Sheet 1.

F. S. DANGERFIELD.

Improvement in Breech-Loading Fire-Arms.

No. 130,984.   Patented Sep. 3, 1872.

Fig 1.

Fig. 2.

Fig. 3.

Fig. 4.

Witnesses.
C. H. Poole.
John R. Young

Inventor.
F. S. Dangerfield, by
Prindle and Co., his Attys

2 Sheets--Sheet 2.

F. S. DANGERFIELD.

Improvement in Breech-Loading Fire-Arms.

No. 130,984.   Patented Sep. 3, 1872.

Fig. 5.

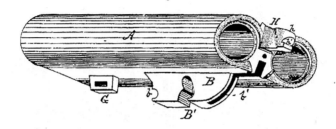

Fig. 6.

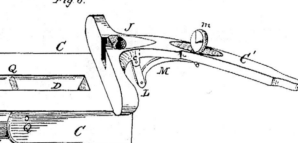

Fig. 7.

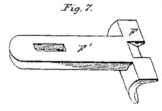

Fig. 8.

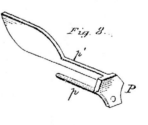

Fig. 9.   Fig. 10.

Witnesses.

C. H. Foote
John R. Young

Inventor,

F. S. Dangerfield, By.
Prindle and Co, his Attys.

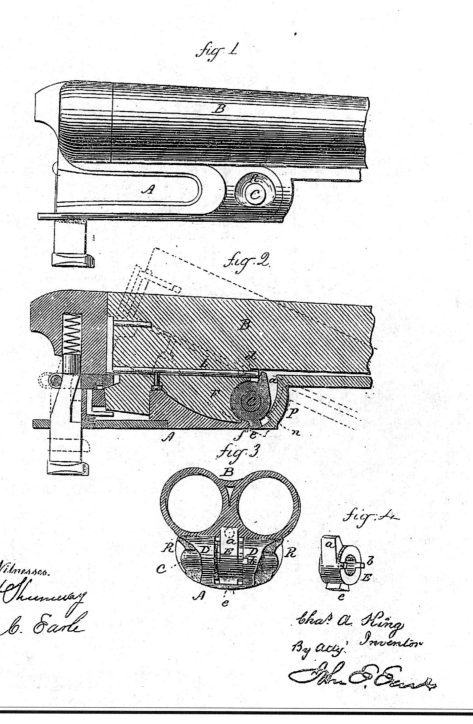

C. A. KING.
Breech-Loading Fire-Arm.

No: 160,915   Patented March 16, 1875.

fig. 1

fig. 2

fig. 3

fig. 4

Witnesses.

Chas. A. King
Inventor
By atty.

W. F. PARKER.

Breech-Loading Fire-Arm.

No. 161,267.   Patented March 23, 1875.

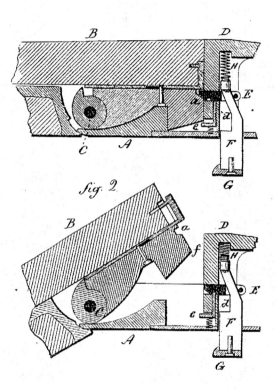

Fig. 1

Fig. 2

Witnesses

J. H. Shumway

Jos. C. Earle

Wilbur F. Parker

Inventor

By atty.

John S. Earle

D. M. LEFEVER.
Breech-Loading Fire-Arm.

No. 205,193.   Patented June 25, 1878.

Fig. 1.

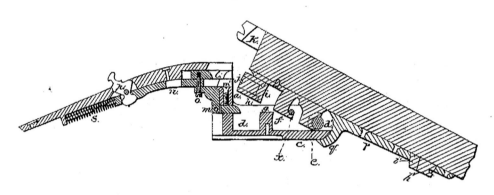

Fig. 2.

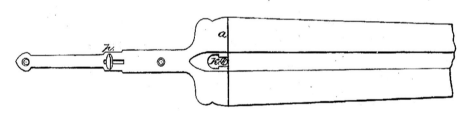

Fig. 4.

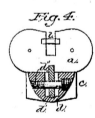

Fig. 3.

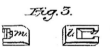

Attest: Inventor:

J. J. Greenough   Daniel M Lefever

Samuel T Jones

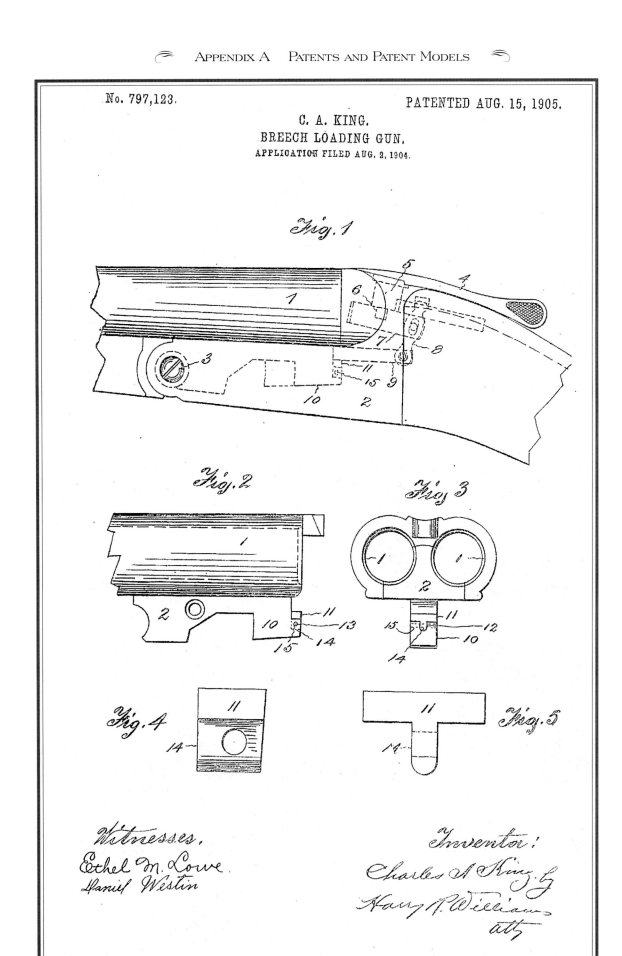

No. 797,123.

PATENTED AUG. 15, 1905.

C. A. KING.

BREECH LOADING GUN.

APPLICATION FILED AUG. 2, 1904.

Fig. 1

Fig. 2

Fig. 3

Fig. 4

Fig. 5

Witnesses,
Ethel M. Lowe.
Daniel Westin

Inventor:
Charles A King
Harry R Williams
atty

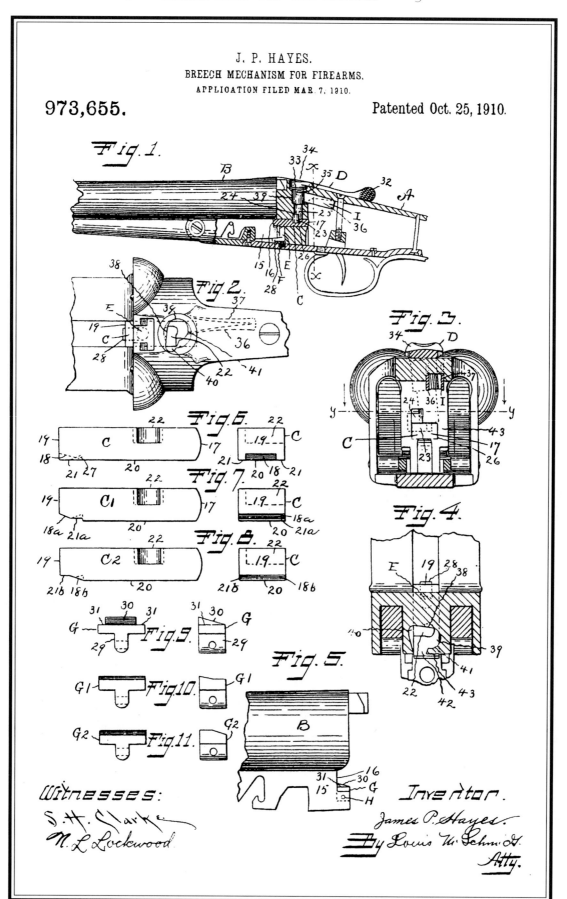

J. P. HAYES.
BREECH MECHANISM FOR FIREARMS.
APPLICATION FILED MAR. 7, 1910.

973,655.

Patented Oct. 25, 1910.

Fig. 1.

Fig. 2.

Fig. 3.

Fig. 6.

Fig. 7.

Fig. 8.

Fig. 4.

Fig. 9.

Fig. 10.

Fig. 11.

Fig. 5.

Witnesses:
S. H. Clarke
N. L. Lockwood

Inventor.
James P. Hayes.
By Louis W. Schm. d.
Atty.

APPENDIX B

DAMASCUS BARRELMAKING

Although a detailed description of Damascus barrelmaking appeared in Parker Brothers' 1880s and 1890s catalogs, the gun works never successfully forged a Damascus, laminated, or twist barrel. All of Parker's Damascus-type barrel tubes were imported as raw materials from England or Belgium. Lack of hands-on forging experience may account for a mistake in Parker's description of Damascus barrelmaking. According to Parker: ". . . the white marks that appear in the finished barrel are iron and the dark ones the steel." Actually, the reverse is true—the white marks are steel, which is more resistant to the browning process, and the dark ones are the softer, more rust-prone iron.

It took three men working together to forge one Damascus steel barrel tube—a very labor-intensive process.

245

According to Major Askins in 1910, ". . . we turn out more shotguns than the remaining world put together, [but] we are not and never have been a barrelmaking nation." Thus, Parker's detailed description of the actual barrel-forging process, and another that appeared in the July 24, 1886, issue of *Scientific American* titled "Making Fine Guns For Sporting Purposes," describe a barrelmaking process "foreign" to American gunmaking. The following was extracted from the *Scientific American* article, and the Figure 2 reference is identical to Figure 2 in Parker Brothers' description of *Shot-Gun Barrel Manufacture*:

Fig. 2 shows the manner in which the metal is worked up to form the gun barrel, to make the Damascus twist. Alternate rods of iron and steel are placed upon one another, and then forged and thoroughly welded together into a solid bar, which is afterward rolled into rods. The rod thus formed is raised to a bright red heat, and one end placed in a revolving chuck, while the other remains fixed, the turning of the chuck subjecting the rod to a severe twisting throughout its whole length, so that it at last acquires the appearance of a screw having a very fine thread. Three of these rods are then placed together, the twist of one being in a contrary direction to that of the other two, and they are welded together and rolled making the strip which is wound around the mandrel, as shown in our illustration, the coil being welded til the spirals unite to form a hollow cylinder. The fine figures that appear in the finished barrel are the result of the skillfulness with which these several operations are performed, after which follows a process of hammering while the barrel is nearly cold, to further condense the metal, and the barrel is ready to be bored, turned, and finished. About three-fourths of the material is cut away in the making, sixteen pounds of iron being used in the first instance to make a pair of barrels which will weigh only eight pounds when the welding is finished, and from three to four pounds after boring and grinding. In the manufacture of laminated steel barrels, the best quality of steel scrap is mixed

4.—Straightening Barrels.
1.—MANUFACTURE OF KRAG-JORGENSEN RIFLES AT THE SPRINGFIELD ARMORY.—[See page 267.]

Finished barrel tubes were checked for straightness by sighting in on a straight line across a window pane. Expert barrel straighteners could tell by reflection of the line along the inside of a barrel tube whether it was straight or required a judicious whack with a hammer. Although Krag-Jorgensen rifle barrels are pictured, the process was the same for Parker shotgun tubes.

with a small proportion of charcoal iron, heated in a furnace, puddled into a ball, well worked up under a forge hammer, drawn out under a tilt hammer into strips of the required length and thickness, and then treated as above described. Such barrels are much esteemed for hardness and closeness of grain, and show a different marking and appearance from those made by the Damascus twist.

[*Author's note*: Barrels built by the above processes exhibiting any pattern are today generically referred to as "Damascus." However, at the time of manufacture, the subtle distinctions between two-blade, three-blade, and four-blade Damascus, Bernard twist, plain twist, and laminated made all the difference when it came to price. The lowest-grade gun on Parker's May 1, 1874, price list had plain twist barrels and cost fifty dollars. The 1878 catalog proudly proclaimed that ". . . we use no decarbonized or plain iron barrels in which the grain of the metal runs lengthwise. Our cheapest guns have genuine twist barrels of good quality and the fine ones, ranging in price from seventy-five to three hundred dollars, have fine Damascus or Laminated steel barrels." Fine Damascus barrels were offered on GH, DH, and CH grades in Parker Brothers' 1920 pocket catalog, and a few Damascus guns were built as late as 1926 or 1927. Surprisingly, the last Parker Brothers ad in the 1934 *Meriden City Directory* pictured a DH grade with Damascus barrels.]

DESCRIPTION OF DAMASCUS BARRELMAKING
FROM PARKER BROTHERS 1899 CATALOG.

Shot–Gun Barrel Manufacture

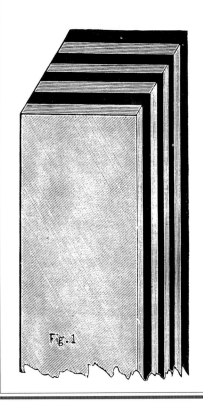

Comparatively few sportsmen realize the amount of labor and expense required to manufacture shot-gun barrels that have a fancy figure and the component parts of which are iron and steel.

These barrels must be light, therefore thin and yet sufficiently strong—conditions which can only be obtained by an extraordinary tenacity of the material. In these combinations this tenacity is secured by mixing and blending the iron and steel so intimately together that the peculiar proportions of each, toughness and elasticity, are imparted to every portion of the mass, and the barrel thus receives the degree of hardness and softness required. Thinking it may be of interest to our customers, we offer the following description of the mode of manufacture, which commences with the operation called piling. This consists in arranging the iron and steel in layers, according to the figures that may be desired. These layers are securely welded together into a compact bar, as shown in Fig. 1, which must be absolutely sound and perfect in every weld, as the slightest spot left unwelded or unsound in this operation will be sure to cause a total loss of the barrel. The process now consists in reducing this bar to such a sized rod as may be required for a certain weight of barrel. This rod is now twisted similar to a rope, as shown at E in Fig. 2, care being taken to have the twist uniform and even. Several of these twisted rods are now placed side by side, being careful to have the inclination of the twist arranged in opposite directions, as shown in the illustrations. These several rods are now welded together with the same care and precision as in the previous operation, to insure perfectly sound barrels. This is now termed a ribbon and is coiled spirally around a mandrel, as shown at F in Fig. 2. This spiral ribbon is now raised to a welding heat and jumped by striking the end against the anvil, thereby welding the edges firmly together, They are then placed upon a welding mandrel, reheated, and welded from end to end. Much skill and care is required in this operation to reduce the outside diameter to correct size and at the same time preserve the calibre, and also maintain the proper taper, the barrel being much larger at the breech than at the muzzle. The fine figure that appears in the figured barrel is dependent upon the correctness of this and the previous welding operations, for if hammered unevenly, the figure itself will be correspondingly uneven. Then follows the process of hammering in nearly a cold state, whereby the texture of the metal is condensed, closing its pores and making it harder. This finishes the operation of barrel-forging, and the barrel is now ready to be bored, turned and finished upon lathes manufactured expressly for the purpose. The curly figure that appears in the Damascus, Bernard and Laminated barrels, as shown at G in Fig. 2, is obtained by twisting the rods before referred to, as appears in the illustration at E in Fig. 2, the variation of figure being obtained by varying the piling. *The white marks that appear in the fnished* [sic] *barrel are iron and the dark ones the steel.* [Emphasis mine—Parker has it backward: The white marks are steel and the dark ones iron.] The fine figure that is on the barrels of the high-priced guns is obtained by an increased number of pieces in the operation of piling. This larger number of pieces necessarily renders the operations of securing perfect welding much more difficult, and the liability of loss is greater. Some people imagine that the curly figures of the barrels are simply etched on the outside, when they are in fact, the visible proof of a superior strength, both desirable and important to every shooter who cares for his personal safety. These fine barrels are not worked and twisted so neatly and nicely that they may look beautiful alone, but rather for the reason that greatest lightness, combined with greatest durability, may be produced. We especially recommend our Damascus barrels as having correct proportions of steel and iron to insure a proper degree of hardness without brittleness.

DATED SERIAL NUMBERS

Parker Brothers and Remington manufactured the Parker gun in callous disregard of collectors, who crave precision when it comes to dates and serial numbers. Larry Baer wrote about a friend who ordered and took delivery of two DHE Parkers in 12-gauge and 28-gauge in 1923—the 28-gauge had number 205,XXX while 171,XXX was the serial number of the 12-gauge. I wrote about some of the last Meriden and first Ilion guns in Chapter 15, "Circumstantial Evidence." My VHE Skeet, s/n 239,826, is date-stamped *XE* (December 1936) by Remington, while another VHE, s/n 239,746, was stamped *ILION* during 1938, and still another VH, s/n 240,807, was shipped from Meriden on July 31, 1937. In this context, a serialization should be thought of as a bell-shaped curve to establish the mode rather than the lowest and highest serial numbers for a particular year.

The serialization below is essentially that of the *Blue Book of Gun Values*, which, in turn, is identical to the list in Larry Baer's book. Although the *Blue Book* doesn't attribute the serialization to Baer, and Baer doesn't attribute it to anyone, the numbers trace directly to a list of 164 dated serial numbers sold by James T. Baker of Decatur, Illinois, perhaps in the late 1960s. I found Baker's list at the Meriden Historical Society. He claimed "forty years experience in fine guns," and listed a series of specific serial numbers broken down by years (six for 1902, with the highest number being 113,113, which was rounded to 113,100 by Baer and the *Blue Book*). Baker's list shows s/n 6,794 as an 1868 gun, and this conspicuous error rounded to s/n 6,800 traces through Baer's book to the *Blue Book*.

Del Grego's gun shop has been the depository of various compilations of dated serial numbers developed by Parker collectors and dealers over the years. Larry "Babe" Del Grego Jr. recalls that the first serialization was compiled by Alfred Stever of Ohio in the 1950s, and another, more definitive list by Cecil Martin of Miami, Florida, in the early 1970s. A copy of Martin's list of dated serial numbers was with Baker's list at the Meriden Historical Society. Martin's serialization is surprisingly accurate for the first ten years of production, but after 1878 it appears to be an interpolation of Baker's array of specific serial numbers. I understand that Cecil Martin reprinted Parker Brothers' 1869 and 1870 catalogs, so it's likely that Parker's earliest guns were his area of expertise. Baker's list seems to be definitive after 1878, but dovetails nicely with Martin's rounded numbers.

What follows is my simplified serialization of dated serial numbers, compiled with much help from Baker and Martin, two men I've never met. My list is submitted with the *caveat* that some of the numbers appeared on my register receipt after I passed Captain du Bray's AA Pigeon Gun across the checkout scanner at the Wal-Mart in San Francisco. Access to the Parker factory records may show that a particular gun was ordered, built, or delivered a year or two earlier or several years later than my list would indicate. Parker's production records may someday be published, and hope springs eternal for a factory letter service to establish provenance for individual guns. But in the meantime, the needs of a casual collector wandering the aisles of a gun show should be served by a photocopy of the list following.

DATED SERIAL NUMBERS—PARKER GUNS

Year	Serial Number	Year	Serial Number	Year	Serial Number
1866-69	1-729*	1892	73,000	1917	178,000
1868	1-100**	1893	78,000	1918	181,000
1869	500	1894	82,000	1919	185,000
1870	1,000	1895	84,000	1920	190,000
1871	1,500	1896	86,000	1921	195,000
1872	2,000	1897	88,000	1922	200,000
1873	3,000	1898	90,000	1923	205,000
1874	4,000	1899	94,000	1924	210,000
1875	6,000	1900	100,000	1925	215,000
1876	8,000	1901	106,000	1926	220,000
1877	10,000	1902	113,000	1927	224,000
1878	13,000	1903	120,000	1928	228,000
1879	18,000	1904	127,000	1929	232,000
1880	21,000	1905	134,000	1930	235,000
1881	24,000	1906	140,000	1931	236,000
1882	28,000	1907	145,000	1932	236,300
1883	35,000	1908	148,000	1933	236,600
1884	38,000	1909	151,000	1934	237,000***
1885	44,000	1910	154,000	1935	238,000
1886	48,000	1911	157,000	1936	240,000
1887	52,000	1912	160,000	1937	241,000
1888	56,000	1913	165,000	1938	241,500
1889	60,000	1914	169,000	1939	242,000
1890	64,000	1915	172,000	1940	242,200
1891	68,000	1916	175,000	1941-47	242,387

*Highest reported Meriden Man'fg Co. for Chas Parker T-Latch shotgun.

**Parker Brothers serial numbers begin over.

***Remington-Parker serial numbers begin between 236,000 and 237,000.

REMINGTON — PARKER DATE CODES

Remington Arms Co. purchased Parker Brothers in 1934 and soon began to stamp Parker guns with Remington date codes as follows:

	B	L	A	C	K	P	O	W	D	E	R	X
Months	1	2	3	4	5	6	7	8	9	10	11	12

Remington's year codes, insofar as they relate to the Parker gun, began with C for 1934, and then D-1935, E-1936, F-1937, G-1938, H-1939, J-1940, K-1941, L-1942, MM-1943, NN-1944, PP-1945, RR-1946, SS-1947, TT-1948, VV-1949, WW-1950, XX-1951, YY-1952, ZZ-1953, and then began over with A-1954, B-1955, C-1956, D-1957, E-1958, F-1959, G-1960, etc. My circa-1936 VHE 12-gauge Skeet is stamped XF3XE and LWW3 on the barrel flats. The number 3 refers to a return for repairs. Accordingly, L means February and WW means 1950, the month and year the gun was returned to Remington for repairs. The XF3XE marking actually consists of two date codes—XF3 means the gun was returned for repairs in December 1937, while XE shows the gun was built in December 1936. The Skeet gun is serial number 239,826, which validates 240,000 on my serialization table as being in the "ballpark" for the end of 1936 production.

PARKER GRADES AND PRICES

The schedule below is a thumbnail sketch of Parker grades and prices over seventy-two years of production. Letter grades were adopted in the early 1880s, so earlier "grades" have been assigned by using 12-gauge pistol-grip catalog prices unless otherwise indicated. All post-1900 guns are priced with ejectors (except Trojan and T-grade hammer gun), but prices exclude other cost-additive options and special features.

	1869	1874	1878	1888	1899	1908	1913	1918	1920	1923	1926	1930	1934	1936	1940
AIS						525	400	550	725	725	675	750	825	865	890
AAH					400	425	325	450	610	610	568	625	688	723	750
A	200	250	300	300	300	325	250	310	410	410	381	425	468	498	530
B	135	200	225	200	200	225	169	225	302	302	281	300	330	355	390
C	110	150	175	150	150	175	131	165	220	220	205	215	237	252	290
D	75	100	125	100	100	125	94	125	166	166	155	160	176	187	195
G		75	80	80	80	105	79	99	129	124	115	115	127	134	159
I*				70	70										
P		60	65	65	65	90	68	84	109	104	97				
T**	50	50	55	55	55	55	41	59							
VH					50	75	56	69	94	90	84	87	96	100	139
TROJAN							28	40	59	55	52	55	61	61	
INVINCIBLE***												1,250			

* 10-gauge pistol-grip with laminated barrels
** T-grade hammer guns
*** Price advertised in magazines

PARKER FRAME SIZES

Special frame sizes for each different gauge were Parker's secret weapon when it came to building look-alike guns of proper scale and balance. Frame-size differences were important to the long-term success of the Parker gun. Parker's 20-gauge was 20-gauge all the way, not just small-bore barrels on an otherwise 12-gauge action and stock. The "hand-fit and finish" manufacturing process was such that the gun works could use the next frame size larger or smaller within a gauge, if necessary, to cater to a customer's request for a heavyweight or lightweight gun.

Each Parker gauge has what can be considered a standard-size frame as determined by the distance between firing-pin centers. For example, a standard 20-gauge size 0 frame has one inch between pins, while a standard 1½ size 12-gauge frame has a 1⅛-inch spread. An in-depth study of all the different dimensions of all the different frame sizes is beyond the scope of this book. Suffice it to say that the distance between hinge pin and standing breech and the width of the barrel-lump slot are the same for all frame sizes while, generally speaking, the external vertical and horizontal dimensions increase or decrease in proportion to larger or smaller bore sizes.

Parker Brothers built guns to different frame sizes even before the adoption of the interchangeable system of gun manufacture announced in its 1877 catalog. I own two circa 1870 back-action 12-gauge Parkers with decarbonized steel barrels: s/n 0895 weighs 7¾ pounds and s/n 01516 weighs nine pounds even. Both guns have thirty-inch barrels and the same overall dimensions. The weight difference results from s/n 01516 having a .10-inch greater spread between the firing pins, which served as a gauge to force thicker barrels at the breech. The heavier gun was described in Parker's 1872 catalog as ". . . decarbonized steel barrels, solid breech, back action locks, number 12-gauge, over 8 lbs. weight . . . $85.00;" the lighter gun cost $75 and was described as ". . . decarbonized steel barrels, solid breech, back action locks, number 12-gauge, 7½ to 8 pounds." Parker's least-expensive gun came in two different frame sizes as early as 1870.

Frame-size numbers were stamped on the bottom of the barrel lug starting in about 1877, and served to indicate whether a particular gun was considered light, average, or heavy at the time of manufacture. The following chart should serve as a general guide to the correlation of gauge to frame size and average weights. But remember, when dealing with general information about Parker guns, all things are possible. As I was preparing this schedule, "Babe" Del Grego told me of a 16-gauge on a number 2 frame. Then Forrest Marshall called to advise that his s/n 220,812 PHE 28-gauge on Number 00 frame weighs five pounds nine ounces, while his s/n 218,476 PH .410 on Number 000 frame weighs five pounds eleven ounces. Both small bores have twenty-six-inch barrels, so thickness rather than length is the variable that caused the "light" 000 frame .410 to be two ounces heavier than its 28-gauge cousin. In this context, the chart below should be considered only a general guide to the correlation of gauge to frame size and average weight.

PARKER FRAME SIZE SCHEDULE

Gauge	Light	Standard	Heavy	Typical Weights *
10	2	3	5	7¾ to 10 lbs
12**	1	1½	2	6½ to 9 lbs
16	0	1	1½	6 to 8 lbs
20	***	0	1	5¾ to 7½ lbs
28	***	00	0	5¼ to 6 lbs
.410	***	000	00	5¼ to 6 lbs

* Weights are from a schedule in Parker's circa-1913 Flying Ducks catalog (except that the .410 weights are from the 1930 large Flying Geese catalog).

** Parker retooled the standard 16-gauge number 1 frame to be number ½ size in 1937; exterior dimensions are scaled down, but the 1¹/₁₆-inch spread between firing-pin centers is the same for both number 1 and number ½ sizes. The half-frame is only known to be used for the 12-gauge. See Chapter 15, "Circumstantial Evidence."

*** Small bores of 20-gauge and less could be built to weigh 5¾ pounds or less on number 0-size frames. Use of number 00 and number 000 frames on 28-gauge and .410 was a matter of proportion and balance, rather than to achieve weight reduction. It's not surprising that circa-1927 small-bore skeet guns weighed between 5½ and 5¾ pounds. Guns built too light tend to lose feel, handling, and follow-through in the hands of adult shooters—Parker small bores weren't built for kids.

INDEX

single trigger, 74

Philadelphia Sterlingworth, 110, 161

Phillips, John W., 87

philosophy, gun collecting, 135–43

Pigeon Gun, 53, 54, 56, 59, 89, 106, 109, 110, 119, 128–9, 151, 181

   scarce, 126

pigeon trap, 45, 73, 91

pinfire, 20, 31, 46

   breechloader, 17

   cartridge, 19

   French and British, 19

pistol grip, 93, 106, 125

   capped, 177

plain twist. See barrel

plunge trap, 70, 73

Posten, Frank, 90

Potter, Clifford, 159

Pottet, M., 19

powder, 19

   American Wood, 49

   bulk smokeless, 180, 207, 213

   charge, 19, 23

   FF Dead Shot, 49

   nitro, 172, 212

   spreader load, 207

   See also ammunition

priming system, 17, 23

   Berdan, Hiram, 25

   Boxer-type (British), 25

   external, 19, 32

   Maynard system, 30

   percussion, 27

production, wartime to peacetime, 37

proof testing, 71, 105, 166, 174, 186

   See also pattern

proofmark, 166

Puglishi Gun Room, Duluth, 27

pull, 73, 136, 173, 174

   long, 174, 213

pump gun, 61, 65

Purdey, James (importer), 102

Purdey guns, 102, 131, 222

Q

quality

   codes, 101–9 (See also individual code letters)

   control (See pattern, percentage)

   detailed grades of, 101–9

   grades of, 101–33

   perceived, 45, 58, 101, 103, 108, 121, 126

Quality A-1. See A-1 Special

Quality CH, 121–2

   See also CH

Quality DH, 119–20

   See also DH

Quality GH, 117–18

   See also GH

Quality PH, 114–16

   See also PH

Queen Victoria, 64

quenching, 167–9

R

R & R Books, 157

R grade, 112

R-S-T- U grade, hammer guns, 106

range of guns, 54

rare guns, 126, 130, 145–54, 153, 154, 159, 173, 174, 177, 210, 218

   vs scarce, 146, 148, 151

reblued, 141, 148

rebounding

   hammers, 41

   lock, 40, 42

Recreation magazine, 63

reestablishing case colors, 168

refinished, 137, 141

   See also restorations

Reilly, E. M., 21

Remington Arms Company, Inc., 3, 8, 14, 79, 92, 168, 169, 209

Remington Arms Museum (Ilion, N.Y.), 16, 47, 151

Remington Custom Shop, 126

Remington gun, 95, 169, 176

Remington-Parker guns, 80, 126, 145, 171, 176, 212, 218

   date codes (See Appendix D)

repeaters, 35, 52, 60, 61, 65, 97, 102, 110, 179

   single barrel, 53

reproduction, 81, 120, 140

restorations, 137, 140, 141, 151, 168, 169, 207

   See also reproduction; upgrade

revolving shotgun, Roper's, 191

rib

   extension, 36, 46, 47, 58, 67, 110

   single (fence), 130

   ventilated, 71, 145, 151, 177, 213

Richards, Wesley, 19, 28, 29, 30, 43, 46

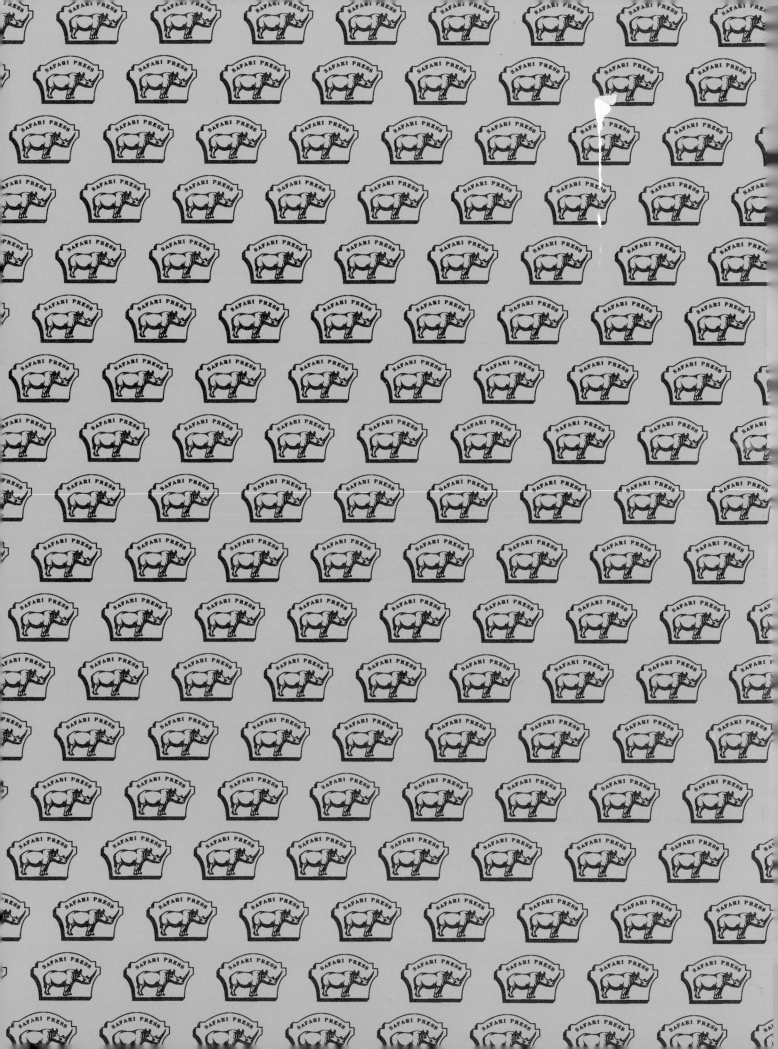